The End of the World As We Know It

THE END OF THE WORLD AS WE KNOW IT

Faith, Fatalism, and Apocalypse in America

DANIEL WOJCIK

NEW YORK UNIVERSITY PRESS
New York and London

NEW YORK UNIVERSITY PRESS
New York and London

Library of Congress Cataloging-in-Publication Data
Wojcik, Daniel.
The end of the world as we know it : faith, fatalism, and
apocalypse in America / Daniel Wojcik.
p.   cm.
Includes bibliographical references and index.
ISBN 0-8147-9283-9 (alk. paper)
1. Millennialism—United States—History—20th century. 2. End of
the world—History of doctrines—20th century. 3. United States—
Religion—*1960-*   I. Title.
BR526.W65   1997
001.9—dc21   97-4781
                    CIP

New York University Press books are printed on acid-free paper,
and their binding materials are chosen for strength and durability.

Manufactured in the United States of America

10 9 8 7 6 5 4 3 2 1

Turning and turning in the widening gyre
The falcon cannot hear the falconer;
Things fall apart; the centre cannot hold;
Mere anarchy is loosed upon the world,
The blood-dimmed tide is loosed, and everywhere
The ceremony of innocence is drowned;
The best lack all conviction, while the worst
Are full of passionate intensity.

Surely some revelation is at hand;
Surely the Second Coming is at hand.
The Second Coming! Hardly are those words out
When a vast image out of *Spiritus Mundi*
Troubles my sight: somewhere in sands of the desert
A shape with lion body and the head of a man,
A gaze blank and pitiless as the sun,
Is moving its slow thighs, while all about it
Reel shadows of indignant desert birds.
The darkness drops again; but now I know
That twenty centuries of stony sleep
Were vexed to nightmare by a rocking cradle,
And what rough beast, its hour come round at last,
Slouches towards Bethlehem to be born?

    —William Butler Yeats, "The Second Coming"

Contents

Acknowledgments

Researching this book has been a lengthy process, and I have many people to thank for suggestions and words of encouragement along the way. I am indebted to Robert A. Georges and Michael Owen Jones of UCLA, who offered guidance during the early stages of this project and helpful insights as my research progressed. I am grateful to Paul Boyer, whose seminar at UCLA on nuclear weapons in American culture helped inspire this project and whose ideas have informed my thinking on contemporary apocalyptic beliefs. I also wish to thank Robert P. Flaherty (whose influence is reflected in chapter 8) for our memorable discussions of apocalyptic topics.

My sincere thanks to Sharon Sherman, Susan Fagan, and Robert Howard at the University of Oregon for reading portions of the manuscript, and to the following colleagues and friends for their contributions and suggestions: Donald Cosentino, Diane Dugaw, Bill Ellis, John Gage, Regan Lee, Steve Poizat-Newcomb, Leonard Norman Primiano, Mike Stamm, Donald Ward, Brennan Washburn, and Catherine Wessinger.

I am especially indebted to Niko Pfund, director at New York University Press, whose initial interest in my research and ongoing encouragement helped bring this book to fruition. I also am grateful for an Individual Research Grant from the American Academy of Religion, and the support provided by the University of Oregon in the form of a Summer Research Award from the Office of Research and Sponsored Programs and a Junior Professorship Development Award from the College of Arts and Sciences. I would like to express my appreciation as well to the artists, authors, and publishers who granted permission for the use of their illustrations, photographs, and quoted material.

Finally, I am grateful for the support and patience of my family: my mother, Beatrice; my father, Gerald; my brother, James; and especially my wife, Wieslawa, and my son, Konrad.

Portions of this book have appeared in the *Journal of American Folklore* (1996), *American Folklore: An Encyclopedia* (1996), *Western Folklore* (1996), and in my monograph, *Punk and Neo-Tribal Body Art* (1995).

The End of the World As We Know It

1

Approaching Doomsday
The Contours of American Apocalyptic Belief

Beliefs and narratives about the end of the world have fascinated people throughout human history. In nearly every society, sacred narratives are told about worldly cataclysm, the regeneration of the earth, and the creation of a terrestrial paradise (Talmon 1968:349–351; Thrupp 1970:11–15). Until recently, the end of the world has been interpreted as a meaningful, transformative, and supernatural event, involving the annihilation and renewal of the earth by deities or divine forces. During the last half of the twentieth century, however, widespread beliefs about a meaningless apocalypse have emerged and now compete with traditional religious apocalyptic worldviews. The creation and proliferation of nuclear weapons, in particular, have fundamentally altered contemporary apocalyptic thought, fueling fears of global annihilation and evoking widespread fatalism about the future of humanity. The dropping of atomic bombs on Hiroshima and Nagasaki in August 1945 initiated an era of nuclear apocalypticism that has flourished in American religious and secular cultures. Popular beliefs about the inevitability of nuclear apocalypse are revealed by a Yankelovich poll taken in 1984, in which 39 percent of a sample population agreed with the statement "When the Bible predicts that the earth will be destroyed by fire, it's telling us that a nuclear war is inevitable" (L. Jones 1985:67). If this sampling of the populace is representative, then approximately eighty-five million Americans believe that nuclear apocalypse is unavoidable (Halsell 1986:10).

Despite the end of the Cold War, anxieties about the possibility of nuclear apocalypse persist today, stemming from the magnitude and seeming uncontrollability of nuclear weapons and the likelihood that they will be developed and used by hostile nations or extremist organizations in the future. In addition to the fear of nuclear annihilation, other threats have emerged as possible causes or signs of impending doom and have enkindled apocalyptic speculation. Perhaps poet T. S. Eliot was right in "The Hollow Men" that the world ends not with a bang but with a whimper: the gradual destruction of the environment, the greenhouse effect, ozone depletion, the AIDS epidemic, widespread famine, overpopulation, incurable strains of pneumonia, ebola, and flesh-eating viruses, and other as yet unimaginable future afflictions may contribute to our eventual extinction. Indeed, the majority of Americans believe that the world will end someday, according to a 1995 Gallup poll, with 61 percent of adults and 71 percent of teenagers agreeing that "the world will come to an end or be destroyed" (Bezilla 1996:26). Fatalism about the future of humanity, especially pervasive among young people, is indicated by an extensive nationwide study of a representative sample of more than seventeen thousand high school seniors; more than one-third agreed with the statement "Nuclear or biological annihilation will probably be the fate of all mankind within my generation" (La Farge 1987:27–28). A 1995 Gallup poll revealed a similar degree of apprehension about the imminence of humanity's destruction, with approximately three teenagers in ten fearing that the world may come to an end during their lifetimes (Bezilla 1996:26).

In view of such attitudes, and the numerous potential disasters that threaten humanity, it is no surprise that with the approach of the year 2000, apocalyptic anxieties have intensified and doomsday speculation flourishes. At the end of the second millennium, ancient apocalyptic traditions converge with recent secular predictions of catastrophe and inflame the popular imagination. Ideas and images about the end of the world permeate American popular culture and folklore, as well as popular religion, and are expressed in films, literature, music, poetry, visual arts, dance, theater, cartoons, comics, humor, and commercial products. Religious apocalypticism and its secular counterpart may differ in terms of underlying premises and the details of doomsday, but the proponents of such beliefs—whether televangelists, authors of best-selling paperbacks on biblical prophecy, seers of the Virgin Mary, New Age visionaries, Hopi prophets, survivalists, or futurologists—agree that global catastrophe is imminent.

This confluence of popular beliefs about approaching doomsday has compelled some researchers to predict that before the century ends, political, economic, and social problems will be interpreted as portents of the endtimes and further contribute to widespread feelings of doom; an apocalyptic fervor will captivate millions of people throughout the United States and the world; a multiplicity of prophets and visionaries will appear; and apocalyptic movements will arise and attain mass followings, with some apocalypticists perhaps even attempting to fulfill their own prophecies by instigating societal catastrophes in order to usher in a new world (see Friedrich 1986:11; Schwartz 1990:8–10; Martin 1982; Barkun 1983). In fact, a self-fulfilling apocalyptic scenario may have been the goal of the Aum Shinri Kyo ("Supreme Truth") sect, alleged to have perpetrated the subway nerve gas attack in Tokyo in March 1995. The sect's scientists supposedly were researching and experimenting with chemical, laser, biological, and conventional weapons so as to fulfill their leader's prophecies of worldly cataclysms.[1]

Popular stereotypes of apocalypticism as a "cult" phenomenon involving fanatics and alienated outcasts have been reinforced by the media coverage of the Aum Shinri Kyo sect, the Branch Davidian tragedy that occurred in 1993, the suicides and murders associated with the Swiss Order of the Solar Temple sect, and most recently the collective suicide of the Heaven's Gate group in March 1997. However, expectations of the end of the world are not limited to a handful of religious groups existing on the social margins. Today, millions of Americans embrace beliefs about the imminence of societal catastrophe. Apocalyptic thinking is an enormously influential and pervasive means of conceptualizing the world and one's place in it, yet scholars have largely neglected the study of contemporary endtimes thought.

The End of the World As We Know It offers a framework for understanding various expressions of apocalyptic belief that exist in the United States today and suggests reasons for the prevalence and enduring appeal of such ideas. The forms of apocalypticism discussed herein are predominately expressions of "folk" or "popular" belief—widespread ideas that are not officially promoted or approved by mainstream organizations but that exist at a grassroots level apart from the formal sanction of these institutions. The work examines the underlying features of differing apocalyptic traditions as expressed through oral narratives, folk religious practices, and the prophecies of visionaries and charismatic leaders, as well as through photocopied fliers, religious tracts, videos, audiocassettes, paperbacks, popular literature and music, humor, and computer newsgroups. Taking a comparative and multidisciplinary approach, this study analyzes the ways that various apocalyptic traditions have been adapted to reflect current concerns and how new religious and secular apocalyptic beliefs have emerged in the latter half of the twentieth century.

This book focuses in particular on how the prospect of nuclear annihilation and other potential catastrophes has influenced apocalyptic thought and explores how the concept of fatalism—commonly understood as the belief that certain events and experiences are inevitable, unalterable, and determined by external forces beyond human control—is central to apocalyptic speculation in the nuclear age. The term *fatalism* is not used here in a pejorative sense; fatalistic thought is an enduring and widespread means of interpreting experiences and understanding the world. The idea of fate embodies the sense of inevitability, both pessimistic and optimistic, that is inherent to religious and secular apocalypticism in the United States today.

The word *apocalypse* (from the Greek *apokalypsis*) means revelation or unveiling. This sense of a revealed, underlying design for history has traditionally characterized apocalyptic ideas and resembles ancient notions of fate as an absolute force in the universe that determines all things. As philosopher and theologian Martin Buber notes, in apocalyptic thought "everything is predetermined, all human decisions are only sham struggles" (1957:201). By asserting that history and worldly renewal are predetermined, religious apocalyptic belief systems affirm that the cosmos is ordered, that evil and suffering will be destroyed, that human existence is meaningful, and that a millennial realm of peace and justice ultimately will be created. Faith and fatalism are thus interwoven into the fabric of apocalyptic thought: a profound fatalism for a world believed to be irredeemably evil is entwined with the faith for a predestined, perfect age of harmony and human fulfillment.

Unlike religious apocalyptic worldviews, secular beliefs about societal cataclysm usually lack this sense of meaning and moral order. Although various secular movements promise or anticipate a radical transformation of the world after the destruction of current society (Nazism, communism, or survivalism, for instance), most secular beliefs about imminent apocalypse are devoid of the component of worldly redemption and therefore tend to be characterized by a sense of hopelessness and despair. This profound pessimism and fatalistic appraisal of the future is especially evident in secular beliefs about a nuclear conflagration. Although the prospect of nuclear annihilation has been readily incorporated into some religious apocalyptic belief systems, and thus mythologized as a meaningful event that is the fulfillment of a divinely ordained plan for the redemption of the world, secular beliefs about an inevitable nuclear war express feelings of fatalism, helplessness, resignation, and universal doom (Chernus 1986:53–62; Lifton 1987:137–147). Exploring the complexities of fatalistic thought and the reasons that motivate people to interpret events fatalistically provides considerable insight into the nature of both religious and secular apocalyptic speculation and their respective visions of a meaningful or meaningless apocalypse and reveals much about current concerns, fears, and hopes for the future.

This study begins with a survey of the landscape of contemporary American apocalyptic belief and then discusses the terminology, "folk" attributes, and fatalistic underpinnings associated with apocalyptic worldviews. Chapter

2 traces the history of American apocalyptic beliefs; subsequent chapters explore the following forms of contemporary endtimes thought: (chapter 3) premillennial dispensational prophecy beliefs as expressed in the books of Hal Lindsey, the most influential prophecy interpreter in the twentieth century; (chapter 4) apocalyptic prophecies associated with visions of the Virgin Mary as expressed in the Bayside apparitions in New York City; and (chapter 5) secular ideas about nuclear apocalypse in American popular culture and folk belief, and within various subcultures. Chapter 6 analyzes the fatalistic aspects and cultural and psychological meanings of these diverse apocalyptic ideas, and chapter 7 examines the transformation of apocalyptic prophecy in the post–Cold War era and the current themes now emphasized with the approach of the year 2000. The last chapter explores the emergent apocalyptic ideas associated with UFOs and extraterrestrial beings and compares these recent beliefs to previous apocalyptic worldviews. The conclusion offers a typology of apocalyptic beliefs, surveys apocalyptic speculation associated with the year 2000, and reflects on the enduring appeal of apocalyptic thought at the end of the second millennium.

Contemporary American Apocalyptic Beliefs

Narratives about the end of the world have existed since the beginning of recorded history. The tale of Noah and the Flood, the Norse myth of Ragnarök (popularized in Richard Wagner's opera *Die Götterdämmerung*), the Hindu myths of recurring worldly annihilation and regeneration, and selected Zoroastrian, Babylonian, Sumerian, Buddhist, Islamic, Greek, Roman, African, Mayan, and Native American myths describe the destruction and transformation of the world, the struggle between the powers of good and evil, and the divinely determined destiny of humanity and the cosmos. As historian of religion Mircea Eliade notes, "The myth of the end of the world is of universal occurrence; it is already to be found among primitive peoples still at a paleolithic stage of culture . . . and it recurs in the great historic civilizations, Babylonian, Indian, Mexican and Greco-Roman" (1975:243). The pervasiveness of such narratives historically and cross-culturally is revealed by the listings in the various folklore motif and tale-type indices, such as Stith Thompson's six-volume *Motif-Index of Folk-Literature* (1955–1958), which classifies particular narrative motifs and identifies their distribution. The major apocalyptic narratives are listed under "World calamities and renewals" (A1000–A1099), which includes subcategories such as "World catastrophe" (A1000), "Deluge" (A1010), "Escape from deluge" (A1020), "World-fire" (A1030), "Continuous winter destroys the race" (A1040), "Heavens break up at end of the world" (A1050), "Earth disturbances at end of world" (A1060), and "Fettered monster's escape at end of world" (A1070). The narratives and motifs listed in this and other folklore indices contain many of the same underlying ideas and structures as contemporary apocalyptic narratives, illustrating the continuities through time of apocalyptic thought.

Christian belief in apocalyptic prophecy, founded in the ancient Jewish prophetic tradition, has an extensive legacy in American culture and consciousness, beginning with the Puritans and continuing to the present day. Scholars have frequently commented on the presence of apocalyptic themes in American religion, history, literature, and "imagination" (see Zamora 1982a). Beliefs about apocalypse and the arrival of the millennium have been central to numerous sectarian groups (such as the Shakers and the Millerites) and the Native American Ghost Dance movements in the 1870s and 1890s, and contributed to much nineteenth-century social reform, including the abolitionist and temperance movements. According to several scholars, such beliefs also served as the ideological catalyst for numerous slave revolts, early feminist consciousness (Moorhead 1987:17–18), and even the American Revolution itself (Bloch 1985:xiii). Studies of American millennialism have examined the relationship between millennialist thought and themes of American destiny (Cherry 1971; Tuveson 1968), millennialist ideas in the fundamentalist and holiness movements (Marsden 1980; Sandeen 1970), the rise and appeal of premillennialism in the late nineteenth century and early twentieth (Weber 1987), the nature and diversity of millennialist thought in eighteenth-century New England (Davidson 1977), millennialist fundamentalist ties with rightist politics (Jorstad 1970), and the ways that millennialist ideas influenced political actions during the Civil War (Moorhead 1978).[2] The prevalence of apocalyptic and millennialist ideas in the United States has even prompted comparisons with American foodways and sporting events: social scientist John Wiley Nelson asserts that apocalyptic ideas are "as American as the hot dog" (1982:179) and historian Leonard Sweet asserts that a preoccupation with the millennium "has become, even more than baseball, America's favorite pastime" (1979:531).

Most studies of American millennialist traditions examine such ideas prior to the Civil War, or among selected sectarian groups, or as expressed in premillennial dispensationalism in the late nineteenth and early twentieth centuries (Buss 1988:19). With the exception of a few recent studies (Boyer 1992;

Brummett 1991; O'Leary 1994; Strozier 1994), surprisingly little research on contemporary American apocalypticism has been conducted, and comparative work on American apocalyptic beliefs in the nuclear era is practically nonexistent.[3] According to historian Paul Boyer, author of an important study of premillennial dispensationalism, "Despite a vague awareness that prophecy belief is rampant 'out there'—in the dark beyond the campfire, so to speak—academics have given these beliefs little systematic attention" (1992:15).

Often the studies that have been conducted consider those who believe in the imminence of the end of the world to be members of marginal social groups, the disenfranchised, the oppressed, or the deprived. Historian Timothy Weber observes, "Traditionally, advocates of apocalypticism have been outsiders, alienated and disinherited from the privileged and powerful. With few exceptions, they looked for their future redemption from beyond the clouds precisely because they had no recourse in the present" (1987:x). Although this association may have been true in the past, as the third millennium approaches, millions of Americans of all backgrounds and socioeconomic levels currently hold beliefs about apocalyptic prophecies.

Today in the United States, belief in apocalyptic prophecy is integral to the worldviews of many evangelical Christians, such as the Southern Baptist Convention (with an estimated fifteen million members) and various pentecostal and charismatic denominations (roughly eight million members), including the Assemblies of God Church, the Church of Nazarene, and thousands of independent evangelical "Bible churches" (Boyer 1992:4). Premillennial dispensationalism, a form of evangelicalism that emphasizes apocalyptic prophecy, is espoused by the majority of televangelists, including Jerry Falwell, Pat Robertson, Jack Van Impe, and Oral Roberts (as well as the once-popular Jimmy Swaggert and Jim and Tammy Bakker), many of whom have stated, at one time or another, that nuclear weapons and the prospect of nuclear war are a fulfillment of biblical prophecies. According to a Nielsen survey of television viewers conducted in October 1985, approximately "61 million Americans (40 percent of all viewers) regularly listen to preachers who tell them nothing can be done to prevent a nuclear war in our lifetime" (Halsell 1986:11). Although such surveys do not reveal the degree to which apocalyptic beliefs are integral to people's lives, the data gathered through various polls suggest that beliefs about biblical prophecy and the Second Coming are much more pervasive than scholars have recognized. For instance, a 1983 Gallup poll revealed that 62 percent of the respondents had "no doubts" that Jesus will return again to earth, and a 1994 poll for *U.S. News and World Report* indicated that 61 percent of Americans believe that

Jesus will return (Gallup and Castelli 1989:4; *U.S. News and World Report,* December 19, 1994, 64). The *U.S. News and World Report* survey also found that 53 percent of those polled believe that some world events in the twentieth century fulfill biblical prophecy, and that a significant percentage of Americans believe the Bible should be taken literally when it speaks of a final Judgment Day (60 percent), a Battle of Armageddon (44 percent), the Antichrist (49 percent), and the Rapture of the church (44 percent) (*U.S. News and World Report,* December 19, 1994, 64).

Widespread interest in apocalyptic prophecy is further indicated by the success of mass-marketed paperbacks on the topic, such as the numerous best-sellers by Hal Lindsey. His book *The Late Great Planet Earth* (1970), sold 7.5 million copies during the 1970s, making it the largest-selling American nonfiction book of that decade (*New York Times Book Review,* April 6, 1980, 27). More than twenty-eight million copies of the book, in fifty-two languages, now have been sold (*Los Angeles Times,* February 23, 1991, F16; S. Graham 1989:249). President Ronald Reagan's interest in biblical prophecies about the imminence of Armageddon, which received national media attention in April 1984, is a further indication that such beliefs are held by not only members of marginal, disenfranchised groups. Although treated as an "aberration" by the press, Reagan's preoccupation with prophecy is like that of millions of Americans who are fascinated by apocalyptic biblical predictions. The ubiquitous nature of apocalyptic prophecy belief also was revealed in 1991, when some premillennialists interpreted the war in the Persian Gulf as the beginning of an endtimes scenario that would culminate in a nuclear conflagration. Suddenly, the otherwise "invisible" beliefs about biblical prophecy held by millions of Americans were activated and apocalyptic speculation escalated. According to a Gallup poll conducted during the Persian Gulf War, 15 percent of Americans thought the war fulfilled prophecy and that Armageddon was at hand (Bezilla 1996:26). John Walvoord's book *Armageddon, Oil and the Middle East Crisis,* originally published in 1974, was updated and reprinted in 1990, and immediately sold over 600,000 copies from December 1990 to February 1991. Another 300,000 copies were ordered and distributed by evangelist Billy Graham, who reportedly discussed the book's predictions about Armageddon with President George Bush (*Los Angeles Times,* February 7, 1991, E2). Walvoord's opinions concerning biblical prophecies and the Persian Gulf War were enthusiastically sought by the mainstream press, and he was interviewed on CNN, CBN, CBS-TV, and sixty-five radio stations nationwide (Boyer 1992:330).

Although premillennial dispensationalism is the most pervasive form of contemporary apocalypticism in the United States, it is only one of many apocalyptic traditions, each of which has a distinctive history and system of beliefs. For example, the expectation of imminent worldly destruction and renewal is an important part of the theology of the Seventh-day Adventists, Church of Jesus Christ of Latter-Day Saints (Mormons), and Jehovah's Witnesses. Apocalyptic prophecies associated with visions of the Virgin Mary and delivered at numerous Marian apparition sites, such as Fatima, Portugal; Garabandal, Spain; San Damiano, Italy; Medjugorje, Croatia; and Bayside, New York, are familiar to millions of Roman Catholics worldwide. Beliefs about Mary's apocalyptic warnings are an expression of Catholic folk religion, existing apart from the approval of institutionalized Catholicism and reinforced by an extensive popular literature about Marian prophecy that interprets recent apparitions as part of a divine plan unfolding in the last days. Apocalyptic prophecy belief was once central to Judaism, and although deemphasized today, persists among members of the Chabad Lubavitch movement, an Orthodox Hasidic sect of Judaism. In 1992, many of the more than 250,000 followers of Rabbi Menachem Mendel Schneerson, of Brooklyn, New York, believed that he had prophesied various events and that he was in fact the Messiah who would bring about the redemption of the world (Chandler 1993:213–215).

Native American beliefs about the end of the world bear some resemblance to the prophecy beliefs in Christian and Jewish traditions, with Hopi prophecies, in particular, foretelling of a period of chastisement, called the "Great Purification," that will occur prior to a fiery worldly cataclysm. Hopi prophecies warn that if sacred knowledge is rejected and if the planet's resources continue to be exploited after this period of tribulation, the world will be destroyed (Timms 1994:150–170). Hopi prophecies have been embraced by some New Age devotees, who have adopted an assortment of previous prophetic and apocalyptic traditions, as well as the predictions of Nostradamus, Edgar Cayce, and Jeanne Dixon, among others, to create an amalgam of apocalyptic prophecy belief.

The eclecticism of New Age prophetic beliefs is epitomized by the Harmonic Convergence, which was organized around a cross-cultural melange of prophecy traditions, the cycles of the Aztec and Mayan calendars, and the configuration of the planets in the solar system. The event was celebrated by tens of thousands of people throughout the world on August 16–17, 1987, dates interpreted as a critical juncture that would help determine the future salvation of the planet (Argüelles 1987). New Age beliefs tend to offer a kinder and gentler apocalypse, emphasizing "paradigm shifts" in global consciousness rather than societal destruction, and the gradual progression into a golden age of harmony and peace brought about by human effort and new forms of spirituality. However, catastrophic apocalyptic beliefs do exist among some New Agers, such as the thirty thousand devotees of the Church Universal and Triumphant, whose leader, Elizabeth Claire Prophet, has been predicting cataclysmic disasters for over a decade.

The syncretic nature of emergent traditions of apocalypticism in the twentieth century is exemplified by UFO beliefs, which comprise a synthesis of Christianity, Theosophy, Spiritualism, Eastern religions, New Age notions, and ideas inspired by science fiction literature and popular films. For the past fifty years, beliefs about UFOs and extraterrestrials have been characterized by expectations of imminent worldly destruction and salvation by superhuman beings, and these apocalyptic themes have been increasingly emphasized as the year 2000 approaches.

Like beliefs about UFOs which arose in the twentieth century, ideas about the senseless and unredemptive destruction of humanity are a predominantly twentieth-century phenomenon and are often diffused with a sense of helplessness and fatalistic resignation. Secular doomsday speculation, whether related to fears about nuclear annihilation, environmental catastrophes, overpopulation, or technological collapse, frequently has scientists and social critics as its main proponents (e.g., Meadows et al. 1972; Schell 1982) and pervades contemporary American literature, art, music, popular culture, and folklore. In popular film, secular doomsday scenarios have become almost a cliche, with portrayals of future nuclear cataclysms especially prevalent, from the early end-of-the-world visions of *On the Beach* (1959) and *Dr. Strangelove* (1963) to the nuclear docudramas in the 1980s, such as *Testament, Threads,* and *The Day After,* and the post–nuclear war action pictures such as the various *Planet of the Apes* films (late 1960s and 1970s) and *Mad Max* films (1979–1985). In recent years, environmental catastrophes have become increasingly popular in post-apocalyptic films; in *Waterworld* (1995), for example, the action takes place in the future after the ice caps have melted, with the hero, a mutant fish-man, battling barbaric, neotribal punk-pirates obsessed with destroying what remains of the earth's resources.

Filmic visions of a post-apocalyptic world often are similar to the scenarios imagined by some survivalist and militia groups that anticipate the collapse of society through a series of catastrophes, such as nuclear war, worldwide economic disaster, or race riots. Stockpiling weapons and supplies, the members of such groups prepare for Armageddon by developing "survival skills" and establishing bomb shelters or refuges in remote areas (see Coates 1987). Although some survivalist groups are not explicitly racist hate groups, white supremacist and neo-Nazi organizations such as the Posse Comitatus, the Order, and Aryan Nations are the most adamantly apocalyptic, expressing the determination to establish an Aryan empire after the occurrence of various societal cataclysms. In this sense, the beliefs of survivalists and militia groups differ from those of most other secular apocalypticists and resemble religious apocalyptic beliefs in that the establishment of a cleansed, new world is anticipated after the apocalypse.

Unlike the expectations of survivalists, members of various post–World War II youth subcultures have expressed a more pessimistic vision of the future, anticipating various societal cataclysms without hope of redemption. The early punk subculture, in particular, exhibited explicit apocalyptic themes, embracing as one of its mottos the idea of "no future" and reveling in visions of societal collapse and destruction (Hebdige 1979:27; Laing 1978:124; Wojcik 1995:9–11). The celebrated apathy and nihilism of so-called slackers and the members of Generation X (reflected in the book *Generation X,* with its preoccupation with nuclear annihilation, impending societal doom, and post–baby boom powerlessness) and the darker ethos of industrial music, with its preoccupation with societal decay and destruction, further illustrate the pervasiveness of secular visions of imminent catastrophe in American culture.

The Terminology of Apocalypse

Contemporary speculation about imminent societal cataclysm is vast indeed, yet not every reference to disaster, decline, or societal transformation is an expression of apocalypticism. The word *apocalypse* has differing connotations among academics, who have reached no consensus on the precise meaning of the term. When used by biblical scholars, *apocalypse* usually refers to Jewish or Christian literature involving revelations and prophecies about the end of time and the establishment of a new world, expressed in esoteric, cryptographic, or symbolic language.[4] The biblical use of the term derives from the Apocalypse of St. John, known also as the Revelation of John or the Book of Revelation, the last book in the New Testament. The term *apocalypse* came into theological use in the second century to designate a specific type of literature characterized by mysterious revelations communicated by a supernatural figure that involve the ultimate defeat of evil, the judgment of the world, and the creation of a new heaven and new earth (J. Collins 1989:3–4).

In contrast, other scholars have favored a broader meaning of the term, using the word *apocalypse* to refer to a sense of an ending, decline, societal crisis, and transformation, whether associated with actual historical events or expressed as themes in modern literature (e.g., Kermode 1967; Ketterer 1974; Robinson 1985; Wagar 1982) or science fiction (e.g., Dewey 1990; Rabkin et al. 1983). In popular parlance, *apocalypse* is now used loosely to refer to any sort of disaster, with no reference to divine revelations about the end of the history, or expectations of a supernatural scenario involving worldly destruction and renewal. As literary critic Frank Kermode notes, "In fashionable use, the word *apocalypse* has no very precise meaning, only vague connotations of doom" (1985:84). Such broad characterizations of *apocalypse* as a reference to any crisis or period of change are too general and arbitrary for a clear understanding of apocalyptic ideas today. On the other hand, definitions that consider the key features of *apocalypse* to be divine revelation, the supernatural defeat of evil, and the creation of a new world are restrictive and eliminate from consideration various emergent forms of endtimes thought, such as secular expectations of imminent and inevitable worldly cataclysm.

In this study the term *apocalypse* refers to the catastrophic destruction of world or current society, whether attributed to supernatural forces, natural forces, or human actions. Although this characterization of *apocalypse* is unconventional and perhaps somewhat controversial, it reflects the emic (or "folk") understanding of *apocalypse* as expressed in the wide range of beliefs, narratives, and behaviors discussed in this book. *Apocalypticism* and *apocalyptic* are used here to refer to those beliefs and discourses that assert that the cataclysmic destruction of the world is inevitable and unalterable by human effort, and these terms are used to describe both redemptive and unredemptive visions of the End.

The sense of fatefulness about the inevitability of worldly destruction, whether believed to be divinely predetermined or the inescapable consequence of the destructive behavior of human beings, distinguishes apocalyptic thought from other types of catastrophic speculation that predict imminent cataclysms but assert that human beings can intervene to prevent them. For example, in his book *The Fate of the Earth* (1982), Jonathan Schell speculates about the devastating effects of large-scale nuclear war, an event that he argues would end civilization. But Schell asserts that human action may lead to nuclear disarmament and thus prevent a nuclear apocalypse. Schell does not consider the end of the world to be inevitable, and because his speculations are not fatalistic, they are not truly apocalyptic but a form of secular cataclysmic forewarning. The belief that worldly destruction is inevitable and determined by uncontrollable external forces is an essential feature of apocalyptic thought that will be explored throughout this study.

The terms *millennialism* and *millenarianism* are usually applied to the study of apocalyptic beliefs, and refer to ideas about the imminent transformation of the current social order and the expectation of a perfect, new world of harmony and justice (Schwartz 1987:521). In Christian tradition, this perfect age is associated with the return of Christ and a predicted thousand-year period of peace and prosperity (the *millennium* or *chiliast*).[5] Millenarianism refers to the expectation of imminent, this-worldly, collective salvation that will be brought about by a divine or superhuman plan (Cohn 1970:15; Talmon 1968:349; Wessinger forthcoming:1). Contemporary millenarianism in the United States generally includes the belief that the transformation of the present world will be cataclysmic and accomplished in accordance with a divine plan, which will eliminate evil and establish a terrestrial paradise. This worldview (referred to variously as *catastrophic millennialism, apocalypticism,* or *premillennialism;* Wessinger forthcoming:2) expresses a pessimistic view of humanity, maintaining that the world is fatally flawed and unredeemable by human effort, and that only a divinely ordained worldly cataclysm can usher in the millennium. Yet not all millenarian beliefs emphasize a catastrophic scenario involving worldly destruction prior to the millennium. Christian postmillennialism, for example, asserts that the millennium will be brought about gradually and noncatastrophically by human beings acting according to a divine plan that will transform the world into a place worthy of Christ's Second Coming.

Mythology and Eschatology

Religious narratives about the end of the world, whether ancient or modern, belong to the category of mythology—sacred narratives that explain the existence of the world as well as the nature of human existence (see Dundes 1984). These sacred stories address absolute realities and issues of ultimate concern, expressing religious values and providing models for behavior. Deities, animals, and culture heroes are the main characters in myths, which are often set in an earlier world different from the world of today or in another world completely (Bascom 1965:9). Creation myths provide a religious account of the origin of things, explaining important aspects of human life and other phenomena: how and why the world originated, the role of deities in the creation of things, why people must suffer and die, why evil exists.

Not all myths address origins; some concern endings, or eschatology (the study of "the last things," from the Greek *eschatos,* "last" or "furthest"), such as the ultimate fate of the world or the fate of the soul after death. Individual eschatology deals with the existence of an afterlife, the transmigration of souls, the judgment of the dead, and the future of the soul in other spiritual realms, such as heaven or hell. Cosmic eschatology is concerned with the destiny of the universe, the end of the world, the end of time, the end of the gods, the end of humanity, the fate of humanity after that ending, and the creation of a perfect age (Werblowsky 1987:149). In traditional eschatology, the end of things is not thought to be a negative event, nor is it perceived as the absolute termination of all things. Religious eschatologies usually regard the end of the world optimistically because the apocalypse promises a new beginning in a redeemed new world. However, in the nineteenth century the belief in an unredemptive and meaningless end developed, what W. Warren Wagar refers to as a secular eschatology, involving the "study of world's ends that ignores religious belief or puts the old visions to use as metaphors for modern anxiety" (1982:4).

Like creation myths such as Genesis that awaken the desire for a lost paradise that once existed in a primordial time, apocalyptic myths frequently appeal to a sense of loss and alienation, inspiring a yearning for a perfect world that is free from suffering and evil. This millennial paradise is envisioned as an entirely new world, although often it is the symbolic equivalent of a mythical golden age or a paradise lost projected into the future and occurring at the end of time. The imagined millennial realm is the antithesis of current society, with its overwhelming suffering, evil, and injustice, none of which can be remedied by the established political, social, and religious institutions. In religious apocalyptic systems of belief, fatalism for the current society is reinforced by the faith in its inevitable destruction and redemption by divine forces. The mythic narratives of apocalyptic traditions thus offer religious solutions for both suffering and injustice by promising the destruction of an evil and oppressive old order, and the establishment of a morally just millennial kingdom of peace and harmony.

Folklore, Folk Religion, and Apocalyptic Beliefs

Much of contemporary religious apocalypticism may be usefully thought of as expressions of folk religion, defined as "the totality of all those views and practices of religion that exist among the people apart from and alongside the strictly theological and liturgical forms of the official religion" (Yoder 1974:14). Although the words *folk* and *folklore* may evoke images of peasants in costumes celebrating at harvest festivals or sitting around a fireside telling tales, folklorists today consider the "folk" to be any group of people with shared cultural traditions and expressive behaviors (their "lore") (Bauman 1992:35; Dorson 1970; Dundes 1965:1–3). The term *folklore* has been defined in varying ways, but folklorists generally agree that the concept refers to expressive behaviors and forms considered to be traditional and usually communicated in informal contexts or face-to-face interactions (see Georges and Jones 1995:1; Oring 1986:16–18). On the whole, contemporary folklorists study grassroots expressive culture and the experiences, beliefs, and behaviors of ordinary people often neglected or otherwise devalued.

Historically, apocalyptic ideas often have been manifestations of folk religion, originating apart from the official sanction of religious institutions and founded in personal experiences rather than prescribed by doctrines. The revolutionary millenarian movements that occurred in Europe between the eleventh and sixteenth centuries, for instance, were forms of apocalypticism that existed outside and in opposition to dominant ecclesiastical structures. In characterizing the popular appeal of these medieval millenarian movements, historian Norman Cohn notes that "the importance of the apocalyptic tradition should not be underestimated; even though official doctrine no longer had any place for it, it persisted in the obscure underworld of popular religion" (1970:30). The leaders of such movements—self-proclaimed messiahs, visionaries, heretics, and mystical anarchists—gained their authority apart from the institutional church and attracted disciples through personal charisma and promises of an apocalyptic end to current suffering and the establishment of a world free from pain, evil, and sin (Cohn 1970:16–17). Members of some groups, such as the Ranters and the Brethren of the Free Spirit, considered the institutional church to be an obstacle to salvation or even the enemy and regarded themselves as divine beings and thus incapable of sin and evil. Acknowledging no authority but their own experiences, these medieval millenarians created their own anarchistic religious communities, free of restraints, believing that they could murder, rob, lie, and engage in "free love" and other hedonistic activities without sin (Cohn 1970:150). This example may be extreme, but it illustrates the degree to which folk apocalyptic thought developed outside official religious institutions and gave rise to specific millenarian social movements.

British and American millenarianism in the late eighteenth century and the nineteenth century also developed apart from formal religious institutions, according to historian J. F. C. Harrison, who notes that "omens and auguries, dreams and divinations, magic, witchcraft and demons . . . the popular literature of chapbooks and almanacs lies close to the world of millenarian manifestations. . . . Folk culture provided the matrix in which millenarian yearnings could be nourished" (1979:39). Apocalyptic traditions of belief frequently have rejected institutional religious dogma and expressed desire for salvation outside established institutions, which are considered to be corrupt or evil and which therefore must be destroyed before a new social order may be established (B. Wilson 1973:19).

Today, many of the leading proponents of apocalyptic worldviews are not formally trained theologians associated with mainstream religious denominations or national organizations but visionaries or prophecy interpreters who derive their apocalyptic authority from their charisma, predictive abilities, or divinely inspired revelations attained outside the formal sanction of dominant social institutions.[6] Filling the void left by the general avoidance of detailed apocalyptic speculation within institutional religion, interpreters of apocalyptic prophecies usually do not lead formal pastorates but promote their ideas through personal ministries and rely primarily on their readership and media constituencies for support rather than affiliation with a particular denomination or a formally organized religious body (Boyer 1992:305). Contemporary apocalyptic belief in the United States is characterized by this "unofficial" and subcultural quality, existing at an informal level and usually transmitted outside the channels of official religious instruction.[7]

Current apocalyptic beliefs are expressed through oral traditions and customary lore and also communicated through photocopied fliers, mass-produced paperbacks, cable television, radio, telephone helplines, communications satellites, and computer newsgroups. Audio-video programs and printed materials are widely distributed by both small-scale groups and large, highly sophisticated promotional organizations. Hundreds of lay groups now operate their own printing presses and audio and video recording studios, arrange lectures and symposia, and conduct advertising campaigns. Even as apocalypticists may bemoan the state of current society and condemn modernity, they tend to embrace print and electronic technologies wholeheartedly, and are thus able to convey apocalyptic ideas to millions of people, spanning religious denominations as well as secular and religious distinctions.[8]

Although apocalyptic ideas are now often transmitted through the technology of mass communications, most of these ideas reflect commonly held worldviews and local folk beliefs. Certainly, some promoters of apocalyptic beliefs are savvy and exploitative entrepreneurs, but the majority of people who disseminate such ideas are sincere in their faith and have simply used new technologies to sustain and promote widespread popular traditions. Their publications and audio and video cassettes are replete with testimonials and beliefs that reflect the real experiences and faith of believers. The popular origin and often ephemeral nature of many of these printed and electronic documents bear some resemblance to the chapbooks and broadsides of previous times. Like these earlier forms associated with ordinary people and existing outside the intellectual mainstream of society, they represent "subliterary forms" of expression that stay close to popular traditions, reflect the beliefs of specific social groups, and ignore and scorn literary refinements (Dorson 1977:208). Print and electronic media are especially valuable sources of information about the subliterary expression of apocalyptic beliefs, revealing much about the spiritual culture of popular apocalypticism, illuminating the common themes, recurring ideas, and adaptability of apocalyptic ideas, and providing insights into the concerns, feelings, and hopes of people who anticipate the end of the world.

Electronic and print technologies have resulted in the increasing privatization of religion, enabling people to experience the sacred outside the sanction of religious institutions and in the privacy of their own homes. Dramatic and impassioned performances of radio and TV evangelists, inspirational videotapes containing poignant testimonials, or publications consisting of do-it-yourself spiritual techniques allow people to engage in religious pursuits apart from formalized religious structures. Formal religious institutions may not, in fact, be the center of religious belief for the majority of people in American society as individuals selectively choose and create belief systems from a variety of sources, formal and informal, mass-mediated and popular (see Luckmann 1967; Primiano 1995).

The privatization of apocalyptic beliefs is exemplified by the profusion of mass-marketed items on apocalyptic prophecy. The consumers of these materials may never come into direct contact with one another but instead may construct a personal vision of apocalypse gleaned from a diversity of sources. Most people who ascribe to or assimilate popular apocalyptic prophecy beliefs have not formed into separatist religious groups (like David Koresh's Branch Davidians) or created specific social movements (like the cargo cults of Oceania). Instead, this interest in apocalyptic ideas is a personalized expression of belief, largely unsanctioned by formal religious institutions and authorities yet existing at an informal level among millions of individuals.

Fatalistic Beliefs and Apocalypticism

Although contemporary apocalyptic ideas have become increasingly privatized, they are not idiosyncratic notions but are connected to larger traditions of belief, some of which have ancient origins. In the past, scholars have attempted to identify and typologize beliefs, using such categories as "magical," "superstitious," "supernatural," "religious," and "scientific" in their efforts to characterize people's behavior. Researchers have long been interested in what have been regarded as "fatalistic" beliefs; however, relatively few studies have been conducted on the meaning and appeal of such beliefs in contemporary societies.[9] For the most part, scholars have assigned negative connotations to fatalistic beliefs, associated them with the doctrines of ancient civilizations and the worldviews of non-Western peoples or considered them to be "survivals"—"animistic," irrational, prescientific, and heathen (see Doob 1988:6; Shaffer 1984).[10] Although the term *fatalism* is infrequently used by researchers to describe contemporary behavior, fatalism not only is central to American apocalypticism but is a pervasive mode of interpreting experiences and perceptions worldwide. One researcher asserts that "belief in fate is surely a cultural universal" (Grambo 1988:11); another estimates that thirteen million people in a dozen countries including the United States and Germany are "resigned to Fate or God's will" (Cantril 1965:277).

The word *fate* comes from the Latin *fatum,* literally "that which has been spoken," implying a sentence or doom of the gods, and originally associated with the spoken word of the Roman god Jupiter, which could not be altered (Leach 1972:371). Fatalism is usually distinguished from related concepts such as determinism, fortune, and destiny by the belief that human will or effort is incapable of altering the outcome of certain events.[11] Whether fate is believed to be derived from a personal power (a god) or an impersonal order, the underlying attitude in both instances is ultimately fatalistic if events are considered to be inevitable, determined by external forces, and unalterable by human will or effort. As folklorist Helmer Ringgren notes, "Theism and fatalism are intertwined, and there is in the realm of religion a great variety of interpretations of destiny in the sense of that which happens to man, the predetermined lot, the inescapable" (1967:11). A broad definition of fatalism thus includes both theistic belief (i.e., God's predetermined plan) and nonreligious belief (i.e., the inevitability of nuclear annihilation) about events that are considered to be unalterable by human action.

The bulk of research by folklorists on fatalistic ideas has focused on the documentation of examples of fate as expressed in folktales, ballads, religious legends, and other narratives.[12] Rolf Wilhelm Brednich (1964), for instance, has examined narratives about the Schicksalsfrauen—the three women of fate—often portrayed as omniscient divinities who spin the life and destiny of all people and whose decrees the gods themselves often cannot alter.[13] Narratives about the three Fates are widespread both cross-culturally and historically, known in Greek tradition as the Moirai, in Norse mythology as the three Norns, in Roman belief as the Parcae and Fata, in Gypsy tradition as the Ursitori, and in Anglo-Saxon tradition as the Wyrdes (and portrayed in Shakespeare's *Macbeth* as the three Weird Sisters; *wyrd* means "fate," or "what is to come" in Old English). In assorted folk traditions, the Fates are portrayed as the three spinners who appear after the birth of a child and spin the web of destiny, and in some folktales the Fates have been transformed into fairy godmothers or malevolent spinsters, their once-omniscient powers reduced to that of granting gifts and good fortune or cursing the lives of human beings.[14]

Other folklorists have proposed typologies of the various ways fate has been conceptualized historically, discussing how fate is conferred, the distinctions between a personal and impersonal determiner of fate, and the relation people may have with fate (see Brøndsted 1967; Grambo 1988; Ringgren 1967). C. J. Bleeker identifies general categories of beliefs about fate, such as the belief that one's destiny is related to the time, place, and circumstances of one's birth; that the "wheel of fortune" is capricious and turns arbitrarily, with one person born lucky, and another born with ill fortune; that fate is tragic and inescapable (the view presented in Greek tragedies); that a world order controls all events for good or bad; and that an all-knowing God predetermines people's destinies (1963:114–116).[15]

The persistence of fatalistic ideas today is indicated by beliefs in portents and omens, which are assertions that the future is predetermined and foretold by premonitions. Numerous common expressions, such as "It was fated that our paths would cross," "It was meant to be," "It's in the cards," "What will be will be—no matter what you do," and "When it's your time, it's your time," demonstrate the ubiquitous nature of fatalistic statements in daily speech. The expression that someone is "gifted," or born with certain natural abilities and talents, has its origins in the ancient belief that the Fates dispense gifts at birth, as well as good and ill fortune, and determine the destiny of the child. After the devastating Los Angeles earthquake of January 17, 1994, some residents described their immediate reactions to the quake in fatalistic terms: "I thought my time had come—my number was up." Widespread belief in astrology and various forms of fortune-telling also indicate that fatalistic thinking is a common means of interpreting the world. Even family courtship narratives often are characterized by the belief that initial romantic encounters and subsequent marriage are not coincidental occurrences but fated events (Zeitlin 1980:24–27).

Although current fatalistic beliefs and behavior often concern the role of fate in individual life, apocalyptic thinking conceptualizes fate as a cosmic, controlling power that determines history and the future of the earth and humanity. As historian Bernard McGinn observes, apocalyptic ideas from various religious traditions and historical periods exhibit "a sense of the unity and structure of history conceived as a divinely predetermined totality" (1979:10). In world mythology, ideas about omniscient and omnipotent fate traditionally are associated with concepts of history, time, the destruction and renewal of the world, and the end of humanity.[16] Such ideas from Greek antiquity are revealed in Hesiod's poem *The Works and Days*, which contains an account of the predestined decline of humanity through the five ages of the world, with each subsequent age becoming increasingly violent or foolish and culminating in Hesiod's own age. This final age is populated by the last generation of humanity, which is condemned to an existence of suffering, sorrow, and endless toil in an evil world that Zeus will finally destroy (Lattimore 1977:31–43). Hesiod lists the various evils in the world that have been ordained by Zeus and concludes, "There is no way to avoid what Zeus has intended" (Lattimore 1977:31).

American apocalyptic beliefs about the foreordained destruction of the world and the divine determination of history resemble these ancient notions about an unalterable and cosmic power that controls history and human destiny. The next chapter surveys the history of apocalyptic beliefs in the United States and explores the role of fatalistic thought in a diversity of American apocalyptic traditions.

2

The American Apocalyptic Legacy

> We, while the stars from heaven shall fall,
> And mountains are on mountains hurled,
> Shall stand unmoved amidst them all,
> And smile to see a burning world.
> —Millerite hymn, 1843

Historically, the United States has been conceptualized by numerous scholars (and characterized in popular sources) as the new Eden, a terrestrial paradise of political, economic, and religious freedom unfettered by the burdens of history. The notion that the "new lands" represented a millennial paradise was expressed by the earliest European explorers, including Columbus, who apparently believed that he was fated to fulfill various prophecies prior to the appearance of the Antichrist and imminent apocalypse (Watts 1985:74). Upon landing, Columbus supposedly quoted scripture from the Book of Revelation about discovering the Terrestrial Paradise—the "new heaven and new earth" cited in the Bible. According to historian Lois Zamora, Columbus believed that this millennial paradise was located at the tip of the earth, which he proclaimed was pear-shaped like a woman's breast, and from which flowed the waters of the Rivers of Eden (1982a:1).[1] Columbus, who intently studied the prophetic implications of biblical scripture and applied these to his own life, declared that his destiny as an explorer was to fulfill God's divine plan in preparation for the millennial kingdom on earth; as he wrote in his journal, "God made me the messenger of the new heaven and the new earth of which he spoke in the Apocalypse of St. John . . . and he showed me the spot where to find it" (Watts 1985:102).

Eschatological beliefs pervade the writings of the Puritans, many of whom maintained that they had been elected by God to fulfill a divinely determined historical plan. Puritan settlements were conceived as communal millennialist prototypes, established in anticipation of Christ's Second Coming. The sermons of Puritan preachers such as John Cotton and Increase Mather often dealt with apocalyptic prophecy. Cotton asserted in *The Pouring Out of the Seven Vials* (1642) that doomsday would occur after the destruction of the Catholic Church, which was identified as the Antichrist. In *The Mystery of Israel's Salvation Explained and Applyed* (1669), Mather maintained that the conversion of the Jews to Christianity would foretell the end of the world. The apocalyptic speculations of Increase Mather's son, Cotton Mather, had an especially strong influence on American colonialist religion. Cotton Mather was preoccupied with prophecy and the specifics of Christ's Second Coming—how Christ would return, who would accompany him, the exact date, and the location of the millennial kingdom on earth—all of which he believed could be predicted by interpreting contemporary events as providences (Erwin 1990:7–8). As folklorist Richard Dorson notes, widespread beliefs in providence, regarded as manifest signs of God's divine will and intention, pervaded colonialist thought: "Since in the Puritan and Reformation concept, God willed every event, from the black plague to the sparrow's fall, all events held meanings for errant man. The Lord worked chiefly through natural or secondary causes, or He might intervene directly in the processes of the world, as a first cause, but whichever the case, He guided every occurrence" (1973:17).

Early Puritan and Calvinist apocalyptic writings express the belief that human actions and historical events reflect God's divine plan, that the world is unredeemable, and that human salvation is predetermined by God. The widespread ideas about predestination that were fundamental to Calvinist and Puritan belief exemplify the fatalistic underpinnings of early American religious thought. According to early Calvinist theology, human beings are completely depraved (because of Adam's fall), God's will is absolute, and humankind cannot be saved by good works but only by God's grace.[2] Most important, according to this view, an elect group has been predestined from eternity for everlasting life in heaven while the rest of humanity is doomed to suffer the eternal torments of hell. As the historian of religion August Dorner observes, "According to Calvin, everything is subject to the omnipotent Will, and a certain number of the human race are rejected from the outset, simply because God willed that they should be sinful and should persist in their sin. . . . God's *horribile decretum* is thus, so far as the reprobate are concerned, neither more or less a Fate from which there is no escape" (1928:776).[3] God's decision for the fate of each person could not be known or influenced; believers could only strive to fulfill God's laws regardless of their ultimate fate.[4]

The apocalyptic ideas prevalent in Puritan belief are reflected in Michael Wigglesworth's poem "The Day of Doom" (published in 1662), which enumerates in graphic detail the Day of Judgment, the imminent destruction of the world, and the punishment of sinners in hell. Wigglesworth based his poem on a dream that he had had nine days earlier, and he wrote it in ballad meter so that it could be easily memorized. The following passage, which depicts Christ's return and his divine judgment of sinners, typifies Wigglesworth's colloquial style:

> For at midnight breaks forth a light,
>   which turns the night to day,
> And speedily an hideous cry
>   doth all the world dismay.
> Sinners awake, their hearts do ache,
>   trembling their loins surpriseth;
> Amaz'd with fear, by what they hear,
>   each one of them ariseth.
>
> They rush from beds with giddy heads,
>   and to their windows run,
> Viewing this light, which shines more bright
>   than doth the noon-day Sun.
> Straightway appears (they see't with tears)
>   the Son of God most dread,
> Who with his Train comes on amain
>   to judge both Quick and Dead.
>   (1867:22–23)

In the poem, the Day of Judgment is initiated with a burst of light, which is then followed by a blast and worldwide fire that would fill all with terror. Despite the emphasis on impending doom throughout its 224 stanzas, Wigglesworth's poem, like the sermons of other preachers of the time, countered the threat of imminent destruction with the promise of the millennium for the righteous. The poem was so popular that no first or second editions of it remain in existence; they were thumbed to shreds. One out of every twenty citizens in the Bay Colony bought a copy of the poem, making it the first American best-seller (Benét 1987:242).

In the seventeenth and eighteenth centuries, influential preachers such as Jonathan Edwards sustained and elaborated upon American prophecy beliefs. As Lois Zamora observes, "It is safe to say that every preacher in New England between 1660 and the Revolution preached a good portion of hellfire and brimstone. The conventional apocalyptic imagery of the Day of Judgment, the seven vials of wrath, the last assize, the devouring flames, the catalogue of pestilences, the chaos of pandemonium were all exploited to the ample extent of their terror" (1982b:104). Edwards, a master of apocalyptic rhetoric, frequently warned of doom in his sermons and portrayed human beings as depraved sinners who were at the complete mercy of a wrathful God. This sense of powerlessness before a deity who controlled all things is illustrated by the famous passage in Edwards's sermon "Sinners in the Hands of an Angry God": "The God that holds you over the pit of hell, much as one holds a spider, or some loathsome insect, over the fire, abhors you, and is dreadfully provoked. . . . You hang by a slender thread, with the flames of divine wrath flashing about it, and ready every moment to singe it, and burn it asunder" (cited in Foerster 1970:68). Edwards was especially fascinated with the prophetic meanings of his era, and a collection of his sermons entitled *A History of the Work of Redemption* (1786), published forty-seven years after they were first delivered, contains his ideas about history, which he regarded as unified by a grand design and a causal chain of events divinely directed by God (Zamora 1982b:105).

Postmillennialist beliefs were widespread during the Great Awakening and stressed the eventual establishment of God's kingdom on earth. The religious revivals during this period deemphasized imminent worldly cataclysm and asserted that the millennial age would be brought about gradually by human beings in fulfillment of God's plan. In various postmillennialist prophecy traditions, the United States was viewed as having a prophetic destiny as a chosen nation that would redeem the world and usher in the millennium (see Tuveson 1968). According to historian Ruth Bloch, assorted millennialist ideas contributed to the development of a revolutionary consciousness prior to the American Revolution, providing "the main structure of meaning through which contemporary events were linked to an exalted image of an ideal world" (1985:xiii). During this time, many Americans anticipated the coming of the millennium, although they differed with regard to their interpretations of its initiation. Some, for instance, saw the Great Awakening as the beginning of the millennium; others interpreted the American Revolution as inaugurating the millennial age on earth.

The late eighteenth century to the middle of the nineteenth century saw the formation of numerous religious groups with utopian and millennialist aspirations. Many of the most popular and successful of these organizations stressed communal living, withdrawal from society, and establishment of a millennial kingdom on earth. The Shakers, also known as the United Society of Believers in Christ's Second Appearing, are perhaps the most celebrated of these religious groups. The founder of the organization was Ann Lee, who emigrated from England to the colonies in 1774, and who based many of the group's teachings on her own ecstatic experiences and visions. "Mother Ann," as she became known, announced that Christ had returned in feminine form and that she herself was the embodiment of Christ's Second Advent. As the result of this proclamation, the Shakers contended that the millennium had been initiated and that it would be attained on earth through their beliefs and practices. Shaker customs included communal living, equality of the sexes, celibacy, and isolation from the sinful influences of the world. By the 1840s approximately six thousand people were members of nearly twenty Shaker communities; a few years ago only a handful of Shaker women were still living (Lippy 1982:44).

The Oneida Community, like the Shakers' community, was also established in the 1830s as the result of millennialist expectations. John Humphrey Noyes, its founder, became better known for his unorthodox ideas about sexual relations and communal living than for his assertion that he had attained a state of millennial perfection and that the millennial kingdom had been established on earth in the form of the Oneida Community (Barkun 1987b:153–172). Other sectarian groups in the nineteenth century, such as the Christadelphians, also anticipated Christ's return, interpreting contemporary events as signs that the End was imminent.

Around the same time, the predictions of William Miller prompted the formation of the Millerites, known for their failed prophecies about the end of the world. Inspired by a conversion experience at a revival, Miller became immersed in interpretation of the apocalyptic sections of the Bible in an attempt to predict the exact date of the end of the world and the beginning of the millennium. Like others before him, Miller believed that the Scriptures contained a numerical cryptogram revealing the exact date of the apocalypse. Convinced that this date could be mathematically decoded, Miller labored fervently to calculate precisely the day of doom. Miller was reluctant to proclaim his views publicly, but his ideas were actively promoted by others, particularly the publicist Joshua Himes. By March 1843, the designated time of Miller's predicted end of the world, he had thousands of followers (Harrison 1979:192–203).

Belief in Miller's prophetic pronouncements persisted even though his predictions failed in 1843 and again in 1844. The following recollection by the Millerite Hiram Edson expresses both the joyful anticipation of Christ's return as well as the sense of profound disillusionment when it did not occur as expected:

[W]e confidently expected to see Jesus Christ and all the holy angels with him . . . and that our trials and sufferings with our earthly pilgrimage would close, and we should be caught up to meet our coming Lord. . . . Our expectations were raised high, and thus we looked for our coming Lord until the clock tolled 12 at midnight. The day had then passed and our disappointment became a certainty. Our fondest hopes and expectations were blasted, and such a spirit of weeping came over us as I never experienced before. It seemed that the loss of all earthly friends could have been no comparison. We wept, and wept, till the day dawn. (Numbers and Butler 1987:215)

After the devastation of what became known as the "Great Disappointment," many disenchanted Millerites were attracted to other millenarian movements, the most notable being that of the Seventh-day Adventists. According to Adventist belief, Miller's predictions were accurate. Adventists asserted that an "invisible" or spiritual apocalypse was initiated in 1843–1844 with the "cleansing of heaven," and it was soon to be followed by the destructive cleansing of earth. Adventist beliefs and practices centered around the teaching of the visionary and prophetess Ellen G. White, who, like Shakers founder Ann Lee, often fell into trance states and then later communicated her divine revelations about the establishment of a millennial kingdom. In one vision, for instance, she was informed that specific restrictions on dietary and health practices were a necessary form of premillennial purity, and she thus denounced the evils of meat, alcohol, tobacco, masturbation, and modern medical science (Williams 1990:215).

This emphasis on the body and health as expressions of spiritual perfection and millennial purity was widespread in the United States in the early and mid-1800s. The evangelist Sylvester Graham, for instance, created the graham cracker in the 1830s as an alternative means of food reform designed to promote physical and spiritual health. The Adventist interest in alternative diet, health reform, and millennial bodily perfection resulted in the experimentation with water cures, the invention of peanut butter, and the creation of cold breakfast cereal, which was developed by devotee John Harvey Kellogg, who perfected the corn flake during his involvement in the Adventist community in Battle Creek, Michigan (Williams 1990:215).

Adventist belief today continues to stress prophetic interpretations of the present and future. According to Adventist doctrine, all of the apocalyptic predictions preceding the end of the world have been fulfilled except one. This final prophecy states that when a group of "prepared people" (interpreted as the Adventists themselves) proclaim that the End is imminent and spread this message throughout the world, Christ will return.

The millennialism of the Church of Jesus Christ of Latter-Day Saints, better known as the Mormons, is based on the revelations that its founder Joseph Smith had in the 1820s. In his visions, Smith was informed by an angel that Christ's Second Advent was imminent and that he had been chosen to help bring about God's will by gathering together the saints in the last days and preparing humanity for the millennium (Harrison 1979:176–178). The millennial kingdom is destined to be established in the United States, according to Mormon belief, and one of the reasons for the Mormon westward movement and settlement in Utah was to found the New Zion in expectation of Christ's Second Coming and millennial reign.

The beliefs of the Jehovah's Witnesses also regard the establishment of the millennium as foreordained. According to founder Charles Taze Russell, the spiritual Second Coming of Christ occurred in 1874 in the "upper air," initiating a "Millennial Dawn." However, Russell asserted that the fulfillment of Christ's millennial kingdom would be completed only after the prophesied destruction of nations, governments, churches, and world leaders, all of which he considered to represent Satan's rule. Characterized by a radical interpretation of the Bible and the rejection of all secular and religious sources of authority, Russell eliminated the concept of hell from his theology, distinguished between Jehovah and Christ as distinct entities, denied the existence of the Trinity, and predicted an elaborate scenario of events to occur in the millennial kingdom (see Penton 1983:169–207).

Russell's ideas were continued by Joseph Rutherford, who named the group Jehovah's Witnesses and established meeting places in the form of Kingdom Halls (rather than churches, which were considered satanic). As a result of this distrust of formal religious and governmental organizations, the Witnesses developed the practice of door-to-door evangelism. All Witnesses are considered ministers who are obliged to proselytize the truth as the apocalypse approaches. The Witnesses' emphasis on personal interaction and proselytizing continues today. Within weeks after I ordered the luxuriantly illustrated *Revelation: Its Grand Climax At Hand!* from the Witnesses' Watchtower Bible and Tract Society located in Brooklyn, New York (the national organization maintained by the Witnesses), several Witnesses came to my residence to hand deliver the book and invite me to a "Saturday memorial of the death of Jesus Christ," held the day before Easter Sunday at a Kingdom Hall in the neighborhood. The introductory remarks in the book exemplify the spirited anticipation of inevitable worldly cataclysm and transformation that pervades much of Witnesses literature:

How do we find happiness through the book of Revelation? We do so by searching out the meaning of its vivid signs, or symbols, and acting in harmony therewith. Mankind's turbulent history will soon reach a catastrophic climax, as God and Jesus Christ execute judgment on today's wicked system, replacing it with "a new heaven and new earth.". . . Here we find, not a mere fatalistic message of world doom, but an uncovering of divine truths that should build in our hearts a radiant hope and an immovable faith. (Watchtower Bible and Tract Society of Pennsylvania 1988:6)

Because Jehovah's Witnesses believe that Christ's millennial age has been initiated on earth, they have often rejected other forms of authority, refusing to support the military, to salute the flag and say the Pledge of Allegiance, and to engage in certain types of health care such as accepting blood transfusions. These refusals, in addition to their earlier targeting of Catholicism as the embodiment of the Antichrist and their door-to-door proselytization, resulted in widespread criticism and marginalization. Despite the ostracism, however, Jehovah's Witnesses continues to be one of the fastest-growing religious groups in the United States.

Not all of the numerous apocalyptic movements that arose in the nineteenth and early twentieth centuries occurred among white Americans. In the 1870s and 1890s, beliefs about the violent transformation of the current social order were essential to the Ghost Dance movement among Native Americans. As a response to cultural oppression and radical cultural change, the Ghost Dance movement stressed the rejection of Western influences, the revival of traditional ceremonies, and the apocalyptic promise of the divine destruction of white settlers, followed by a millenarian return to the world as it was before the white man's arrival (see Linton 1943). Millenarian expectations have also been a part of African-American religious experience, particularly Pentecostal and Holiness groups, although several observers have stated that these groups tend to stress conversion, sanctification, perfection, rigid morality, and millennialist aspirations rather than beliefs about imminent apocalypse (see Lippy 1982:51).

In the 1960s, apocalyptic beliefs became increasingly popular among Christian youth movements, such as the Jesus people or "Jesus Freaks." As one researcher notes, "Everything in the Jesus Movement is colored by apocalyptic mentality. Bumper stickers flaunt it; songs repeat it; witnessing returns to it over and over again; sermons and personal conversations are obsessed by it" (Enroth et al. 1972:179–180). Offshoots of the Jesus Movement, such as the Alamo Christian Foundation, the Love Family (known officially as the Church of Armageddon), and David Berg's group the Children of God, have similarly asserted that the annihilation of current society and the transformation of the world is imminent and inevitable.

Apocalyptic visions have characterized the beliefs associated with an extraordinary diversity of recent religious organizations in the United States: the Unification Church of Reverend Sun Myung Moon, the International Society of Krishna Consciousness, Baha'i organizations, and other movements based in non-Western religious traditions; various New Age religious groups, exemplified by the apocalyptic predictions associated with the Church Universal and Triumphant, the Harmonic Convergence, and spirit channeler J. Z. Knight/Ramtha. Although known primarily for its publication *The Plain Truth* and its celebrity concerts held at Ambassador College Auditorium in Pasadena, the Worldwide Church of God, founded by Herbert W. Armstrong, continues to stress the prophetic role of the United States and Britain in God's endtimes plan.

The most publicized American apocalyptic group, prior to the Branch Davidians, was Jim Jones's "Peoples Temple," which ended in the mass murder-suicide of 914 people who drank Kool-Aid laced with cyanide in the remote jungles of Guyana on November 18, 1978 (Chidester 1988:15). Jones and his followers viewed the current world, which they said dehumanized women, African-Americans, and the elderly, as corrupt, and Jones pronounced himself to be a messenger sent to establish a socialist millennial kingdom after an evil capitalistic society was destroyed by a nuclear cataclysm. When the Peoples Temple was threatened by U.S. government investigation, damaging news coverage, and defections, the majority of the community chose to commit collective suicide, which was considered to be a heroic act that would transform members into a higher level of existence and provide salvation from an irredeemably evil world (Chidester 1988:155; Wessinger 1995:4, 9).

In the United States today, a multitude of contemporary popular prophets declare that apocalypse is foreordained and part of a supernatural plan for humanity. Millions of people currently believe that the present is divinely patterned and that the world will end in the near future (D. Wilson 1977:12). As noted, the extent to which apocalyptic beliefs permeate American culture was illustrated in April 1984, when President Ronald Reagan's interest in biblical prophecies about Armageddon received national attention in the press and on radio. An article in the *Washington Post* asserted that Reagan held millennialist beliefs about the inevitability of a nuclear Armageddon and that his foreign policy had been influenced by these beliefs (Dugger 1984). In a presidential debate on October 21, 1984, when questioned by Marvin Kalb of NBC about his beliefs concerning apocalypse, Reagan said that he had discussed the topic of Armageddon as the fulfillment of divine prophecy with various theologians. Reagan had previously stated in a telephone conversation in 1983:

> You know, I turn back to your ancient prophets in the Old Testament and the signs foretelling Armageddon, and I find myself wondering if—if we're the generation that's going to see that come about. I don't know if you've noted any of those prophecies lately, but believe me, they certainly describe the times we're going through. (Conversation with Thomas Dine, executive director of the American-Israeli Public Affairs Committee, October 18, 1983; published in the *Jerusalem Post*, October 28, 1983; cited in L. Jones 1985:65)

Reagan's interest in biblical prophecies about the last days and his relationships with Christian theologians who had expressed apocalyptic views (Jerry Falwell, Billy Graham, Jimmy Swaggert, Pat Robertson, Jim Bakker, and Hal Lindsey) caused fearful speculation about the possibility of an apocalyptic religious coalition influencing foreign policy and initiating what they believed would be a divinely sanctioned nuclear war (Halsell 1986:40–50; L. Jones 1985). These fears escalated when people learned that Secretary of the Interior James Watt and Secretary of Defense Caspar Weinberger expressed interests similar to Reagan's about the imminence of the coming of Christ and the end of the world.

As these examples indicate, beliefs and behaviors expressing a fascination with prophecy have thrived in American popular belief, despite the fact that most orthodox churches deemphasize prophecy and reject outright the practice of predicting events relating to the end of the world. Televangelists such as Jerry Falwell, Pat Robertson, Rex Humbard, Jim Robison, Oral Roberts, Jimmy Swaggert, Jack Van Impe, and Billy Graham, among many others, have popularized and reinforced such beliefs through broadcasts that regularly reach more than sixty million Americans (Halsell 1986:11). In addition to premillennialist televangelism, a profusion of mass-marketed paperbacks on apocalyptic prophecy in recent years depict current disasters and contemporary political events as portents indicating the inevitability of the end of the world. For individuals interested in current updates of the signs of the End, periodicals such as *Prophecy 2000, The Endtime Messenger, Countdown, Rapture Alert Newsletter, It's Happening Now, International Intelligence Briefing,* and *Bible Prophecy News* provide the latest interpretations of recent events in terms of biblical prophecies. In addition to hundreds of nationwide radio broadcasts on prophecy, mass-marketed video and audio cassettes, seminars, slide presentations, lectures, and retreats organized by independent ministries are available. Films and video cassettes that portray apocalyptic prophecies, such as *A Thief in the Night, A Distant Thunder, Image of the Beast, Prodigal Planet, The Final Hour,* and *The Road to Armageddon* are regularly shown in premillennialist evangelical settings. According to estimates by its producers, *A Thief in the Night* (1973) has been seen by one hundred million people in the United States (Balmer 1988:426). Apocalyptic comic books distributed by Jack Chick Publications and end-times picture books by the prolific author Salem Kirban are accessible guides to the end of the world, with color illustrations of the tribulation period, the rise of the Antichrist, the forced laser-tattooing of the "Mark of the Beast" in the last days, the horrors of doomsday, and the joys of the millennial kingdom.

These diverse contemporary manifestations of Christian apocalypticism have their origins in the ancient Jewish prophetic tradition, which asserted that God's plan for humanity was revealed through divinely inspired prophets (Bergoffen 1982:27–28). The concept of human history being divinely determined and ultimately resulting in the establishment of an earthly paradise has been dated at least as far back as the prophecies of Isaiah in the eighth century B.C.E. (Bloch 1985:xi). The profound influence of apocalyptic ideas on Christian thought has been noted by numerous scholars and illustrated by theologian Ernst Käsemann's assertion that "apocalyptic was the mother of all Christian theology" (1969:40).

The inspiration for most contemporary Christian prophecy stems from specific apocalyptic passages in the Bible, particularly the books of Revelation, Daniel, Zechariah, and Ezekiel, which are generally considered to be the most complete of the biblical apocalyptic writings. The prophetic messages suggested in these sections of scripture have captivated Christian thought for centuries, and continue to fascinate a significant portion of the populace today. Understandings of the prophetic imagery associated with the end of the world have varied considerably in different historical and cultural contexts because of the esoteric language and ambiguous allusions in these ancient biblical passages. The symbolism of the opening of the seven seals, the pouring of the seven vials, the judgment and fall of Babylon, and the return of Christ described in the Book of Revelation has been interpreted in numerous ways and assumed to represent often entirely different incidents. The apocalyptic language and unusual tone expressed in the Book of Revelation, in particular, have motivated diverse explanations and have been commented on by countless observers. The novelist D. H. Lawrence, for instance, offered the following interpretation of its imagery and popular appeal:

And this is Jesus: not only the Jesus of the early churches, but the Jesus of popular religion today. There is nothing humble nor suffering here . . . it is a true account of man's *other* conception of God; perhaps the greater and more fundamental conception: the magnificent Mover of the Cosmos! To John of Patmos, the Lord is *Kosmokrator*, and even *Kosmodynamous*, the great Ruler of the Cosmos, and the Power of the Cosmos. . . . Now again we realize a dual feeling in ourselves with regard to the Apocalypse. Suddenly we see some of the old pagan splendour, that delighted in the might and the magnificence of the cosmos. Suddenly we feel again the nostalgia for the old pagan world. (Cited in Kawada 1985:74–75)

Other writers have said that for many people the symbolism of the Book of Revelation has supplanted other aspects of Christ's message; the atomic bomb, the apocalyptic attitude of the sixties, and perceptions of societal upheaval have inspired not so much a revival of belief in Jesus as a fascination with the Book of Revelation (Ventura 1985:223). Historian and psychoanalyst Charles Strozier, commenting on the popular appeal of the apocalyptic sections of the Bible, observes, "If all the bombs go off or we choke ourselves in a haze of pollution, the human story will die in ways that make little sense in a theology based on the compassion of the Sermon on the Mount. The focus on violence by way of tribulation gives the traditional Christian story the edge it needs to fit our crumbling and maybe dying world" (1994:89).

Although interpretations of the apocalyptic passages in the Bible vary, the eschatological visions promoted by popular premillennialists are relatively consistent in one respect: most assume that the events of the present are signs that foretell of the ultimate destruction of an unredeemably corrupt society predicted in the Bible as a part of God's divine plan. Perhaps the most persistent theme in contemporary prophecy is that the end of the world will occur as a result of nuclear apocalypse.

Images and visions of nuclear annihilation have been easily incorporated into traditional Christian eschatology, with the symbolic and cryptic language of the Book of Revelation regarded as prophetic descriptions of the realities of nuclear war. The inevitability of nuclear annihilation not only has been integrated into traditional apocalyptic belief systems but has been sanctified as a meaningful occurrence that is necessary for the redemption of humanity.

Before the invention of nuclear weapons, biblical references to a fiery cataclysm at the end of time were interpreted in terms of natural disasters, such as earthquakes, comets, and volcanic eruptions. After the bombing of Hiroshima and Nagasaki, many interpreters of prophecy were convinced that the Scriptures had predicted the invention of atomic weapons and foretold of their apocalyptic use (Boyer 1992:115). From the beginning of the atomic age prophecy believers searched the Bible for possible allusions to nuclear confla-gration and found persuasive evidence for the inevitability of nuclear apoca-lypse. References to fiery destruction in the Book of Revelation, for example, suggested atomic warfare—an allusion to "hail and fire mixed with blood" which burns a third of the land and trees and "all green grass" sounded like nuclear war (Rev. 8:7); an allusion to scorching heat and malignant sores might describe the aftermath of atomic radiation (Rev. 16:2–8). For some believers, Zechariah's (14:12) account of human flesh being consumed as peo-ple stand on their feet appeared to resemble the effects of a nuclear firestorm, as do the predictions of a coming day that shall burn like an oven and set peo-ple on fire (Malachi 3:19) and flames burning all the trees of the field (Joel 1:19). The compatibility of ancient prophecies about "fire from the heavens" and visions of nuclear cataclysm is illustrated by the often-cited passage of a melting earth from 2 Peter: "The heavens shall pass away with a great noise, and the elements shall be disintegrated with intense heat; the earth also, and all its works, shall be burned up" (3:10). Convinced that nuclear weapons were the means by which ancient prophecies of "fire and brimstone" raining down from the heavens would be realized, prophecy believers from various traditions embraced the development of nuclear weapons as a portent indi-cating that humanity had accelerated its progression toward an apocalypse that was inevitable. As one prophecy believer remarked: "The holocaust of atomic war would fulfill the prophecies. . . . The Bible and science go right down the line together on the forecasting of future events for earth" (Reid 1968:160, 165).

The endtimes that occur prior to nuclear apocalypse and Christ's return are envisioned by prophecy enthusiasts as times of oppression, suffering, and the apparent triumph of evil over good. The last days are characterized as a period of signs and portents that reveal the imminence of doomsday and Christ's Sec-ond Coming, at which time all existing evil will be judged and abruptly destroyed. Consequently, apocalypse is anticipated by many believers with joy-ful expectation. This enthusiasm about the inevitability of the end of the world is exemplified in a fund-raising letter by singer Pat Boone, sent out by the inter-national evangelistic organization Bibles for the World: "My guess is that there isn't a thoughtful Christian alive who doesn't believe we are living at the end of history. I don't know how that makes you feel, but it gets me pretty excited. Just think about actually seeing, as the apostle Paul wrote it, the Lord Himself descending from heaven with a shout! Wow! And the signs that it's about to happen are everywhere" (Woodward et al. 1977:51). Boone is an advocate of premillennial dispensationalism, the most influential form of religious apocalypticism in the United States today.

Dispensationalism is a form of Christian fundamentalism, often associated with Pentecostalism and espoused by the majority of televangelists and successful apocalyptic authors, including Hal Lindsey, Pat Robertson, Jerry Falwell, John Walvoord, Kenneth Copeland, Rex Humbard, Tim and Beverly LaHaye, Jack Van Impe, Salem Kirban, and the once-popular Jimmy Swaggert and Jim and Tammy Bakker. Dispensationalism, like Christian fundamentalism, is characterized by its emphasis on biblical literalism and inerrancy, supernaturalism, support for conservative political causes, and its condemnation of communism, secularism, science, and ecumenicism. Although the character and motives of dispensationalists Jimmy Swaggert and Jim Bakker came into question as the result of sex scandals (and Bakker's being found guilty of fraud and misappropriation of funds), and although other fundamentalists have been accused of being motivated by the desire for fame, influence, and wealth, most are sincere in their efforts to save souls, which involves teaching the gospel of Jesus Christ and converting others to this gospel before Christ's imminent return (Hadden and Swann 1981:13–14).[5] The centrality of apocalyptic beliefs in the lives of fundamentalists is explored in detail by Charles Strozier in *Apocalypse: On the Psychology of Fundamentalism in America* (1994). Examining the ways that apocalyptic beliefs reflect the life experiences and affect the everyday lives of fundamentalists, Strozier notes that "the apocalyptic is more than the subtext. It is the ground of fundamentalist being" (1994:11).

The dispensationalist beliefs embraced by many fundamentalists have their origins in the nineteenth century, when this belief system emerged as a competing interpretation of the meaning of millennialism in America. The three distinctive types of Christian millennialism, as Timothy Weber (1987) notes, are generally identified as amillennialism, postmillennialism, and premillennialism. The term *amillennialism* involves the belief that biblical references to the millennium are symbolic and figurative, with the millennial rule of Christ occurring in the hearts of believers (Weber 1987:9). *Postmillennialism* is characterized by an expectation of the gradual transformation of society brought about by Christian ideals, the belief in the idea of human progress and perfection, and a relatively liberal perspective. The millennium, this view maintains, will be brought about by humans working in accordance with a divine plan and will be achieved by means of religious revivals, social reform, and the triumph of Christian principles. This steady progression toward goodness will ultimately result in the defeat of all evil and the establishment of a golden age, after which Christ will return (Weber 1987:9–14). In the nineteenth century, some postmillennialists regarded slavery, alcoholism, child labor, and other social ills as impeding the establishment of God's kingdom on earth and they worked to improve society in an effort to attain a state of millennial perfection. This movement, known as the Social Gospel, remained a popular means of millenarian social reform through the 1920s.

Christian premillennialism, on the other hand, has been identified as involving an interpretation of humanity and the world as unrecuperably evil. Premillennialists assert that an inherently sinful world can be redeemed only through catastrophe and supernatural intervention. Holding that the imminent return of Christ is the only means of rectifying the world's problems, premillennialists believe that a thousand-year reign of peace on earth will be established after Christ returns. Prior to the Second Coming of Christ, humanity will become increasingly evil (a state that is generally thought to be occurring during the believers' own lifetimes) and the Antichrist will rise to power, persecute Christians, and wreak havoc upon the world during a period of tribulation. The Antichrist will be destroyed at the Battle of Armageddon by Christ and his legions and a millennial realm will then be established that will last for one thousand years, after which Satan and the forces of evil will rise up to do battle with Christ once again. The final defeat of Satan and all evil in this battle will be followed by the resurrection of the dead, the last judgment, and the creation of a new heaven and a new earth for God's people (Weber 1987:10–11).

Contemporary premillennial dispensationalism is derived from a belief system that developed in England in the 1820s and that quickly became a predominant expression of apocalyptic ideas in the United States. Early American dispensationalism was initially promoted by John Nelson Darby (1800–1882), a member of the Plymouth Brethren. Influenced by Darby's system and relying on Cyrus I. Scofield's Reference Bible (1909), dispensationalists divide history into seven epochs and maintain that humanity has been predestined to pass through each of these dispensational periods, during which God tests and communicates with humankind in differing ways. One of these dispensational epochs ended with Christ's resurrection, and the next will be initiated by the Rapture, when the Christian faithful are removed from the earth (Weber 1987:16–24).

Dispensationalism gained increasing popularity after the Niagara Bible Conferences that began in 1875, and this system of belief had replaced postmillennialism as the dominant form of millenarianism by the early twentieth century. As a response to the Protestant liberalism of the time, dispensationalism ultimately converged with the fundamentalist movement, emphasizing doctrine over religious experience and insisting on the absolute authority of the Bible as a divine document dictated by God. Regarding the Scriptures as literally true and inerrant, dispensationalists use the Bible not only as a sacred guidebook for individual behavior but as a means of determining God's plan for human history.

Although scholars have noted that visions of catastrophe and social transformation as well as social progress are found in both premillennialist and postmillennialist systems of belief, and that the distinctions between the two are not absolute, premillennialism tends to be more pessimistic in its appraisal of the world (Schwartz 1976:6). Humanity is generally regarded as irredeemably evil, and social problems are interpreted as omens of a bankrupt society on the verge of imminent apocalypse. Premillennial dispensationalist attitudes appear overtly fatalistic, emphasizing inevitable cataclysm and deemphasizing the efficacy of human effort to improve the world. Responsibility for bringing about the millennium is attributed to supernatural forces, and human beings cannot really effect any significant change in an unrecuperably evil world. As A. G. Mojtabai notes in her discussion of dispensationalist perspectives on the arms race, "The repeated theme of the dispensationalist vision is that humans are powerless to build a just and peaceful future, powerless to avert the destruction to come" (1986:149). Because human beings are destined to fail each of God's seven dispensations and are incapable of improving the world, dispensationalists emphasize enduring the evils of this world while vigilantly looking for the signs of the End that offer the promise of the Rapture and a redemptive, new realm. In the next chapter, the dispensationalist belief system will be examined in detail, specifically as it is expressed in the writings of Hal Lindsey, the most popular and influential proponent of apocalyptic prophecy in the twentieth century.

3

Signs of the Endtimes

Hal Lindsey and Dispensationalist Prophecy Beliefs

> To the skeptic who says that Christ is not coming soon, I would ask him to put the book of Revelation in one hand, and the daily newspaper in the other, and then sincerely ask God to show him where we are on His prophetic time-clock.
>
> —Hal Lindsey, *There's a New World Coming*

Premillennial dispensationalism, with its emphasis on interpreting current events as the prophetic fulfillment of a precise endtimes scenario, is the predominant form of popular apocalypticism in the United States today. From the early 1970s through the 1990s, the individual most responsible for promoting dispensationalist beliefs about the imminence and inevitability of the end of the world has been Hal Lindsey. Lindsey's role as the primary popularizer of contemporary prophecy belief is indisputable, and the apocalyptic scenario that he presents in his writings is familiar to most premillennialists today. As noted, his book *The Late Great Planet Earth* (1973 [1970]) was the largest-selling American nonfiction book of the 1970s, outselling every other work except the Bible (Halsell 1986:4); by 1991, the volume had sold more than twenty-eight million copies, making Lindsey the most widely read interpreter of prophetic apocalypticism in history (*Los Angeles Times*, February 23, 1991, F16; S. Graham 1989:249; Weber 1987:211). Lindsey's subsequent books have been extremely successful as well, with sales in the millions. He is one of the few authors ever to have had three books on the *New York Times* best-seller list at the same time (Lindsey 1981:179). Within the dispensationalist subculture he is referred to as "the father of the modern prophecy movement," and his books are estimated to have had a combined worldwide sales of more than thirty-five million (Lindsey 1994:back cover).

Prior to his interest in biblical prophecy, Lindsey was an agnostic, a business major, a member of the Coast Guard, and a tugboat captain on the Mississippi River (Kirsch 1977:30). After a conversion experience and then later hearing a sermon on prophecy in 1956, Lindsey became convinced that many recent historical events were forecast in the Bible. He soon launched his lifelong career of decoding the symbolic meanings of Scripture (S. Graham 1989:247–248), pursuing his interest in biblical literalism at the Dallas Theological Seminary, which is the main center for such studies in the United States and from which numerous independent, nondenominational dispensationalist expositors have received their education. Lindsey later worked as a missionary for the Campus Crusade for Christ in California, proselytizing on UCLA's Bruin Walk in the 1960s and on other campuses, and ultimately heading the campus ministry at UCLA, to which he gave the title "The Jesus Christ Light and Power Company" (Kirsch 1977:31).

In 1970, Lindsey collaborated with writer Carole C. Carlson to publish *The Late Great Planet Earth*. In this work, as in all his subsequent books, Lindsey declares that biblical prophecies are being fulfilled and that the Battle of Armageddon is imminent and inevitable. At the outset of the book, he attempts to establish his credibility as a prophecy interpreter, noting the failure of previous prophets and Bible students who, he asserts, have been overly anxious in their attempts to interpret the signs of the End. According to Lindsey, these earlier prophets overlooked the importance of the nation of Israel in biblical prophecy: the establishment of a Jewish nation in the land of Palestine in 1948 and Israel's taking of Old Jerusalem in 1967 are the crucial events prophesied in the Bible that conclusively indicate that the end of the world is at hand. Once these events occurred, the doomsday clock was accelerated: "This has now set the stage for the other predicted signs to develop in history. It is like the key piece of a jigsaw puzzle being found and then having the many adjacent pieces rapidly fall into place" (Lindsey 1973:47).

At the beginning of the book, Lindsey also attempts to establish the legitimacy of the tradition of Christian prophecy, declaring that Christ's life had been completely foretold in detail by the Old Testament prophets and that Christ "showed simply and clearly how prophecies were being fulfilled by His life" (1973:21). Calling these fulfilled predictions Christ's "credentials," Lindsey says that "Jesus said that the signs leading up to His coming were just as clear as the face of the sky. Let's examine these signs, these credentials" (1973:22). After enumerating various fulfilled prophecies regarding Christ's life, Lindsey examines predictions about the Second Coming of Christ that "are related to the specific pattern of world events which are precisely predicted as coming together shortly before the coming of the Messiah the second time" (1973:31). Employing what he calls a "deductive" means of analysis, Lindsey subsequently infers and decodes the meaning of prophecies that he believes God literally or symbolically has communicated in the Bible. For instance, biblical references to flashes of lightning are interpreted by Lindsey as missiles; hailstones are ICBMs; beasts and "locusts with scorpion tails" are armored tanks and Cobra helicopters spraying nerve gas from their tails. The biblical passage "And the ten horns out of this kingdom are ten kings that shall arise" is presumed to be the revival of the Roman Empire in the form of ten nations belonging to the European Common Market (what is now the European Community; Lindsey 1973:82–85). Other signs predicted in the Bible that foretell the end of the world include the invention of nuclear weapons; the prominence of a Russian confederacy as the powerful "nation of the North"; the rise of China as the "nation in the East" with an army of 200 million soldiers; disasters (earthquakes, famine, strange diseases, unusual weather changes); increased crime, drug abuse, and violence; and widespread interest in the occult, new religions, and the appearance of false prophets, all identified as manifestations of the "Babylonian Mystery Religion" that Lindsey declares is predicted in the Book of Revelation.

The following scenario, which Lindsey maintains is foretold in the Bible, embodies many of the basic elements of dispensationalist endtimes belief. Prior to Armageddon, the "Roman Empire" will be revived through an alliance of ten European Common Market nations, and this new world power eventually will be controlled by a great charismatic leader who will protect Israel, resolve disputes in the Middle East, and bring peace to the world. This global leader, who will have miraculously recovered from a fatal head wound, is the Antichrist, and he will be worshipped as the world's savior in the form of a one-world religion consisting of secular humanism, "faithless Christianity," and "occult practices" such as astrology, witchcraft, and drug-induced mind expansion (Lindsey 1973:103–123). The Antichrist, who will dominate the world through the European Common Market, will be symbolized by some representation of the number "666" (the "Mark of the Beast"), which will be required of all individuals for buying and selling. To control people economically, the Antichrist will demand that the number be imprinted or tattooed on the hand or forehead (1973:100–102). The Antichrist's rise to power will initiate the seven-year tribulation period of Christian and Jewish persecution, disasters, and worldly suffering that "will make the regimes of Hitler, Mao, and Stalin look like Girl Scouts weaving a daisy chain by comparison" (Lindsey 1973:99). During his rule the Muslim Dome of the Rock Mosque in Jerusalem

will be destroyed and the ancient Jewish Temple of Solomon rebuilt on its original site in its place. (Jewish terrorists actually have been convicted of plotting
to destroy the Dome of the Rock and allegedly have received financial support
from Christian Zionist organizations intent on expediting Christ's return
[Halsell 1986:9].)

According to Lindsey, once the Temple is rebuilt, the end of the world is
imminent. At this point, a Russian confederacy (assumed to be the Soviet
Union during the Cold War) and its Arab and African allies will invade Israel
and take Jerusalem. Lindsey states that the European forces, led by the
Antichrist, will then obliterate the "Red Army" in Israel, as well as the Russian
confederacy, most likely in a nuclear attack. Soon afterward, an army of 200
million "Red Chinese" will mobilize and challenge the Antichrist's world domination, attacking his forces at the Mount of Megiddo and the plain of Jezreel
(Lindsey 1973:135–157). In the ensuing battle one-third of the population and
all the major cities of the world will be destroyed, and just as the carnage esca-
lates to its climax, Christ will return to defeat the evil forces, judge the faithless, and protect the faithful. The "bright spot" of this scenario, according to
Lindsey, will be the conversion of a great number of Jews to Christianity
(1973:156). These recent Jewish converts living in Jerusalem will be miraculously saved from the devastation of Armageddon when the ground separates
at the Mount of Olives in Jerusalem. Jesus' feet will first touch the earth there
when he returns, creating a crack in the earth into which the converts will
escape. After Armageddon, an earthly paradise, established out of "atomic
materials," will then exist for one thousand years. At the end of that time, this
millennial paradise will be threatened by a rebellion of unbelievers led by Satan,
which Christ will suppress, after which a new heaven and new earth will be created and the faithful will become immortal (Lindsey 1973:158–168).

Throughout this and other books, Lindsey emphasizes the rise of the
nation of Israel as the most important fulfillment of endtimes prophecy; in
one book he refers to Israel as the "Fuse of Armageddon" (1973:34), and in a
documentary film he says that "the most important sign of all—that is the Jew
returning to the land of Israel after thousands of years of being dispersed"
(Lindsey 1973:ii). From the Puritans to the present day, the return of the Jews
to Palestine and their conversion to Christianity in the endtimes has been an
enduring theme in numerous American prophecy traditions and an idea that
has been especially embraced by dispensationalists. As Paul Boyer notes, current dispensationalist beliefs about the role of the Jews and Israel in God's plan
have precedent in ancient prophecy traditions and are a complex and para-
doxical phenomenon, privileging the Jews as the chosen people and express-

ing support for Israeli causes and yet encouraging the view that anti-Semitism is foreordained by God and that the future persecution of the Jewish people is inevitable (1992:180–224). Lindsey, for example, condemns anti-Semitism and attributes it to Satan's influence but asserts that previous tragedies suffered by the Jewish people are foretold in the Bible and that the prophesied persecution of the Jews will inevitably increase in the last days before the end of the world (1984:159, 1973:35).

The prophetic significance of Israel's role in the last days is so important to the worldview of dispensationalists that some advocate military support for Israel in order to accelerate the prophetic timetable and hasten Armageddon in the Middle East. This dispensationalist-Israeli relationship has been examined by journalist Ruth Halsell (1986), who traveled to Israel as a member of one of Jerry Falwell's tour groups that was intended to establish ties between Israeli Jews and the Moral Majority. In her discussion of the political dimensions of "Armageddon Theology" and its promotion by televangelists, Halsell notes that numerous individuals with political and financial power in the United States assert that the Battle of Armageddon is foreordained and that any attempt to prevent a nuclear scenario in the Middle East is heretical. For instance, television evangelist Jim Robison, who was invited by Ronald Reagan to deliver the opening prayer at the 1984 Republican National Convention, states, "There'll be no peace until Jesus comes. Any preaching of peace prior to this return is heresy; it's against the word of God; it's Anti-Christ" (Halsell 1986:16). Like Robison, Lindsey also declares that world peace is impossible, promising his readers that Judgment Day and Jesus' return will occur a generation after the establishment of Israel, which was proclaimed a nation on May 14, 1948.[1]

The concept of the "Rapture," a word used to describe the protection and salvation of the Christian faithful prior to worldly cataclysm, is central to dispensationalist visions of the end of the world. Belief in the Rapture is characterized by the notion that devoted Christians will be physically "lifted up" to meet Christ in the air at some point prior to doomsday and exist with Christ in the heavens until the Second Coming, at which time they will return to earth with glorified bodies. Popular beliefs about the Rapture stem from the following biblical quote from the apostle Paul:

> For the Lord himself shall descend from heaven with a shout, with the voice of an archangel, with the trumpet of God; and the dead in Christ shall rise first. Then we which are alive and remain shall be caught up together with them in the clouds, to meet the Lord in the air; and so shall we ever be with the Lord. (1 Thessalonians 4:16–17)

Although the Rapture is generally interpreted by mainstream Christian theologians to represent the Second Coming of Christ, premillennial dispensationalists such as Lindsey say that there will be two Second Comings and that a secret Rapture will actually occur prior to Christ's final return, involving the divine rescue of the Christian faithful, who will be the only people who will see Christ in the clouds. The timing of the Rapture within God's prophetic plan is a subject of debate among premillennialist Christians. Pretribulationists believe that the Christian faithful will be raptured prior to the coming of the Antichrist and the seven-year tribulation period. Midtribulationists believe that the Rapture will occur sometime during the tribulation period, after the Antichrist has risen to power, but prior to the period of divine retribution involving God's vengeance and judgment of humanity. People who identify themselves as posttribulationists believe that the Christian church and the faithful will endure the tribulation period and be raptured at the time of Christ's return (Weber 1987:11).

Beliefs about the Rapture are quite pervasive. According to wide-ranging estimate, somewhere between 30 percent and 44 percent of Americans embrace beliefs about the Rapture of the church (see Tufts 1986:vi; *U.S. News and World Report,* December 19, 1994, 64). In her study of attitudes about nuclear war among fundamentalist Christians in Amarillo, Texas, A. G. Mojtabai writes that dispensationalist Rapture beliefs are characterized by the theme of "blessed assurance," involving the promise of exemption from the disasters and suffering that will befall others. She states, "For millions of Christians in the United States today, the Rapture is seen as the final solution for all our human ills" (Mojtabai 1986:xi). Jerry Falwell, who in the past has asserted that the faithful will be raptured prior to nuclear Armageddon, describes the Rapture as follows:

> You'll be riding along in an automobile. You'll be the driver perhaps. You're a Christian. There'll be several people in the automobile with you, maybe someone who is not a Christian. When the trumpet sounds you and the other believers in that automobile will be instantly caught away—you will disappear, leaving behind only your clothes and physical things that cannot inherit eternal life. That unsaved person or persons in the automobile will suddenly be startled to find the car is moving along without a driver, and the car suddenly somewhere crashes. (Cited in Lukacs 1986:7)

Rapture believers may proclaim their views through bumper stickers with slogans ("The Rapture—What A Way To Go!"; "Warning—driver will abandon car in case of Rapture"; "Beam me up, Jesus!") and by purchasing framed paintings, postcards, watches, and other items depicting the Rapture, which are sold at Christian bookstores and are available through mail order. The Bible Believers' Evangelistic Association in Sherman, Texas, for instance, distributes an assortment of Rapture merchandise, such as laminated Rapture dinner place mats, which depict an open-armed Christ returning above the skyscrapers of an urban center as raptured Christians float out from automobiles crashing on a freeway and dead Christians rise from their graves in a cemetery. Some people who anticipate the Rapture have arranged for their unraptured relatives or friends to become the legal heirs of their property after they are lifted up to meet Jesus; the Mutual Insurance Company of New York has even agreed to allow individuals to draft riders to their life-insurance policies that guarantee raptured Christians the same status as deceased clients, with the benefits of the policies going to the next-named beneficiary (Woodward et al. 1977:51).

Hal Lindsey is a pretribulationist. In his books he assures his readers that the true church will have already been raptured prior to the seven-year tribulation period and the Battle of Armageddon. Referring to the Rapture with vernacular expressions such as "The Ultimate Trip" and the "Big Snatch," Lindsey describes Jesus' lifting up the believers to be reunited with Him in heaven: "He is coming to meet all true believers in the air. Without benefit of science, space suits, or interplanetary rockets, there will be those who will be transported into a glorious place more beautiful, more awesome, than we can possibly comprehend" (1973:126). Like other dispensationalist writers, Lindsey also offers descriptions of the startled reactions of the nonraptured when the true believers suddenly disappear, as well as the ensuing disasters and worldwide panic that will occur immediately after the Rapture. For instance, he provides numerous conversational portrayals of how nonbelievers will interpret the mysterious disappearance of Christians, such as the following: "There I was driving down the freeway and all of a sudden the place went crazy . . . cars going in all directions . . . and not one of them had a driver. I mean it was wild! I think we've got an invasion from outer space!" (1973:125). Lindsey's promise that the faithful will be delivered in the Rapture from the terrors of nuclear apocalypse and the horrors of the tribulation period has an obvious psychological appeal, the escapist and fatalistic implications of which will be discussed later in this study. The assurance of planetary escape by means of the Rapture is especially appealing given Lindsey's assertions that nuclear apocalypse is predicted in the Bible and thus an inevitable part of God's ultimate plan.

In each of his books, Lindsey details the ways that nuclear war and its aftermath are important parts of the divine script, methodically interpreting

Scripture that refers to mass destruction or fiery cataclysm in terms of nuclear annihilation. A passage from Revelation (6:14) about the atmosphere being torn and pushed apart like a scroll rolled together, for example, is regarded as a "perfect picture of an all-out nuclear exchange" which will shake every mountain and island from its present position (Lindsey 1984:98). The fourth seal judgment in the Book of Revelation (6:7–8) about the arrival of a "pale horse" of death is viewed as a prediction indicating that between one-fourth and one-half of humanity will be killed in a global nuclear war (Lindsey 1984:88); the catastrophic trembling of the earth that is part of the sixth seal judgment (Rev. 6:12) leads Lindsey to believe "that the Apostle John is describing an earthquake set off by many nuclear explosions"; the prophesied darkening of the sun and the moon (Rev. 6:12) resembles the radioactive contamination of "dirty" cobalt bombs and an ensuing "nuclear winter" scenario (Lindsey 1984:96–98).

Lindsey declares that the ancient biblical prophets could not adequately describe the sophisticated technologies of nuclear destruction conveyed in their revelations and thus referred to ICBMs and nuclear firestorms, for example, in terms of "hail and fire mixed with blood." (Lindsey asks, "How could God transmit the thought of a nuclear catastrophe to someone living in the year A.D. 90!" [1984:12, 117].) The invention of nuclear weapons suddenly has made these unfathomable prophecies comprehensible:

> [Zechariah 14:12] predicts that "their flesh will be consumed from their bones, their eyes burned out of their sockets, and their tongues consumed out of their mouths while they stand on their feet." For hundreds of years students of Bible prophecy have wondered what kind plague could produce such instant ravaging of humans while still on their feet. Until the advent of the atomic bomb such a thing was not humanly possible. But now everything Zechariah predicted could come true instantly in a thermonuclear exchange! (Lindsey 1984:210–211)

Lindsey also provides descriptions of the effects of nuclear cataclysm in terms of the biblical seven trumpet judgments and the seven bowls of wrath, each of which involves a preordained scenario of suffering that will be unleashed on humanity and that will ravage the earth. The devastation and slaughter will be unparalleled: "Imagine, cities like London, Paris, Tokyo, New York, Los Angeles, Chicago—obliterated! John [in the Book of Revelation] says that the Eastern force alone will wipe out a third of the earth's population (Revelation 9:15–18). He also predicts that entire islands and mountains would be blown off the map. It seems to indicate an all-out attack of ballistic missiles upon the great metropolitan areas of the world" (1973:155). According to Lindsey the devastation will be so enormous that "coastlines and continents will be changed and all the mountains will be shifted in elevation . . . the cities of the world will have been reduced to rubble. The world will look just as you'd expect the 'end of the world' to look" (1984:214). As the result of this mass destruction, Christ will ultimately have to create a new world for humans to inhabit during the millennium, in which "the sky will be bluer, the grass will be greener, the flowers will smell sweeter, the air will be cleaner, and man will be happier than he ever dreamed possible!" (1984:255).

Lindsey's subsequent books, films, radio broadcasts, and lectures expand on themes first presented in *The Late Great Planet Earth*, providing updates that interpret recent world events in terms of prophecy and that further illustrate God's design for humanity. For instance, in *The Rapture: Truth or Consequences* (1983), Lindsey elaborates on the concept of the Rapture and the role of nuclear cataclysms in the last days, slightly modifying his previous interpretation of the meaning of the opening of the seven seals and the trumpet judgments. In *Satan Is Alive and Well on Planet Earth* (1972), he identifies the satanic influences and manifestations of evil that he believes have overtaken Western civilization and now permeate all aspects of American life. He describes the demonic "thought bombs" set off by individuals such as Darwin, Marx, Freud, Hegel, Kant, and Kierkegaard and provides an inventory of satanic phenomena and influences, ranging from psychic powers and speaking in tongues to rock music, television (the demonic "eye in our living room"), and the behavioral psychology of B. F. Skinner (in the section entitled "Skinner Dipping," Lindsey asks, "Could it be that the long-dreaded figure of Bible prophecy, the Antichrist, will rise up to implement Dr. Skinner's basic tenets into reality?" [1972:101]). In one lurid passage involving a two-page interview with a Los Angeles police commander, the topics of satanism, drug use, blood sacrifice, and sexual orgies are combined to paint a picture of youth culture running amuck: "Blood is put into cauldrons, mixed with LSD and used as a drink during their rites or ceremonies. . . . Not long ago there was a 'Kiss-In' on a Santa Monica beach. . . . they were just one big mass swaying to the throb of drums and weird music . . . some began to indulge in open sex . . . most of them wore charms around their necks" (1972:18–19). Lindsey's portrayals of the evils that pervade contemporary society reflect the view that American culture is irredeemably corrupted, a belief that he shares with other dispensationalists and premillennialists in general.

Conspiratorial notions about widespread satanic influences in American society are substantiated in this and other books through Lindsey's use of quotations from "experts" and numerous firsthand accounts of his own interactions with satanists and evil personages. Lindsey's somewhat haphazard technique of documentation consists of statements from members of the Club of Rome, Nobel Prize winners, "renowned futurists," Albert Einstein, John F. Kennedy, professors from M.I.T., anonymous "authorities," "researchers," police officers, daily news reports, the *Bulletin of Atomic Scientists*, and the *National Enquirer*, all of which are treated as equally credible. Although Lindsey's scholarship may be questionable and somewhat indiscriminate, his books give the impression that he has a vast knowledge of contemporary events. His interpretations of current affairs in terms of biblical prophecy convey a sense of privileged information and an understanding of the present and the future. Lindsey's assurances that biblical predictions are being continually fulfilled in God's countdown to Armageddon undoubtedly motivate many readers to purchase his new publications in order to receive updates on prophecy and fully understand God's plan.

Each of Lindsey's publications reinforces the ideas presented in his previous books, with revisions and enumerations of various prophecies that have been subsequently fulfilled. In *The 1980s: Countdown to Armageddon*, which was on the *New York Times* best-seller list for more than twenty weeks, Lindsey recounts the various predictions presented in *The Late Great Planet Earth* that have come to pass: "During the 25 years I have been studying prophecy I have seen incredible things forecast 3,000 years ago happen right before my eyes. . . . The decade of the 1980's could very well be the last decade of history as we know it" (1981:8). Lindsey retrospectively interprets the events of the 1970s in terms of his prophetic framework, declaring that he successfully predicted the Soviet invasion of Afghanistan, the overthrow of the shah of Iran, the superiority of Soviet military strength, the decline of U.S. military power, and the addition of new nations to the European Common Market to reach the biblically predicted number of ten.

In addition to verifying his previous predictions, in this book Lindsey reiterates his endtimes scenario but diverges somewhat from the traditionally apolitical tone of dispensationalism. In the last two chapters he advocates right-wing political causes and a substantial military buildup in order to thwart communist global dominance and curtail moral decay within the United States. Lindsey still maintains that God has determined history and that the decline of the United States and the destruction of the world is inevitable, but he asserts that military strength, a conservative political agenda, and increased capitalistic enterprise can temporarily delay the prophesied decline until the occurrence of Rapture, after which the deterioration of the country will be of little consequence to raptured Christians. In this way, Lindsey has politicized the dispensationalist tradition, incorporating right-wing ideology into basic dispensationalist tenets, in a move similar to the politics of Pat Robertson and Jerry Falwell.

As previously noted, numerous contemporary premillennialists express ideas similar to Lindsey's (though they may not share his somewhat sensationalistic interpretive approach). Pat Robertson, for instance, also has stated that the European Common Market nations are the ten-nation confederacy mentioned in the Book of Revelation, that the rise of the Antichrist is imminent, that the Soviet Union will invade Israel, and that strange natural disasters will occur prior to Christ's return, which he expected in the early 1980s (Hadden and Swann 1981:96). Best-selling authors Tim and Beverly LaHaye, who have been instrumental in the fundamentalist Christian campaign of identifying "secular humanism" as a force of evil, also declare, like Lindsey, that nuclear apocalypse is inevitable, that the faithful will be raptured prior to Armageddon, and that world peace organizations such as the United Nations and World Council of Churches are potentially satanic institutions foretold in the Book of Revelation (1972, 1975). Numerous books by Salem Kirban similarly identify current events and institutions as signs of God's unalterable plan. In his *Guide to Survival* (1973), for instance, Kirban concludes, "The world is rapidly coming to an end. It is on an irreversible course" (1973:21). The picture-book version of his *666* (Kirban 1981) provides a colorfully illustrated account of the tribulation period, the rise of the Antichrist, and the infernal strategies that will be used to force people to bear the "Mark of the Beast," identified as the number 666. Evangelist Billy Graham, who professes to have "presented the gospel face to face to more people than any other man in history" (B. Graham 1983:back jacket cover), and who has advocated social activism rather than premillennial passivity, nonetheless embraces prophecy beliefs about foreordained worldly catastrophe. In fact, it appears that Graham rose to fame in the 1950s initially because of his apocalyptic interpretations of current events. Two days after President Harry Truman announced the first Soviet atomic test on September 23, 1949, Graham, unknown at the time, highlighted the apocalyptic capabilities of atomic weapons and interpreted the rise of communism as a sign of impending doom (Boyer 1985:239). Hundreds of thousands of people flocked to Graham's tent revival, which was extended from three weeks to two months.

Although previous premillennialists have made similar assertions and the themes and underlying eschatological structures of Lindsey's books are not new, his interpretations of the Bible as prophetic text are innovative and accessible. Like any talented storyteller or writer, Lindsey weaves a compelling and imaginative narrative from traditional story structures, motifs, and images. Lindsey's books, inspired by Revelation and other biblical texts and bolstered by the prognostications of scientists and secular doomsayers, are creative interpretations of current events that directly address contemporary concerns about earthly destruction and worldly evil. Nuclear annihilation, environmental disaster, war, famine, disease, drug addiction, divorce, increased crime, violence, and a sense of overwhelming evil in the world are explained as a fore-ordained and meaningful part of God's countdown to Armageddon.

In addition to the graphic interpretations and innovative updating of traditional dispensationalist eschatological narratives, the appeal of Lindsey's books may also be attributed to his writing style, which is engaging, often humorous, and easily understandable. He says that his books are written in a way that is simple and free of jargon in an attempt to reach the "common person," particularly skeptics and the irreligious: "As I wrote, I'd imagine that I was sitting across the table from a young person—a cynical, irreligious person—and I'd try to convince him that the Bible prophecies were true" (Kirsch 1977:31). Chapter titles such as "Sheik to Sheik" (the role of the Arab nations in prophecy); "Russia Is a Gog" (Russia identified as the prophesied Gog that will invade Israel); "The Ultimate Trip" (the Rapture); and "The Main Event" (the Second Coming of Christ) illustrate Lindsey's use of catchy phrases to introduce his ideas (Lindsey 1973).

The content of Lindsey's books, his writing style, and his innovative reworking of the dispensationalist tradition certainly account for much of his popularity, but the marketing of his books has greatly contributed to their widespread appeal as well. From the beginning of his writing career, Lindsey's ideas have been skillfully promoted through the paperback publishing industry. He insists that his books be published in both hardcover and paperback simultaneously so as to reach a greater number of people; he says he is "writing for the youth culture—and the average young person doesn't even look at hardbacks of any kind" (Kirsch 1977:31). Not only are his books affordable, they are available in general bookstores nationwide and often have sensational cover art that resembles other mass-marketed paperbacks. The cover of *The Late Great Planet Earth*, for instance, depicts the earth in flames, soaring through space leaving a trail of fire; the cover of *The 1980s: Countdown to Armageddon* has an illustration of an hourglass, with a green and blue planet earth inside the upper section, trickling down into a blackened pile of cinders in the bottom portion.

The widespread appeal of Lindsey's ideas is also attributable to their promotion through his management firm, Hal Lindsey Ministries, as well as through his radio news and call-in talk show heard in more than one hundred cities in the United States every Saturday morning. Lindsey also travels on a nationwide lecture circuit and apparently is one of the most sought after lecturers in the country (S. Graham 1989:247). Various videotapes and film versions of his books also promote his apocalyptic predictions. In the film rendition of *The Late Great Planet Earth* (produced in 1977 and featuring Lindsey, and narrated by an ominous-sounding Orson Welles), the events preceding Armageddon are presented in a documentary style, enhanced with gruesome special effects and including a surrealistic portrayal of the Revelation of St. John, with the Whore of Babylon slurping blood from a goblet, for instance, and dying sinners shown suffering the wrath of God in the last days.

Lindsey's interpretations of the dispensationalist tradition have become codified, legitimized, and seemingly "institutionalized" as the result of their promotion through print and electronic technologies. In this manner, the mass media have allowed grassroots and individualistic explications of apocalyptic prophecy to rapidly gain credibility and an enormous following. Unlike those apocalypticists who base their authority on charisma or direct communication with supernatural forces, the source of authority for prophecy interpreters such as Lindsey is not dependent on trance states but obtained indirectly through textual exegesis. Traditional charismatic prophets convey direct messages from supernatural beings; Lindsey and other literalist prophecy enthusiasts are popular theologians and folk exegetes who derive their authority from an apparent knowledge of current events and world history and from their ability to decipher symbolic information about the future as revealed in the Bible. If anything, such speculations about the end of the world resemble divinatory practices rather than prophecy because they are based on interpreting symbolic messages rather than direct revelation involving the immediate communication of information from deities who speak through an inspired individual (see Overholt 1989:140–147; Aune 1983:339). Divination, prophecy, and oracles are similar in that they involve determining the will of supernatural entities and forces; the individuals involved are intermediaries between the supernatural and natural worlds. These practices are often implicitly fatalistic, implying that certain future, present, or past events have been ordained and that their causes may be determined by consulting supernatural forces. The predictive techniques employed in the books of dispensationalist prophecy interpreters resemble the practice of "technical divination": their predictions are a form of scriptural divination, based on personal knowledge and training. This method of "scientific" or "rational" prophecy is presented as if it is based on scientific inference involving the analysis and decoding of esoteric messages from God hidden in the Bible and correlating these with contemporary events.

Although prophecy interpreters such as Lindsey do not profess to be divinely inspired prophets, they do imply that they possess unique insights and special abilities in interpreting the Bible. For example, Lindsey states that he does not believe prophets are currently receiving direct revelations from God but that "we do have prophets today who are being given special insight into the prophetic word" (1973:78). Biblical prophecy has been "unsealed" in recent times, says Lindsey, and he portrays himself as one who has special skills in interpreting the prophetic meanings of biblical passages. Although Lindsey and other prophecy interpreters are not charismatic leaders in the traditional sense, they do imply that they possess "exceptional powers or qualities" of exegesis that enable them to unravel and decode God's blueprint for the end of history.

Popular prophecy books such as Lindsey's are written for lay readers who may not have formal religious training, and the authors assert that knowledge of God's plan is accessible to everyone, not only the ecclesiastical elite. In fact, popular interpreters of biblical prophecy (like other apocalypticists in general), often situate themselves in opposition to official religious institutions, portraying theologians as corrupt, depicting dominant religious organizations as controlled by apostates, and informing readers that although they constitute the "true church," they are in the minority. Even though millions of people have read such books, they are depicted as marginalized and frequently reminded that their beliefs exist outside or in opposition to the dominant theological trends in Christianity.

Folk Beliefs, Omens, and Apocalyptic Prophecies

The content, structure, and cause-effect relationships that characterize Lindsey's predictions and those of other dispensationalists resemble traditional folk beliefs about doomsday portents in which perceived threats, social turmoil, anomalous occurrences, and unusual cosmic and natural phenomena are interpreted as signs that foretell of imminent worldly destruction. Wayland D. Hand's monumental *Popular Beliefs and Superstitions from North Carolina*, for example, lists meteor showers, an eclipse of the sun, comets, strange lights in the sky, and the disappearance of pawpaws as doomsday signs (1961–1964:573). Stith Thompson's *Motif-Index of Folk-Literature* (1955–1958) also contains various references to the End, such as birds dripping blood on doomsday (B259.5); bleeding wood as a doomsday sign (A1091.2); the moon shining by day (A1053.1) and the sun shining at night as doomsday signs (A1052.2); talking stone at doomsday (A1091.3); and unusual migrations of birds at doomsday (A1091.4). In addition to natural and cosmic inversions and doomsday reversals occurring before the end of the world, reversible dates, such as those that can be read back to front or upside-down (e.g., 1881 or 1961) also have been assigned doomsday significance (Simpson 1978:562–564).[2] The date of doomsday has been frequently attributed to round numbers, and thus the end of every century is a time of apocalyptic angst for many. The two-volume *Popular Beliefs and Superstitions* from the Ohio collection of Newbell Niles Puckett (Hand et al. 1981) includes cows lowing at night, bad thunderstorms, women wearing glass high heels, and the disappearance of the Eastern European folk custom of painting on Easter eggs as signs that foretell the end of the world (1981:1516). The collection *Popular Beliefs and Superstitions from Utah* (Hand and Talley 1984) contains belief statements about meteors and comets (11686, 11700), the eclipse of the sun (11710, 11722, 11724), blood on the moon (9999, 10001, 10002), and chickens laying more eggs than normal (9989) as signs of the last days. This collection also includes statements about certain social and political events that foretell doomsday. Fathers will turn against sons, mothers against daughters, and neighbors against neighbors; parents and children will hate one another; the United States and the USSR will unite to fight against China in the last days (9991, 9994, 9996). Bleached hair (9997), hooped earrings, and the confusion of gender distinctions (9998) are also signs that the end of the world is approaching.

Unlike "active" (or "magical") beliefs, in which human action is prescribed in order to cause an effect, these doomsday portents foretell various events by themselves and do not involve human agency. In 1926, Puckett distinguished between active and predictive beliefs, which he labeled "control signs" and "prophetic signs"; the former allow for a degree of human control and the latter involve "those undomesticated causal relationships in which the human individual has no play . . . man has no control and submits helplessly to the decrees of nature" (1926:312). Scandinavian ethnologist Albert Eskeröd (1947) also differentiated between passive and active superstitions, characterizing the condition-result relationship typical of passive beliefs such as omens as *ominant-ominat*, and that of action beliefs as *causant-causat*. The first type of belief involves the reading of signs or omens (*ominant*) that predict occurrences or states of being (*ominat*) and does not involve volition or causality. The second type of belief is characterized by a cause-and-effect relationship between actions and the results of those actions (*causant-causat*).[3] Omens and passive beliefs (or what Alan Dundes calls "sign superstitions") predict the future, and active beliefs make the future; the former allow one to foretell death, bad luck, or the weather, and the latter enable one to produce results by means of magical practices (Dundes 1961:31).

Similar to the noncausal *ominant* that foretells events and does not involve human action or volition, Lindsey's predictions express the notion that particular occurrences are predetermined and that humans are helpless to avert these inevitable events. Although Lindsey's prognostications are more elaborate than the isolated belief statements about doomsday assembled in folklore collections, his predictions are similar in structure and in the assertion that future events are foreordained. Dispensationalist prophecies indicate that the present reveals the future and that the future cannot by altered in any way by human action. Characterized by a belief in inevitability and human helplessness concerning certain occurrences, portents and prophecies reveal the fundamental human desire to predict future events and to attribute meaning to that which is regarded as unchangeable or unavoidable.

Unlike traditional portents and omens that usually consist of a single condition and result, Lindsey's predictions include multiple and general conditions that allow for wide-ranging prophetic speculation. The somewhat vague nature of his predictions is indicated by many of his statements about the future, such as the following: "In the Bible, He [Jesus] told us that seven signals—war, revolution, plague, famine, earthquakes, religious deception, and strange occurrences in space—would alert us that the end of the old world and the birth of the new was near" (1981:19). All of these conditions can be said to be occurring now; on the other hand, one could argue that they have occurred throughout most of human history. Lindsey's predictions are ambiguous enough to allow for many events to be interpreted as a fulfillment of signs that foretell specific results. For instance, his prediction of an attack on Israel from a northern nation might be understood by some readers in terms of the Iraqi launching of Scud missiles at Israel during the Persian Gulf War, even though Lindsey's original prediction forecasts the massive destruction of Israel by a northern confederacy. During the 1980s, Lindsey's prophecy of ten nations in the European Common Market was in fact fulfilled, until Spain and Portugal were added and the number increased to twelve.

Some of Lindsey's predictions are sufficiently vague to enable a multiplicity of interpretations; others are logical assumptions about political and social events that may occur in the future (e.g., "Keep your eyes on the Middle East. If this is the time we believe it is, this part of the world will become a constant source of tension for all the world" [Lindsey 1973:173]). Lindsey asserts that his numerous unfulfilled predictions will all be realized within this generation, such as the rise of a one-world religious organization, the appearance of the Antichrist, the rebuilding of the Jewish Temple, and the sudden disappearance of the Christian faithful in the Rapture. His failed predictions (e.g., that the "Jupiter Effect," caused by the alignment of the planets in the solar system would initiate the world's most disastrous earthquakes in 1982 [Lindsey 1981:29–30]) are simply disregarded or modified in subsequent books.

In the well-known sociological study *When Prophecy Fails*, Leon Festinger (1956) and his fellow fieldworkers focus on the beliefs and behaviors of a group of individuals in the 1950s who were convinced that the destruction of the world was imminent. The researchers concentrated on one particular prophecy by the seer Mrs. Keech, who predicted a widespread cataclysm, to occur on a specific date, involving a flood that would submerge and destroy the western portion of the North and South American continents. Devotees believed that prior to the day of destruction, they would be saved by UFOs (a notion similar to the dispensationalist belief in the Rapture prior to the tribulation period). In their attempt to understand how cognitive dissonance is resolved, Festinger and his colleagues were particularly interested in the explanations and rationalizations that occurred after the prediction failed. Lindsey's predictions, unlike Mrs. Keech's, which were specific enough to be disconfirmed, are generally so ambiguous and open to multiple interpretations that they rarely can be refuted. Lindsey's predictions and those of other dispensationalists in some ways resemble the speculations of futurologists more than those of previous doomsday prophets, such as Mrs. Keech or William Miller, who not only provided precise information about the details of doomsday but anticipated its occurrence on a specific date. The abstract and symbolic nature of biblical apocalyptic writings allows dispensationalists like Lindsey to interpret retrospectively a diversity of events—from bar-coding and international terrorism to the establishment of the European Community and the Trilateral Commission—as fulfillments of prophecy.

Divine Determination and a Sense of Coherence and Control

Underlying the predictive beliefs expressed in Lindsey's books is the notion that history resembles a narrative that has been deliberately designed and is ultimately meaningful. The story of human existence is presented by Lindsey and other dispensationalists as coherent from beginning to end, characterized by dramatic, preordained events and an ongoing battle between good and evil.

Lindsey's account of the end of the world affirms that present and future disasters are not arbitrary and meaningless but explicable as part of a divine structure. His books directly address various dominating concerns and offer resolutions to the anxieties and uncertainties that these concerns evoke.

As the research of folklorists and anthropologists indicates, a primary human aim is to maintain a sense of control over the environment and consequently over one's experiences and the outcomes of events. Anthropologists such as Bronislaw Malinowski, E. E. Evans-Pritchard, and A. R. Radcliffe-Brown, among others, have discussed the relationship of belief and behavior to anxiety, uncertainty, and dominating concerns. Evans-Pritchard (1937), for instance, states that among the Azande in Sudan causality is attributed to supernatural forces particularly in cases of uncertain, inexplicable, or tragic occurrences. He notes that belief in witchcraft provides the Azande with a sense of understanding about the causes of unusual events and in some instances affords individuals an opportunity to act or retaliate, thus gaining a sense of control over unfortunate circumstances. Malinowski's (1954) well-known hypothesis that magical beliefs are expressed more frequently in situations of anxiety and uncertainty has been verified by numerous subsequent researchers (see Mullen 1969; Vogt 1952). Albert Eskeröd (1964), in an attempt to avoid the potentially negative connotations of Malinowski's concept of anxiety, has proposed the notion of "dominating interests" (*Interessendominanzen*) to characterize the emotional and discerning attitudes of individuals in situations of extreme importance, uncertainty, or concern which are subsequently endowed with supernatural significance (1964:89). These and other researchers have demonstrated that uncertain situations and dominating concerns may motivate people to attribute causality to supernatural forces, whether in the form of magic, witchcraft, fate, or God's will. In such cases, the attributing of supernatural causality not only may reduce and explain uncertainty, but may enable people to gain a sense of control over inexplicable events and obtain a sense of meaning concerning such events. Lindsey's books are inventories of contemporary anxieties, uncertainties, and dominating concerns. In chapter after chapter he discusses the threat of nuclear war, the destiny of the reader's soul, and the meaning of recent historical events, political turmoil, widespread social ills, disasters, wars, famine, and disease. As assertions about the supernatural predetermination of worldly events, Lindsey's apocalyptic predictions provide a means of making sense of otherwise incomprehensible, tragic, or distressing occurrences identified as divine signs that are a part of God's plan. As such, they are deliberate sources of information about Christ's return and humanity's place on the apocalyptic clock as it winds down to doomsday. Like other forms of apocalyptic belief that depict history as foreordained and human action as ineffectual in altering the outcome of events, Lindsey's writings may be considered a tragic form of discourse offering explicit religious theodicies: assertions of order and meaning that provide symbolic solutions to questions of why there is evil, suffering, and death in the world (O'Leary 1994:14, 200–201). Apocalypticism, as a tragic and fatalistic mode of thought, offers privileged explanations that "unveil" the otherwise obscure meanings behind events and experiences, reassuring believers that current crises and social evils are part of a predetermined endtimes scenario orchestrated by God.

Lindsey admits that his predictions may sound like a "wild fairytale" to some readers but declares that for others the "realization of what's in store for them in eternity is so thrilling that they can hardly wait to get there!" (1984:279). He asserts that knowing and contemplating God's plan for the future as it is revealed through prophecy is necessary because "this life has many disappointments and heartaches, but knowing there *is* a new world coming for God's people gives us patience and strength to joyfully bear the burdens of this life" (1984:279). Providing his readers with the promise of this new world and a systematic framework for interpreting the existing world, Lindsey clarifies life's uncertainties in an authoritative tone, and his writings assert that God is not only controlling human history but personally involved in people's lives. Lindsey also promises that believers will meet this personal and approachable God in the millennial kingdom to come: "God will be there in person, and we'll see Him face-to-face" (1984:273); "It's exciting to think about kneeling at God's feet one minute and sitting beside His throne the next! There's no chance of eternity being boring with that kind of challenge alternating with adoring service" (1984:278).

Many prophets in the past have maintained that worldly disasters were warnings of God's wrath and the imminence of apocalypse if humans did not repent, but the calamities and prophecies highlighted by Lindsey are not interpreted as warning signs from God or catalysts for action. Instead, these are noncausal indications of God's timetable, codified in the Bible thousands of years ago. In the dispensationalist view, the reform and repentance of all humanity cannot avert a doomsday that has been divinely determined. Although the supernatural motivation for allowing suffering and the spread of specific evils prior to Armageddon is unknowable or attributed to the inevitable evils of human nature and Satan's influence, Lindsey's writings affirm that all that occurs is ultimately meaningful within God's larger design. The belief in divine determination and the inextricable connection between

God's plan, human history, and one's own life has been identified as one of the cornerstones of Christian fundamentalist thought:

> The Bible also instructs fundamentalists that a rationale for life apart from God cannot exist. Nothing in life is an accident; rather, all is a part of God's plan. Bad things happen as God's chastisement of us or as God's way of closing doors on mere human plans. God is always good, but His goodness is sometimes rather terrible. . . . Fundamentalists cannot think or speak of their history, their present, or their future apart from God as *deus ex machina* who makes all things happen. (Hadden and Swann 1981:89–90)

Within this framework of ultimate control in divine hands, suffering, death, and tragedies are not cruel or absurd occurrences in an insensitive universe but have a larger, symbolic meaning as part of a transcendent order.

Lindsey's writings offer readers a sense of the significance of their own lives within the divine plan once they are saved by belief in Christ, as well as a sense of the importance of living at the end of history. Although worldly cataclysm is inevitable, specific actions to save oneself and one's family and friends from the horrors of apocalypse and eternal damnation are prescribed. Fatalistic resignation about the irredeemability of this world does not result in total passivity. Lindsey states that "far from being pessimistic and dropping out of life, we should be rejoicing in the knowledge that Christ may return any moment for us. This should spur us to share the good news of salvation in Christ with as many as possible . . . we should plan our lives as though we will be here our full life expectancy, but live as though Christ may come today" (1973:176). Lindsey urges his readers to accept Christ into their lives, regularly read the Bible, and attempt to convert others so that they will be rescued in the Rapture.

In an essay on weather portents and magical beliefs, folklorist Michael Owen Jones (1967) discusses the behavioral responses that certain beliefs motivate, noting also his informants' own interpretations of these beliefs. He proposes the concept of "implicit activating beliefs," which are similar to Alan Dundes's notion of sign superstition, but Jones demonstrates that the act of reading portentous signs may implicitly motivate action. Lindsey's belief propositions resemble implicit activating beliefs in that they are signs indicating that certain events are inevitable, but that human action can counteract inevitability at a personal level if one acts in accordance with divine decrees. These prescriptions for action are spiritual—an act of faith or a conversion experience—and involve evangelization rather than explicit instructions for social or political action. At the conclusion of a chapter entitled "World War III" in *The Late Great Planet Earth*, after he describes worldwide destruction

ular apocalypticism in the United States. Although less frequently studied, the prophecy beliefs associated with apocalyptic visions of the Virgin Mary, familiar to millions of Roman Catholics worldwide, are another expression of popular apocalypticism in America today. As will be explored in the next chapter, apocalyptic Marian worldviews share the premillennial dispensationalist belief that the imminence of doomsday is revealed through prophecy and that the world is pervaded by evil, yet they differ in terms of the forms of prophecy used, the apocalyptic scenario imagined, and the underlying fatalism of such beliefs.

4

Apocalyptic Apparitions of the Virgin Mary in New York City

And there appeared a great wonder in heaven: a woman clothed with the sun, and the moon under her feet, and upon her head a crown of twelve stars.   —Revelation 12:1

O My children, My heart is torn that you will not turn about and get down on your knees. Throughout your world now there will be great trials set upon mankind: Upheavals of nature, discord in governments, nations at war, fire raining from the sky! My children, you ask for peace, but you are traveling to your own destruction as you build up armaments to kill your brothers and maim!
                              —Message from the Virgin Mary delivered to
                                       Veronica Lueken, July 15, 1977

Contemporary belief in apocalyptic prophecy is usually associated with Protestant premillennialism, but speculation about the end of the world pervades popular Roman Catholic thought as well. Beliefs about apocalyptic apparitions and prophecies associated with visions of the Virgin Mary are familiar to Catholics worldwide. Hundreds of apparitions of the Virgin Mary have been reported since the beginning of the nuclear age, many of which have warned that nuclear apocalypse is imminent. Apocalyptic messages have been delivered at numerous Marian apparition sites that continue to attract pilgrims, such as Fatima, Portugal; Garabandal, Spain; San Damiano, Italy; Akita, Japan; Medjugorje, Bosnia; and Bayside, New York. Belief in the prophetic importance of Marian apparitions remains a strong undercurrent in American Roman Catholic faith and is supported by a vast popular literature on Marian prophecy.

For more than a decade, advertisements publicizing apparitions of the Virgin Mary occurring in the borough of Queens, New York City, have appeared in newspapers and on billboards throughout the United States. The following headline, for instance, was published regularly in the classified section of the *Los Angeles Times* in January 1990: "JESUS & MARY Predict Great Earthquake For Los Angeles Area." The ad states that "we are now in the end days of the world just preceding the great tribulation and the 2nd return of Her Divine Son to Earth. It has been Her mission to now prepare mankind for the coming Chastisement from God, which is to consist of nuclear World War III and our planet being struck by the 'Ball of Redemption,' a fiery comet of Divine origin" (January 19, 1990, A14).

This advertisement was paid for by a group called Our Lady of the Roses, Mary Help of Mothers, which celebrates the prophecies of Mrs. Veronica Lueken, through whom the Virgin Mary, Jesus, and various saints are believed to communicate to humanity, initially at Bayside, and then at Flushing Meadows-Corona Park, New York. Similar to Hal Lindsey's predictions, the prophetic messages delivered at this apparition site identify the evils of contemporary society, reveal the signs of impending apocalypse and God's plan in the endtimes, and prescribe specific behavior for personal salvation. These prophecies and the supernatural occurrences associated with the site are a folk religious phenomenon, promoted outside the official sanction of clerical authorities, through word of mouth and an assortment of print and electronic technologies.

Visions of the Virgin Mary and Popular Marian Devotion

Apparitions of the Virgin Mary have been a component of Roman Catholic folk religious experience for centuries and have often been the basis for the continuing popularity of Marian devotion (Carroll 1986:xiv). The apparitions at Bayside and the divinely inspired messages of Mrs. Lueken have numerous antecedents in the twentieth century: hundreds of apparitions and miracles associated with the Virgin Mary have been reported since the end of World War II. Many of the most prominent and active contemporary Marian shrines—at such places as Lourdes, Fatima, Guadalupe, and Medjugorje—were established as the result of sightings of the Virgin Mary. In each instance Mary appeared to humble, poor, and theologically unschooled individuals. The sites at which these events occurred have become centers of devotion, attracting millions of pilgrims each year.

Approximately five million people annually visit the shrine at Fatima, where apparitions of the Virgin Mary appeared in 1917 to three peasant children. More than four and a half million individuals make annual pilgrimages to the apparition site at Lourdes, where Bernadette Soubirous had visions of the Blessed Mother in 1858; and roughly twelve million people each year visit the Basilica of Our Lady of Guadalupe near Mexico City, where Mary appeared in 1531 to Juan Diego (Carroll 1986:115). The most internationally celebrated of recent apparition sites is in Medjugorje, in the former Yugoslavia, where, until the outbreak of civil war, an ever-increasing number of pilgrims (estimated to be at least one million a year) transformed the small village where the Virgin Mary appeared to six children in 1981 into the largest Marian apparition site in Eastern Europe. Numerous other shrines established as the result of apparitions of the Virgin Mary attract several hundred thousand pilgrims annually as well, such as those at Knock (Ireland), La Salette and Pontmain (both in France), Beauraing and Bannuex (both in Belgium), Garabandal (Spain), San Damiano (Italy), Betania (Venezuela), Hrushiv (Ukraine), and Zeitoun (Egypt), among others.

In addition to the millions of pilgrims who journey to these apparition sites, even larger numbers belong to organizations that promote devotion to the Virgin Mary, primarily through the dissemination of the divine messages communicated during her appearances on earth. Catholic lay organizations such as the Militia of the Immaculate Conception (founded in 1917), the Legion of Mary (1927), the Slaves of the Immaculate Heart of Mary (1940), and the Blue Army of Our Lady of Fatima (1947) are all committed to "winning the world for Mary" (Carroll 1986:219). For instance, supporters of the Blue Army, which was formed at the beginning of the Cold War, distributed the apocalyptic and anticommunist messages supposedly revealed at Fatima. The primary goal of the Blue Army was the "conversion of Russia" and the defeat of the "atheistic Red Army" by means of praying the Hail Mary. At one time this organization claimed twenty-five million members in 110 countries (Geisendorfer 1977:46).

The impact of Marian apparitions on Catholic belief is illustrated by the fact that the rosary, the Brown Scapular of Our Lady of Mt. Carmel, and the Miraculous Medal (the three religious objects most often associated with devotion to the Virgin Mary) were revealed during Marian visions (Carroll 1986:116). Belief in visions of the Virgin Mary and widespread popular devotion to her have played a significant role in the Catholic Church's approval of Marian apparitions. Traditionally, the church has taken a restrained position toward acceptance of Marian sightings, sanctioning only a few of the thousands of visions that have been reported. In those instances in which Marian apparitions have been accepted by the church hierarchy, official approval is not considered dogma because Catholics are not required to believe in the reality of the visions. Rather, the church issues an official statement that the evidence is sufficient to "justify a purely human faith in the reality of the apparition" and that the apparition does not display any characteristics antithetic to Catholic faith and morals (Graef 1963:83–84; Carroll 1986:116). The Bayside apparitions are among those that have not been approved. After an investigation in 1973, the Diocese of Brooklyn declared that it had no basis for belief that Veronica Lueken had seen the Virgin Mary. The diocese issued another statement to the same effect in 1986 (Mugavero 1989:209–211).[1]

Although official approval of modern Marian apparitions may take decades (or, as in most cases, be denied by the church completely) and despite the fact that the Second Vatican Council in the early 1960s attempted to deemphasize Mariology, belief in the prophetic importance and apocalyptic reality of Marian visions appears to have increased among Catholics worldwide. Popular devotion to the Virgin Mary has a long history, illustrated by the festivals in the Middle Ages held in honor of Mary's Immaculate Conception (December 8), despite church opposition, and the fact that Marian feasts on the day of the Nativity (September 8) and the Assumption (August 15) were celebrated for centuries without the approval of church officials and often against their recommendations (Matter 1986:85). Various unsanctioned traditions and festivals celebrating the Virgin Mary were eventually made official by the church hierarchy, with the Immaculate Conception considered dogma in 1854, and the Assumption achieving official recognition in 1950. The somewhat recent nature of church sanction of these two holy days indicates the obvious "lag" between folk religion and institutional codification and reveals that official approval of Marian devotion is a relatively modern phenomenon.

The theological basis for devotion to the Virgin Mary originates in the doctrine of the communion of saints, which proclaims that a spiritual relationship exists between the faithful on earth, the souls in purgatory, and the saints in heaven (Turner and Turner 1978:203). According to Catholic tradition, the saints may be petitioned and may respond to the prayers of individuals, interceding with God on behalf of the faithful, and communicating with the living through apparitions, prophecy, visions, dreams, and by miracles (Turner and Turner 1978:203–205). Accounts of Jesus, various saints, and the devil intervening in human affairs have a long history in Catholic belief, yet it is the Virgin Mary who has appeared most frequently, inspired the greatest degree of observable devotion, and attracted the largest number of pilgrims (Carroll 1986:115; Rahner 1963:72–73).

For centuries the Virgin Mary has been worshiped as the "Mother of God" among the Catholic populace, particularly in regions in which an antecedent tradition of goddess worship existed (Gimbutas 1982:199–200). During the Middle Ages, when Marian devotion was extremely widespread, the depiction of the Virgin holding the infant Jesus was the most pervasive image associated with the cult of Mary. Although the Virgin Mary performed no miracles during her life and was not martyred, as were the majority of saints, she became the most popular devotional figure of Catholicism: "Mary was more powerful than the saints and less awful than God; as His Mother she had a quite peculiar influence with Christ, and her position between man and maker, as the Middle Ages pictured it, is exactly expressed by St. Bernard, when he says that Christ desires us to have everything through Mary" (Power 1928:xiii).

The scant biblical references to the Virgin Mary have become the basis for the varying roles and attributes assigned to Mary in her earthly appearances. As E. Ann Matter notes, not much is known about the life of Mary of Nazareth; the majority of references that mention her actually focus upon Jesus and her relationship to him as his mother (1986:81). The Gospel of St. Luke (1:26–38) states that Mary was a virgin who was betrothed to a man named Joseph when the angel Gabriel revealed to her that she had been chosen by God to conceive a son by the Holy Spirit. After an account of the Annunciation, the Bible states that Mary visited her relative Elizabeth, who was pregnant with John the Baptist. Elizabeth's womb "leaped for joy" (Luke 1:44) as Mary approached; and Elizabeth joyfully cried, "Blessed art thou among women, and blessed is the fruit of thy womb." These words were later combined with the angel Gabriel's words at the Annunciation, "Hail Mary, full of grace; the Lord is with thee," to form the Hail Mary, the prayer of the rosary (Matter 1986:81–82).

Belief in the Virgin Mary as "mediatrix," or divine intercessor between human beings and God (one of her primary functions in Marian apparitions), seems to have its basis in the biblical account of the miracle at the wedding of Cana (John 2:1–11). Mary states that the wine has been depleted and more is needed. At her request, Jesus transforms water into wine in the first of his miracles, thus exemplifying Mary's capacity to influence the behavior of her son.

The biblical reference to the Virgin Mary most significant for an understanding of modern Marian apparitions occurs in chapter 12 of the Book of Revelation. The passage speaks of "a woman clothed with the sun," with the moon under her feet, appearing in the sky. It is the scriptural precedent for the appearance of the Virgin Mary in the sky during her visitations, as well as for the apocalypticism expressed in these apparitions. This citation, like much of the Book of Revelation, is vague and open to innumerable interpretations. Although the woman mentioned in this reference is never specifically identified as the Virgin Mary, interpreters since the Middle Ages have assumed that the passage refers to Mary (Matter 1986:83). The text prior to this excerpt (Revelation 12:1) is essential for an understanding of the apocalyptic explanations assigned to the passage. After the opening of the seventh seal, the plague of locusts, the "beast that ascendeth out of the bottomless pit," and various other foreboding events, the following passage precedes the reference to the Virgin: "And the temple of God was opened in heaven, and there was seen in his temple the ark of his testament: and there were lightnings and voices, and thunderings, and an earthquake, and great hail. And there appeared a great wonder in heaven: a woman clothed with the sun. . . ."

The section later reveals that the woman is pregnant, that a "red dragon, having seven heads and ten horns, and seven crowns upon his heads," attempts to devour the child as soon as it is born. The woman, however, gives birth safely to a "man-child, who was to rule all nations with a rod of iron: and her child was caught up unto God and to his throne" (Revelation 12:1–5). After the child is taken to heaven, the woman escapes to a place in the wilderness, under the protection of God, as angels fight the dragon. Later the serpent persecutes the woman, sending a flood of water from its mouth to drown her, but the earth saves the woman, swallowing up the flood (Revelation 12:15–16). The serpent then departs to "make war with the remnant of her seed," identified as all of humanity familiar with the testimony of Jesus Christ (Revelation 12:17).

The obscure and fantastic symbolism embodied in this passage has motivated many to try to decipher its cryptic meaning. Catholic theologians generally regard the image of the woman to be a symbol of the early church, and the dragon is usually interpreted as representing the Roman Empire, which, at the time, threatened the existence of the church. Some theologians regard the woman's triumph over the serpent as a symbol of the Second Eve's overcoming the original curse brought to humankind by Eve (Warner 1976:383). However, for Veronica Lueken, her followers, and millions of Catholics interested in prophecy worldwide, "the woman" refers to the Virgin Mary, who is now appearing to warn humankind of imminent worldly cataclysm. According to this interpretation, the prophetic passage in Revelation specifically refers to the Virgin as the one who will do battle and triumph over a multitude of evil forces in the world symbolized by the serpent.

The Tradition of Apocalyptic Marian Apparitions

Although prophecy has been associated with Marian apparitions for centuries, apocalyptic themes in Marian prophecies are a relatively recent phenomenon, expressed in the apparitions at La Salette, France in 1846, and later with increased fervor at Fatima in 1917, and at the ecclesiastically unsanctioned apparition sites in Garabandal (1961–1965) and San Damiano (1964–1981). The visions reported in Medjugorje have apocalyptic overtones as well: the Virgin Mary told the visionaries that she appears so frequently there because it is the last place she will appear on earth before the Chastisement (Shinners 1989:175–176). Marian apparitions in Lubbock, Texas, in 1988–1989, also included apocalyptic prophecies, one of which described a star that would hit the earth within two years (*Los Angeles Times*, April 10, 1989, pt. I, 1, 19–20). The apparitions of the Virgin Mary and Jesus seen by housewife Nancy Fowler that began in 1987, in Conyers, Georgia, also warn of imminent divine punishments to be unleashed because people have rejected God. Historian of religion Sandra L. Zimdars-Swartz refers to this popular apocalyptic worldview among Roman Catholics as a "transcultural apocalyptic ideology," and asserts that Marian devotees regard Mary's recent appearances as part of a pattern of endtimes warnings revealing an "all-encompassing divine plan" occurring at the end of history before the return of Christ (1991:246). In her role as intercessor, the Virgin Mary represents divine mercy, the nurturing mother intervening on behalf of her children to rescue them from the apocalyptic punishments of an angry God (Zimdars-Swartz 1991:247–248). The Bayside apparitions, possibly the most apocalyptic of contemporary Marian visitations, represent an intensification of the eschatological, anticommunist, and conspiratorial themes of this modern Marian worldview, with Mary appearing as an apocalyptic prophetess who reveals God's plan in the last days.

Perhaps the most familiar legend among Roman Catholics associated with the tradition of apocalyptic Marian apparitions involves the "third secret of Fatima," which was communicated by the Virgin Mary to the seer Lucia dos Santos on July 13, 1917. According to legend, the secret message was delivered in a sealed envelope to the Vatican and was to be revealed to the world by the pope in 1960. However, the third secret has never been revealed publicly by the Catholic Church, and stories circulate about the adverse reactions of various popes who opened the envelope and read the prophecy (fainting, weeping, suffering heart failure, going into comatose state). The third secret is commonly believed to predict a fiery apocalypse during the term of the fifth pope after the letter was unsealed (John Paul II, who was chosen to be pope in 1978, is the third pope since the letter was opened). Rumors suggest that the church will not reveal the secret for fear that people will become suicidal and immoral if informed of the end of the world. The third secret is also rumored to predict World War III, various other cataclysms, and crises in the Roman Catholic Church.

To determine the extent to which apocalyptic beliefs and stories such as the third secret of Fatima are known among Catholics is difficult, but the people who come to Flushing Meadows Park are well versed in the apocalyptic themes and messages of previous apparitions. For instance, a number of the Baysiders that I spoke with told me that they either had been or would like to go to Fatima or Garabandal, the places where the messages from Mary have been the most apocalyptic. Few mentioned Lourdes, Guadalupe, or Medjugorje, where apocalyptic ideas are subordinate to other themes or nonexistent. As noted earlier, not all Marian apparitions have apocalyptic overtones, but the Baysiders seemed to prefer the shrines with obvious end-of-the-world messages. At Lourdes, for instance, no explicit apocalyptic sentiments were expressed, nor have ensuing discussions of the messages reinterpreted them as apocalyptic. Instead, the Lourdes messages emphasize universal penance and traditional Catholic doctrine. Although the Medjugorje messages exhibit a degree of apocalypticism, this theme is secondary in importance to the larger message of universal peace and a return to Catholic traditions. For this reason, many Baysiders believe that the Medjugorje apparitions are a fraudulent ploy influenced by Satan, involving a false, New Age Madonna preaching love, peace, and a one-world religion. They claim that the authentic Mother of God is currently appearing only on the apparition grounds in Flushing Meadows Park and that other Marian apparitions, such as those at Medjugorje, are spurious and spiritually dangerous.

Since the Fatima visions, modern apparitions of the Virgin Mary not only have become increasingly apocalyptic but have been repeatedly interpreted as identifying communism as the "serpent," the "beast," and the "red dragon" referred to in the Book of Revelation. According to the messages communicated at Fatima and several other apparition sites including Bayside, the conflict of ideologies between communism and democracy is in fact a cosmic battle between Satan and God, to be fought in a world seething in sin and teetering on the edge of total destruction.

The Fatima apparitions were perhaps the most spectacular Marian visions in history, purportedly involving strange occurrences in the sky. For instance, during the October 13, 1917, apparition, rain clouds parted, the sun turned into a silver disk surrounded by a multicolored light, the sky seemed to revolve, and then the sun appeared to spin and plunge toward the earth, where it hovered for a moment and then ascended. These supernatural phenomena were witnessed by many of the seventy thousand people assembled at the site, several of whom were reporters (Gracf 1963:82). Although some controversy surrounds this sighting as well as the messages delivered at Fatima, the church recognized the apparition in 1931, and, according to popular belief, Pope Pius XII consecrated the world to the Immaculate Heart of Mary in 1942 because of the Fatima messages. A major emphasis of the second message of Fatima involves the Virgin Mary's request that "Russia be consecrated to Christianity," which allegedly was revealed to Lucia dos Santos in 1917. The Virgin Mary's political views about Russia and communism were disclosed years later in Lucia's memoirs, written in a convent between 1935 and 1941. Evidence suggests that Lucia's pronouncement of the Virgin Mary's anticommunist stance may have been based on experiences that occurred between 1925 and 1935, during a period of extreme anticommunist sentiment among Portuguese Catholics (Kselman and Avella 1986:408–409; Perry and Echeverría 1988:184–193).

Lucia's second message from the Virgin Mary at Fatima reinforced and provoked anticommunist sentiment, and this zealous anticommunism finds full expression in the messages communicated by Mrs. Lueken at Bayside. In addition to anticommunism and apocalypticism, the Bayside messages emphasize a return to traditional Catholic teachings, as do previous apparitions. Penance, fasting, and praying the Hail Mary are stressed as a means of preventing global war, disease, starvation, natural disasters, and various divinely ordained cataclysms. Devotion to the Virgin Mary is seen as the only remaining solution in a world gone astray; veneration of Mary will divert the wrath of an angry God and prevent the destruction of the planet.[2]

Our Lady of the Roses, Veronica Lueken, and the Bayside Apparitions

The Bayside phenomenon began on June 5, 1968, the day that Robert F. Kennedy was assassinated. Veronica Lueken, a housewife from Queens, New York, and mother of five children, experienced a perfume of roses in her car as she prayed for the dying New York senator. Shortly thereafter, Mrs. Lueken had a vision of Saint Thérèse of Lisieux, who later gave her sacred writings and poems by dictation. On April 7, 1970, the Virgin Mary appeared to Mrs. Lueken in her home, instructing her to establish a shrine on the grounds of the Saint Robert Bellarmine Church in Bayside, New York, and promising to make a personal appearance if vigils were held there on June 18, 1970. The Virgin Mary requested that this shrine be named "Our Lady of the Roses, Mary Help of Mothers." The Virgin Mary also promised to appear and speak through Mrs. Lueken (who would act as a "voice box" repeating words from heaven) in the evenings of all the great feast days of the Catholic Church, if vigils were faithfully kept on those days. In addition, Mary told Mrs. Lueken to spread the messages from heaven throughout the world.

An essential component of Mrs. Lueken's messages is her constant reference to prophetic signs that indicate that the end of the world is near. These portents, often similar to those described by other proponents of imminent apocalypse, predict various disasters to be provoked by increased social and moral decay in the world. Worldwide cataclysm, or what is referred to as the "Great Chastisement," may be averted through personal penance, prayer, and adherence to traditional Catholic teachings, and particularly through the conversion of Russia to Christianity.

Beginning in 1970, vigils were held regularly at the Bayside shrine. Several hundred messages have been transmitted by Mrs. Lueken, who declares she repeats the Virgin Mary's messages word for word, although she often adds her own descriptions of what she sees in her visions. In 1975, the apparition site was moved from Bayside to Flushing Meadows-Corona Park because of the objections of the residents around Saint Bellarmine's Church to the Saturday night vigils and the controversial nature of the messages. Although the apparitions now occur at Flushing Meadows Park, they are still referred to as the "Bayside apparitions," and Mrs. Lueken's followers continue to call themselves "Baysiders." Mrs. Lueken has been told by the Virgin Mary that the Baysiders will eventually be allowed to return to the original site, that a basilica will be built there, and that a miraculous spring of curative waters will come forth from the sacred grounds, similar to Lourdes (the shrine's literature refers to the Bayside phenomenon as "The Lourdes of America"). Baysiders maintain that Bayside will eventually become the national Marian shrine in the United States, like Lourdes in France or Our Lady of Guadalupe in Mexico.

The number of Baysiders is difficult to estimate. According to the shrine literature, between twelve and fifteen thousand people attended the thirteenth anniversary celebration of Mrs. Lueken's visions on June 18, 1983, and as many as ten thousand purportedly attended the nineteenth anniversary celebration in June 1989, at which I was present. On other occasions that I have attended, only a few dozen devotees were at the Saturday evening vigils. Publications from the shrine refer to "thousands of followers" and the "tens of thousands" of newsletters and messages that regularly are mailed to those who subscribe to the shrine's literature (see *Rose Notes* 5, no. 10 [August 1993]:3).

Groups dedicated to promoting the Bayside messages have formed in numerous cities in the United States and throughout the world; a radio program about the Bayside prophecies, entitled "These Last Days," airs in various cities in more than thirty states; and the Bayside prophecies have been translated into more than twenty languages. In 1994, the shrine organization placed a full-page advertisement entitled "The Virgin Mary in America . . . the world's refuge at the last hour," in the *Weekly World News* (December 13, 1994), a tabloid magazine with a circulation of 560,000. According to the shrine's literature, the ad elicited 5,000 phone calls and 1500 written responses, and more than 3,000 of the shrine's introductory packets were sent as a result (*Rose Notes* 7, no. 17 [March 1995]:2). In 1995, upwards of 1200 people attended a banquet celebrating the twenty-fifth anniversary of Mrs. Lueken's visions, and pilgrimages to the apparition site were organized in more than 150 cities in eleven countries. The shrine's newsletter predicts, "The day is not long coming when millions throughout the world will come to acknowledge Bayside for what it truly is—the last refuge at the last hour" (*Rose Notes* 7, no. 18 [June 1995]:2).

The apocalyptic messages and prophesies conveyed to Mrs. Lueken by the Virgin Mary are documented and disseminated by Our Lady of the Roses Shrine and a network of other organizations through an assortment of electronic and print technologies. Each time Mrs. Lueken speaks to Mary and Jesus at the apparition site, she allegedly is recorded on audiotape. The messages are then transcribed and printed by the Our Lady of the Roses Shrine and distributed to thousands of Baysiders. Audiocassettes of Mrs. Lueken in a trance state receiving the divine communications are also available, as are an introductory pamphlet describing the shrine (*Our Lady of the Roses, Mary Help of Mothers: An Introductory Booklet on the Apparitions of Bayside*, henceforth referred to as *OLR Booklet*) and the larger, 168-page *Our Lady of the Roses, Mary Help of Mothers "Blue Book"* (referred to as *OLR Book*), which provides detailed information about the messages and the shrine. The complete transcriptions of Mrs. Lueken's visions are collected in two large books, *Roses from Heaven: Jesus and Mary Speak to the World—1970–1976*, Volume 1, and *Roses from Heaven: Jesus and Mary Speak to the World—1977–1986*, Volume 2. Other literature, inspirational pamphlets, videotapes, and various sacramental items, such as rosaries, medallions of saints, crucifixes, scapulars, and laminated rose petals believed to be blessed by Jesus and Mary during the apparitions, are available as well.

The literature and audio- and videocassettes distributed by the shrine provide commentaries on a litany of topics: nuclear weapons, natural disasters, communism, AIDS, famine, abortion, pornography, terrorism, drug abuse, and corruption and conspiracy in the government and especially in the Roman Catholic Church. The imminence of nuclear annihilation is a predominant theme in the Bayside messages, but current disasters are discussed as well, such as earthquakes, floods, drought, famine, starvation, and epidemics, all of which are regarded as further proof that these are the endtimes (*OLR Book* 1986:52–53). Mrs. Lueken's apparitions also provide divine commentary on a wide range of various satanic influences in American society, including discussions of things like rock music, immodest dress, sex education, television, the Illuminati, UFOs, and test-tube babies. Some of the shrine's literature addresses contemporary issues, but much of the distributed material attempts to establish the shrine's place within the tradition of Marian apparitions and often highlights the supernatural phenomena associated with the apparition site.

Although knowledge of the apparitions of Our Lady of Bayside is transmitted verbally, this is by no means the predominant mode of disseminating information about the shrine. The apparitions have been promoted largely through religious tracts, videos, cable TV, advertisements, audiocassettes, public presentations, and a twenty-four-hour-a-day, 1-800 telephone number. The use of print and electronic technologies accounts for much of the popularity and continuing interest in the apparitions, and without these technologies to transmit the messages and raise money, it is questionable whether the Bayside movement would exist as a viable organization.

As a visionary, Veronica Lueken derives her source of authority from direct miraculous experiences and revelations, and she maintains this charismatic authority by her continuing visionary abilities. Like other seers, Mrs. Lueken acts as an intermediary between humans and the supernatural order, directly communicating God's will and plan for humanity. She is, as she states, a "voice box for heaven," repeating word for word the pronouncements of supernatural entities. Her visionary and oracular capabilities resemble what was referred to in antiquity by thinkers such as Cicero and Plato as "natural divination" (*naturalis divinatio*), defined as the ability to understand the conversation of gods through direct inspiration, trance, ecstasy, and visions (Aune 1983:339). Trance states are commonly characterized by revelations, visions, hallucinations, and out-of-body experiences, and are distinguished from possession states, which are associated with certain types of prophetic and particularly shamanistic experiences (Bourguignon 1976:1–10). Although I have not personally witnessed Mrs. Lueken in a trance state—she is surrounded by bodyguards during the vigils because of alleged attempts on her life—I have seen photographs and videotapes that show her conversing with various deities in which she is trembling, weeping, waving, and smiling, and clearly seems to be in an altered state of consciousness. The charismatic and miraculous abilities attributed to Mrs. Lueken emphasize the subjective, experiential aspects of her divine calling over formalized religious education. Divinely inspired prophets and charismatic seers like Mrs. Lueken often are the catalysts for apocalyptic fervor, serving as "channels" for supernatural criticism of the existing religious, social, economic, and political institutions. Their personal experiences form the basis for the mythos of the apocalyptic movement, and their revelations provide explicit explanations for current ills and prescribe specific behavior for individual and societal salvation.

The Virgin and the Bomb: Nuclear Destruction and the Fireball of Redemption

The imminence of divine punishment and worldly catastrophe is the most prominent idea addressed in Mrs. Lueken's visions. The apocalyptic scenario prophesied in the Bayside apparitions describes a global "Warning," followed by a "Great Miracle," and then a "Chastisement" that will destroy three-fourths of humanity. The Chastisement will consist of two parts. The first will be World War III; the second, a God-sent "Fireball of Redemption." Prior to the Chastisement, a great Warning will be sent to humanity, as the following message from the Virgin Mary indicates:

> There will be a tremendous explosion and the sky shall roll back like a scroll. This force shall go within the very core of the human. He will understand his offenses to his God. . . . There will be tremendously high waves roaring and taking with them cities; buildings shall disappear from their moorings; the atmosphere shall spew forth currents of great heat; a darkness of spirit and a darkness of atmosphere shall settle in a deadly quiet upon mankind. As the day follows night, so shall this warning follow soon. Beware of the sunrise! Do not look up to the sky, the flash! Close your windows! Draw your shades! Remain inside! Do not venture outside your door, or you will not return! (*OLR Book* 1986:44–45)

In another vision, Mrs. Lueken experienced the Warning, and describes it as follows: "It is as though everything exploded in the sky—the flash! It is very hot, very warm. It feels like a burning. Now—the sky is very white . . . it's like a huge explosion. NOW—this VOICE, the VOICE, the VOICE, Our Lady says it is a voice within you: 'YOUR WARNING BEFORE THE CHAS-TISEMENT—FLASH, FIRE, AND THE VOICE WITHIN YOU'" (*OLR Book* 1986:44).

Mrs. Lueken's predictions of the Warning have precedents in the messages communicated by the Virgin Mary at Garabandal, Spain (1961–1965). According to one of the seers there, Conchita Gonzales, the Warning will be like an internal fire, and although it will not cause physical injury, "dying is preferable to a mere five minutes of what is awaiting us" (*OLR Book* 1986:44). Conchita also said that the Warning will involve the realization of one's sins and be experienced by everyone in the world, and be clearly divine in origin. Mrs. Lueken's visions of the Warning are also similar to descriptions of the sun hurling toward the earth at Fatima, which was interpreted by some who experienced it as a terrifying chastisement from heaven and a prelude to the end of the world.

The messages delivered by the Virgin Mary at Garabandal about the Warning appear rather general (see Zimdars-Swartz 1991:232–233), but Mrs. Lueken's messages provide specific details and clarify the nature of this event: the Warning will appear after a revolution in Rome in which the pope flees the Vatican, seeking refuge in another country. In Mrs. Lueken's graphic descriptions, the Warning seems to resemble a divinely sent nuclear explosion, although the cataclysmic consequences of the Warning are not exactly clear. Unlike the Garabandal messages, Mrs. Lueken's visions imply that the Warning will cause death and physical injury (*OLR Book* 1986:44–45), but that the faithful will not be harmed: "All who remain in the light of grace will have no fear. They will pass through this great Warning without suffering" (*OLR Booklet* n.d.:2). Although previous Marian apparitions foretell of cataclysmic events such as the Warning, Mrs. Lueken's visions expound on the destructive nature of these events, emphasizing in greater detail the devastation and violence that will occur in the endtimes.

According to Mrs. Lueken's visions, following the Warning a "Great Miracle" will be sent to encourage humanity to change its sinful behavior. The Miracle will occur in the sky, for many to see, and will be the greatest miracle that God has performed for the world. It will occur through the intercession of the Virgin Mary, but agents of Satan will attempt to disprove its divine nature (*OLR Book* 1986:45). The details of the Miracle are vague in Mrs. Lueken's messages, but if humanity does not change after this supernatural spectacle, the Chastisement will follow, the first portion of which will involve nuclear war: "A war far greater than any war fought in the history of creation shall come upon mankind soon. Flames shall engulf many nations, burning the skin from bones, and the skin shall dry up and blow away as if it had never been!" (message from the Virgin Mary, May 20, 1978 [Skovmand 1993:91]). A message communicated from Jesus confirms the imminence of a nuclear conflagration: "The greatest loss of life, My children, will come with the explosion of a nuclear warhead upon mankind! The Ball of Redemption shall follow, and not much shall be left of flesh upon earth" (message from Jesus, July 25, 1977 [Skovmand 1993:87]).

In another apparition, Mrs. Lueken has a vision of a nuclear explosion, "Oh, I see a great horrible war. I see . . . it looks like a mushroom. A tremendous explosion and everything is gone! Oh! [The Virgin Mary then says:] 'Satan, My child, shall have his hand upon the button'" (*OLR Book* 1986:49). Later in the message, Mrs. Lueken speaks of uniformed soldiers with "red stars on their hats," and concludes with a command from the Virgin Mary to pray for the conversion of communist Russia to Catholicism in order to avert nuclear catastrophe. In the Bayside prophecies, like dispensationalist predictions, the proliferation and use of nuclear weapons is often portrayed as inevitable, with peace efforts and nuclear disarmament viewed as hopeless:

> The cries of peace going throughout your world are just a cover for armaments that are being gathered now to enslave and ensnare the world into a war of major proportion. My children, all of the cries of peace that go out throughout your world cannot prevent the explosion of nuclear warfare upon mankind! The hand of God that withheld this punishment upon mankind is being withdrawn. . . . (message from Jesus, June 16, 1977 [Skovmand 1993:87])

Unlike dispensationalism which attempts to correlate current events with scripture through impressive feats of biblical exegesis, such interpretative acrobatics are rare in the Bayside literature, and regarded as unnecessary by Baysiders because prophecies of the endtimes are directly communicated by Mary, Jesus, and the saints. At one of her apparitions, however, Mrs. Lueken does interpret biblical scripture, citing the vision of Zechariah in which he describes a "flying roll," twenty cubits long by ten cubits wide, which brings a curse over the face of the whole earth, and which consumes the timber and stones of houses (*OLR Book* 1986:50; Zechariah 5). Mrs. Lueken then explains his vision in terms of nuclear weapons:

> The flying roll as given in the Bible, described in the Bible, destroys their houses. The houses are burned and consumed. Now the size of the flying roll

would be about the size of the new multiple warhead ICBMs or orbital bombs, the ones that will carry ten H-bombs each. Now that message is specifically one reason why Heaven allowed me to be here this evening: because of the urgency of the times and the necessity to pray for Pope John Paul II. (*OLR Book* 1986:50)

This uncommon interpretive venture on the part of Mrs. Lueken reveals the preoccupation with nuclear armaments and their destructive capabilities that characterizes her apparitions and pervades the worldview of her followers.

The sense of the imminence of nuclear war and communist invasion is also conveyed through the illustrations in the shrine's publications. On one page of the shrine's "Blue Book," for example, is an illustration of a communist demon emerging from Russia with blood dripping from his fingers, another illustration of a cemetery filled with crosses, and a photograph of a mushroom cloud, under which is the boldfaced subheading "The Good Will Also Die With The Bad" (*OLR Book* 1986:49). Such imagery, along with the prophecies and repeated references to nuclear annihilation in the Bayside literature, presents a vision of the nuclear threat as a menacing presence, a dark, radioactive cloud looming over all humanity, with nuclear war regarded as an imminent event that human beings are powerless to prevent.

The details of this impending nuclear scenario are revealed in another one of Mrs. Lueken's visions, in which she is shown a map by the Virgin Mary depicting Jerusalem, Egypt, Arabia, French Morocco, and Africa, and is told that World War III will start in this region (*OLR Book* 1986:50). According to Mary, communist Russia will unite with China and attempt to take over the world; Syria will be instrumental either in creating world peace or the third world war; and a satanic leader from Egypt will start a world war (Skovmand 1993:84–92). In a message delivered May 30, 1978, Mary also told Mrs. Lueken that a single, insane individual will initiate a global nuclear inferno: "Your world shall soon be visited by a baptism of fire. Is this what you want? You shall not escape this baptism of fire, for sin is insanity, and one insane mind shall plunge you into a bloodbath and a destruction by fire" (Skovmand 1993:90).

In other visions, Mrs. Lueken is shown wars in Africa, a hammer and sickle floating above the African continent, and the continent fading into darkness. Finally, she sees "an actual globe of the world, like we have on our desk in school. And the first place to burst into flames is Africa. Now Our Lady is pointing farther up on the globe, and She's saying now: 'Listen, My child, and repeat this well. The United States of America is fast approaching on the start of the THIRD WORLD WAR" (July 1, 1985 [Skovmand 1993:84–85]). After the war in Africa, communist Russia will invade the United States, attacking with nuclear missiles. This nuclear conflagration and other nuclear exchanges will exterminate millions of people, and the United States will be destroyed because it has become a nation of sin and increasing paganism. This third world war is considered to be a "man-made chastisement," a punishment for sins that God will permit unless humans repent.

The Bayside prophecies repeatedly declare that as sinfulness increases, so will disasters and social problems, resulting ultimately in God's wrathful condemnation of the human race in the form of the "Fireball of Redemption," a comet that will eliminate more than three-quarters of the world's population. An apocalyptic scenario involving a divinely sent comet that will cleanse the earth is not unique to the Bayside apparitions but is mentioned in various popular books on Catholic prophecy. The privately published *Prophecies, the Chastisement, and Purification* (Herbert 1986), written by an interpreter of Catholic prophecy, surveys various Marian chastisement scenarios prophesied by seers and visionaries, one of which is by a fireball of redemption. *Catholic Prophecy* (Dupont 1973), whose traditionalist Catholic author says he has studied hundreds of prophecies, has a chapter entitled "The Comet." Its narratives about a fiery comet and beliefs about a divine chastisement are not sanctioned by the Catholic Church but are a form of folk apocalypticism, learned through popular publications and discussions that Catholics have with one another.

Mrs. Lueken's descriptions of the Fireball chastisement are as extensive as her depictions of the nuclear chastisement. In one of her apparitions she describes the Fireball as follows:

> Now I see coming through the sky a tremendous huge ball, Oh! It's like a giant sun. But as it is travelling through the sky now it seems to be turning colours, white and orange, and spinning so fast, that it's like it's hurtling through space. Aaah! It has tremendous heat! . . . Now I'm looking into the street—it's a very large city and I see people pointing up to the sky and they look like they are filled with terror; they're running and they're all running but they seem to be running from the cities. . . . Oh, my goodness—Oh!! I see back as I look back— I see what look like bodies but I can't recognize them because they look . . . Oooh! They look like they've been burnt, burnt black! Ooh! . . . Oooh! . . . I see everything is flattened back there. It looked like it was a city—but it's flat and there's smoke rising, and everything looks like it was just knocked over, like a stack of cards. (*OLR Book* 1986:46)

Although the imagery might be interpreted as a metaphor for nuclear war— the atomic fireball—Mrs. Lueken's messages make it clear that this is a God-sent comet of destruction. Humanity will not be solely responsible for the final apocalypse; the fury of God will be unleashed and most of humanity will perish. As the world itself becomes increasingly sinful and violent, God will repay human violence with the violence of apocalypse.

Mrs. Lueken's messages make a distinction between the nuclear chastisement and the comet chastisement, yet one cannot help but consider the Fireball in terms of the imagery of nuclear conflagration. Mrs. Lueken's visions of bodies burnt black and cities completely leveled evoke the images of the leveling of Hiroshima and Nagasaki by nuclear bombs and the blackened bodies amid the ruins. It is tempting to consider visions of the Fireball to be a projection of fears of nuclear destruction, with the comet the symbolic equivalent of the bomb, disguised and recast as a fireball hurled by an angry God. Visions of a fiery apocalypse and its aftermath, whether by means of nuclear weaponry or divine fireball, are easy to imagine in the nuclear age and imbue Mrs. Lueken's prophecies with a disturbing visual power.

In contrast to the apocalyptic anger of God, the tone of the Virgin Mary in her apparitions to Mrs. Lueken is that of concern and love for humanity gone astray: "My children, as a Mother, My heart is torn for you. O mothers who come to Me, hearts bleeding in sorrow, I will comfort you, for I, too, know the suffering of loss" (October 6, 1979; *Directives from Heaven* 1, no. 8 [December 27, 1991]:1). Like previous Marian visitations, the Virgin Mary of Bayside appears as a compassionate and loving mother who is warning her children of imminent disaster and attempting to save and comfort them. Mrs. Lueken's predictions fluctuate between visions of devastation, with Mary depicted as a warrior deity who will lead the battle against Satan and ultimately crush him beneath her heel, and Mary as nurturing and loving mother, pleading with her children to prevent the prophesied catastrophes through repentance, prayer, and conversion. Despite the apocalyptic ethos and violence of the visions at Bayside, Baysiders emphasize the role of the Virgin Mary as the forgiving and compassionate Mother, the Mother who nurtures all, who suffers and weeps over her children, and protects them from the wrath of God the Father. Devotion to the Virgin Mary, at Flushing Meadows Park and elsewhere, is appealing not only because it may represent the worship of the feminine side of God but perhaps because it expresses deeply felt emotions about our own mothers as well as the yearning for divine maternal protection otherwise denied in the Christian tradition dominated by male deities and principles (see Cunningham 1982; Greeley 1977; Jung 1970; Kselman and Avella 1986).

Unique Aspects of the Bayside Apparitions

The Bayside apparitions have antecedents in previous Marian apparitions, but they also have new, idiosyncratic elements that modify the existing corpus of beliefs and narratives and that further contribute to the tradition of Marian sightings. One such element, for instance, is the belief in the concept of the Rapture, normally associated with premillennial dispensationalism. Like dispensationalist beliefs, Mrs. Lueken's prophecies imply that a select group of the chosen few will not have to endure the horrors of apocalypse because they will have been raptured prior to this event. Her ideas about the Rapture may well have been influenced by dispensationalist thought (perhaps even Hal Lindsey's books, which were popular during the decade in which her visions began), although her descriptions of the Rapture differ from those of dispensationalists and are somewhat vague. In a message delivered by the Virgin Mary, Mrs. Lueken states:

> I give you grace of heart, My children, to know that many shall be taken from the earth before the great chastisement. It will be of great mirth, My child, to reveal to you that there will be much consternation and conflicting thought when these beloved children disappear from the earth. Many of your news media shall state that they have been carried off by flying saucers. Oh no, My children, they were carried off into a supernatural realm of the Eternal Father to await the return of My Son upon earth. (*OLR Booklet* n.d.:2)

Unlike Lindsey, Mrs. Lueken does not develop a systematic articulation of what will occur during the Rapture, and it is unclear whether the Rapture will involve only Baysiders or include other traditionalist Catholics or Christians in general.

The ambiguous nature of Mrs. Lueken's Rapture scenario is indicated by other messages that specify that the faithful may have to endure the horrors of the last days, suffering the ordeal of large-scale nuclear war and the Chastisement, during which three-fourths of humanity will be destroyed. Some of the prophecies assert that believers will survive the coming destruction; other messages from Mary declare that the innocent will be killed in the cataclysms (*OLR Book* 1986:49). The prophecies encourage believers to prepare for the catastrophes and sufferings ahead: to store food, nail crucifixes to their doors, pray, and protect themselves with their "spiritual armor"—scapulars, crucifixes, rosaries, religious medals, and saints' statues. The importance of these spiritual objects is continually emphasized in the prophecies: "Both front and back doors must have a crucifix. I say this to you because there will be carnage within your areas, and this will pass you by if you keep your crucifix upon your doors" (*OLR Booklet* n.d.:11). Praying the Hail Mary is also frequently mentioned as an act that will protect Baysiders from imminent catastrophes. Another feature that distinguishes Mrs. Lueken's visions from those of previous Roman Catholic seers is that she has received prophecies from numerous figures in the Roman Catholic pantheon, not just the Virgin Mary. Mrs. Lueken frequently receives messages from Jesus, and occasionally from Saint Michael the Archangel, who is venerated as the guardian of the church, the conqueror of Satan and the fallen angels cast into hell for eternity for rebelling against God. Other figures that have accompanied the Virgin Mary in her appearances at Bayside and Flushing Meadows Park include Saint Thérèse of Lisieux, Saint Joseph, Saint Paul, Saint John the Evangelist, Saint Gabriel the Archangel, Saint Teresa of Avila, Saint Francis of Assisi, Saint Anne, Saint Joachim, Saint Bernadette of Lourdes, Saint John Neumann of Philadelphia, Saint Gemma Galgani, Saint Aloysius Gonzaga, Saint Thomas Aquinas, Saint Robert Bellarmine, Saint Catherine Labouré, Jacinta Marto (one of the visionaries of Fatima), and Padre Pio (the stigmatic Capuchin friar). The Bayside literature explains that the appearance of all these saints indicates the Virgin Mary's desire to reestablish "the cult of the Saints, which the modernists in the church have tried to destroy, mainly by the removal of the statues and Sacred Images from the Catholic Sanctuaries of the World" (*OLR Book* 1986:81).

Along with apparitions of saints, Mrs. Lueken has had visions of people who have recently died, such as a vision of her son (who was shot to death in an accident), ascending a golden staircase into heaven. Pope Pius X, known for his antimodernist views, has appeared to Mrs. Lueken, as have several other popes, who sometimes speak to her directly. Pope John Paul II appeared in one vision and said, "My children of the world pray for me" (*Directives from Heaven* 1, no. 7 [December 13, 1991]: 1). The profusion of saints and other holy figures who have appeared at the apparition site not only confirm Mrs. Lueken's visionary powers for Baysiders but indicate that God's intermediaries are actively involved in communicating and implementing God's plan in the last days.

Mrs. Lueken's lengthy and detailed accounts of what she sees in her visions is another distinctive aspect of the Bayside apparitions. In her visions, Mrs. Lueken describes the color of the sky, the clothing, the gestures, and the expressions of the divine beings with whom she communicates:

> The sky has been a very misty, subdued colouring of pink . . . but there is blue now . . . Our Lady's call, Her call signal is blue in the sky, blue dots. But the whole area surrounding the call colours of Our Lady, the area is turning into a velvety-looking plush . . . almost like a floor covering . . . a carpeting of deep blue

velvet. . . . Our Lady now is coming forward, and She's stepping onto this very beautiful, blue carpet. Our Lady is dressed in a white gown, a beautiful, almost translucent colour of white. And She has on a golden type of belting around Her waist. . . . Our Lady has a mantle of deep blue, a beautiful colour blue, and all along the border of the mantle, there's a golden trim. Oh, from here it would appear to be around an inch and a half trim. . . . (*OLR Book* 1986:18)

Such descriptions usually continue for several paragraphs and are typical of most of Mrs. Lueken's apparitions. The common expressions and colloquialisms used by Mrs. Lueken, as well as the inclusion of her emotional interjections, give the messages an unpretentious or "unrefined" quality that non-Baysiders may find humorous but that Baysiders do not seem to mind at all. Skeptics might facetiously remark that such accounts describe the Virgin Mary as if she were participating in a divine fashion show, yet this emphasis on exact detail and visual imagery enhances the perceptualization of Mrs. Lueken's visions and gives graphic testimony to their authenticity for Baysiders.

The Bayside literature provides a reason for the necessity of these lengthy descriptions: the Virgin Mary has adapted her appearances to the needs of Americans:

In the United States, Our Blessed Mother knows the American people. She knows their hunger for details. . . . And so, at each vigil, Veronica while in ecstasy, describes in detail Our Lady's appearance, Her manner of movement, the celestial beings that accompany Her, and a wealth of other particulars dear to the hearts of those who love Her and pray to Her. . . . In appearing in New York City, Our Lady has come to the capital city of a nation of television addicts. They have been conditioned to demand the details of the visual. And with Her typical graciousness, Our Lady seeks to accommodate them. (*OLR Book* 1986:18)

In the past, visionaries usually have briefly described the Virgin Mary and conveyed Mary's concise messages some time after their visions had occurred; Mrs. Lueken's extensive descriptions and divine communications occur in the immediate present, with devotees hearing her narration shortly after she receives the messages from heaven. Because they are told exactly when Mary, Jesus, and the saints are present at the shrine, Baysiders actively participate in the apparitions, responding immediately to the messages as they are conveyed. During my visits to the apparition site, Baysiders began noticing increased supernatural phenomena on the apparition grounds as soon as Mrs. Lueken indicated that Mary and Jesus were approaching in the sky, and her descriptions of them made their presence palpable for many Baysiders, providing a heightened sense of involvement in a numinous event as the apparitions occurred.

Miraculous Photography and Apocalyptic Divination

The widespread use of photography by Baysiders to document the miraculous phenomena associated with the shrine is perhaps the most compelling innovation on previous Catholic traditions concerning Marian apparitions and miraculous images. Baysiders have adapted the image-making qualities of photography to document the signs of the apocalypse and reproduce these signs in tangible form on film (Wojcik 1996b). Referred to as "miracle photos" or "Polaroids from Heaven" by Baysiders, these photographic images are said to contain allegorical symbols and are interpreted as divine communications offering insights of prophetic relevance. Taking miraculous photographs at the apparition site is central to the religious experiences of many Baysiders and an important means by which imminent apocalypse is foretold.[3] The shrine's literature states, "Our Lady has said that the Eternal Father is making use of modern technology 'to communicate with a fallen generation,' a generation whose hearts are so hardened, and eyes so blinded, that they need some kind of tangible proof of the authenticity of the Bayside visions" (*OLR Booklet* n.d.:9).

Mrs. Lueken's messages explicitly encourage Baysiders to use Polaroid technology to document the supernatural occurrences at the apparition site, and a booklet distributed by the shrine organization states that "in view of the fact that the [Book of] Apocalypse itself makes extensive use of symbols, Heaven seems to be using the same method by communicating with symbols in the miraculous pictures" (*OLR Booklet* n.d.:9). According to the shrine's literature, the Virgin Mary has directed Baysiders to use "Polaroid or other self-developing cameras, since these pictures develop on the spot and therefore eliminate later accusations of tampering with the negatives" (*OLR Book* 1986:22). The miraculous photographs are examined by Baysiders not only for prophetic information about the imminence of apocalypse but for personal revelations as well, and are valued as tangible souvenirs of supernatural manifestations. Baysiders are familiar with the legend of Saint Veronica and her veil, a piece of cloth that is said to have been imprinted with a miraculous and true image of Christ, somewhat like a photograph, after Veronica wiped his sweating and bleeding face with it on his way to Calvary. Baysiders note that their visionary's name is also Veronica, which they claim comes from the Latin *vera icona*, or "true image," and they say that heaven, through miraculous photography, is showing its "true face" to humanity.

When I was present at the apparition site, I observed Baysiders taking photographs throughout three-hour Saturday evening vigils, although most began taking pictures once Mrs. Lueken entered a trance state of divine ecstasy. As she described the approach of Jesus and Mary in the heavens, Baysiders fervently snapped photographs of the sky and shrine. The sound of clicking and fluttering camera shutters and then the whirl-buzz of film being ejected from hundreds of Polaroid cameras could be heard all over the apparition site. Once the sheets of Polaroid film are dispensed from the cameras, images begin forming almost immediately, and the photos are completely developed within sixty seconds as the photographers and other anxious Baysiders look on. The supernatural symbols and figures manifested on the photos include streaks and swirls of light; images representing Mary, Jesus, and various saints; symbols for angels and demons; the "red bear of communism"; the Fireball of Redemption; the world in flames. Dotted lines and beads of light appear in many of the photos; these are said to be the Baysiders' rosary prayers ascending to heaven. Some Baysiders tape rose petals believed to have miraculous powers to the side of their cameras in order to enhance the possibility of taking a miracle photograph. The petals are said to have been blessed by Jesus and Mary during previous apparitions at the site. Several individuals I spoke with told me that they also had their cameras blessed by a priest.

Various publications and videocassettes distributed by the shrine organization contain reproductions of some of the more famous miracle photos, which Baysiders often show to the public during lectures and video presentations. Non-Baysiders have difficulty seeing the miraculous imagery in the photos and may even laugh at the pictures, but many Baysiders believe that the photographs defy all scientific analysis, that they are proof of the miraculous nature of Mrs. Lueken's visions. Rationalistic explanations attribute the imagery on the photos to accidental double exposures, long hand-held exposures, and the fact that Baysiders usually take the photos at night, without a flash. This results in a slower shutter speed, thus exposing the Polaroid film to the various light sources on the apparition grounds and creating unusual photographic imagery. For the skeptical, the Baysiders' misunderstanding of photographic technology has resulted in the mystification and sacralization of the Polaroid process. Baysiders confidently deny such explanations and openly discuss their own views about how the photos are miraculously created. One explanation that I frequently heard was that the Holy Spirit enters the camera and "directs" the content and symbolism of the photos. Other explanations are that Mary, Jesus, the saints, and previous visionaries actually draw or create the images inside the camera. The photos are considered by Baysiders to be graces bestowed for private revelation.

Baysiders are not unique in their use of cameras to document miraculous phenomena at a Marian apparition site. Miraculous photos have been taken of the Virgin Mary appearing over a Coptic church in Zeitoun, Egypt; over a tree in San Damiano, Italy; and in the sun at Medjugorje. Many pilgrims at the apparition site in Lubbock, Texas, in 1989, took pictures of the miracles associated with that shrine, as do followers of Nancy Fowler's Marian apparitions in Conyers, Georgia. The creating of sacred images through photography is an emerging Catholic folk tradition associated with contemporary Marian apparition sites. As a folk religious phenomenon, miraculous photography is an institutionally unsanctioned expression of the doctrine of the communion of saints. This tenet that the sacred manifests itself in matter and intervenes in the lives of people may pose problems regarding communication between an invisible spiritual world and the faithful on earth because one is never sure that one's prayers have been heard by God or a saint (Turner and Turner 1978:205). Miraculous photography resolves this dilemma, providing Baysiders with direct and palpable experiences of supernatural intervention in their lives, as well as permanent photographic records that verify the reality of contact with the divine.

As a means of predicting apocalypse, determining the will of God, and interpreting the present, miracle photography is a form of divination, a technique of interpreting symbolic messages communicated by supernatural forces believed to shape the destiny of individuals and history itself. Historically, some of the more popular forms of divination have included numerology, palmistry, astrology, decoding the behavior of animals or reading their entrails, interpreting natural phenomena, analyzing dreams, and communicating with the spirits of the dead (G. Foster 1972). In the Greco-Roman world, the primary forms of divination included kleromancy (the casting of lots), ornithomancy (the flight and behavior of birds), haruspicy (the entrails of animals), cledonomancy (various omens, sounds, chance remarks, or events), and oneiromancy (dreams) (Aune 1983:23). According to classicist Georg Luck, "Almost anything that could be experienced or observed, anything that attracted attention, anything that could be manipulated" was used to predict the future and divine the meaning of events (1985:256–257). In an age in which people have become increasingly dependent on technology, the use of Polaroid cameras as devices of divination should not be surprising.

Various shrine publications about the Bayside phenomenon provide a guide to the main symbols that appear on the Polaroids, similar to a divinatory chart, giving Baysiders a basis for deciphering the miracle photos. The types of symbols are divided into four categories: numbers, letters of the alphabet, concrete symbols, and colors. For instance, the number 2 symbolizes a man or woman; the number 3 means warning; the letter *M* means Mary; *W* is for worldwide warning. The omega sign means the End is at hand. Concrete symbols often include snakes, which represent the forces of hell. And among colors, blue equates with the Virgin Mary; pink, Jesus Christ; green, Saint Michael; and purple, suffering or sorrow (*OLR Book* 1986:22).

The divinatory practices of Baysiders resemble what usually is characterized as "technical divination," which is based on the knowledge and abilities of the diviner to interpret signs, sacrifices, or dreams (Aune 1983:23, 349). Although the symbolism that is manifested on miracle photos is divinely communicated, the meanings of the photos are not, nor are Baysiders divinely inspired, with the exception of their visionary, Veronica Lueken. The photos must be decoded by Baysiders, and interpretation is based on one's knowledge of the established divinatory system. The symbolism on the photos is ambiguous and undecipherable to non-Baysiders, and the cryptic meanings are not always apparent even to Baysiders themselves. For instance, after I took a Polaroid photo at the apparition site, various people at the site offered somewhat general interpretations of its meaning. One person stated that the scrawls on the side of the photo represented the Baysiders' rosary prayers, said at the apparition site, ascending to heaven. But the person was unable to decipher the other imagery on the photograph. Later, another Baysider—who had previously asked me about my religious background and knew that I was not a Baysider, that I did not necessarily believe in miraculous photography—confidently deciphered various images on the photo, identifying various symbols, such as the Baysiders' rosary prayers ascending to heaven, as well as a symbol of the Freemasons, identified as enemies of the church, and a green streak representing Saint Michael. I was told that the photo indicated that evil forces were battling for my soul and that Saint Michael could protect me. After explaining this imagery, this individual discussed the Bayside apparitions at length, his own initial doubts about them, and Veronica Lueken's miraculous abilities. He also said that he did not understand some symbolism in my photo, but that Veronica would be able to tell me what it meant. He advised me to examine the photo further and contemplate its meaning.

The vague symbolism of miracle photos permits a multitude of interpretations, influenced by individual and social contexts. I did not provide the interpretation of the photos; their meanings were formulated in situational context, suggested by others present who were familiar with the divinatory system and the Bayside literature. In my case, miracle photography served as a means of spiritual diagnosis and as a basis for a discussion about the Bayside apparitions, the folk theology of the shrine, and Mrs. Lueken's supernatural abilities. Later, after I took another photograph that had streaks of light in it, I asked the man who had suggested that I take a photo, and from whom I borrowed a Polaroid camera, what it meant. He replied, "Well, do you see anything in it that relates to your own life? What did you ask for?" When I responded that I had no idea what it meant, he told me to take yet another photo, this time concentrating on a specific subject or "asking heaven" a specific question. Like a religious Rorschach test, the ambiguous imagery on miracle photos allows for a variety of attributed meanings, which reflect both the theology of the shrine and the dominating concerns of individuals at the apparition site.

Some of the photos are diagnostic in nature and provide information about one's current spiritual state or an understanding of current evils; others are predictive and reveal information about the fate of the world. On another visit to the apparition site, I noticed that many people were taking photos of the sky. I decided to try this and took several pictures of the sun. My Polaroids contained an image of a white orb surrounded by a blackened sky. People began gathering around me and attempted to interpret the photos. One person exclaimed loudly, "It's the Fireball—the Fireball of Redemption!" The photos were passed around and scrutinized. I was temporarily treated as if I, or perhaps my camera, had special divinatory powers, and several people waited for me to take more photos, which I did. In this instance, photodivination reaffirmed Mrs. Lueken's predictions of imminent worldly destruction by a divinely sent comet, provided a means to discuss the imminence of future disasters, and momentarily afforded me a certain degree of social status. Although the predictive and diagnostic images on miracle photos are not necessarily interpreted as explicit prescriptions for behavior, the imagery often motivates people to pray, proselytize, or engage in other activities believed to be spiritually efficacious. Photodivination is thus a means of spiritual instruction that reinforces the messages of the Bayside apparitions and reveals God's design for the world and for one's own life. For Baysiders, Polaroid photography has become the technology of prophecy, providing a lens through which God's plan is revealed and brought into focus, literally unveiling images of the endtimes.[4]

The Bayside Movement, Roman Catholic Traditionalism, and Conspiracy in the Church

The Bayside phenomenon is an expression of the broader Roman Catholic traditionalist movement that arose after the reforms initiated during the Second Vatican Council (1962–1965). Catholic traditionalism developed as a response to the liberalizing changes in church doctrine and policy, such as the Mass being said entirely in the vernacular, the priest facing the congregation during the consecration of the Holy Eucharist, increased participation in services by members of the congregation, and less emphasis on religious ceremony and more on the word of God. Although the majority of Roman Catholics welcomed these changes, the Council's *aggiornamento* ("updating") was regarded by some as a betrayal of the Catholic faith and the abandonment of a rich heritage of sacred traditions.

Like many traditionalist Catholics, most Baysiders regard Vatican II as heretical or the result of a conspiracy and reject its modernist theology, its liturgical changes, and its sacramental rites. Many traditionalists condemn Pope Paul VI, who approved the reforms of Vatican II, and some reject outright the authority and infallibility of the pope as Christ's representative on earth. This view, held by the sedevacantist traditionalists (from the Latin, meaning "vacant see") asserts that all the popes since Pius XII are invalid, considering them "deposed, excommunicated, or improperly elected," and that currently Rome has no legitimate pope (Dinges 1991:88). Baysiders say that the authentic pope, Paul VI, was poisoned and replaced by an imposter pope who, with his satanic allies, then implemented the modernist changes in the church. Consequently, Baysiders believe that they do not oppose the authority of the actual pope, Paul VI, because, they maintain, he had nothing to do with the progressive reforms of the church.

Conspiracy theories about the changes instituted by the Second Vatican Council are not unique to the Baysiders but are a persistent feature of traditionalist Catholic worldview. Traditionalist literature consistently proclaims that the church is infiltrated by evil forces and that the reforms of Vatican II are a part of a plot by the enemies of Christ to destroy the church, with communists and Freemasons as ubiquitous conspirators (Dinges 1991:89–90). According to many traditionalists, post-Vatican II revisions were not the result of reasonable, negotiated changes in Catholic religious culture but part of a diabolic plan orchestrated by devious forces to undermine the church's sacred traditions and contaminate its institutions. The nature and range of changes brought about by Vatican II and the speed with which these were implemented by an institution perceived as immutable are cited by traditionalists as further proof of a conspiracy.

A conspiratorial view of the world associated with Marian apparitions is encountered in the form of the supposed "secrets" conveyed by the Virgin Mary in her appearances at La Salette and especially at Fatima. The third secret of Fatima, rumored to predict various cataclysms, was supposed to be disclosed in 1960, but the Catholic Church has never revealed the secret. Soon after the 1960 deadline, however, the alleged contents of the secret were published in various periodicals, with the most famous and influential appearing in the German weekly *Neues Europa* on October 15, 1963. The account, which was purported to reveal the main points of the message, predicted that Satan would infiltrate the highest positions of the Catholic Church and confuse its leaders, would convince world leaders to manufacture nuclear weapons in great numbers, and then initiate a massive war in the second half of the twentieth century in which millions of people would die. This apocalyptic scenario was inevitable unless people converted, the church and world leaders encouraged such conversions, and the buildup of nuclear warheads was prevented (Zimdars-Swartz 1991:213–214). Rumors also circulated that the seer Lucia had warned that if the church did not reveal the secret, communist Russia would soon bring about the end of the world (Alonso 1979:54).

The apocalyptic messages conveyed to Mrs. Lueken by the Virgin Mary not only reflect these rumors and popular beliefs about the third secret of Fatima but call for Lucia (who was living in a Carmelite convent in Coimbra, Portugal, in the 1980s) to reveal the secret because the Catholic Church will not and the End is near: "The hourglass is almost empty; days can be counted by hours. For at this very moment We see a most terrible explosion, with the loss of many lives about to take place . . . have Lucy [Lucia] come forward and tell the Third Secret word for word" ("Roses" newsletter, message from the Virgin Mary, June 18, 1986).

Mrs. Lueken's messages concerning the third secret especially emphasize the idea of the "satanic infiltration" of the church, interpreted as the changes that occurred as the result of the Second Vatican Council. For instance, on May 13, 1978, Mary revealed to Mrs. Lueken "how I warned and warned that Satan would enter into the highest realms of the hierarchy in Rome. The Third Secret, My Child, is that Satan would enter into My Son's Church" (*OLR Book* 1986:113). According to the Bayside literature, the disclosure of the third secret of Fatima in 1960 would have alerted the faithful of the insidious takeover of the church, and perhaps prevented the liberalizing changes that occurred after Vatican II. Like other traditionalists, Baysiders regard the struggle for the restoration of traditional Catholic doctrines and rites as a conflict between good and evil, an eschatological battle between the sinister minions of Satan and righteous army of Christ.

Antimodernist and Nativistic Aspects of the Bayside Apparitions

The Bayside phenomenon is not unique among apocalyptic movements in its emphasis on a return to previous traditions. Numerous apocalyptic movements in the past have advocated a restoration of traditional values when accepted systems of meaning were being destroyed by change or when the world was perceived to be in a state of severe spiritual, moral, or cultural crisis. In such situations, established beliefs and practices are reasserted while individuals await the imminent and supernaturally ordained destruction of the present world, which is regarded as irredeemably corrupt. Ralph Linton identifies such worldviews as expressions of "nativistic movements," defined as any "conscious, organized attempt on the part of a society's members to revive or perpetuate selected aspects of its culture" (1943:230). Although this concept is usually applied to non-Western societies to describe responses to cultural contact, conflict, and oppression, it seems to be an appropriate characterization of the themes expressed in the Bayside apparitions as well as the behavior of Baysiders. Nativistic movements, according to Linton, place emphasis on restoring and preserving practices considered to be traditional, and attempt to eliminate specific foreign influences from the society. An often-cited example of a nativistic response is the Ghost Dance movement of various Native American tribes in the 1890s, which was characterized by the rejection of Western cultural influences, the revival of traditional ceremonies and games, and the millenarian promise of the destruction of the new settlers and a return to an idealized condition prior to the white man's arrival (Linton 1943). Like previous nativistic movements, the emphasis on the restoration of traditions that characterizes the Bayside phenomenon is a response to a sense of religious and cultural crisis, and especially a sense of loss—the loss of one's religious heritage and one's religious identity.

Another concept useful for understanding the ideas communicated in Mrs. Lueken's visions is the notion of "revitalization," proposed by Anthony Wallace (1956) and defined as a deliberate and organized religious response that attempts to rejuvenate and reinterpret existing cultural patterns in order to save the culture and construct a more satisfying existence. Wallace asserts that religious revitalization is a response to cultural disintegration, situations of stress and crisis, and widespread dissatisfaction, and he demonstrates that nativistic movements, messianism, and millenarianism may all be subsumed under this general term.

The nativistic and revitalistic aspects of the Bayside apparitions are illustrated by the repeated pronouncements that contemporary society is in a state of social crisis and decay. Mrs. Lueken's visions enumerate the ways that traditional Catholic attitudes about God, morality, community, family, sexuality, and the roles of women and men, among other things, have been challenged or destroyed. The restoration of traditional beliefs, practices, and spirituality is regarded as the only means of averting worldly destruction. Against the assertions of science, relativism, ecumenism, and modernism, Mrs. Lueken's prophecies demand a return to immutable Catholic traditions and completely reject the recent innovations in the church: "My Son's Church has been laid out and the course to Heaven, the way to Heaven has been given by Him. Therefore, change causes confusion and error. When you have something beautiful, when you have a firm foundation, you don't start boring holes in it, or you will weaken it" ("Roses" newsletter, message from the Virgin Mary, March 18, 1983). Mrs. Lueken's messages are a direct response to the changes brought about by the Second Vatican Council, which transformed the nature of Catholicism worldwide, dramatically altering the traditional liturgy, doctrines, and rituals that had been associated with the Catholic Church for centuries. Her apparitions not only describe the end of the world but portray the end of triumphalist Catholicism, the end of beliefs, rituals, values, and religious forms that millions of Catholics learned and expressed throughout their lives and that many people continue to find meaningful.

The Bayside visions are aggressively antimodernist, like other Marian apparitions and the Catholic traditionalist movement in general. The antimodernist sentiments of Marian visions and pilgrimages have been noted by Victor and Edith Turner, who state that modern (postmedieval) pilgrimages have become a significant means of defense against the secularization that characterizes the post-Darwinian world, and that Marian apparitions "give emotional expression to doctrines under fire from scientific and rational criticism" (1978:210), reaffirming the reality of the supernatural and the doctrines of the church. Thomas Kselman (1983), Barbara Corrado Pope (1985), and Nicholas Perry and Loreto Echeverría (1988) also note that Marian apparitions and devotion were used in the nineteenth century to refute modernist and rationalist ideas. Veronica Lueken's apparitions, like previous Marian visions, condemn modernist ideas as the source of contemporary ills and assert that they will precipitate the destruction of humanity: "The world has become polluted with all forms of 'ism': communism, atheism, humanism, all destructors of the soul" ("Roses" newsletter, message from Jesus, June 18, 1991). Secularism, communism, science, and Vatican II are all considered by Mrs. Lueken to be part of a diabolic conspiracy. She, like Hal Lindsey and other premillennialists, offers criticism of the major societal developments of the twentieth century and insists upon a return to traditional beliefs and practices in the last days before Christ's return.

Apocalyptic Admonitions and the Concept of Fate

Apocalyptic apparitions of the Virgin Mary and dispensationalist prophecies of a precise doomsday scenario both express the view that human history is unfolding according to a divine endtimes plan. However, unlike the predictions of dispensationalists, who say that the end of the world is imminent, inevitable, and unalterable by human will or effort, the messages of Veronica Lueken, and other Roman Catholic visionaries, assert that apocalypse is imminent but that the divine timetable may be postponed if people repent and return to God's ways. The apocalypse predicted by Mrs. Lueken will occur at a specific historical moment not because it is completely fated to occur at that time but because of God's anger at humanity's increasing sinfulness. As the literature from the shrine states:

> Our Lady has been chosen by the Eternal Father to alert mankind now of the scriptural predictions of a cleansing of the earth with fire unless mankind makes a complete reversal of his sinful ways. A world-wide Warning according to Our Lady shall precede this Chastisement in an effort to recall God's children to a life of grace. She has also promised that God will perform a great Miracle after this Warning, and if men still refuse to change, then God will be forced to send the Chastisement. (*OLR Booklet* n.d.:1)

Although overwhelming evil on earth and the corruption of the Catholic Church may soon provoke God to destroy the world, future chastisements and worldly destruction are not unalterable or predetermined because the purpose of the Virgin Mary's appearance as intercessor is to save humanity, restore traditionalist devotion, and encourage the consecration of Russia to the Immaculate Heart of Mary.

Like previous Marian visionaries, Mrs. Lueken maintains that worldly disasters are both chastisements for sinful behavior and portents of the end of time. This interpretation of worldly catastrophes as supernatural warnings and admonishments is represented by the following message from the Virgin Mary: "Earthquakes in your country, . . . know it comes but from the hand of God. Famine, starvation, your crops will rot. The heat will burn, the cattle will starve. And why? Because you refuse to turn back, complacent in your arrogance" (*OLR Booklet* n.d.:3–4). In enumerating the reasons for God's anger—communism, secularism, modernism, social and moral decay, corruption in the church, homosexuality, abortion—Mrs. Lueken's messages occasionally specify the precise punishments to be unleashed. In one message that predicts a plague to be sent to the United States, for instance, the cause of God's outrage is specifically identified: "Your city and many cities throughout your country shall feel the plague. It is for the murders of the unborn that your city receives the plague" (*OLR Booklet* n.d.:4). In this way, cause-and-effect relationships are posited between human behavior, worldly disasters as chastisements, and the signs of the End. The predictions of dispensationalists such as Hal Lindsey, on the other hand, interpret the signs of the End as noncausal markers on a foreordained timetable of irreversible doom. Repentance, prayer, righteousness are encouraged by Lindsey, but not as an effectual means of averting the end of the world.

According to Mrs. Lueken, the intercession of the Virgin Mary on behalf of humanity has delayed the destruction of the world, as the following message from Mary makes clear: "All I can say is I stand before the Eternal Father and continuously plead your cause before Him. If this was not to be, you would have received the Ball of Redemption already. I do not know, My children, how long I can hold the hand of the Eternal Father back. I can say at this time, that when the Ball of Redemption hits the earth, only a few will be saved" ("Roses" newsletter, June 18, 1991). Mary can petition and interact with God, but the prophecies reiterate that once worldly sin reaches a specific anti-Christian critical mass, Mary's merciful pleas will be powerless to hold back the punishing hand of God and avert the end of the world. This belief is indicated by the following message delivered to Mrs. Lueken from the Virgin Mary: "My child and My children, there are scoffers who will say there shall not be a Third World War. They do not know and cannot conceive of the plan of the Eternal Father. Be it known now that the Father has great heart for all His children, but when the sin reaches a peak only known to the Father . . . then the Father will take action" ("Roses" newsletter, May 5, 1983).

The "Eternal Father" mentioned in Mrs. Lueken's prophecies resembles Jehovah, the warrior God of the ancient Israelites, who controls all earthly phenomena and sends divine punishment to the wicked while showing mercy to his chosen people (see Ringgren 1966:69–104). Unlike the distant God characterized by dispensationalists, who is personally uninvolved with the inevitable disasters and dispensations foreordained in the Bible, the wrathful Eternal Father in Mrs. Lueken's visions actively participates in the destruction of the world, sending warnings and chastisements in the form of plagues, disasters, and earthquakes to those who disobey his divine will. Although angry with humanity, this God responds to the appeals and petitions of human beings through his intermediaries, the saints, and Mary in particular.

The prophecies of Mrs. Lueken reveal God's wrath toward those who have deviated from a divinely prescribed sacred order and plan for humanity, while offering the hope that the world will be transformed through human behavior as ordained by God. Popular Roman Catholic prophecy, because of its emphasis on the personal relationship between the saints in heaven and the faithful on earth, is less overtly fatalistic than dispensationalism, with its emphasis on biblical literalism, inerrancy, and predetermined dispensations. Because the saints may intercede with God on behalf of the faithful and also convey God's will to those on earth, the fate of world and human history is not utterly determined—as it is in the dispensationalist worldview. The sacramental quality of Catholicism is epitomized by the Virgin Mary's role as mediatrix between humanity and an otherwise distant and inaccessible God, and Baysiders, like many other Roman Catholics today, believe that through Mary the destiny of the world may be altered.

Yet even as Mrs. Lueken's apparitions assert that apocalypse may be averted if people fulfill God's requests for reform, a sense of inevitability about imminent catastrophe as well as the unrecuperability of humanity also pervades these predictions. Nearly all of the messages state that humanity is living in the last days prior to Christ's return. Some messages imply that apocalypse is inevitable, asserting that the Chastisement and coming Ball of Redemption are preordained: "Do not be affrighted, My child; you must see this, for it is important. Within this century this Ball will be sent upon mankind" (*OLR Booklet* n.d.:4). This combination of imminence and inevitability—an overwhelming sense of impending doom—characterizes the Bayside prophecies. Mrs. Lueken's lengthy descriptions and the specific details about future cataclysms that will take place give the impression that these events are in fact fated. The messages imply that humans will not heed these divine warnings and will continue on a sinful path to destruction: "My child, you must pray more, do much penance, for the Warning is coming upon mankind . . . this warning shall be of short duration, and man shall continue upon their road to perdition, so hard are the hearts now, My child" (*OLR Book* 1986:44). This divinely sent Warning is said to be inevitable, and will be followed by the Miracle, and then the Great Chastisement. Mrs. Lueken's visions of a millennial realm that will exist after the Chastisement also indicate that the destruction of the present world is inevitable:

> And now, Our Lady is going back. It's becoming very bright: "My child, I am not leaving, I am only moving so that you can see the world as it will be after the purification." . . . [T]he sun is shining. . . . It's like summer. I see these green trees and a beautiful lake. And now as I'm looking at the most beautiful, restful place I have ever seen . . . and now, through the trees . . . Oh! I can see Jesus coming! Oh, it's like another world! It's . . . Oh! A beautiful land—oooh!!! . . . Now it must be warm because Jesus doesn't have anything on His feet and He's coming now through the foliage in the trees. . . . Oh, now Jesus is saying: "You see, My Child, there will be a renewed Earth. You are watching, My Child, soon after my arrival upon Earth." (*OLR Book* 1986:47)

These descriptions, similar to Lindsey's depictions of a new earth that will follow Armageddon, promise that the current world will be cleansed in a "baptism of fire" and then renewed in the form of a terrestrial paradise.

Mrs. Lueken's apparitions repeatedly assert that the Fireball of Redemption and the ensuing apocalyptic scenario will be divinely sent and beyond human power to avert, and her forecasts of worldly cataclysms in the form of earthquakes, plagues, famine, and other disasters, as supernaturally ordained events, are believed to reveal God's plan in the last days. This belief in inevitable disasters prior to doomsday is expressed in the introduction to a publication on the Bayside prophecies that states,

> With these new prophecies you will discover how to prepare your family and loved ones for the days just ahead. You will be free from the anxiety and worry of the things to come. This is the most important book you could read, along with the Holy Bible, in these last days before that glorious day when Jesus returns to earth. . . . Most of all you will discover how to protect yourself from the great misfortunes coming to North America. (*The Incredible Bayside Prophecies* 1991:v).

The book delineates Mrs. Lueken's predictions about imminent destruction and maintains that most Baysiders will escape the impending cataclysms through the spiritual protection offered by the Virgin Mary and the use of various sacramental objects.

Although Baysiders may interpret worldly calamities to be divinely sent "imminent merciful warnings of Almighty God" (*OLR Book* 1986:44), these large-scale disasters that indiscriminately destroy complete families, cities, or regions are somewhat difficult to explain as part of a benevolent and merciful God's plan because the innocent are punished as well as the sinful. The Bayside prophecies acknowledge the seeming cruelty of God's wrath and the fatefulness implicit in divinely sent disasters, proclaiming that these are the inevitable result of human sinfulness:

> My children, I hear voices of disdain shouting, sadism!! Is this a sadist God who promises such destruction upon His creation? I say unto you, as your God, I bring not your destruction; you will bring about your own destruction, for I leave you, as your God, to the exercise of your free will. In your free will, if you reject your God and the plan for man's redemption as given from the beginning of time, I say unto you—*you will destroy yourselves!!*" (*OLR Booklet* n.d.:3; message from Jesus, May 18, 1977).

This message maintains that human beings have free will and their sinful behavior is the cause of current and future disasters, yet it also implies that history and human behavior are divinely prescribed. Individual salvation and the salvation of the world is dependent upon humans acting in accordance with the divine will, with the acceptance or rejection of God's prescriptions for behavior and belief the only two options available. In either case this interpretation of the results of human action appears to express an underlying fatalism; humans, through their own efforts, cannot save themselves or the world from apocalypse unless they follow God's will and behave in ways decreed. Human beings are free to choose, but ultimately God's will determines the final fate of all things. The apparent contradiction between God's will, free will, and divine inevitability is not unique to the theology of Baysiders but has characterized Christian thought for millennia, with the omniscience of God seeming to imply the inevitability of everything that occurs (R. Taylor 1967:362). Those who act according to God's mandates "perform God's will" ("accept the decrees of fate") and are promised salvation. The Bayside prophecies encourage people to accept and act to fulfill God's will, from which collective and individual fate is derived. If people ignore or oppose that which is supernaturally decreed and go against God's will, humanity will be destroyed.

Fatalism has been characterized as "the view that whatever happens must happen of necessity and whatever does not happen of necessity does not happen at all. . . . It is generally taken to be an obvious consequence of fatalism that nothing a man does is ever really up to him. What he has done he had to do; and what he will do he must do" (Adams and Kretzmann 1969:3–4). Mrs. Lueken's prophecies prescribe what people must inevitably do and assert that human beings are helpless to save the world through their own efforts. The will of God as communicated by Mrs. Lueken is a fatalistic mandate and adherence to this mandate is required for salvation: "The world has not progressed as the Eternal Father has asked. Man has become obsessed with sin. I tell you now, in the Trinity, that unless you listen now, your world will be planet-struck" ("Roses" newsletter, message from Jesus, June 18, 1991).

Although individual fate and the fate of the world may be conceptualized as originating either from a personal deity or an impersonal source (Ringgren 1967:8), in either case fate is assigned, determined, and inescapable, except in those instances in which human beings obediently fulfill divinely prescribed behaviors. Mrs. Lueken's prophecies assert that one cannot escape from the unalterable decrees of God and that humans must either accept them or be destroyed and eternally damned. Any attempt to save the world or oneself from disaster that is outside God's will is rejected as futile.

The sense of fatefulness inherent in beliefs about an omniscient God's absolute knowledge and will over all things has been debated for centuries by theologians who have attempted to reconcile the concept of free will with divine will, usually subordinating individual freedom to God's power and acknowledging the helplessness of humanity apart from God:

> St. Augustine and virtually every other theologian who contributed greatly to the development of Christian thought assumed without question that God, as thus conceived, must know in advance every action that every man is ever going to perform. . . . A man is helpless to do anything except sin unless he is assisted by the power and grace of God. . . . Accordingly, no man can be saved by the exercise of his own will, which can lead him only to damnation. He can be saved only by being chosen by God. (Taylor 1967:363)

Through prophecy, Baysiders discover God's will, and by following God's decrees they obtain God's grace as well as knowledge of the fate of the world, derived from the will of God and contingent upon human behavior as prescribed by God.

Prophecy and photodivination not only provide information about God's will concerning the future but also serve as a means of interpreting events in the present and the past as part of a divine endtimes scenario. The repeated assertions by Baysiders that Mrs. Lueken's prophecies are continually being fulfilled further reinforce the belief that disasters and current crises are not senseless but meaningful occurrences that reveal God's wrath in the last days. Claims of prophecies fulfilled also support Mrs. Lueken's status as a soothsayer while confirming that the supernatural is actively involved in human history. According to Mrs. Lueken's prophecies, an omnipotent God, along with Jesus Christ, the Virgin Mary, and the saints, oversees the fate of Baysiders and the fate of the world, and the inescapable duty of human beings is to carry out God's unalterable will.[5]

In contrast to religious apocalypticists who believe in a redemptive and divinely ordained apocalypse, many people in the United States today believe that the end of the world is an inevitable but not a meaningful or supernatural event. The next chapter explores selected secular apocalyptic ideas in American society, focusing specifically on attitudes about nuclear apocalypse, and the differences between these ideas and religious concepts about the end of the world.

5

Secular Apocalyptic Themes in the Nuclear Era

> Our tragedy today is a general and universal physical fear so long
> sustained by now that we can even bear it. There are no longer
> problems of the spirit. There is only the question: when will I be
> blown up?   —William Faulkner, Nobel Prize speech, 1954

Apocalyptic ideas traditionally have been associated with religious
eschatologies, but American secular culture also has contributed to widespread beliefs, images, and expectations about the end of the world. The concept of a meaningless apocalypse brought about by human or natural causes
is a relatively recent phenomenon, differing dramatically from religious apocalyptic cosmologies. Instead of faith in a redemptive new realm to be established after the present world is annihilated, secular doomsday visions are usually characterized by a sense of pessimism, absurdity, and nihilism.

Secular apocalyptic ideas have become increasingly pervasive in contemporary American society; these notions, however, are not unique to the twentieth century. Visions of the world destroyed by humans, as well as by natural
cataclysms, began appearing in fictional literature in the 1800s. According to
Warren Wagar, Mary Shelley's *The Last Man* (1826) was the first of such works,
and the majority of these early secular doomsday writings, like religious apocalyptic visions, offered the hope of a renewed and transformed society after
the destruction of the world (1982:11–13). Nineteenth-century secular visions
of worldly destruction and renewal were not limited to literature; the Marxist
promise of world revolution and redemption of the working class is an explicit
form of secularized millenarianism. As Eric Hobsbawm notes in his *Primitive
Rebels*, the political ideals of socialism and communism resemble the millenarian "hope of a complete and radical change in the world" (1965:57,

93–107). These nineteenth- and early-twentieth-century visions of worldly destruction and transformation were usually optimistic in their evaluation of apocalypse, viewing it not as the end but the beginning of the transformation of society.

Since the end of World War II, visions and beliefs about the end of the world appear to have become increasingly pessimistic, stressing cataclysmic disaster as much as previous millenarian visions emphasized the imminent arrival of a redemptive new era. Numerous observers have noted that the romantic, millennial vision of America as a redemptive paradise or pristine wilderness has been challenged and altered during the latter half of the twentieth century, becoming more bleak and apocalyptic in nature (see Rovit 1968; Ketterer 1974; Zamora 1982a). Literary critics have made similar assertions in their attempts to characterize the "postmodern condition" as an apocalyptic psychological and social milieu involving individual and collective perceptions of the decay and destruction of art, culture, philosophy, and meaning (see Baudrillard 1988; Jameson 1984; Kamper and Wulf 1989): "a *fin-de-millennium* consciousness which, existing at the end of history . . . uncovers a great arc of disintegration and decay against the background radiation of parody, kitsch, and burnout . . . a suicidal nihilism . . . on the violent edge between ecstasy and decay" (Kroker and Cook 1986:8–9). Numerous scholars have suggested that the prophetic apocalyptic imaginings of the past have become secular apocalyptic realities in recent decades. As one writer notes, "Images of Hiroshima and Nagasaki, the Holocaust, Vietnam (rendered by filmmaker Francis Ford Coppola as *Apocalypse Now*) give unalterable contours to the landscape of contemporary memory. Apocalypse is no longer a dark shapeless terror, but a statistically documented event, complete with date, time, and place" (Kawada 1985:x).

The pervasiveness of secular apocalyptic ideas became particularly evident in the 1970s and 1980s. Many books written by academics, scientists, and social critics predicted or warned of the cataclysmic destruction or gradual decline of humanity as the result of human and natural causes. As Michael Barkun notes, these influential forecasts of imminent global disasters began appearing in the early 1970s with Barry Commoner's *The Closing Circle* (1971) and the Club of Rome's publication *The Limits to Growth* (Meadows et al. 1972) (Barkun 1983:263). Among the more prominent of numerous books that address the possibility of naturalistic or human-made cataclysms are Roberto Vacca's *The Coming Dark Age* (1973), Robert Heilbroner's *An Inquiry into the Human Prospect* (1974), L. S. Stavrianos's *The Promise of the Coming Dark Age* (1976), Isaac Asimov's *A Choice of Catastrophes* (1979), Fred Warshofsky's

Doomsday: The Science of Catastrophe (1977), and Jonathan Schell's *The Fate of the Earth* (1982). These and other works delineate various destructive scenarios, ranging from astrophysical, climatological, and geological disasters to nuclear disasters, societal breakdown, the "population bomb," economic exploitation and collapse, the greenhouse effect, pollution, ozone depletion, toxic waste, and technological collapse.

In addition to secular apocalyptic literature, secular organizations exist that warn of imminent apocalypse, such as DOOM: The Society for Secular Armageddonism, which is "a non-religious group dedicated to promoting public awareness of the coming end of the world." Based in San Francisco, the organization has established a telephone "Hotline of Doom," which provides callers with a brief message about the causes of the end of the world:

> We believe the apocalypse is at hand, and our reasons for this belief are overwhelming: chemical and biological weapons, nuclear proliferation, deforestation, the greenhouse effect, ozone depletion, acid rain, the poisoning of our air and water, rising racism, massive species loss, toxic waste, the AIDS pandemic, the continuing population explosion, encroaching Big Brotherness, and at least another thousand points of blight. These aren't just conversational topics for cocktail parties; they're Grade-A, unadulterated harbingers of destruction. One hundred percent, bona fide specters of doom. And they're all proof that we don't need God to end it for us. The coming end will be a strictly do-it-yourself apocalypse.

The message ends with a bell tolling in the background and with a promise that future telephone messages will provide profiles of specific global threats and refer callers to groups resisting these threats. The society received more than ten thousand calls from September to December 1990 (Dial-a-Bummer 1990:22).

Emphasizing the destructive capabilities of human beings, secular predictions of doom describe unredemptive worldly cataclysm brought about by ignorance, technology, or chance natural disasters. Of the various secular apocalyptic scenarios imagined, visions of and beliefs about the world destroyed by nuclear weapons remain among the most widespread and fatalistic. In this regard, many secular apocalypticists are in agreement with religious apocalypticists who consider nuclear apocalypse to be inevitable.

Since the development of nuclear weapons, a sense of profound anxiety and uncertainty has existed in American society about a future in which nuclear warfare is a possibility. As Paul Boyer's *By the Bomb's Early Light* (1985) and Spencer Weart's *Nuclear Fear* (1988) demonstrate, the development and use of nuclear weapons in the mid-1940s dramatically altered American thought and culture. For some Americans, nuclear weaponry represented military superiority or the promise of a techno-utopian future; for others, the bomb evoked feelings of helplessness and fatalism about the future of humanity. In his study of the effect of nuclear weapons on American culture and consciousness between 1945 and 1950, Boyer notes, for instance, that the dropping of atomic bombs on Japan in August 1945 fueled fears of irrational mass death and collective annihilation, as well as a loss of faith in technology, progress, and the future (1985:278–281). The feeling of fatalism that arose after the bombing of Hiroshima and Nagasaki, and that persists today despite the end of the Cold War, is described by Alfred Kazin: "The bomb gave the shape of life, outer and inner, an irreversible charge; a sense of fatefulness would now lie on all things . . . we are still struggling—often enough without knowing it, all too often in total resignation—with every effect and implication of that change" (1988:1).

Since the bombing of Hiroshima and Nagasaki, enormous developments in nuclear weaponry and delivery systems have further increased contemporary fears about nuclear annihilation. The bomb dropped on Hiroshima, the equivalent of 12,500 tons of TNT, was small by current standards, with warheads of that size now considered to be merely "tactical" weapons (Schell 1982:36). A typical nuclear warhead currently has an explosive capability of 2,000,000 tons of TNT, the equivalent of all the bombs exploded in World War II (Sagan 1986:13). Experts estimate that in the mid-1980s the United States had approximately 27,000 nuclear weapons and the Soviet Union roughly 33,000 (Broad 1992:4A), enough destructive power to obliterate more than a million Hiroshimas (Sagan 1986:13). The doctrine of nuclear deterrence, or Mutual Assured Destruction (MAD), based on the premise that nuclear war can be avoided if each nuclear superpower has an arsenal that can completely destroy the entire society of any aggressor in a retaliatory second strike, made the self-destruction of humanity a genuine possibility during the Cold War era. A large-scale nuclear war not only might result in the complete destruction of civilization in less than an hour but could conceivably result in human extinction and the extinction of other life forms (Sagan 1986:13–18; Schell 1982:93–96).

Despite the end of the Cold War and the resulting arms control treaties and unilateral actions that have designated a significant portion of the nuclear stockpile to be "retired," nuclear fears and the nuclear threat persist today. Concerns have been expressed about the control of nuclear weaponry in the now-independent former Soviet republics, stemming from the fear of clandestine sales to black marketeers, theft by terrorists, nuclear disasters resulting from the improper storage of radioactive materials, and the possibility of former Soviet scientists disseminating knowledge about nuclear weapons by working for other countries (Broad 1992:4A). Current nuclear anxieties are also related to the export of nuclear technology and the possibility that nuclear weapons will be developed and used by hostile nations or terrorist groups within the United States. At the turn of the millennium, the nuclear bomb remains the most concrete embodiment of humanity's potential for global self-destruction, continuing to fuel fears and fatalism about inevitable apocalypse.

Bomb Culture and Nuclear Lore

Ideas about the inevitability of nuclear apocalypse were expressed immediately after the detonation of the first atomic bomb at Alamogordo, New Mexico, on July 16, 1945. Popular images, narratives, and conceptions at the time often implied that after the invention of the bomb, humanity could not reverse its inevitable path to destruction, and that scientists had created an uncontrollable weapon that would ultimately destroy the world. For instance, stories about Robert Oppenheimer, the director of the first atomic bomb tests, correlate his interest in ancient mythology with ideas of inevitable apocalypse. Upon seeing the first atomic mushroom cloud in the New Mexico desert, Oppenheimer supposedly envisioned the Hindu deity Krishna in the form of the All-Devourer, and then recalled the following verse from the *Bhagavad Gita*:

> If the radiance of a thousand suns
> Were to burst into the sky
> That would be like the splendor of the Mighty One.
> I am become Death,
> The shatterer of worlds.   (Chilton 1986:129–130)

In this account, and in many others, the atomic blast is associated with cosmic destructive power, a manifestation of mythic images of death and worldly destruction. Numerous reports compared the blast to the creation of the world and the Second Coming of Christ. The published accounts of the first bomb test described it in almost euphoric terms, with prose and imagery resembling the language of the Book of Revelation. For instance, General Thomas F. Farrell characterized the explosion as follows:

The effects could be called unprecedented, magnificent, beautiful, stupendous and terrifying. No man-made phenomenon of such tremendous power had ever occurred before. The lighting effects beggared description. The whole country was lighted by a searing light with the intensity many times that of the midday sun. It was golden, purple, violet, grey and blue. It lighted every peak, crevice and ridge of the nearby mountain range with a clarity and beauty that cannot be described but must be seen to be imagined. It was that beauty the great poets dream about but describe most poorly and inadequately. Thirty seconds after, the explosion came, first the air blast pressing hard against people and things, to be followed almost immediately by the strong, sustained, awesome roar which warned of doomsday and made us feel that we puny things were blasphemous to dare tamper with the forces heretofore reserved to The Almighty. (Groves 1962:303–304)

The sinister connotations of nuclear weapons as devices of inevitable apocalypse were also reinforced by popular depictions of the physicists who worked on the development of the atomic bomb. Similar to the legendary Faust character, atomic scientists were often portrayed as evil geniuses or maddened technological wizards engaged in nuclear alchemy, obsessed with harnessing the sacred powers of the universe, who would ultimately destroy the world in the pursuit of divine, forbidden knowledge (Weart 1988:21).

In contrast to these apprehensions and negative depictions, the commercial exploitation and enthusiastic promotion of "atomic" goods and styles began immediately after the bombing of Hiroshima and Nagasaki. Countless businesses adopted the word "Atomic" as part of their title; bartenders concocted "Atomic Cocktails" (a luminous green beverage of Pernod and gin); burlesque clubs in Los Angeles advertised "Atom Bomb Dancers"; department stores had "Atomic Sales"; atomic bomb songs proliferated in popular music; and designers created atomic jewelry (in some instances from the greenish, glass-like, and perhaps still radioactive melted sand from the Alamogordo test site) (Boyer 1985:10–12).[1] This lighthearted adoption of the signifier "atomic" seems to have been a reaction to deeper anxieties about the bomb, serving as a means of subduing the fear of the atomic threat; by associating the atomic bomb with commodities and commonplace events, its destructive capability was domesticated and incorporated into everyday life.

Widespread beliefs during this time expressed ambivalence about new technologies and reflect feelings of individual helplessness concerning the prospect of nuclear apocalypse. In the 1950s, push-button devices were symbols of convenience, modernity, and technological ease; yet the destructive potential of technology was represented by beliefs about the "Doomsday Button," a red button that, when pushed, would destroy the world. As one observer notes, "there was one common household object that was inextricably linked to the threat of nuclear annihilation—the push button. The President of the United States was widely viewed as having a push button on or in his desk that would trigger atomic war as surely as a housewife could activate her dishwasher. And in the Kremlin there was another push button, with just about the same power" (Hine 1989:132). The push-button efficiency of dishwashers, television sets, washing machines, and vacuum cleaners simplified life and provided entertainment, but the same technological efficiency had made a push-button apocalypse a reality. The belief that the world could be ended by pressing a button both reflected and reinforced feelings of helplessness and apocalyptic inevitability. Once the button was pushed, nothing could be done to stop the process because the technology was for the most part overwhelmingly sophisticated and beyond one's understanding and control. Apocalypse was no longer a cosmic event executed by supernatural deities; it was now reduced to a mundane, technological absurdity.

While adults have pondered the possibility of a push-button apocalypse, the culture of the bomb and an awareness of the threat of the nuclear cataclysm have also been a part of the experiences of children growing up in the postwar era. Youngsters sent away for atomic-bomb-ring toys promoted on the back of Kix cereal boxes, ate red-hot candies called Atomic Fireballs (still marketed today), read comic books that described the nuclear destruction of worlds, and played A-bomb games on playgrounds.[2] By the late 1950s, the imminence of a nuclear attack pervaded the consciousness of most American schoolchildren living in large cities as they sat through lectures about the atomic bomb and civil defense and practiced air-raid drills. Children in some school districts in high-risk target areas were issued metal dog tags for the purpose of identifying them if they were lost or burnt beyond recognition in a nuclear attack (in New York City, free dog tags had been issued to 2.5 million children by 1952) (Jonas and Nissenson 1994:39).

Duck-and-cover drills were common in major cities: at the sound of the school siren or when the teacher yelled, "Drop!" children would dive under their desks with their hands clasped behind their necks and their faces shielded. The ever-present threat of nuclear attack was further conveyed by civil defense films, such as the well-known reel starring Bert the Turtle, who teaches children to "Duck and Cover." In actuality the duck-and-cover strategy offered little protection in the event of major nuclear attack, and at least some children seemed aware of this, as the following interview with sixth graders in 1963 reveals:

Teacher: Are there shelters at your school, Susan?

Susan: No, there aren't any. . . . But I don't really think these drills would do much good at all. Because in such bombings as an atom bomb and if it was as close as one hundred miles off, the radiation would in time reach you. . . .

Teacher: And what do you think, Robert?

Robert: I think that if a radiation-type bomb were to be dropped near or on you, you wouldn't have a chance. . . .

Susan: It wouldn't seem right to me at all if I were one of the only people who lived. And so, I would really prefer to die in a bombing. . . .

Teacher: Kathy?

Kathy: I'd rather die and let some person live who would be more helpful to whoever survives—like a doctor. (interviews with Mrs. Elsa Knight Thompson's sixth-grade class, San Francisco, California; cited in Barasch 1983:86)

Though not necessarily representative of children's responses to the prospect of nuclear war, these statements express recurring ideas associated with the nuclear bomb: imminent death, the futility of efforts at personal survival, and feelings of guilt if one were to survive. In reality, duck-and-cover drills may have been performed more for adults than for children, providing a semblance of safety, order, and personal control when confronted with the massive destructive power of the bomb. Such drills not only offered a sense of protection in the face of an uncontrollable threat but emphasized the efficacy of human effort and personal action through a ritualized duck-and-cover response, a secularized version, perhaps, of magico-religious practices customarily performed in situations characterized by danger, uncertainty, and helplessness.

The fallout shelter frenzy that climaxed in 1961 may have served similar functions, providing people with an active response to the threat and perceived inevitability of nuclear destruction. Although shelters were established in public buildings (still identifiable by yellow and black "Fallout Shelter" signs), the U.S. government encouraged people to build fallout shelters beneath their homes or in their backyards. Individual initiative and personal survival in the event of nuclear attack were stressed rather than the survival of the larger community. Entrepreneurs and popular magazines marketed bomb shelters to families, promoting them as practical additions to suburban homes.[3] Offering the hope of survival through proper preparation and resourcefulness, bomb shelter dealerships boomed and merchants sold items thought necessary for life underground in the event of a nuclear attack.[4] Although *Life* magazine's cover story on September 15, 1961, claimed that ninety-seven out of one hundred people would be protected from the bomb in a shelter, in actuality, most fallout shelters within ten miles of ground zero would have functioned as crematoria, incinerating or asphyxiating people.

For a while belief in the effectiveness of fallout shelters persisted, and moral debates arose concerning the ethics of sharing one's shelter with negligent neighbors who had not bothered to build one for themselves, and whether gunning them down if they attempted to break into the family shelter was okay. Fallout shelter lore also involved speculation about what emerging from a shelter after a nuclear war would be like. Often these imagined scenarios were compensatory fantasies in which the problems of current society were eliminated—after the apocalypse, life would be simpler, the world would be less crowded and perhaps purified, and the duty of the surviving men and women would be to get down to the business of repopulating the planet.

The mania for shelters not only reflected popular perceptions concerning the imminence of nuclear war but may have been a momentary outburst of the hope of survival in the face of the nuclear threat. This hopefulness gradually deteriorated after the acknowledgment that shelters offered little protection against intercontinental ballistic missiles that could annihilate entire cities within thirty minutes and that, launched from submarines, could obliterate coastal targets within a couple of minutes. Once the facts about a post-nuclear-holocaust world and the horrors of nuclear winter were revealed—worldwide fallout, subfreezing temperatures, and the destruction of the ozone layer—fallout shelters and civil defense seemed increasingly futile. With increased knowledge about the realities of a full-scale nuclear conflagration and its aftermath, fatalistic resignation appears to have become the predominant response, even among some civil defense authorities, as the following statement by the deputy director of New York City's Office of Civil Preparedness indicates:

> A Russian submarine forty miles off New York can lob missiles at New York City that from launch to detonation will take seven seconds. In that time, the military command has to discern the attack at its headquarters in Colorado, and notify Albany, and they notify us, and we have to notify fifty-six precincts to turn on the sirens, and the people who hear them will run into buildings and will be turned into sand in a few seconds anyway. (Lieutenant Robert Hogan, August 1979; cited in Barasch 1983:85)

Nuclear Apocalypse in Popular Literature

American literature expresses similar themes of inevitability and resignation concerning nuclear apocalypse. Although apocalyptic ideas historically have been widespread in literary works, critics have observed that the notion of apocalypse and entropy became increasingly common concepts in the 1950s and 1960s and have been dealt with by many contemporary American writers (Lewicki 1984:xvi; Zamora 1982b:97).[5] Among the better known popular works that address the idea of accidental and meaningless nuclear annihilation are Nevil Shute's *On the Beach* (1957) and Eugene Burdick and Harvey Wheeler's *Fail-Safe* (1962) (later made into successful films). Secular apocalyptic ideas are particularly prevalent in the science fiction and fantasy genre, and works with increasingly pessimistic and fatalistic themes seem to have proliferated in the nuclear era (see Boyer 1985:257–265; Rabkin et al. 1983). Ward Moore's satiric *Greener Than You Think* (1947), for instance, chronicles the end of the world brought about by an aberrant strain of grass created by scientists (a metaphor for nuclear fallout) and describes the fatalistic worship of inevitable doom that ensues. Another particularly fatalistic depiction of the end of the world is *Level 7* (1989 [1959]) by Mordecai Roshwald, in which the inhabitants of a seven-tiered fallout shelter are slowly killed level by level by radiation from a nuclear cataclysm. As the lethal radiation seeps toward them, the inhabitants of the deepest level create a new religion in which strontium embodies the elemental force of evil (Boyer 1985:354). Themes of inevitability and helplessness concerning nuclear apocalypse are also central to Walter Miller's *A Canticle for Leibowitz* (1982 [1959]). Miller describes a post-apocalyptic religious order—the pious monks of the Order of St. Leibowitz the Engineer—who live in a monastery in the Utah desert, where they worship the relics of their physicist founder and venerate the blessed nuclear blueprints housed in the shrine of the sacred fallout shelter. The monks' efforts to keep the knowledge of nuclear physics from secular society ultimately fail, and the world is destroyed by humans once again. *The Martian Chronicles* (1950) by Ray Bradbury also contains several stories with explicit secular apocalyptic themes; the best known is probably "There Will Come Soft Rains," in which the machines in a techno-utopian home continue to perform their functions long after the extinction of the human species by nuclear catastrophe.

Similar themes are expressed in the writings of Kurt Vonnegut, Jr., who often depicts the inevitable destruction of society from an absurdist viewpoint. In *Cat's Cradle* (1981 [1963]), for instance, the protagonist describes the approach of doomsday brought about by the substance *ice-nine*, created by a scientist known as the Father of the Atom Bomb. When accidently dropped into the ocean through a series of absurd occurrences, *ice-nine* triggers a chain reaction that freezes the earth's oceans and waterways, leading to the eventual extermination of all life. In *Slaughterhouse Five* (1984 [1969]), the time-traveling Billy Pilgrim has visions of inevitable apocalypse, which are in fact prophetic, with the end of the world brought about by a test pilot from the planet Tralfamadore who accidently ignites the universe while testing a new fuel for his flying saucer.

A sense of doom and decline is also exemplified by much of the writing associated with the Beat movement in the 1950s, the first generation of writers after the invention of the bomb. Whether in the form of the apocalyptic transcendentalism of Alan Ginsberg's "Howl" and Jack Kerouac's *On the Road,* the melancholy fatalism of Paul Bowles, or the unredemptive vision of decadence and decay of William S. Burroughs, Jr., the writing of numerous Beats is often characterized by a sense of inevitable societal destruction. Ginsberg's "Howl," for instance, with its revelatory language condemning the modern world, proclaims the doom of American civilization—"Moloch whose fate is a cloud of sexless hydrogen!"—and presents banal images of waiting for the H-bomb: disillusioned, exhausted beatniks sit "through the stale beer afternoon in desolate Fugazzi's, listening to the crack of doom on the hydrogen jukebox" (Ginsberg 1965:17, 10). Ginsberg's apocalyptic indictment of America disputes the prophetic vision of the American millennial paradise, declaring instead the end of American innocence and glory.

The writings of William S. Burroughs, Jr., in particular, provide an emphatically unredemptive vision of American society in a state of disintegration and decadence. According to one biographer, Burroughs's preoccupation with nuclear apocalypse is the basis for much of his writing: "For Burroughs, the Bomb and not the birth of Christ was the dividing line of history. The Bomb stole the relevance from all that had preceded it, and from its ramifications Burroughs constructed a worldview. . . . After the Bomb, Burroughs had a sense of everything going wrong. He had visions of world death and death-in-life" (Morgan 1988:55). Burroughs's surrealistic sense of doom, anarchy, and nihilism is exemplified in *Naked Lunch* (1966 [1959]), in which there is little plot or character development but instead a sequence of macabre occurrences in a hellish, post-apocalyptic, drug-addicted society. Burroughs depicts a world destroyed, characterized by violence, fear, paranoia, and a sense of fatalism. The characters in the novel wander through a wasteland devastated by nuclear war, hopelessly addicted, with incurable diseases and afflictions, resigned to their fate. Burroughs's *Cities of the Red Night* (1981), in which a lethal virus destroys humanity, and his *Apocalypse* (1988), a collaborative project with graffiti artist Keith Haring, also express a sense of imminent, unredemptive, worldly doom. Burroughs's vision of the End is conveyed without remorse or sentimentality—a nihilistic, nuclear-age Book of Revelation, which accepts the inevitability of the End without hope of renewal.

The complete absence of the theme of millennial redemption characterizes these works and much recent apocalyptic literature. As one critic observes, "More representative of recent decades is a reversion to the savagery and destructiveness of the original biblical paradigm, but without its sanction in a transcendent other world. Much of our literature of absurdity and black comedy is a form of black apocalypse—grotesque visions of an ultimate violence which destroys not to renew but to annihilate a world which is regarded as an affront to being" (Abrams 1971:426–427). The visions of a meaningless apocalypse presented in recent literature vary in terms of the nature of the destruction of the human species. In some instances the extermination of humankind occurs in an immediate and violent manner; sometimes it happens slowly, a gradual decline. The themes of helplessness, despair, and fatalism in these writings most often directly reflect the threat of nuclear annihilation.

The Nuclear Bomb in American Art

Images of an inevitable and meaningless apocalypse also pervade contemporary art, although according to several observers, depictions of nuclear apocalypse did not become a frequent subject in the arts until the 1980s, with most artists actually avoiding nuclear apocalyptic themes or responding with a sense of despair, denial, or psychological numbing (Lifton 1987:257–272; Weart 1988:391–404).[6] Although explicit nuclear apocalyptic imagery was uncommon, apocalyptic attitudes may have been implicitly expressed in much of the art that appeared after the bomb:

> Abstract Expressionists shut out the world to paint the insides of their minds, but the images came out explosive, splayed and splattered over the canvas with the violence of an irrational force. . . . The style contained large amounts of self-destructiveness and denial: the canvas had to suffer violent transformations— wiping out, covering over, continually destroying in order to go beyond. . . . Only now is a connection becoming visible between the mushroom cloud and de Kooning's disintegrating "Women," Pollock's tangles of debris, Still's creviced darkness, Rothko's spreading reddish glow, Gottlieb's cold orbs, or Reinhardt's absolute negation. (Levin 1988:38)

Several art critics have asserted that the emphasis on ephemeral and "dematerialized" art, as well as the pop art glorification of banal commodity culture and its insistence that all objects are equally meaningful and thus utterly meaningless, reveals distinct apocalyptic tendencies (Gumpert 1983:47). The emphasis on the process of creating art rather than the final art product itself, exemplified by action painting or performance art and "happenings," has been interpreted as being possibly related to nuclear apocalyptic fears and feelings of futurelessness (Schell 1982:164–165).[7] Such observations about the influence of images and fears of nuclear apocalypse may appear somewhat overstated, but the personal statements of some artists themselves seem to confirm these interpretations (see Gumpert 1983:55–81).

During the 1980s, artists began to express explicitly nuclear apocalyptic themes and fears. Numerous exhibits and group shows dealt with apocalyptic ideas in art, such as the Terminal New York show in Brooklyn in October 1983; the Apocalyptic and Utopian Images in Contemporary Art exhibit in Bethlehem, Pennsylvania, in 1983; and the extensive The End of the World: Contemporary Visions of the Apocalypse show held at the New Museum of Contemporary Art in New York City in 1983–1984. Similar to contemporary apocalyptic literature, the art exhibited in these shows was characterized by a sense of imminent worldly disaster and social decay, the banality and meaninglessness of the end of the world, and apocalyptic gallows humor.[8]

Atomic Bombs, Nuclear Apocalypse, and Societal Catastrophe in Film

Many filmic portrayals of the End also express a sense of the meaninglessness, absurdity, and inevitability of nuclear apocalypse. The two best-known films that portray a nuclear doomsday, *On the Beach* (1959) and *Dr. Strangelove* (1964), have been seen by millions of individuals. Other doomsday films from the same period include *Fail-Safe* (1964), *The Day the Earth Caught Fire* (1961), and *Panic in the Year Zero!* (1962). In these and numerous other films of the apocalyptic genre, technology is often portrayed as awesome, unmanageable, and yet banal in its destructiveness. In *Fail-Safe*, for instance, the nuclear annihilation of Moscow occurs as the result of a technological malfunction. *On the Beach* depicts the lives of a handful of people who survive a large-scale nuclear war and await their fate as a radioactive cloud approaches. As the lethal fallout draws near, the scientist (played by Fred Astaire) contemplates the causes of the End and concludes, "The world was probably destroyed by a bunch of vacuum tubes and transistors." In *Crack in the World* (1965), a scientist searching for new energy sources sets off an atomic bomb in the center of the earth and the world begins cracking in two; in *The Day the Earth Caught Fire*, the earth is knocked out of orbit and sent spinning toward the sun as the result of coincidental and concurrent nuclear bomb tests in the United States and Soviet Union. As the earth gets hotter and people prepare for the End, teenagers cope with the prospect of doomsday by engaging in rock-'n'-roll riots in the streets.

The masterpiece of apocalyptic gallows humor is Stanley Kubrick's *Dr. Strangelove—Or, How I Learned to Stop Worrying and Love the Bomb*. In this film a paranoid General Jack D. Ripper launches a preemptive nuclear attack on the Soviets in order to preserve "our precious bodily fluids," which he believes are being contaminated by a global communist conspiracy to fluoridate the world's water supply. Ripper's assistant frantically tries to stop the attack and breaks the secret recall code, recalling the B-52's. However, one bomber gets through and the bomb is dropped, straddled by a wahooing airforce major played by cowboy actor Slim Pickens. The bomb activates the Soviets' doomsday machine, and the world is destroyed. *Dr. Strangelove* satirizes the Cold War fears of the 1950s, but its underlying theme is the inanity of the end of the world. Human attempts to avert the preemptive attack ultimately fail, and once the technology of annihilation is activated, apocalypse is unalterable by human effort. The film's title exemplifies the psychological transformation of nuclear fear into a helpless, fatalistic acceptance of the bomb and ultimate doom. Human powerlessness to avert apocalypse is further represented by the destruction of the world by a "doomsday machine" that cannot be stopped once set in motion, a metaphor perhaps for nuclear proliferation leading humanity down an inevitable road to destruction.

In addition to films that depict a meaningless nuclear apocalypse are the dozens of atomic bomb mutation films, particularly in the low-budget, "B-movie" category. In such films, nuclear bombs and radioactivity inevitably result in the creation of monsters, mutants, and threats to society and individual existence. Among the better-known of such films are *Them!* (1954), in which massive, migrating ants exposed to radiation at an atomic test site invade the sewers of Los Angeles and *Attack of the Crab Monsters* (1957), with atomic radiation creating, on an isolated island, oversized crabs that decapitate scientists, eat their heads, and gain their intelligence. In the *Beginning of the End* (1957), radioactive fertilizer results in monstrous grasshoppers who converge on Chicago; in *It Came from Beneath the Sea* (1955), San Francisco is attacked by a radioactive octopus that destroys the Golden Gate Bridge and Market Street Tower before being torpedoed to bits.

A related film type involves dinosaurs being revived from their primordial slumber by an atomic blast. In *The Beast from 20,000 Fathoms* (1953), a prehistoric creature brought to life by an atomic bomb test in the Arctic swims to New York City and attacks Manhattan, stomping on people in Times Square and Wall Street, and taking a bite out of the roller coaster at Coney Island. The first Godzilla film, *Godzilla, King of the Monsters* (1954), released in Japan a year later, had similar themes, with the four-hundred-foot radioactive dinosaur trampling Tokyo. The same basic plot is used in a British version entitled *The Giant Behemoth* (1959), in which a brontosaurus with radioactive breath burns the skin off people, attacking London and destroying the House of Parliament. By the end of the 1950s, films about oversized monsters created or unleashed by atomic energy—likely personifications and projections of the fear of nuclear annihilation and radioactivity—had become a sci-fi subgenre. By ultimately defeating or taming these cinematic beasts, the otherwise uncontrollable threat of imminent nuclear destruction was perhaps symbolically vanquished in the context of a movie theater.

The mutating effects of radiation on human beings served as the basis for numerous other films. In *The Incredible Shrinking Man* (1957), the protagonist passes through an atomic cloud and suddenly begins shrinking, so that his suburban home ultimately is transformed into a place of terror. In *Creature with the Atom Brain* (1955), atomic zombies—nuclear death made manifest—stage a mass attack; and in George Romero's cult classic *Night of the Living Dead* (1968), radioactive material brought back to earth by a space vehicle causes corpses to return to life. Like similar films in the radioactive-mutants-battle-humans genre, flesh-eating zombies become the personification of the invisible, deathly power of radioactivity, threatening to destroy civilization as they stalk and cannibalize the living. In other films the invisibility of radioactivity is transmuted into tangible, creeping, blob-like monsters that destroy everything in their path. For example, in *X The Unknown* (1956), radioactive mud from the center of the earth dissolves people as it searches for isotopes; in *The H-Man* (1958), fallout changes people into an oozing green slime that then eats other humans. In *The Blob* (1958, starring Steve McQueen), the radioactive goo is a bright red color from the blood of people consumed in a supermarket, a theater, and a diner. Like the threat of nuclear annihilation and radioactivity, these atomic blobs are mindless, inhuman, and impersonal, disintegrating and devouring unsuspecting victims.

A related subgenre consists of movies that portray a post-apocalyptic world, from cult classics such as *World without End* (1955), *Teenage Cave Man* (1958), *The Omega Man* (1971), *A Boy and His Dog* (1975), and the numerous *Planet of the Apes* films (late 1960s and 1970s), to the highly successful *Mad Max* (1979),

The Road Warrior (1982), and *Mad Max Beyond the Thunderdome* (1985), and the more recent *Judge Dredd* (1995) and *Waterworld* (1995). These films depict life on earth in the aftermath of nuclear war or some other global catastrophe, such as the melting of the ice caps (*Waterworld)* or a plague (*Omega Man*), with the survivors usually living in a state of post-apocalyptic savagery or often battling mutants in the ruins of destroyed cities. In Roger Corman's first science-fiction film, *The Day the World Ended* (1956), an atomic blast has transformed those exposed to radiation into horned, three-eyed, four-armed mutant cannibals with telepathic powers who attack unradiated humans sheltered in a mountain cabin. In *Beneath the Planet of the Apes* (1970), the mutant humans dwell underground and worship a nuclear bomb in the buried ruins of Grand Central Station. In one scene they congregate before the nuclear missile, the "Holy Weapon of Peace," and chant, "I reveal my inmost self unto My God!" In the same film the splitting of the atom serves as the source for an apocalyptic nursery rhyme, as children sing a post-nuclear-holocaust version of "Ring around the Rosie":

> Ring-a ring o' neutrons
> A pocketful of positrons,
> A fission! A fission!
> We all fall down.

Whether the survivors of nuclear cataclysm deify or fear the bomb, they usually have been transformed by it into subhumans—mutants, monsters, savages—who live underground, under siege, or enslaved by evil tyrants. In a few films (for example, *The World, the Flesh, and the Devil* [1958] and *Five* [1951]) the remnant survivors are portrayed as postwar Adams and Eves who will remake the world, liberated by the bomb from a corrupt, overly technological civilization. But in the majority of such films, the post-apocalyptic world is inhabited by degenerated barbarians and inhuman creatures, victims of forces beyond their control, battling for survival on a brutal and ruined planet.

Humor in the Nuclear Age

With the exception of a few films, such as *Dr. Strangelove*, explicit apocalyptic gallows humor is relatively infrequent in film. Cartoonists and illustrators, on the other hand, generally have had fun with the topic of doomsday. In particular, the stereotyped image of a bearded and robed doomsayer holding a sign with some humorous twist or wordplay is a frequent object of parody. For instance, an illustration by Gahan Wilson depicts an anguished, bearded doomsayer in sandals attempting to sell balloons, pennants, buttons, and baseball caps that read "THE WORLD IS COMING TO ITS END" (Griffin 1979:xiv). In another cartoon, a bearded doomsayer in sandals is shown racing into a bar with a sign that reads "THE END IS UPON US!" and frantically shouting to the bartender: "Double Scotch, and *hurry!*" (*Medical Economics*, February 3, 1990, 169). The series "Grin and Bear It" shows a bearded doomsayer in a suit in an urban setting carrying a sign that reads "DOOMSDAY IS NEAR"; a cheerful-looking woman asks him, "Will there be a doomsday sale?" (July 29, 1988, "Wagner," North America Syndicate, Inc.).

Cartoons and illustrations about doomsday are pervasive and usually satirize doomsayers, but jokes about nuclear apocalypse seem to be relatively scarce and express a sense of ironic inevitability:

Did you hear the World War III knock-knock joke?"
No.
Knock, Knock.
Who's there?
(Silence!).   (Dundes 1987:viii)

What do you do if they drop the bomb?
What?
Hide under a table, put your head between your legs, and . . . kiss your ass
    goodbye!

What should you do in case of a nuclear attack?
What?
Get a shovel and a sheet and walk slowly . . . to the nearest cemetery.
Why slowly?
You mustn't start a panic.   (Weart 1988:239)

What do you do if they drop the bomb?
I don't know, what?
Get a six-pack, go up on your roof, and enjoy the show.[9]

Parodying civil defense instructions, these jokes express an absurdist sense of helplessness in the face of nuclear doom. The third joke, for instance, not only mocks civil defense evacuation plans as ludicrous, but also the instructions to "stay calm" in the event of a nuclear attack, with doomed citizens marching fatalistically to their own graves. Similar themes of futility and absurdity characterize the fourth joke, with its gallows humor derived from the equation of nuclear apocalypse with Fourth of July celebrations or some other public display. The spectators have no choice but to embrace doomsday, watching the End from their rooftops and perhaps even cheering, between swigs of beer, as the apocalyptic fireworks illuminate the sky.

Comparable humor about the futility of civil defense efforts and the possibility of surviving a nuclear attack is reflected in what is commonly referred to as "Xeroxlore"—printed or written materials that are reproduced by means of photocopiers, Xerox machines, and fax machines. Such xerographic lore tends to be a reflection of popular beliefs and concerns, and usually is unofficially or illicitly reproduced and informally displayed (see Dundes and Pagter 1987; Dundes and Pagter 1992).[10] The following example of Xeroxlore was widely circulated in the 1970s:

NOTICE

Office of Civilian Defense

Washington, D.C.

INSTRUCTION TO PATRONS ON PREMISES

IN CASE OF NUCLEAR BOMB ATTACK

UPON THE FIRST WARNING:
1. STAY CLEAR OF ALL WINDOWS.

2. KEEP HANDS FREE OF GLASSES, BOTTLES, CIGARETTES, ETC.

3. STAND AWAY FROM BAR, TABLES, ORCHESTRA, EQUIPMENT AND FURNITURE.

4. LOOSEN NECKTIE, UNBUTTON COAT AND ANY OTHER RESTRICTIVE CLOTHING.

5. REMOVE GLASSES, EMPTY POCKETS OF ALL SHARP OBJECTS SUCH AS PENS, PENCILS, ETC.

6. IMMEDIATELY UPON SEEING THE BRILLIANT FLASH OF NUCLEAR EXPLOSION, BEND OVER AND PLACE YOUR HEAD FIRMLY BETWEEN YOUR LEGS.

7. THEN KISS YOUR ASS GOODBYE.   (Dundes and Pagter 1992:105)

Like other types of xerographic folklore, this example imitates the style and rhetoric of an "official" document but ultimately mocks institutional instructions, expressing cynicism about surviving a nuclear attack, like the joke mentioned above with the same punchline.

Folklorist and noted scholar of humor Alan Dundes states that people joke about that which is of utmost concern and that jokes serve as a means of projecting anxieties or allowing for psychological catharsis (1987:viii). The infrequency of verbal humor about doomsday indicates that apocalyptic fears and anxieties are scarce, that fears associated with the subject are so great that people consciously avoid joking about it, or that this avoidance is unconscious. Numerous psychologists have demonstrated that a common response to perceptions of imminent death or disaster is denial (e.g., Becker 1973). Robert Jay Lifton, in particular, says that a common response to the threat of nuclear war is conscious or unconscious denial and "numbing" (Lifton and Falk 1982:3–12). This denial is one possible explanation for the relative lack of explicit verbal humor about the end of the world.

Certain topical joking cycles, however, particularly disaster or "sick joke" cycles, may indirectly express fears and anxieties about nuclear apocalypse. According to Willie Smyth, the graphic images of death and mutilation that characterize Challenger Shuttle jokes, for instance, express not only disillusionment with capitalism and fears of personal death but widespread anxiety about global annihilation and fears of destructive technology that can no longer be controlled (1986:254). In an article on the same subject, Elizabeth Simons states that the gruesome imagery and prevalence of sick jokes is directly related to the events of World War II and the influence of the media: "Since World War II the world itself seems to have grown sicker. The Holocaust and the dropping of the atomic bomb broke all earlier sense of the limits of people's inhumanity. . . . The explosion of the Challenger Seven was yet another unprecedented death (to be added to death by Holocaust, atomic explosion, and nuclear accident)" (1986:265–266).

Images of large-scale disaster and the distrust of technology were also manifested in Chernobyl jokes and popular responses to the accident at the Three Mile Island nuclear power plant near Middletown, Pennsylvania, in 1979. After the Three Mile Island disaster, facetious greetings among residents included "My, you look radiant!" or "You're glowing today!" but beliefs and rumors about the dangers of exposure to radioactivity (e.g., sterility, genetically mutated offspring, increased rates of infant mortality) spread rapidly, a reflection of the suspicion that authorities were withholding information, as well as uncertainty about the long-term effects of radiation (Milspaw 1981;

Malsheimer 1986). The nuclear disaster that occurred in Chernobyl, Ukraine, in 1986, provoked similar beliefs and rumors, as well as jokes with ironic and macabre themes that expressed anxieties about uncontrollable nuclear technology ("What has feathers, glows in the dark, and cooks by itself? Chicken Kiev"; "What do you serve with Chicken Kiev? A black Russian"; "What's the weather report from Kiev? Overcast and 10,000 degrees"). These jokes were responses to specific nuclear disasters, but they also express underlying fears and anxieties about nuclear doom.

Cultural critic Kim Levin asserts that the invention of nuclear weapons had a direct influence on American humor and vernacular speech: "The bomb spawned the humor of the '50s, the sick jokes, the Little Willie rhymes, the moron jokes. It crept into the slang: teenagers trying to shut out the world only succeeded in 'bombing around' in crowded Chevy's" (1988:38). In his analysis of the phenomenon of "Dead Baby Jokes" that proliferated in the 1960s, Alan Dundes states that these jokes reflect widespread anxieties about abortion, contraception, and the carnage of the Vietnam War, but also express fear of technology: "Certainly a large percentage of the dead baby jokes explicitly describe babies being ground up by a variety of modern conveniences, e.g., lawnmowers, blenders, razors blades, garbage disposals. Is the joke cycle warning of the possible or probable fate of modern man? Are we doomed to be destroyed by uncaring machines that we ourselves have created allegedly to make life easier and more pleasurable?" (1979:153). Although dead-baby jokes do not explicitly refer to nuclear war, the gruesome imagery of babies being mutilated, burned, and obliterated may unconsciously or symbolically express prevailing fears of nuclear annihilation, which intensified around the time the jokes became current. Children represent, as Robert Jay Lifton remarks, a "symbolization of our own future, of the process of being part of the great chain of being and the flow of generations" (1987:23). The mutilation and obliteration of children (the symbolic destruction of the future) that characterizes the sick and cruel joke cycles that have become especially popular since the 1950s may express to some degree the sense of radical futurelessness that is often a psychological response to threat of nuclear war.

Speech forms, neologisms, and euphemisms associated with nuclear weapons also seem to express a sense of futurelessness and the view that nuclear apocalypse is an inevitability beyond human control. The common use of the expression "the bomb" when referring to the multitude of nuclear warheads that exist in the world reflects popular perceptions of nuclear weapons as a single, massive, inescapable, omnipresent force of destruction. Often in popular speech "the bomb" is described as if it were a superorganic or supernatural entity with a power and will of its own, beyond human comprehension and control, that ultimately will destroy humanity. According to Paul Chilton, the rhetoric about the bomb frequently has religious connotations associated with supernatural awe and the notion that the bomb's development was somehow destined and inevitable (1986:127–142). He refers to this specialized language associated with nuclear weaponry as "nukespeak," and declares that nuclear metaphors and even grammatical constructions evoke the supernatural character of the bomb and serve to condone nuclear proliferation and acceptance of the idea of nuclear war (1986:128). The bombing of Hiroshima and Nagasaki, for instance, has often been referred to as inevitable, rather than something that might have been avoided. Statements about nuclear weapons harnessing the "basic power of the universe" or being a "force from which the sun draws its power," "a vast and mysterious power," embodying the "revelation of the secrets of nature," equate the bomb with supernatural agency. As Chilton observes, "One is left with the supposition that men were not ultimately responsible for the invention and use of the atomic bomb; it was given to them by some outside force" (1986:132). Nuclear weapons, rather than human action, become the agents of apocalypse, with the bomb bestowed with an uncontrollable power that is out of the hands of human beings.

A sense of helplessness and fatalism in the midst of overwhelming forces may evoke what Rudolf Otto, in his book *The Idea of the Holy*, describes as a sense of the numinous: an ineffable sense of terror, magnificence, and limitless power ("absolute overpoweringness"), as well as feelings of personal powerlessness, mystery, danger, and a sense of the "wholly other" (1958:12–24). Thoughts about the enormous destructive power of nuclear weapons and the inevitability of nuclear annihilation may precipitate feelings similar to what Otto called the *mysterium tremendum*—a sense of overwhelming awe, fear, dread, and "a terror fraught with an inward shuddering such as not even the most menacing and overpowering created thing can instil" (1958:14).

The sense of the numinous, like fatalistic beliefs and behavior, is often characterized by the admission of one's own powerlessness and the submission of one's self to a greater power, whether God, fate, or some other external determining agency. As the embodiment of incomprehensible and terrifying destructive power, nuclear weapons may be ascribed with a numinous terror that in the past was associated only with the supernatural, and may inspire similar feelings of helplessness and perhaps an embracing of one's powerlessness. In this way, perhaps, the bomb itself may become a symbol of unalterable, supranormal fate for the secular apocalypticist, as a numinous and uncontrollable power that will determine individual fate and the fate of humanity.

Survivalists and Secular Millenarianism

Even though secular apocalyptic ideas pervade American literature, art, film, popular culture, and folklore, secular apocalypticists themselves are not as easily identifiable as religious apocalypticists because they generally do not form into groups or actively solicit members. Some do, however, share and express their beliefs in imminent apocalypse with like-minded individuals.

Many people who identify themselves as survivalists, for instance, anticipate the destruction of current society through a series of catastrophic occurrences, such as nuclear war, worldwide economic collapse, epidemic disease, environmental disasters, or race riots. Preparation for imminent worldly destruction involves developing "survival skills," stockpiling food and weapons, and establishing refuges in remote areas. Determining how widespread survivalism is can be difficult because most survivalists consider anonymity and secrecy crucial to their safety during these cataclysms. The few studies that exist on the subject indicate that survivalism tends to appeal to Caucasian males of conservative or independent political affiliations, but also that survivalists are an eclectic group of individuals and not easily categorized (Coates 1987; Houglum 1986; Linder 1982; Myers 1982). The proliferation of survivalist books, magazines, newsletters, catalogs, and supplies, as well as survivalist shops, conventions, and consultants, reveals that interest in survivalism seems to have increased in recent years, with as many as three million people estimated to be involved in this movement (Linder 1982:11).

The sense of unavoidable cataclysm that motivates much survivalist behavior is exemplified by the following statement by survivalist writer Mel Tappan, who is generally acknowledged as one of the "founding fathers" of the survivalist movement:

> We are about to witness the profound disruption of this country and, possibly, the entire civilized world. Barring some *deus ex machina* miracle, there is no longer any practical way to prevent it and, unless you are willing to believe for yourself that what I am telling you here is truth, you will probably become a victim of this holocaust without ever having the opportunity to strike a blow in behalf of your country or yourself. (Tappan 1981:1)

Survivalist publications and newsletters consistently maintain that impending catastrophes will completely destroy society as it currently exists. According to one writer, "What all survivalists share is a belief that something terrible will happen soon, and that people had better get ready for it" (Myers 1982:12). Whether that eventuality is envisioned as economic collapse, racial conflicts, or nuclear war, many survivalists insist that these future catastrophes are inevitable.

Of the various apocalyptic scenarios prepared for by survivalists, nuclear conflagration is by far the most predominant (Coates 1987:9; Houglum 1986:69–70; Myers 1982:13). Unlike individual responses to the threat of nuclear war that are characterized by denial, avoidance, or escapism, survivalists have developed specific plans for dealing with the nuclear destruction of society. Researcher James Coates maintains that survivalism is a means of directly coping with the fear of nuclear annihilation and "the terrors of post-Hiroshima life on a fragile and unfriendly planet. . . . Instead of worrying about how to prevent the coming holocaust, these Survivalists have devoted their energy to planning how to prosper by it" (1987:9).

In his book *Life after Doomsday*, prominent survivalist author Bruce Clayton states that of the numerous potential cataclysms that threaten the United States (such as famine, epidemic disease, economic collapse, political and religious disruption, and various natural and environmental calamities), "nuclear war is both the greatest possible catastrophe our nation could ever face and the most immediate and continuous threat to our lives" (1980:14). After conducting a statistical analysis on the probability of a nuclear cataclysm occurring in the near future, Clayton concludes that "under these circumstances, the advent of nuclear war can be regarded as a certainty. Only the date is unpredictable" (1980:15). Like religious apocalypticists, the beliefs and rhetoric of many survivalists assert that predicted future events are unalterable by human effort. Instead of being part of a divinely ordained plan for the world, survivalists contend that these cataclysmic events will inevitably occur as the consequence of "natural laws," human ignorance and violence, uncontrollable technology, governmental ineptitude and deceit, or conspiracies by sinister groups.

Survivalist literature assures readers that with the proper planning, preparation, and training they will endure even the most devastating catastrophes. As Clayton states, "Believe it or not, *even a nuclear war is survivable*. With an eye toward realistic preparation, you can see to it that your family and a small group of friends will be able to live through the holocaust and the post-attack period with a minimum of unpleasantness" (1980:17). Clayton provides extensive information about survival strategies, discussing in detail various types of shelters, plans for evacuation, food storage, foraging, alternative energy sources, weapons, emergency medicine, the tactics of self-defense, and the psychology of managing people during a disaster. Some survivalists have formed groups and purchased property in rural areas that they plan to inhabit once society collapses or when urban areas become too dangerous. The more retreatist survivalists have relocated to remote areas where they await the apocalypse. By providing individuals with a plan of action, survivalism may transform a sense of helplessness or resignation about inevitable societal destruction into an ethos of self-reliance and self-salvation.

Although there are some religious survivalists (midtribulationists and post-tribulationists) who believe that coming catastrophes are part of the foreordained tribulation period that they will have to endure prior to the Rapture, it appears that the majority of survivalists expect that imminent worldly cataclysms will be natural or human-made. Some of these secular survivalists, however, envision the renewal of society after its destruction. Like other millenarians, these individuals are pessimistic about the current society and believe that future disasters will hasten the transformation of the world. Similar to dispensationalists and the Baysiders, who regard apocalypse as a purification of the earth prior to the establishment of a millennial paradise, these millenarian survivalists anticipate a catastrophic cleansing of the planet, the abolishment of government, and a state of unlimited, anarchistic freedom.

As Michael Barkun notes, some Christian Identity survivalists envision an apocalypse that will involve the genocide of specific racial or religious minorities (1990; 1994:213–217). The racist millenarian tendency of this paramilitary minority within the survivalist movement is exemplified by the writings of Kurt Saxon, who states that World War III "will be a blessing for survivors. We can start anew, hopefully avoiding past errors . . . the earth's surplus population is long overdue for a culling" (Myers 1982:45). Saxon's writings anticipate a WASP golden age free from "foreign," nonwhite inhabitants, who, he asserts, will have been eliminated during the collapse of civilization. Another racist post-apocalyptic scenario is described by researcher James Coates, who observes that the survivalist right is characterized by the idea "that the world is on the verge of some form of catastrophic renewal, after which the stage will be set for them to eliminate the Jews, blacks, Hispanics, Catholics, and others who are their targets" (1987:10). Using the eschatological images of the Bible to support its ideology, the apocalypse imagined by the survivalist right is the pivotal moment in which a contaminated society will be destroyed and humanity "cleansed" of racial and religious "impurities." Life after apocalypse often is envisioned as an Edenic terrestrial paradise with white Adam-and-Eve-like survivors repopulating a pristine planet.

The millenarian aspects of survivalism clearly resemble religious apocalyptic traditions that emphasize the salvation of a select few rather than society as a whole. The dangers and crises that threaten humanity are viewed as unsolvable by human effort, and, like many religious apocalypticists, most hard-core survivalists have "given up" on a corrupt society that they consider to be doomed. Although human action is regarded as futile in averting catastrophes and saving society, personal salvation is possible through self-sufficiency, retreatism, and the development of certain prescribed skills and behaviors. The feelings of powerlessness otherwise evoked by fears of nuclear annihilation and other imminent disasters are displaced by elaborate preparations that provide the hope of surviving doomsday. Unlike the promise of planetary escape in the Rapture, the protection afforded by the Baysiders' "spiritual armor," and other assurances of supernatural intervention or protection, secular survivalists must rely on their own skill, resourcefulness, and rugged individualism to endure societal destruction. The majority of survivalists seem to embrace the fatalistic view that nuclear war and other cataclysms are inevitable, envisioning themselves as post-apocalyptic pioneers who will be the dominant inhabitants of a devastated new frontier and who will gradually rebuild society from the ruins.

Visions of Apocalypse in Punk Subculture

Survivalism is one of the more obvious examples of secular apocalyptic thinking, but ideas about imminent societal destruction also have been a part of the worldview of numerous other subgroups in the United States during the past four decades, particularly so-called countercultures and youth subcultures.[11] Unlike various groups in the 1960s and 1970s that expressed the millenarian hope that society would be transformed and redeemed, the behavior and rhetoric of members of the punk subculture in the late 1970s was characterized by pessimism, nihilism, and a sense of impending societal destruction. Apocalyptic ideas were not necessarily the defining characteristic of punk worldview; however, a sense of imminent doom was a dominant theme, consistently expressed in song lyrics, fanzines, newsletters, posters, manifestoes, beliefs, and behavior. As Dick Hebdige observes, "The rhetoric of punk was drenched in apocalypse: in the stock imagery of crisis and sudden change" (1979:27). Greil Marcus, commenting on early punk music, notes that it "was millenarian from the beginning, certain to lead the listener into the promised land, or forty years in the wilderness" (1989:5). The apocalyptic temperament of punk ethos and aesthetic is also suggested by Ted Morgan, who observes that "the punk scene flourished with the coming of the age of the first generation raised on the concept of nuclear annihilation, the Soviets having announced in 1950 that they had the Bomb" (1988:537). Although the apocalyptic themes of punk worldview have been noted by other writers (cf. Laing 1978:124), as well as punks themselves, extended analyses of this aspect of punk rhetoric, belief, and style have not been made. This discussion concentrates on various manifestations of the punk culture in late 1970s and early 1980s, before punk was transformed into a variety of other subcultural and musical movements.[12]

Punk made its debut in the popular media in the summer of 1976, primarily as the result of the scandalous antics of the rock band the Sex Pistols. Much of the attention focused upon their style of body adornment, their loud and "obnoxious" music, their "self-mutilation" (burning their arms with lighted cigarettes and scratching their faces with needles), and their obscene behavior (cursing on a nationally televised talk show and performing a "spitting and vomiting act" at Heathrow Airport). It was not long before a variety of other punk bands appeared, the members of which generally had little or no prior musical training. These initial groups emphasized a raw, amateur musical style and a self-effacing, "anti–rock star" approach. The do-it-yourself attitude of punk is epitomized by the often-cited advice in the punk fanzine *Sniffin' Glue*, which has an illustration of three finger positions on the neck of a guitar and the caption, "Here's one chord, here's two more, now form your own band."

In general, early punk subculture was characterized by antiromanticism, anticommercialism, and the lack of distinctions between musicians and fans. It also quickly became renowned for a style of adornment calculated to disturb and outrage: dyed hair, mohawks, studded leather jackets, torn clothing, bondage wear, profaned religious articles, tattooing, and safety pins piercing the nose, lips, and ears. Claiming to be anarchists and nihilists, punks offended as many people as they could: some were distressed by the profanation of religious objects and the use of sexually "deviant" paraphernalia; others were disgusted by the emphasis on the sordid and obscene. Punk behavior and rhetoric evoked a "moral panic"—a general horror and condemnation in the popular media that spread throughout society. Punks were demonized and depicted in stereotypical ways as "folk devils" that threatened national morals and the social order (Hebdige 1979:157–158).

Punk became popular when it did because it was a grassroots reaction to the mass marketing, commercialism, and elitism that characterized mainstream rock music; it also captured the mood of the time, giving expression to many of the frustrations and concerns of youth, such as a high unemployment rate, dismal economic conditions, and a pervasive attitude of desperation and futility (Laing 1978:123–125; Hebdige 1979:23–29). The fatalistic underpinnings of punk are noted by Tricia Henry, who states that punks "felt they had 'no future' (one of the slogans which became synonymous with the punk world view), and that their lives had been predestined by a society run by people with unfair advantages (i.e., money and political power). When they finished high school, if they did, they either couldn't find work or were doomed to jobs which they found unbearably boring, and which offered no creative challenge and very little pay" (1989:1). The punk motto "no future," which summed up the sense of fatalism inherent in early punk ethos, comes from the Sex Pistol's song "God Save the Queen" (1977), which became an international punk anthem. In it, Johnny Rotten screams:

> God save the Queen
> The fascist regime
> It made you a moron
> A potential H-bomb
>
> God save the Queen
> She ain't no human being
> There is no future
> In England's dream
>
> No future
> No future
> No future
> For you. . . .

The sense of cultural pessimism, futurelessness, and nihilism expressed by the Sex Pistols appealed to disaffected youth around the world, and punk quickly became a global phenomenon. Because early punk music was generally not promoted by the record industry or played on the radio, knowledge about the subculture was communicated primarily by word of mouth at record stores, nightclubs, and other meeting places, as well as through correspondences and hundreds of fanzines run by punks themselves, such as *Punk, Sniffin' Glue, Search and Destroy, Rotten to the Core, Slash, Maximumrocknroll, Damage, World War III,* and *Flipside.* The grassroots character of punk is exemplified by the fact that even though "God Save the Queen" was banned on British radio and some stores refused to sell the record, it rose to the top of the music charts in England.

Unlike British punk, the American punk movement was not so much a response to economic oppression as an expression of alienation from and disgust for mainstream values. Like their British counterparts, however, American punks often embraced a sense of societal disintegration, fatalism, and futurelessness. As a former punk from New York put it: "I liked that time of decay. There was a nihilism in the atmosphere, a longing to die. Part of the feeling of New York at that time was this longing for oblivion, that you were about to disintegrate, go the way of this bankrupt, crumbling city. Yet that was something almost mystically wonderful" (Savage 1991:133).

The sentiment that there was no future and that society was collapsing pervaded American punk fanzines and lyrics. The well-known documentary film about punks in Los Angeles, *The Decline of Western Civilization* (1981), by Penelope Spheeris, captures this sense of pessimistic inevitability, epitomized by singer Darby Crash of the band the Germs, who was one of the first and most influential punk singers in Southern California. Crash performed in a state of drug- and alcohol-induced oblivion and eventually committed suicide. Punk self-destructiveness often has been interpreted as an aesthetic style rather than an expression of a genuine sense of despair or fatalism, yet there were many punks who were absolutely fatalistic and completely serious about destroying themselves, and many did. The destructive aspect of the punk movement became ritualized in the form of slam-dancing, ceremonial violence, drug and alcohol abuse, and other forms of actual or symbolic self-negation.

This emphasis on destruction was palpable at punk concerts, which often felt like symbolic enactments, or perhaps celebrations, of the collapse of all social order, a momentary, cathartic release from societal constraints. The music shook the walls of the ramshackle clubs and ruined auditoriums in which it was played; band members screamed, collapsed, spit on the audience, had seizures, lacerated their bodies, and threw themselves into the crowd. Fans leaped up on the stage and did the same, hurling bottles and chairs, spitting their approval rather than applauding, and diving head first or somersaulting into the crowd. Punk dances also expressed this sense of destruction and negation: slam-dancing involved running and throwing oneself into the other dancers; and the pogo was a denial of all previous dance aesthetics, as individuals hopped up and down with their arms at their sides and crashed into one another. The editor of *Punk* magazine, John Holmstrom, who authored one of many initial punk manifestoes, states that a punk concert "is like an

1. Fearful Sights and Great Signs. The portents of the last days shown in this nineteenth-century Millerite illustration include earthquakes, eclipses, erupting volcanoes, and showers of falling stars. (From a reprinted edition of S. S. Brewer, *The Last Day Tokens: Nos. 1, 2, 3,* 1874.)

2. The Theater of the Universe on the Eve of Time. This eighteenth-century depiction of the dead rising from their graves on the Day of Judgment illustrates a tract that uses the metaphor of the theater for conveying a sense of history's predestined plot. While the righteous few are being allowed into the Gallery to watch the end-times drama unfold, a mob of sinners is being cast into the Pit, which "is very wide and commodious, which causes great numbers to flock to it, [and] it is generally crowded." (From a publication by G. S. Peters, Harrisburg, Pennsylvania, no date; from the collection of the Library of Congress.)

3. This portrayal of the return of Jesus Christ and his angels to gather up the faithful illustrates a home-study lesson on "The Four Horsemen of Revelation" distributed by Seminars Unlimited, a Seventh-day Adventist ministerial supply and resource center. (Courtesy of Seminars Unlimited.)

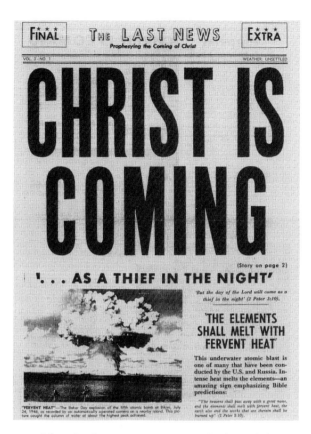

4. The Last News. The role of atomic weapons in God's plan and the inevitability of nuclear apocalypse prior to Jesus Christ's return are recurring preoccupations in popular prophecy, conveyed by this cover of a prophecy tract (circa 1990) styled after the front page of a tabloid. (Courtesy of Feral House.)

5. Apocalypse at a Theater Near You. Hal Lindsey's endtimes scenario was not only promoted in the 1970s by his best-selling book *The Late Great Planet Earth* but also by a documentary-like film featuring Lindsey and narrated by Orson Welles (some ads claimed that the film was the "ultimate disaster movie"). (From the advertisement for the film *The Late Great Planet Earth*, a Pacific International Enterprises release.)

6. Rapture Place Mat. Charles Anderson's painting of the Rapture, well known in dispensationalist circles, is available as a place mat, postcard, or framed print. (Courtesy of the Bible Believers' Evangelistic Association, Inc.)

7. The Great Snatch! The comic book version of Hal Lindsey's *There's a New World Coming* (1974), illustrated by Al Hartley, presented dispensationalist beliefs to teenagers in the 1970s in the vernacular style of the times. (From the Spire comic book *There's a New World Coming*.)

8. Like previous prophecy interpreters, Hal Lindsey recast ancient biblical passages in terms of modern concerns and contexts, in this instance identifying the locusts mentioned in the Book of Revelation as swarms of apocalyptic helicopters. (From the Spire comic book *There's a New World Coming.*)

9. According to premillennialist interpretations of the Book of Revelation, the major armies of the world will converge at the Battle of Armageddon where the Antichrist and the forces of evil will be finally defeated by Jesus Christ and the forces of good. (From the Spire comic book *There's a New World Coming.*)

10. Left Behind Mowing the Lawn. This illustration of the Rapture in suburbia from *The Rise of the Antichrist* by Salem Kirban warns that some family members may miss the Rapture and be forever separated from their loved ones. (Courtesy of Salem Kirban.)

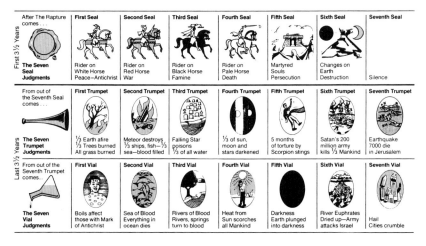

	First Seal	Second Seal	Third Seal	Fourth Seal	Fifth Seal	Sixth Seal	Seventh Seal
After The Rapture comes . . . The Seven Seal Judgments	Rider on White Horse Peace–Antichrist	Rider on Red Horse War	Rider on Black Horse Famine	Rider on Pale Horse Death	Martyred Souls Persecution	Changes on Earth Destruction	Silence
	First Trumpet	Second Trumpet	Third Trumpet	Fourth Trumpet	Fifth Trumpet	Sixth Trumpet	Seventh Trumpet
From out of the Seventh Seal comes . . . The Seven Trumpet Judgments	⅓ Earth afire ⅓ Trees burned All grass burned	Meteor destroys ⅓ ships, fish—⅓ sea—blood filled	Falling Star poisons ⅓ of all water	⅓ of sun, moon and stars darkened	5 months of torture by Scorpion stings	Satan's 200 million army kills ⅓ Mankind	Earthquake 7000 die in Jerusalem
	First Vial	Second Vial	Third Vial	Fourth Vial	Fifth Vial	Sixth Vial	Seventh Vial
From out of the Seventh Trumpet comes... The Seven Vial Judgments	Boils affect those with Mark of Antichrist	Sea of Blood Everything in ocean dies	Rivers of Blood Rivers, springs turn to blood	Heat from Sun scorches all Mankind	Darkness Earth plunged into darkness	River Euphrates Dried up—Army attacks Israel	Hail Cities crumble

(First 3½ Years / Last 3½ Years)

11. The Judgments of the Tribulation Period. This prophecy chart details the predetermined punishments to be inflicted upon humanity—the Seven Seal Judgments, the Seven Trumpet Judgments, and the Seven Vial Judgments—during the seven year tribulation period prior to Jesus Christ's return. (Courtesy of Salem Kirban.)

12. Body Art in the Last Days. In this illustration, the Mark of the Beast is depicted as a fashionable form of body modification that people will embrace willingly in the endtimes in order to buy, sell, and express their allegiance to the Antichrist. (Courtesy of Salem Kirban.)

13. Some prophecy enthusiasts believe that the Mark of the Beast will be required for all financial transactions in the future and will take the form of an invisible tattoo on the back of the right hand which will be scanned by lasers, similar to the way Universal Product Codes are now scanned at check-out counters at supermarkets. (Courtesy of Salem Kirban.)

14. Business as Usual in the Endtimes. A business man with the Mark of the Beast on his hand and forehead hails a taxi during the reign of the Antichrist. From the cover of *Signs of the Times,* a Seventh-day Adventist publication. (Courtesy of Jim Starr.)

Be a witness to
your loved ones and friends! Wear a

RAPTURE   WATCH

This unique Rapture watch will give
you an opportunity to witness to others
and it will also remind you, as each
hour passes, we are **One Hour Nearer
The Lord's Return!**

Each time you look at this watch you
will recall our Lord's promise in
Matthew 24:44 and Mark 13:33
that He will come "...*in such an hour
as ye think not.*"

The RAPTURE WATCH is pictured <u>full size</u> above.   It is a
Quartz watch and has a battery powered movement.   It also
has conventional hands plus a second hand.   It is housed in a
gold plated case and comes with a genuine leather band.

15. Rapture Time. Prophecy believers may purchase an assortment of inspirational endtimes products such as this "Rapture watch" with the reminder that each passing hour brings the wearer "one hour nearer the Lord's return." (Courtesy of Salem Kirban.)

16. An illustration of the Virgin Mary appearing to three children at Fatima in 1917, perhaps the most famous apparition site where Mary is believed to have delivered apocalyptic, anticommunist, and traditionalist messages. (From a newsletter published by St. Paul's Guild.)

WARNINGS⁺FROM HEAVEN!

MOST RECENT APPARITIONS AND VISIONS OF
CHRIST, ST. MARY, SAINTS & ANGELS IN U.S.A.,
MEXICO, ITALY, SPAIN & FRANCE WARN OF
WAR, SCHISM, UFOs, ANTI-CHRIST, SATAN, &
MUCH MORE IN NEW ALARMING MESSAGES.

Send $2.00 for KIT of over 50 documents and sacra-
mentals (for protection). Includes Rosary, Scapular,
Miraculous Medal and Icon.

ST. PAUL'S GUILD
GRANITEVILLE, VERMONT 05654

17. Warnings from Heaven. At various contemporary Marian apparition sites, visionaries claim that the Virgin Mary has warned of the imminence of nuclear apocalypse, symbolized in this advertisement by an image of Mary framed by a mushroom cloud. (From a newsletter published by St. Paul's Guild.)

18. Promoting the Virgin Mary in America. This full-page advertisement by Our Lady of Roses Shrine about the Bayside apparitions appeared in the *Weekly World News* in December 1994 and elicited nearly fifteen hundred written responses and five thousand phone inquiries. (Courtesy of Our Lady of the Roses, Mary Help of Mothers Shrine.)

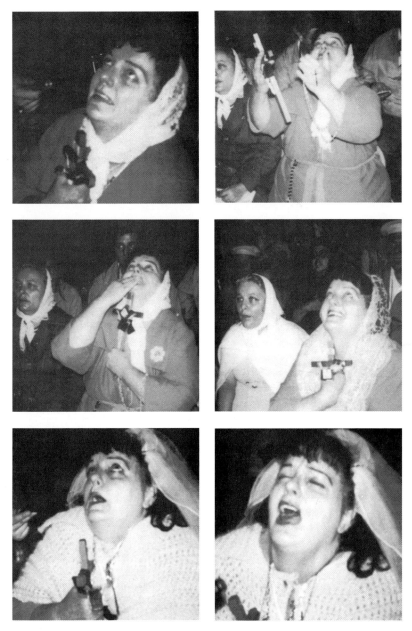

19. Veronica in Ecstasy. These photographs from a publication that promotes the Bayside apparitions document Veronica Lueken's ecstatic visions of the Virgin Mary. The first three photos show her envisioning the gate of heaven, holding Baby Jesus, and blowing a kiss to the Blessed Mother; the fourth photo shows her in ecstasy, while the last two pictures document her response to a vision of hell. (Courtesy of Apostles of Our Lady.)

ROSES

ST. MICHAEL GUARDIAN OF THE FAITH

REDEMPTION GRACE PEACE

BAYSIDE, "THE LOURDES OF AMERICA"

Our Lady of the Roses, Mary Help of Mothers Shrine
Box 52, Bayside, New York 11361-0052

MESSAGE OF OUR LADY AND OUR LORD TO VERONICA LUEKEN

VATICAN PAVILION SITE, FLUSHING MEADOW PARK

March 26, 1983 — Eve of Palm Sunday

" Russia plans to invade the United States with missiles " — Jesus

★ Warhead In Abandoned N.Y. Subway Tunnel ★

BACKGROUND STORY

Veronica Lueken, the seer of Bayside, is a wife and mother of five children. She is in her late fifties and lives on Long Island, New York. The story of her heavenly visitations goes back to the year 1968 when St. Theresa started appearing to her and giving her poems and sacred writings by dictation. Prior to this, Veronica had not received any manifestations from Heaven.

Our Lady Herself appeared to Veronica in her home on April 7, 1970, informing her that She would appear on the grounds of the old St. Robert Bellarmine Church in Bayside on June 18, 1970, that vigils of prayer be held there, and that full directions be given to the clergy of the parish to prepare for Our Lady's first visit there. Our Lady also requested that a Shrine and Basilica be erected on this Her chosen Sacred Site, which is to be named "Our Lady of the Roses, Mary Help of Mothers". She promised to come on the eve of the great feast days of the Church, which dates would be given to Veronica beforehand. The Blessed Mother also instructed Veronica to disseminate the Messages given to her throughout the whole world.

Our Lady has requested that the Rosary be recited aloud by the crowd during the whole of the Vigil. All are requested to kneel in the presence of Jesus. The Message is repeated word for word by Veronica. Veronica also describes what she sees. All is recorded by tape.

Veronica—I was startled to see the lights, the blue lights, coming out from among the trees. And there are two—you could explain them as being, like ball in shape; it is very difficult...round. And these lights—in human language I would find it very difficult to explain to you the beauty of them and where they came from. Well, strictly from Heaven because it is a miracle in itself to see these lights—which have been caught on camera, too—coming from the sky and branching outward. Now that is the usual call mark for us to know that Jesus and Our Lady are approaching.

And now just above Our Lady's statue, about fifteen

Veronica in ecstasy at this same Vigil of March 26, 1983.

the sign of the cross—She's extending it forward, like this: In the name of the Father, and of the Son, and of the Holy Ghost.

Now Our Lady is moving over. She had floated. She's not walking; Jesus and Our Lady both float. It's

standing at Our Lady's left side; Our Lady's now by His right side. And Our Lady is looking up. And Jesus now is looking all about Him. He has on His burgundy cape. And it's down from His back—I can see Jesus' hair—and the cape is extending down to His footsteps, down to His feet.

Now, Jesus is now taking His hand out, like this, and making the sign of the cross: In the name of the Father, and of the Son, and of the Holy Ghost. Now Jesus also is turning to His left, our right side, and making the sign of the cross: In the name of the Father, and of the Son, and of the Holy Ghost.

Now He's moved over. He's floated over a bit to the uppermost branch on our right side of the trees. And now He's turning and going back to standing next to Our Lady—oh, about—now They're about—I can't judge the distance through the sky, but I would say They're standing about sixteen feet above Our Lady's statue.

Now Jesus is taking His first finger and placing it to His mouth; that means to listen and repeat.

Jesus—"My child, I will not continue the discourse at this time over the matter of obedience, charity, and other virtues that have dimmed the working force within the circle. You must pray more. And do not allow yourselves to falter in bringing out the Message to the world because of slight differences of opinion and others that send you like rabbits scurrying here and there, and bringing nothing back.

"My child and My children, as I told you in My

---

20. The messages from Jesus and Mary communicated to Veronica Lueken are transcribed and disseminated through an assortment of print and electronic media; this tract (dated March 26, 1983) contains a message from Jesus that expresses a recurring theme in the Bayside apparitions despite the end of the Cold War—the imminence of a nuclear attack on the United States by communist forces. (Courtesy of Our Lady of the Roses, Mary Help of Mothers Shrine.)

21. Photo of Exterminatus. This photograph is believed by some Baysiders to be a miraculous picture of "Exterminatus, the angel of death," a skull-faced figure on horseback brandishing a sickle who will soon claim those who are not in a state of grace. (Courtesy of Our Lady of the Roses, Mary Help of Mothers Shrine.)

22. Take Cover. As a part of school routine in the 1950s and 1960s, duck-and-cover drills offered a sense of protection from the uncontrollable and ever-present nuclear threat; here, second grade children practice taking cover in the event of a surprise attack by the Soviets. (Photo by Sondak, courtesy of FPG International Corp.)

23. Soon after the detonation of the first atomic bombs, the word *atomic* was used by hundreds of businesses to promote an assortment of products and services marketed as modern, powerful, or scientifically advanced. Atomic Fire Ball candy, first released in 1954 by the Ferrara Pan Candy Company and still sold today, transforms the terror of the atomic bomb into the jawbreaker "with the red hot flavor." A more cynically apocalyptic commercial use of the image of the mushroom cloud occurred in 1985 when Topps Chewing Gum, Inc. issued Garbage Pail Kid trading cards, the trademark for which was an image of "Adam Bomb" pressing a button on a remote control device as a mushroom cloud explodes out of the top of his head. (From the Ferrara Pan Candy Company and Topps Chewing Gum, Inc.)

24. Doomsayers holding signs pronouncing the end of the world have been frequent objects of caricature and mockery, but Gahan Wilson's gallows humor goes one step further in this illustration of the earth in pieces and an endtimes sign in space. (Reproduced by special permission of *Playboy* magazine; copyright © 1961 by *Playboy*.)

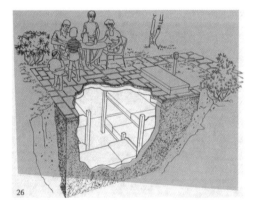

25. This illustration of a family fallout shelter beneath a patio, from a pamphlet issued by the Civil Defense Preparedness Agency in 1977, depicts the perpetual threat of imminent nuclear catastrophe underlying everyday life and leisure during the Cold War era. (From *Protection in the Nuclear Age*.)

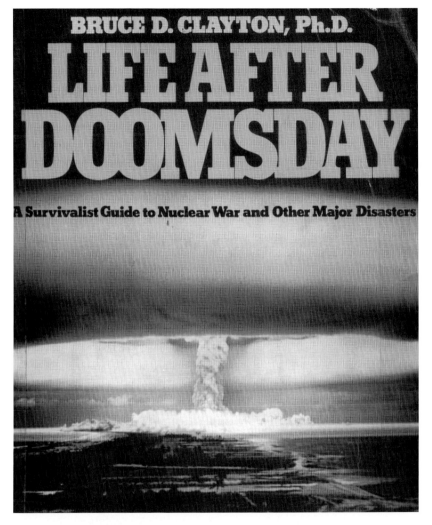

BRUCE D. CLAYTON, Ph.D.

LIFE AFTER DOOMSDAY

A Survivalist Guide to Nuclear War and Other Major Disasters

26. Survivalist publications during the Cold War era directly addressed nuclear apocalyptic fears, exemplified by this cover of *Life after Doomsday*, a guide for preparing for and surviving nuclear war and various other cataclysms. (Courtesy of Paladin Press.)

27. Images of mushroom clouds were ubiquitous in early punk fanzines, reflecting nuclear apocalyptic fears and the idea of "no future," illustrated here by a modified version of Edvard Munch's *The Scream.* (From the cover of *Fallout* fanzine.)

28. This illustration from a sixteenth-century German broadsheet depicts strange objects sighted in the sky over the city of Nuremburg on April 14, 1561, which were interpreted at the time as apocalyptic warnings from God; today various UFO enthusiasts consider accounts of this medieval aerial spectacle to be evidence of flying saucers in the Middle Ages. (From the collection of the Zentralbibliothek, Zürich.)

29. The Space Brothers Want You to Survive Doomsday. This advertisement for the book *Psychic & UFO Revelations in the Last Days* depicts a UFO evacuation of the "chosen ones" prior to worldly catastrophe, a scenario that resembles Christian Rapture beliefs about planetary escape prior to the tribulation period. (Courtesy of Inner Light Publications.)

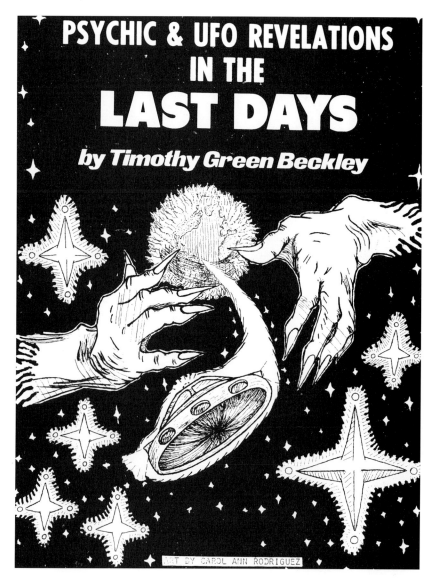

PSYCHIC & UFO REVELATIONS
IN THE
LAST DAYS
by Timothy Green Beckley

ART BY CAROL ANN RODRIGUEZ

30. The sense of cosmic fate controlling earth's final days is conveyed by this cover of *Psychic & UFO Revelations in the Last Days* which depicts the earth engulfed in flames as an escaping UFO slips through the sinister looking hands of some interstellar entity. (Courtesy of Inner Light Publications.)

31. At the beginning of the atomic age, UFO contactees described the Space People as beautiful, benevolent, and human-like in appearance. According to early encounter narratives, these angelic beings, frequently depicted in jumpsuits with flowing, shoulder-length hair, had come from utopian planets in an attempt to save humanity from destroying itself. (From *The Book of Spaceships and Their Relationship with Earth.*)

32. In this syncretism of Christian and UFO symbolism, Jesus Christ is portrayed as a Space Being in an astronaut-like jumpsuit. (From "Angeles ayer extraterrestres hoy," by La Asociacion Adonai para la Fraternidad Cosmica Desojo.)

33. George Adamski, the first person to claim direct contact with space beings (in the California desert on November 20, 1952), poses with a painting of a Space Brother. Although Adamski's encounter narrative has been dismissed as a hoax by some ufologists, its emphasis on the dangers of atomic weapons influenced subsequent contactee accounts in the 1950s and 1960s. (Courtesy of *UFO Magazine*.)

34. Members of the Aetherius Society charge a spiritual battery with "prayer power"; Aetherians believe that this spiritual energy may be discharged in the future during times of crisis to avert worldly cataclysms. (Photograph by Douglas Curran, from *In Advance of the Landing*.)

35. Ruth Norman, known as Uriel by students of the Unarius Academy of Science, stands beside a hand-crafted replica of STARCENTER ONE, consisting of a tower of UFOs from each of the planets of the Interplanetary Confederation. Unariuns believe that these starships will land on earth in the year 2001 and interlock to form a two-mile-high "college of cosmic wisdom," the interplanetary inhabitants of which will lead humanity into a golden age of peace and prosperity. (Courtesy of the Unarius Academy of Science.)

36. A persistent belief in the UFO faith is that extraterrestrials are monitoring the development and use of nuclear weapons on earth and that they either will intervene to prevent worldly destruction or rescue a chosen few prior to global annihilation. (Illustration by Jefferson R. Weekley, courtesy of *UFO Magazine*.)

37. A depiction of an alien abduction, illustrating the aliens' ability to pass through matter and abduct victims anywhere and at any time against their will. (Illustration courtesy of Darryl Anka, from *Beyond My Wildest Dreams: Diary of a UFO Abductee*.)

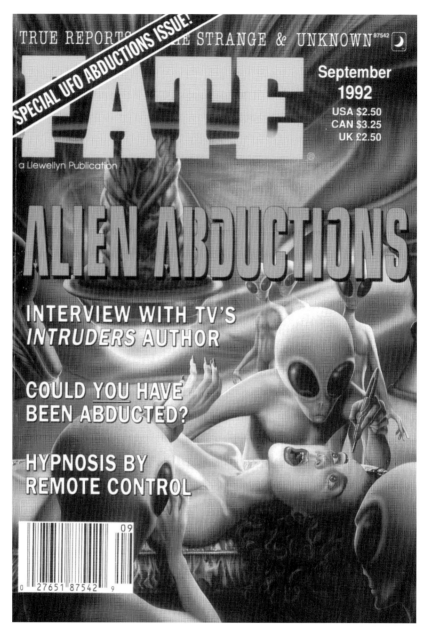

39. Some alien abductees assert that extraterrestrials are engaged in a process of genetic engineering and are interbreeding with human beings and then later removing the hybrid fetuses in order to ensure the survival of the human race prior to worldly cataclysm. (Illustration courtesy of Darryl Anka, from *Beyond My Wildest Dreams: Diary of a UFO Abductee.*)

40. An artist's depiction of alien/human hybridization—and a representation of the continuation and evolution of the human experiment in the form of a genetically transformed and transhuman offspring—from the cover of Kim Carlsberg's book *Beyond My Wildest Dreams: Diary of a UFO Abductee* (1995). (Illustration courtesy of Darryl Anka.)

41. Like angels, extraterrestrials are depicted in some accounts as otherworldly beings with omnipotent powers who have intervened to save the lives of people, in some cases curing them of AIDS, cancer, and other illnesses. In this illustration, benevolent ETs are shown using crystals to heal a terminally ill woman. (From *UFO Universe*.)

42. God or Extraterrestrial? This illustration accompanies an article in a UFO magazine that discusses some of the attributes of benevolent and malevolent extraterrestrials. Unlike the Space Beings in the early flying saucer faith who generally were de-picted as benevolent and often Christ-like, recent UFO beliefs and encounters increasingly have asserted that some aliens are amoral or sinister entities with an evil plan for world domination. The caption alongside this illustration warns, "Beware of any extraterrestrials or entities who say they are your creators or who put down Jesus or God." (From *International UFO Library*.)

43. With the advent of World Wide Web sites and Internet forums, the communication of apocalyptic beliefs is being transformed by new technologies, satirized in this caricature of a stereotypical doomsayer holding an endtimes sign with a World Wide Web–site address. (Drawing by Robb Armstrong; copyright 1996. Courtesy of The *New Yorker* Magazine, Inc.)

assault, you know. What the kids want is World War III, and we're giving it to them" (Selzer 1979:119).

Although feelings of despair and anomie have been expressed by members of numerous youth groups, many punks elevated the idea of personal and societal negation to an aesthetic. The names of various punk bands illustrate this emphasis on destruction, futility, and decay: The Last; Damned; Damage; U.K. Decay; Dead Kennedys; Living Abortions; Null and Void; Suicidal Tendencies; Dead Boys; Wasted Youth; Rotters. The pseudonyms that punks often assumed emphasized the same themes, as well as self-effacement, parody, and the absurd: Johnny Rotten; Sid Vicious; Lorna Doom; Jello Biafra; Adam Bomb; Steve Havoc; Rat Scabies; Tequila Mockingbird; Alan Suicide; Phester Swollen.

The pessimistic and apocalyptic roots of punk music and aesthetics can be traced to earlier influences of musicians such as Lou Reed and the Velvet Underground, Iggy Pop, Patti Smith, Richard Hell, the New York Dolls, and the Ramones. In addition to celebrating street life, urban decay, and social outcasts, these musicians frequently expressed pessimistic, fatalistic, and apocalyptic sentiments. The abusive and destructive aspects of these punk predecessors are exemplified by Iggy Pop, who cut himself with broken glass during performances while he harassed and spit on his audiences. In his well-known song "Search and Destroy" (1973) he screams, "I'm the runaway son of the nuclear A-bomb / I am the world's forgotten boy / The one who searches and destroys." The association of nuclear weapons and the threat of global annihilation with images of personal or societal destruction is a recurring theme in punk and protopunk lyrics. Another source of punk doomsday imagery was reggae music, which is inspired by the millenarian beliefs of Rastafarianism, with its prophecies about the destruction of Babylon (identified variously as white colonialism, oppression, and capitalism). The music of David Bowie, who frequently addressed the theme of societal destruction and decay, also served as an inspiration for early punk apocalypticism. On his album *The Man Who Sold the World* (1970), Bowie sings, "The world is doomed / We can't make it any better"; and the predominant theme of the albums *The Rise and Fall of Ziggy Stardust and the Spiders from Mars* (1972) and *Aladdin Sane* (1973) is that of an alien who visits the earth, which is teetering on self-destruction. As Patricia Henry notes, "Punk rockers embraced Bowie's interests in gender ambiguity and doomsday imagery, while rejecting what they perceived as a distasteful interest in commercial appeal and monetary gain" (1989:36–37).

Punk lyrics about nuclear doomsday are blunt and explicit, and usually accompanied by extremely loud and fast music; sometimes the lyrics are screamed; occasionally they are spoken with sarcasm or remorse. For instance, in the song "Random Relations" (1981), the lead singer of The Suspects sings slowly and fatalistically:

> I'm living in a world I really hate
> What can I can do?
> Reluctantly I take the bait
> Just like you. . . .
> We've been threatened with a terrible death
> Nuclear war. . . .
> There ain't no fallout shelter,
> No food to eat
> We'll have to take our chances
> With the shriveling flesh on the street.

Punk lyrics about doomsday are generally characterized by themes of total helplessness and despair. In some songs the lyrics are nearly unintelligible; however, the sense of inevitable doom is clear. In the song "4 Minute Warning" by U.K. Chaos (1982), the only comprehensible words, screamed at regular intervals, are "Hiroshima is here again! / Hiroshima is here again! / Four minute warning! / Four minute warning!" In "When the Last Day Comes" by The Insane (1982), the lyrics are mostly incomprehensible, but the song ends with sound effects simulating a nuclear explosion.

Graphic depictions of nuclear catastrophe are also common, narrated as if the bomb had just been dropped, and often detailing the gruesome aftereffects of a nuclear attack:

> I saw a blinding flash of light
> I felt the heat burn through my bones
> A giant mushroom in the sky
> The smell of burning human flesh
> The people scream in agony
> I stumble blindly through the heat
> Memories of life before. . . . (St. Vitus
> Dancers; "The Survivor," no date)

The gritty descriptions that frequently characterize punk visions of nuclear destruction are often provided by a dying punk survivor wandering through the radioactive rubble, who comments on the meaninglessness of apocalypse and condemns politicians. The image of the punk apocalyptic survivor is exemplified in one strip from the comic "Jimbo," by Gary Panter, in which the protagonist, a punk Everyman preoccupied with fears of nuclear annihilation, survives an atomic explosion and runs barefoot and on fire through a burning, decimated city (Panter 1988). The band Vice Squad, in their song "Last Rockers" (1982), provides a comparable vision of nuclear doom:

> Stepping through the rubble
> My head's in a spin
> I hear them fighting the war
> No one can win
> I'm too young to die
> It's too late to live
> As politicians do the thing
> No God can forgive. . . .
> The time has come for us to die
> No memories left to cry
> No chance of a rebirth
> For the last rockers on earth. . . .
> Our job here is to remind
> A day may come in future time
> For we who fought on city streets
> And perished in atomic heat.

Whether consisting of angry or sarcastic statements, or candid, personal reflections that reveal individual fears about nuclear annihilation, punk lyrics often emphasize the destructive power of uncontrollable technology and depict the government as the immoral agent of doomsday. A fatalistic endorsement of nuclear annihilation is expressed in the Passion Killers' "Start Again" (no date):

> Nuclear forces out of control
> Let's start again
> Let's start again
> All buried down in an A-bomb hole
> Let's start again
> Let's start again. . . .
> Nothin's left, not a single soul
> Let's start again
> Let's start again.

In its simplicity, this punk rant epitomizes attitudes about the threat of nuclear apocalypse—feelings of helplessness, pessimism, gallows humor, and perhaps even a yearning for the End and a new beginning.

Numerous other songs, such as Mutual Assured Destruction's "Holocaust," Nick Cave's "City of Refuge," the Minutemen's "Dream Told by Moto," Crucifix's "Annihilation," Elvis Costello's "Hurry Down, Doomsday (The Bugs Are Taking Over)," and the Crass's "Where Next Columbus?" express apocalyptic themes, describing the destructive capabilities of technology and various doomsday scenarios. In songs like Elvis Costello's "Waiting for the End of the World," Fishbone's "Party at Ground Zero," and R.E.M.'s cheerful "It's the End of the World as We Know It (and I Feel Fine)," the doomsday theme becomes a metaphor for other concerns and topics or is subordinate to other ideas. Punk expectations of doomsday are most often associated with nuclear apocalypse and resemble other contemporary secular visions that regard the End as an absurd event brought about by human ignorance, violence, or accident.

In addition to punk song lyrics and rhetoric, themes of worldly destruction also pervade punk art, album covers, posters, fliers, and fanzine illustrations. Images of demolished cities with punks, mutants, or punk skeletons with mohawk hairstyles wandering through the rubble are common, as are images of nuclear annihilation. For example, artist Winston Smith modified Edvard Munch's woodcut *The Scream* for the cover of *Fallout* fanzine, drawing a mushroom cloud behind the shrieking skeletal figure (*Fallout*, no date, issue 3). The depictions of mushroom clouds scattered throughout punk publications acquired an iconic quality; some were accompanied by nihilistic, gallows humor captions such as "SUPPORT NUCLEAR ANNIHILATION!" or "GOD Listens . . . PRAY FOR NUCLEAR ANNIHILATION" (*NO MAG*, "Close-ups' 83" issue, 1983, 15, 20).

Certain aspects of punk body adornment also may be interpreted as symbolic expressions of feelings about personal and societal doom. Some punks explicitly dressed like irradiated survivors of a nuclear catastrophe; others, pale and emaciated, resembling zombies or corpses, presented themselves as symbols of death or physical ailment, portraits of a diseased society that reflected the idea of futurelessness. Adorned in torn and tattered clothing, early punks decorated themselves with emblems and debris that signified depravity, doom, and decay (e.g., images of death, garbage, sexual fetishistic objects, swastikas). Hair was shaved in patches; the body pierced, mutilated, scarred, tattooed, tied with bondage wear, or smeared with fake blood. Makeup was used to give an impression of lifelessness, with lips painted in colors associated with death—black, dark brown, or gray-purple. The overall impression, as one ex-punk stated, was "kinda mealy looking—you know, kinda dead, like after World War III—the walking dead." Punk style was rife with images of death, destruction, and futility, with punks expressing their alienation through communal rituals of symbolic negation and personal acts of self-abuse. Presenting themselves as symbols of a disintegrating and doomed society, punks enacted their own drama of societal cataclysm, creating the overall impression that they were sacrificing their bodies on the altar of postmodern despair (Wojcik 1995:7–20).

Although images of nuclear apocalypse pervade punk music, literature, art, and adornment to an extent unprecedented in previous youth subcultures, punk feelings about nuclear war may in fact be fairly representative of nuclear anxieties among contemporary youth. As research on fears of nuclear war among children and adolescents has indicated, a sense of fatalism, hopelessness, and resignation about the inevitability of nuclear war seems to be extremely pervasive among young people (Mack 1982). For instance, in a study that surveyed the attitudes of 1,424 adolescents, 82 percent believed that civilization would be destroyed in their lifetimes (Blackwell and Gessner 1983). Another study, mentioned previously, revealed that more than 33 percent of seventeen thousand high school seniors surveyed said they feared that nuclear or biological annihilation would be the fate of humankind within their lifetimes (La Farge 1987:27–28). A survey of the literature on children's fears of nuclear war concludes that "over the past 25 years, separate surveys of children and adolescents in varying locales have repeatedly indicated that children are expressing emotional distress related to the threat of nuclear war. Themes of fear, powerlessness, resignation, hopelessness, and despair are present to some extent in all samples" (Duncan et al. 1986:33). In another study, involving interviews with children from 1961 to 1982 about their thoughts on nuclear war, it was found that the primary means of coping with nuclear war anxieties was by denying the existence of the threat (Schwebel 1982:610), a response that supports Lifton's hypothesis about pervasive psychological numbing associated with the thought of nuclear war. The study also states, however, that those who did think about the possibility of nuclear war generally felt powerless and helpless, with some expressing feelings of bitter resentment and a sense of betrayal toward adults for bringing about a world with nuclear weapons (Schwebel 1982, cited in Duncan et al. 1986:30).

The sense of resentment, betrayal, anger, and helplessness associated with the threat of nuclear war is clearly expressed in the early punk subculture. Punks, in general, did not appear to be desensitized to nuclear fears but through their rhetoric and style often evoked graphic images of nuclear apocalypse, confronting the terror of the bomb directly. The grassroots, participatory, and noncommercial nature of the punk subculture allowed for the articulation of diverse ideas and concerns, particularly apocalyptic ones, that might not otherwise be expressed in dominant discourses.

Although any punks embraced the imagery and rhetoric of societal destruction, for others, apocalyptic themes were simply an expression of punk style, a fashion statement, a way to shock, or a means of articulating a sense of nihilism or anger. When I asked one ex-punk if the punk movement expressed ideas about the end of the world, he replied, "We didn't really talk about it that much, but there was the general attitude of 'Who cares? Everything's fucked and it'll probably get worse.'" Another ex-punk stated, "I would say, *definitely*, punk was apocalyptic. The bomb, the feeling that there was no future, no opportunities. But there were other things too—a lot of political ideas being thrown around." Another individual replied, "Some of it is [apocalyptic], but more nihilistic really. But punk was also a way to shock society, to wake up a dead society, show people how bad it is, that maybe everything's not all right." For some punks, then, the metaphor of apocalypse was adopted as a means of expressing a sense of social rebellion and societal dissatisfaction, as well as general feelings of fatalism and futurelessness.

Many of the ex-punks I spoke with stated that the punk worldview was characterized by its pervasive emphasis on destruction, epitomized, according to several individuals, by the lyrics of the song "Anarchy in the U.K." (1976), by the Sex Pistols:

> I am an antichrist
> I am an anarchist
> Don't know what I want,
> But I know how to get it
> I wanna destroy passers-by
>
> 'Cos I wanna be
> Anarchy. . . .
> Destroy. . . .

When I asked about the meaning of this emphasis on destruction, one ex-punk responded that it had no "meaning": "It was just destruction for destruction's sake." Another stated: "Punk was revolutionary in a way, but punk really didn't have a plan—just mindless anarchy—we just wanted to destroy everything."

This emphasis on "destruction"—personal destruction, societal destruction, the destruction of all dominant discourses—reveals the apocalyptic themes in punk. Having no political and economic power, and believing that they had no possibilities for improving their situation, many punks regarded their own lives as "doomed" and "fated." The punk emphasis on destruction and futurelessness seems to be an extension of feelings of personal helplessness, anger, and a desire for the obliteration of an unjust society that punks felt had condemned them from birth. In this regard, the punk worldview bears some resemblance to the ideas of religious apocalypticists who express a contempt for society, reject the achievements of the modern world, regard the current social order as corrupt and unredeemable, and feel that the present world will be, or must be, destroyed. A shared sense of powerlessness and fatalism is integral to these visions of imminent societal destruction, in addition to the desire for an end to the suffering associated with a debased and evil world.

Although punk rhetoric calls for the destruction of a corrupt and bankrupt society, the punk Day of Judgment is not formulated as part of a coherent eschatology, and punks generally had no articulated plans for a redemptive new realm to replace a world destroyed. Devoid of the promise of societal redemption, punk ideas about the future often were both fatalistic and nihilistic, characterized by a sense of meaninglessness and doom.

The apocalyptic rhetoric that pervades the punk subculture and the other ideas and images about doomsday discussed in this chapter depict societal destruction as inevitable and offer little hope for the salvation of humanity. These secular doomsday visions are a radical departure from traditional apocalyptic beliefs and narratives that offer some promise of human survival, redemption, or worldly transformation. Although recent secular doomsday speculation may share themes with religious apocalyptic views, such as the wickedness and unrecuperability of humanity, it differs in its emphasis on the meaninglessness of doomsday brought about by destructive technology and human ignorance. The senselessness and absurdity of worldly annihilation is expressed repeatedly in secular doomsday thought—whether in the punk culture, in gallows humor of numerous authors and artists, in films such as *Dr. Strangelove* and *On the Beach*, or in popular jokes about the bomb.

Interpretations of worldly destruction as meaningful or meaningless are determined by the ways that individuals attribute causality in their explanations for the apocalypse. For example, nuclear weapons, famine, and environmental disaster, identified by dispensationalists as divinely determined signs that reveal God's foreordained plan, are considered by secular apocalypticists to be the causes, not the signs, of a meaningless End brought about by human beings. Although much secular speculation about worldly destruction is not fatalistic and postulates that people can prevent predicted cataclysms, many secularists do agree with their religious counterparts in their pessimistic evaluation of the present, the unrecuperable state of the human condition, and the sense that human beings are powerless to alter the fate of the world. Attributing no meaning to worldly destruction, secular visions of the End are pervaded by images of the helplessness of human beings and their manipulation by larger, determining forces (the government, multinational corporations, the bomb).

Survivalism is an exception to this view of human powerlessness in the face of inevitable apocalypse. Rather than feelings of helplessness, survivalists seek a sense of personal control and self-salvation by preparing to endure anticipated cataclysms, perhaps even harboring the expectation of worldly renewal following the catastrophes. Survivalists, however, are atypical among secularists in their expectations of living through an apocalyptic scenario. Ideas about the unalterable destruction of the world, when lacking the mythic component of worldly renewal and the belief in divine control, ultimately may be expressed as a form of nihilistic fatalism. The next chapter further explores the nature of fatalism and its role in contemporary apocalyptic thought, and suggests reasons for the persistence and continued appeal of apocalyptic belief and behavior.

6

Fatalism and Apocalyptic Beliefs

As noted in chapter 1, relatively few comparative studies of contemporary American apocalyptic beliefs and behavior have been undertaken. However, numerous studies exist that analyze and compare such beliefs historically and in other cultures, with many of the best-known and most influential theoretical works focusing on non-Western societies. These studies offer assorted typologies and interpretations of millenarian movements, identified variously as "nativistic" (Linton 1943), "revitalistic" (Wallace 1956), "messianic" (Lanternari 1963), "crisis cults" (LaBarre 1971), and "cargo cults" (Cochrane 1979; Jarvie 1977; Worsley 1957). In general, millenarian movements have been interpreted as responses to societal crises, the disintegration of previous ways of life, cultural conflict, and colonialism. The phenomenon of the cargo cult, for instance, exemplifies a millenarian response resulting from the cultural crisis caused by colonialism and the exposure of indigenous peoples in Melanesia to the material goods of Western societies.

Predicting that supernatural forces would one day deliver an abundance of Western goods in the form of a ship's cargo, members of cargo cults believed that their ancestors, deities, or local heroes would return to destroy their Western oppressors and initiate a terrestrial paradise free of injustice, illness, and death (Worsley 1957). Cargo cults and other millenarian movements frequently have been explained in terms of the concept of "relative deprivation," which may occur among people who feel that they are being denied specific material, social, and symbolic benefits (Aberle 1970:209). The sense of deprivation resulting from the exclusion from certain benefits is said to motivate people to anticipate and prepare for another, more perfect world, a supernaturally created ideal age that will remedy current inequities.

In addition to the many analyses of millenarian movements in non-Western cultures, numerous studies focus on apocalyptic groups that have arisen in Western societies in the past.[1] Similar to anthropological approaches, many of these works conceptualize ideas about the end of the world in terms of millenarian responses resulting from cultural crisis, conflict, and a sense of deprivation, and often occurring among the disenfranchised, the marginalized, and the oppressed. In his influential *The Pursuit of the Millennium*, for instance, Norman Cohn (1970 [1957]) asserts that millenarianism has been a persistent and highly adaptable worldview in Western civilization, and he shows that medieval revolutionary millenarian movements arose during times of social upheaval and turmoil among the poor and marginalized masses. According to Michael Barkun, millenarian movements "almost always occur in times of upheaval, in the wake of cultural contact, economic dislocation, revolution, war, and natural catastrophe" (1974:45). After surveying selected studies of apocalyptic ideas, Barry Brummett concludes that "scholars are agreed that apocalyptic stems from a sense of unexplained and inexplicable change or crisis, from a sense that received systems of explanations have failed, and from a resulting sense of anomie, disorientation, lawlessness, and impending chaos" (1991:23). Anthony Wallace (1956) refers to the experience of prolonged societal crisis and individual stress as a "period of cultural distortion," which he says is characterized by the perceived breakdown of previous meaning systems, and subsequent feelings of disillusionment, meaninglessness, anxiety, and apathy.

Conceptualizing apocalyptic beliefs as fatalistic seems to support these previous interpretations, which have shown that perceptions of societal upheaval, crisis, and disintegration frequently precipitate feelings of powerlessness, anomie, and anxiety. Scholars from varied disciplines agree that such feelings often cause people to interpret events and experiences fatalistically (see Doob 1988; Grunig 1971; Nielsen 1975). Communications studies researchers Everett Rogers and Lynne Svenning, for instance, describe fatalism as "the degree to which an individual perceives a lack of ability to control his future. Hence fatalism is a sort of generalized sense of powerlessness, one of the five dimensions of alienation" (1969:273). Folklorist Åke Ström makes a similar assertion, noting that "trends in modern psychology have appeared to give scientific sanction to certain ideas of fate: What we call fate is the totality of those psychological mechanisms against which we feel ourselves powerless" (1967:78). Fatalistic beliefs and behavior, as these and other researchers have suggested, are associated with feelings of helplessness and alienation, especially as these are related to perceptions of unmanageable societal crises and the belief that events cannot be controlled by one's own actions.

The concept of "locus of control," used by psychologists to study the sense of control that individuals feel over their environment, is particularly useful for an understanding of the fatalistic aspects of apocalyptic beliefs. This concept is used to identify the ways that people interpret events, as either determined and controlled by one's own efforts ("internal locus of control") or externally determined by forces outside of oneself ("external locus of control") (Rotter 1966:1). Fatalistic beliefs exemplify the notion of an external locus of control because such beliefs are characterized by the assertion that outside forces beyond one's control determine the outcome of events. In contrast, so-called magical beliefs, in which human action is believed to cause a specific outcome, reveal an internal locus of control. Certain experiences, especially tragedies and disasters, and situations of great concern, uncertainty, or threat often motivate people to attribute causality to external forces, whether God's will, the devil, fate, the government, one's parents, or the configuration of the planets at birth (Doob 1988:20–29). Extraordinary or extremely fortuitous events may also prompt individuals to attribute the outcome of events to external sources. Although people use both externally and internally directed orientations to interpret the world, individuals may emphasize one orientation over the other, depending on previous experiences, personal characteristics, and context (Spilka et al. 1985:21–26).

The concept of "learned helplessness," which is related to the notion of external locus of control, also is helpful in examining both fatalistic and apocalyptic belief and behavior. The term was coined by Martin Seligman (1975), who, in a classic operant conditioning experiment, found that dogs exposed to inescapable shock learned that their responses did not diminish the negative stimuli; as a result they "learned to be helpless" and were unable to learn to escape in later experiments. Learned helplessness in humans is frequently associated with anxiety, depression, and alienation and is characterized by the perception that events and outcomes are considered to be uncontrollable and that all responses are futile (Abramson, Garber, and Seligman 1980:4).

Feelings of helplessness, defined by one researcher as "a perceived inability to affect one's fate meaningfully" (Lefcourt 1976:21), are characterized not only by a sense of uncontrollability but by uncertainty and apprehension. Yet all people seek, to some degree, a sense of control, certainty, predictability, and inevitability. As Leonard Doob has stated, "The quest for inevitability is a basic, conscious activity that is unavoidable and hence inevitable. . . . We cannot plan, we cannot avoid danger, we cannot achieve goals unless some uncertainty is removed and replaced with inevitability" (1988:124). Fatalistic modes of thought provide a framework for interpreting events otherwise considered to be haphazard, uncontrollable, or incomprehensible, reducing uncertainty and offering a sense of control and meaningful explanations for situations in which personal action is believed to be futile. As assertions about the inevitability of important life events, fatalistic beliefs are a pervasive means by which people cognitively structure their experiences and attempt to make sense of that which appears uncontrollable. Although fatalistic beliefs are often ascribed in retrospect to explain events that appear beyond mere accident or chance, such beliefs may also involve the projection of a fated plan into the future, with anticipated events attributed to external causes. Apocalyptic ideas exemplify this latter, future-oriented form of fatalistic thinking.

The underlying fatalism that characterizes the apocalyptic beliefs, behaviors, images, and rhetoric examined in this study is directly related to perceptions of uncontrollable societal crisis and inevitable disaster. Contemporary society is depicted as being in a state of upheaval or disintegration, with the current turmoil attributed to an assortment of unmanageable factors. Hal Lindsey, for instance, asks his readers, "Has there ever been a time when the potential for self-destruction was as great as it is today?" (1973:89–90) and then provides them with inventories of unprecedented crises: wars, revolutions, political tensions, pollution, disease, famine, crime, drugs, lawlessness, the destruction of the family, and the threat of nuclear war (1980:xi–xii; 1984:65). Lindsey, Lueken, and other religious apocalypticists attribute these current calamities to liberalism, secularization, and the evils of the modern world, but ultimately regard these crises as a meaningful part of God's endtimes scenario. Secular apocalyptic speculation is pervaded by a similar sense of societal crisis, with the causes of the current predicament identified variously as the threat of nuclear war, economic collapse, environmental destruction, disease, famine, and increasing lawlessness. Although these imminent disasters are explained in terms of human ignorance, violence, exploitation, and the misuse of technology rather than as part of a divine plan, they nonetheless tend to be regarded as inevitable and determined by forces beyond one's control.

Fear of Nuclear Annihilation and Fatalism

The sense of powerlessness and fatalism associated with perceptions of imminent societal cataclysm is most clearly and persistently expressed by beliefs about nuclear annihilation. Various researchers have noted the relationship between apocalyptic ideas and fears of nuclear war, but few have explored the inherent fatalism in such ideas. The predictions of nuclear annihilation by religious apocalypticists and widespread secular fears associated with the thought of nuclear warfare are characterized by a sense of helplessness and inevitability. Popular endtimes thought rarely conceptualizes nuclear destruction as a "tactical" or limited war, assuming instead that such an event will be uncontrollable and total in its devastation. This view is typified by the statement of survivalist Bruce Clayton: "The long term effect which a full-scale nuclear war will have on Western civilization is fairly easy to define. Western civilization as we know it will cease to exist" (1980:36). The total destruction of society is similarly predicted by Lindsey, who maintains that the final Battle of Armageddon will involve a nuclear conflagration, during which "every city in the world is going to be leveled" (1984:213). Lueken's prophecies also envision complete worldly destruction caused by nuclear war: "My child, look and weep with Me, for you are witnessing the total destruction that will come upon mankind in the Great War, your third World War" (*OLR Booklet* n.d.:2).

The prolonged effect of nuclear fears and Cold War tensions on people's lives has only recently been explored by scholars, who generally agree that the development of nuclear weapons has precipitated widespread perceptions of societal crisis, feelings of uncertainty about the future, and fears of imminent doom (see Boyer 1985; Lifton and Falk 1982; Weart 1988). E. P. Thompson sees the self-identity of many Americans and Soviets as having been conditioned by the tensions of the Cold War (1982:171), and Robert Jay Lifton asserts that the threat of nuclear warfare formed the "context" of life during the Cold War period, with the image of the bomb casting an ever-present "shadow that persistently intrudes upon our mental ecology" (Lifton and Falk 1982:3). As Paul Boyer demonstrates, nuclear weapons have fundamentally altered the basis of existence, and this sense of radical change and crisis was immediately evident and felt by people after the bombing of Hiroshima and Nagasaki: "Most such changes occur gradually; they are more discernible to historians than to the individuals living through them. The nuclear era was different. It burst upon the world with terrifying suddenness. From the earliest moments, the American people recognized that things would never be the same again" (1985:3–4).

The initial feelings of imminent crisis, fearfulness, and fatalism that arose at the dawn of the atomic age continue to pervade and influence American culture and consciousness today. Lifton, in particular, tells us that anxiety about nuclear destruction has generated new orientations toward concepts of history and time and motivated "a new wave of millennial imagery—of killing, dying, and destroying on a scale so great as to end the human narrative" (1979:3). He contends that the threat of nuclear annihilation also has radically changed perceptions about the continuity of life after individual death. Declaring that people need a sense of human continuity, or what he calls "symbolic immortality," to enable them to confront and transcend the reality of death, Lifton maintains that a sense of symbolic immortality is achieved in five general ways: biologically, through one's descendants and family; theologically, through belief in the survival of the "immortal soul" and an afterlife; creatively, through one's human influences, material creations, and contributions; through belief in nature and in its unending existence; and experientially, through belief that mortality can be transcended through ecstatic experiences (1987:10–27).

Images of nuclear annihilation and other impending catastrophes threaten or negate perceptions of all of the forms of symbolic immortality advanced by Lifton. Rather than a sense of human continuity, the nuclear age is characterized by images of extinction and widespread feelings of imminent and inevitable death, not only individual death but the death of all humanity. Although the imagery of extinction is associated primarily with nuclear annihilation, Lifton thinks that events such as the genocide committed by the Nazis in World War II, widespread famine, various nuclear accidents, and environmental disaster and depletion have altered perceptions of symbolic immortality as well (Lifton and Falk 1982:60–61; Lifton 1987:19). He states that individual responses to pervasive images and perceptions of extinction may include psychological avoidance, denial, death anxiety, and feelings of meaninglessness and radical futurelessness (Lifton and Falk 1982:1–11).

One of the most frequent psychological reactions to the threat of nuclear war is what Lifton calls "psychic numbing," a mental and behavioral response to painful or disturbing feelings caused by perceptions of overwhelming threat. Lifton (1967) coined the term to describe the psychological state of survivors of the bombing of Hiroshima who walked among the corpses and the dying and later stated that they felt no emotion. Psychic numbing may occur in situations characterized by a lack of control and a sense of complete helplessness; extreme examples of psychic numbing were the Muselmänner, or "walking corpses" of the Nazi concentration camps, who labored dispassionately with no apparent fear of death (Levi 1961:82).[2]

Psychic numbing, associated with thoughts of nuclear war, is characterized by a sense of apathy and futility, the purposeful denial of thought about the bomb, and the belief that one personally can do nothing to avert inescapable doom—from which resignation ensues ("Well, if it happens, it happens—and it will happen to all of us") as well as cynicism ("They'll drop it all right and it will be the end of all of us—that's the way people are, and that will be that!") (Lifton and Falk 1982:100–105, 10–11). This psychic numbing clearly appears to be a manifestation of fatalism. The fatalistic response to thoughts about the bomb is described in the following way by Gunther Anders: "What stuns and panics us at such moments is the realization not of the danger threatening us, but of the futility of our attempts to produce an adequate response to it. Having experienced this failure we usually relax and return shamefaced, irritated, or perhaps even relieved, to the human dimensions of our psychic life commensurable with our everyday surroundings" (1962:296). Confronted with the enormous destructive capabilities of nuclear weapons, feelings of helplessness and vulnerability are not "irrational" or "pathological" responses but appropriate and normal reactions (Lifton and Falk 1982:14).

Fatalistic thoughts about nuclear cataclysm are characterized by an external locus of control, associated not only with the unfathomable destructive power of the bomb but with the perception that nuclear technology is now unmanageable and beyond human control. Such thoughts about uncontrollability often result in a sense of complete powerlessness: "Compared to the bomb's infinite, mysterious killing power, we feel ourselves to be nothing—to be vulnerable creatures whose lives and very humanity can be snuffed out instantaneously. We feel ourselves to be unable to break out of the death-trap we know to be of our own making" (Lifton and Falk 1982:14). These behavioral responses and the pervasive public apathy concerning the threat of nuclear cataclysm indicate that fatalism is a dominant, if not the predominant, reaction to thoughts about the nuclear menace. The undercurrent of nuclear fatalism that has permeated American thought and culture for more than half a century continues to serve as a primary means of coping with feelings stemming from perceptions of nuclear war as uncontrollable and inevitable.

But the feelings of imminent disaster expressed by contemporary apocalypticists are also related to broader perceptions of societal turmoil. As Ira Chernus has noted, "The feeling of powerlessness and victimization, although intensified by nuclear weapons, was a dominant feature of the modern age before these weapons were invented. Mass culture, mass technology, and mass political movements—some leading to totalitarianism—all created an increasing sense that individuals counted for little and could do little to shape the circumstances of their lives" (1986:56). Numerous writers have described the twentieth century as a time of unprecedented change in technology and in social and cultural norms, as well as a time of a multitude of unrivaled crises. Lifton believes that the latter half of the century is a time of "psychohistorical dislocation," a crisis period caused by a sense of radical historical change, the breakdown of traditional meaning systems and symbols, the mass-media revolution, and the pervasive imagery of human extinction associated primarily with nuclear weapons (1987:16–23). D. S. Russell has compared the contemporary era to that of the years just prior to the life of Christ: "Each is an age of crisis—politically, socially, and religiously—when long established institutions and deeply rooted beliefs have come under severe attack, sometimes from within and at other times from an external source" (1968:5). Victor Turner, applying Arnold van Gennep's concept of liminality to transitional moments in human history, describes such times as being "betwixt and between" cultural periods that are characterized by heightened anxiety, ambiguity, and a sense of crisis (Turner 1969:94–113). Turner notes that liminal historical periods may evoke millenarian aspirations and scenarios, the imagery of which resembles a rite of passage, with similar themes of the destruction of the old condition, marginality and transition, and transformative rebirth involving the establishment of a new status or condition.

Perceptions of Evil and Fatalism

The relation between perceptions of severe societal crisis and fatalism is illustrated by the widespread view among apocalypticists that contemporary society is irreversibly evil. Beliefs about overwhelming evil and omnipresent satanic influences characteristic of much religious apocalyptic thought reveal feelings of powerlessness and a lack of faith in the effectiveness of human effort to remedy societal ills. Lueken proclaims, for instance, that the Virgin Mary's appearances in New York City are occurring because of the overwhelming evil in the world (*OLR Booklet* n.d.:i). Dispensationalists such as Lindsey declare that humans are powerless to save an unrecuperably evil world, with emphasis placed instead on personal salvation.

The conspiratorial view of the world that undergirds much apocalyptic thought also reveals the inherent fatalism of such ideas. Lindsey, Lueken, and many other apocalypticists attribute specific historical events and much human suffering to the machinations of a secret cabal of evil groups: the Freemasons, the Catholic Church, the Elders of Zion, the Trilateral Commission, the United Nations, the media, international bankers, communists, or secular humanists. The Bayside messages, for instance, ascribe the liberalizing changes in the Catholic Church that occurred during the Second Vatican Council to the infiltration of satanists who have obtained the highest hierarchical positions and are in league with various other demonic forces, including the communists, the Freemasons, the secular humanists, and the Illuminati—an alleged "Luciferian" secret society committed to the destruction of Christian principles that has been plotting to control the world since the

French Revolution. As noted previously, Lueken also asserts that Pope Paul VI was poisoned by agents of Satan and replaced by an imposter pope, hastening the evil infiltration and ensuring that the demonic changes would occur at the Second Vatican Council. Lindsey similarly attributes unfavorable events in world history to secret and powerful agencies, asserting that Satan is the mastermind behind the current corruption of society and that various organizations unknowingly may be part of Satan's evil plan: "I believe the Trilateralist movement is unwittingly setting the stage for the political-economic one-world system the Bible predicts for the last days. It's happening in concert with all the other pieces of the prophetic scenario described in this book. What the trilateralists are trying to establish will soon be controlled by the coming world leader—the anti-Christ himself" (1981:128).

These conspiratorial modes of thought view history as controlled by massive, demonic forces engaged in a cosmic struggle with the forces of good. According to Richard Hofstadter (1967), conspiratorial thinking is characterized by a "paranoid style," involving a rigid, dualistic view of the world, suspiciousness, and feelings of persecution. Hofstadter notes that although the paranoid style may be structurally similar to clinical paranoia, it differs in that these paranoid modes of thinking are part of shared systems of belief expressed by relatively normal people rather than private delusions (1967:4). Like apocalyptic worldviews, conspiracy theories offer explanations for perceived ills and the problem of evil in the world and similarly appear to be related to perceptions of crisis and fear of catastrophe (Hofstadter 1967:39). Apocalyptic conspiracy theories maintain that evil must inevitably proliferate in the end-times (epitomized by the Antichrist's reign) before it is ultimately defeated by supernatural forces at the time of the apocalypse. This fatalistic view of history and societal ills asserts that human beings are basically helpless against overpowering, sinister forces and that human effort is ineffectual in saving an increasingly evil and doomed world.

Secular apocalypticists also may embrace the belief that the current world is evil, corrupt, and unrecuperable by human effort. Thoughts about the possibility of nuclear annihilation, for example, may motivate such feelings, with nuclear weapons and nuclear destruction interpreted as manifestations of overwhelming and uncontrollable evil. (Catholic bishops, Methodist ministers, and other religious leaders have in fact labeled nuclear war "evil" in their attempts to prevent such an event [Lifton 1987:5].) Secular apocalyptic speculation is also rife with a sense of other types of evil in the world, attributable to various malevolent forces such as uncontrollable technology, bureaucracy, the military industrial complex, and big business, which ultimately will lead to the collapse of society. Many survivalists, for instance, are disillusioned with societal institutions and distrust the government, which they maintain is the primary cause of impending catastrophes. Survivalist Mel Tappan, who insists that government representatives have ruined the American economy, driven the country to bankruptcy, and periodically initiate wars in order to unite the country against a common enemy and delay imminent economic collapse, exemplifies this mistrust of the government (1981:3, 15). Some survivalists assert that the government has neglected to educate citizens about bomb shelters and civil defense issues and that it is not adequately prepared to handle large-scale disasters. Other survivalists maintain that society has been corrupted by many of the same evil forces identified by religious apocalypticists, such as a conspiracy of world communism, international bankers, Trilateralists, and other sinister groups. Secular apocalyptic interpretations of historical events and current problems as being part of an evil plan orchestrated by secret groups resemble the "paranoid style" endemic in much religious apocalypticism. Such thinking in both cases is characterized by an external locus of control, exemplified by the belief that societal corruption as been determined by clandestine, powerful, and uncontrollable forces. These beliefs reveal not only a sense of powerlessness and fatalism but also the profound alienation from contemporary society that is central to much apocalyptic thought.

Meaning, Divine Control, and the Apocalypse

Religious and secular apocalypticists may agree that the world is characterized by uncontrollable crisis, evil, and the threat of imminent disaster; however, they assign different meanings to the present turmoil. As noted, with the exception of some survivalists secular apocalyptic speculation is usually not marked by the belief that current crises are meaningful or that a "plan" underlies historical events. Predicted cataclysms such as nuclear annihilation, societal breakdown, economic collapse, or environmental disasters are regarded as meaningless events brought about by human ignorance, error, or corruption.

Religious interpretations of apocalypse are appealing precisely because of their insistence that events and history itself are fated, that a controlling and meaningful plan underlies all things. By placing current crises within a divine pattern, religious apocalyptic beliefs explicitly address feelings of helplessness and uncontrollability, converting them into an optimistic vision of worldly redemption and salvation. Such beliefs reinforce perceptions of inevitable and uncontrollable crises on the one hand, and simultaneously provide hope and comfort in the face of seemingly inexplicable events on the other. In this way, the inherently fatalistic attributes of apocalyptic worldviews reduce the anxiety and uncertainty evoked by perceptions of intractable crises and offer a sense of control and meaning. By obeying and advancing God's will as mandated by apocalyptic pronouncements, powerlessness and chaos are replaced with the assurance that everything is in "God's hands." Accepting God's will and acquiescing to God's plan is a means of participating in the power of the deity, as well as knowing the concealed fate of human history.

The sense of control, meaning, and order provided by apocalyptic worldviews is illustrated by interpretations of worldly disasters as part of God's plan. The significance of historical events is deciphered in relation to a supernaturally determined pattern, with current crises explained as part of a design that orders the universe. Dispensationalism demonstrates this fatalistic interpretation of phenomena, regarding recent events as signs that foretell the imminence of Christ's return (the proliferation of wars, earthquakes, famine, plagues, pollution, and drug use); as Lindsey states, "Even though many of these signs are appalling in themselves, their tremendous significance should gladden the heart of every true believer in Christ" (1984:65). Disasters and misfortunes, interpreted as preordained portents, promise imminent salvation and an end to suffering.

Apocalyptic belief systems provide fatalistic explanations for localized or personal tragedies as well, attributing these to pervasive satanic influences or God's plan for each human being. Every human life and human decision may thus be in accord with God's will or God's plan. In a discussion of the determining role of the Holy Spirit in people's lives, for instance, Lindsey remarks, "The Spirit assures you that you're right where God wants you to be and that He has you there for some tremendous purpose. You may not be able to see the future, but you *know* the One who holds it. God wants every believer to be under the control of the Spirit all the time" (1984:21). Personal suffering and worldly disasters may be inexplicable in scientific terms or attributable to random events or extremely complex factors, but apocalypticists' interpretations are clear and concise. Nonbelievers may consider these explanations intellectually insupportable, but such beliefs offer an appealing and inclusive structure of meaning and explanation for otherwise enigmatic events, assuring believers that matters are progressing as God planned.

The appeal of apocalypticism may also be attributable to the fact that such beliefs enhance the self-esteem of believers. Revelation of the secret order of events in the midst of seeming chaos makes devotees privy to arcane knowledge of the meaning of history. Believers are assured membership in an elect, righteous group that will be rescued from apocalypse and enjoy eternal life. By living in the last days and by being members of the "terminal generation," as Lindsey puts it, one's life takes on a renewed importance because one is participating in the cosmic drama that will end in the grand culmination of history. The sense of enhanced self-esteem that apocalyptic knowledge may provide is illustrated by Lindsey's describing his readers as wise and discerning, descriptors he deems appropriate because the prophet Daniel "observed that at the end of time the 'wise' would understand. In biblical terminology the 'wise' are people who study what God has to say and become enlightened to its meaning by the Holy Spirit" (1984:12).

The prophecies of Veronica Lueken similarly assure her followers that they are privy to a special endtimes wisdom and that they are a select remnant of the "true Church" whose current suffering will be avenged by an angry God. Baysiders are told that they are among the few chosen by deities themselves, who through Lueken promise believers heavenly rewards, as the Virgin Mary declares in the following words: "I hold deeply in my Heart all who will help us in this battle to save our children. We will reward you with the greatest of expectations" (*OLR Booklet* n.d.:26). The self-esteem of Baysiders is also enhanced through their direct experiences of the supernatural at the apparition site and especially by taking miraculous photographs, which preserve on film both God's sanction of their activities and involvement in their lives.

Apocalyptic beliefs provide individuals with a sense of empowerment as well by assuring them that the suffering they now endure at the hands of the unjust and the corrupt will be rectified by an avenging God. Apocalypticism emphasizes a rigid polarity between good and the evil, the righteous and the sinful, and promises that the wicked will be punished or destroyed. Lindsey provides the following description of what is to come: "There are two rewards—one a dazzling robe of white linen given to each believer as he enters heaven, and the other a blinding flash of the naked power of Jesus Christ as He reduces to a sea of blood all those who wave their fists in defiance with their last ounce of strength!" (1984:236). The element of divine retribution and expectations of revenge, even at one remove, may be a means of empowerment to those who feel victimized, disempowered, or alienated. This sense of vindication insists on a larger moral order underlying the universe, making meaningful the perceived crises and injustice of contemporary existence by promising that a new world of complete justice and perfect order will replace a world gone seriously awry.

The way that fatalistic doctrines enhance self-esteem, alleviate anxieties, and provide a sense of control is exemplified by religious interpretations of nuclear annihilation. Although secular speculations about nuclear war are fraught with a sense of helplessness and futility, the predictions of numerous religious apocalypticists speak of nuclear war as a divinely determined phenomenon that will purify and redeem a corrupt world. As noted previously, the nuclear threat was immediately interpreted in terms of traditional apocalyptic myths, symbols, and imagery, and the bomb imbued with supernatural significance, giving credence to a divine underlying plan. Fears of human extinction and perceptions of senseless global destruction are transformed into visions of a redemptive apocalypse, promising worldly salvation and offering the prospect of eternal life.

Fate and the Fulfillment of God's Will

Fatalism is commonly seen as involving resignation, helplessness, and passivity, and thus as motivating no action or behavioral response to alter events. However, some fatalists may actively "embrace their fate" and act to fulfill God's will or fate's plan. As Max Weber notes, the Calvinist doctrine of predestination did not lead to a passive fatalism but motivated individuals to prove that they were among the elect through hard work and success in a worldly calling (1958:232). The millenarian ideology of the National Socialist Workers Party repeatedly appealed to a sense of fate, proclaiming that Germans were the elect members of a pure-blooded Aryan "master race" destined to establish the Third Reich. Nazi rhetoric often assured followers that they were acting in accordance with a fated plan, and through their efforts the world would be cleansed of evil forces and a thousand-year period of Aryan rule would be created. This notion of actively fulfilling one's fate is epitomized by Adolf Hitler's chilling statement "I go the way fate has pointed me like a man walking in his sleep" (Gordon 1993:486). Whether promoted by totalitarian leaders or regarded as the decrees of the gods, the authoritarian certitude of fatalistic doctrines has the potential to motivate individuals to work with absolute determination to fulfill their fate, their nation's fate, or specific historical mandates that they believe are predestined.

Most millenarians anticipate the total destruction of the current social, economic, and political order and its replacement by a millennial society. Others, according to Michael Barkun, "couple this anticipation with an active desire to speed the inevitable result, often through violent, revolutionary means" (1974:18). Premillennial dispensationalists, certain of planetary escape in the Rapture, not only eagerly await doomsday and the return of Christ but may attempt to hasten the End. A case in point: premillennialist support of militant Israeli groups intent on destroying the Dome of the Rock in Jerusalem exemplifies the notion that an endtimes plan can be expedited if predetermined conditions are fulfilled.

Modern-day apocalypticists, like their historical precursors—whether medieval millenarians, Millerites, members of cargo cults, or participants in Ghost Dance movements—are confident that an unalterable pattern underlying history will culminate in the redemption of a world in which, it is thought, good rarely triumphs, evil prevails, and human effort changes very little. Directly countering feelings of helplessness, despair, and uncontrollability, apocalyptic belief systems promise the annihilation and regeneration of contemporary civilization through radical supernatural transformation, a promise that brings to individuals a sense of control, meaning, and self-esteem. Apocalyptic traditions offer comprehensive meaning systems that explain current crises as well as personal turmoil, bestow individual salvation upon believers, and fulfill the universal yearning for an ideal, harmonious world free from suffering, sorrow, and injustice. Faith in imminent worldly destruction is accompanied by optimism about and confidence in a divine fate, in the form of God's plan, that is moral and benevolent.

In contrast, secular apocalypticism, devoid of optimism about worldly redemption and belief in an underlying moral order, is pervaded by a sense of the cruelty of fate. The end of the world is not viewed as the culmination that will reveal the pattern determining history but simply as the termination of human existence that will lay bare its meaninglessness and randomness. Doomsday will not be a morally just day of reckoning that will cleanse the world of evil, but, rather, an unjust catastrophe without purpose.

Like the pessimistic notion of fate in classical Greek tragedy, secular apocalypticism often expresses the belief that human beings are struggling against an unhappy fate that will end in ruin and that will be brought about by human flaws. In numerous secular apocalyptic scenarios, worldly destruction is considered immanent in human nature rather than externally prescribed, fulfilled by the actions and character of human beings rather than determined by outside forces. Generally finding no underlying moral purpose for present suffering, secular apocalypticists commonly blame human failings for current crises and predicted catastrophes, implying in some cases that human extinction is warranted because of innate human ignorance, greed, evil, or destructive capabilities. This gloomy appraisal of human nature as flawed and incapable of improving the world has some resemblance to religious apocalyptic ideas that regard human beings as inherently evil, in a state of sin, and completely incapable of redeeming themselves or the world.

As noted, the fatalism that pervades the religious and secular apocalyptic beliefs of the Cold War era is often directly related to perceptions of nuclear cataclysm as uncontrollable and inevitable. With the end of the Cold War and the decreased threat of nuclear war, American apocalyptic beliefs are being reformulated and new endtimes traditions are emerging. Although visions of nuclear annihilation remain a central feature in much recent apocalyptic speculation, other cataclysmic scenarios involving ecological disasters, plagues, Islamic fundamentalism, and global economic and political unification increasingly have fueled current apocalyptic thought. The next chapter examines the transformation of apocalyptic beliefs in the post–Cold War era and the degree to which fatalism remains an important aspect of apocalyptic thinking as the third millennium draws near.

7

The Transformation of Apocalyptic Traditions in the Post–Cold War Era

The changes and current emphases within prophecy belief systems in the post–Cold War era illustrate the adaptability and dynamic nature of apocalyptic traditions. Interpreters of apocalyptic prophecy are masterful *bricoleurs*, skillfully recasting elements and themes within the constraints of their respective traditions and reconfiguring them to formulate new, meaningful endtimes scenarios. Traditions are not unchanging "products" passed from one generation to the next but continuities in human thought and behavior over time, configurations of ideas, and ways of thinking and doing things that symbolically connect the present with the past.[1]

Although the basic themes and formal elements of Christian apocalyptic traditions have remained fairly stable through time, they have been imbued with the culturally relevant flavor of particular historical epochs. Interpreters at different historical moments have pinpointed potential Beasts or described the breaking of the seven seals and the pouring of the seven vials referred to in the Book of Revelation in terms of real catastrophes that threatened humanity and that reflected the cultural milieu.[2] The varying beliefs about the rise to power of the Antichrist in the endtimes exemplifies this updating of tradition, with the actual identity of the Antichrist having been repeatedly revised to reflect perceived enemies of Christianity (i.e., Nero, Napoleon, Hitler, Saddam Hussein). Books identifying Mikhail Gorbachev as the Antichrist may now gather dust on the bottom shelf of the "Prophecy" section at Christian bookstores, but new publications detailing prophetic events in the Middle East, imminent ecocatastrophes, and the role of the European Community in the endtimes have taken their place. This chapter first examines current beliefs about nuclear cataclysm in post–Cold War apocalyptic prophecy and the reformulation of ideas about the role of Russia in the endtimes. It then explores several current emphases in Christian premillennialist traditions, including the preoccupation with the endtimes role of Islamic nations; a "false peace," global unification, and the New World Order; the rise of the

Antichrist; new technologies and the Mark of the Beast; and deadly viruses and ecological disasters.

The Nuclear Bomb in Post–Cold War Prophecy

Although the fear of imminent nuclear catastrophe has decreased in secular culture with the end of the Cold War, predictions of nuclear annihilation remain a central feature in apocalyptic prophecy traditions even as new cataclysmic endtimes scenarios have emerged. Many religious apocalypticists still regard nuclear weapons as a fulfillment of prophecy and predict their use in the near future, emphasizing that existing nuclear arsenals have the capability to destroy the world and that nuclear weapons eventually will be used by hostile nations, terrorist organizations, or a "mad-man" military dictator in the future. Furthermore, visions of nuclear conflagration remain compatible with biblical prophecies about the destruction of the world by fire. As Hal Lindsey puts it: "In this nuclear age, it makes sense to us that the mass annihilation we read about [in the Bible] might well be the result of a nuclear exchange. Because the Bible talks about mass destruction by fire and brimstone (melted earth), this scenario seems to make sense" (1994:197).

In contrast to diminishing secular concerns about global nuclear war, many prophecy enthusiasts declare that the end of the Cold War has brought the possibility of nuclear Armageddon even closer. Lindsey, for instance, in discussing the arms buildup in Arabic nations, asserts that "Planet Earth is more unstable today than it has been at any time in human history. We must never put our faith in false prophets preaching about false peace" (1994:62). He remains "thoroughly persuaded" that the world will soon experience international nuclear war and devotes a chapter in *Planet Earth—2000 A.D.* to a discussion of this inevitability (1994:255–265). While acknowledging the end of the Cold War, Lindsey continues to emphasize the Russian nuclear threat: "The Soviet Union is gone. The Cold War is over. But the Bible tells us Russia is going to play a critical role in the final moments of history. And the world stage is clearly being set for the drama. . . . Russia still poses a real danger to the United States, with its modernized nuclear force which took decades to build aimed at our nation like a gun to our head" (1994:188). A change in leadership or a coup, Lindsey states, might put communist hardliners back in power and quickly reverse recent political transformations.

Other prophecy writers also remind their readers that Russia still has the nuclear capacity to destroy the United States and the entire world. Ed Hindson, Minister of Biblical Studies at Atlanta's nine-thousand-member Rehoboth Baptist Church, cites recent estimates from the Center for Defense Information to confirm the continuing nuclear apocalyptic threat: the hundred-megaton H-bombs in the former Soviet Union have the capacity to create all-consuming firestorms 170 miles in diameter; twenty could destroy three-quarters of the U.S. population in less than an hour; and a retaliatory U.S. nuclear force could kill 400 million people in countries formerly in the Soviet Union and in China within half an hour (1996:86–87).

A number of prophecy interpreters assert that the Russian nuclear arsenal has not diminished but is, in fact, being enlarged. The "devastating truth," according to Grant Jeffrey, is that Russia and its allies are developing new weapons to complete "the most overwhelming military build-up in history to place themselves in a position to put a gun to the head of the West" (1994:186). Lindsey agrees, writing that although some nuclear weapons, such as MIRV ICBMs, are being eliminated under the terms of START I and START II treaties, the Russian nuclear arsenal is also being modernized to have greater accuracy and more destructive power, hence an improved ability to annihilate the United States in a first strike (1994:197–198). Conspiratorial ideas permeate such beliefs and are exemplified by the Bayside messages: "For it is their plan to subdue you, once they get the billions that they need in aid, to bring up the economy and buy more armaments. They have not disposed of their armaments, My child and My children. They store them in other nations. They have the same goals as their forefathers" (message from the Virgin Mary, June 18, 1992; *Directives from Heaven* 3, no. 57 [November 12, 1993]:1).

Along with assertions about Russia's stockpiling of arms, premillennialists from various prophecy traditions continue to predict endtimes nuclear scenarios. They speculate, for instance, that Russia will eventually attack the weakened armed forces in the West and that the United States will answer with a nuclear attack. The response will provoke a second Russian attack annihilating most of the American population and that of the Western world (see Jeffrey 1994:186).

Regardless of the imagined scenario, nuclear cataclysm remains a central part of premillennial prophecy traditions, with the eventual use of nuclear weapons regarded as foreordained. The end of the Cold War has had little effect on prophecy beliefs about nuclear apocalypse, revealing how deeply embedded they are in a wide range of catastrophic millennialist traditions. Fears and feelings about the bomb have fueled eschatological thought since the dawn of the nuclear age, and in light of the continued existence of large nuclear arsenals, the possibility of nuclear terrorism, and the covert attempts by some nations to develop nuclear weapons, predictions of nuclear Armageddon are unlikely to fade from apocalyptic speculation. As a permanent fixture in the American cultural and religious landscape, the bomb will remain an ominous endtimes sign until the day nuclear war is no longer a possibility.

Russia in Post–Cold War Prophecy

In Cold War apocalyptic prophecy, the Soviet Union was often assigned a crucial role as an evil, atheistic nation that would be one of Satan's allies in the last days. Identified in a biblical passage as the northern nation named Gog that is the enemy of Christianity (Ezekiel 38), common prophecy belief was that the Soviet Union would attack Israel and thereby initiate a worldly cataclysm. Historically, the reasons for Gog's invasion of Israel have been a topic of debate based on various geopolitical factors, but after the Bolshevik Revolution many prophecy believers concluded that the Soviet Union, a "godless nation," would naturally attempt to destroy God's chosen people (Boyer 1992:156).

With the thawing of the Cold War and the end of the official Soviet ideology of atheism, this scenario suddenly seemed in question, but the apocalyptic view of worldly events as foreordained and the adaptability of religious apocalyptic worldviews have readily accommodated the changed circumstances. A currently popular interpretation is that the easing of tensions between the East and the West is only temporary or that it is a "false peace" prior to the end of the world. In either case, the changes that have occurred in the Soviet Union, the creation of the Commonwealth of Independent States, and the rise of market economies throughout most of the former Soviet bloc are regarded as prophetic events on God's timetable, the newest pieces in the endtimes puzzle.

Post–Cold War Christian apocalyptic prophecy belief for the most part still identifies Russia as the prophesied Gog that will invade Israel in the last days, although some recent attempts to identify Gog have focused on Syria, Iraq, and new Islamic nations with nuclear weapons that were once part of the former Soviet Union. Post–Cold War prophecy interpreters viewed glasnost with suspicion, and many still assert that changes in the Soviet Union are simply a subterfuge prior to an attempt at world domination. According to numerous premillennial dispensationalist prophecy writers, Russia will revive its Cold War ideology after receiving a wealth of assistance from the United States and European nations. Once it has increased its financial and technological strength, it will become increasing belligerent and ultimately play a central role in some sort of nuclear exchange.

Some prophecy believers have said that the overthrowing of Soviet President Mikhail Gorbachev in August 1991 by a coup led by the KGB and the army, as well as the struggle between Parliament and Boris Yeltsin in October 1993, were staged to deceive the West further. Grant Jeffrey, discussing this theory at length in *Prince of Darkness: Antichrist and the New World Order*, calls reports about the end of the Cold War and the death of communism "a Russian fairy tale," and the coup, "Russian theater at its best" (1994:168–171). In 1991, Pat Robertson stated that the coup was a managed event whose purpose was to assuage any lingering suspicions that recent reforms were a deception. Glasnost, he explained, is a ploy to gain billions of dollars in aid from Western democracies and to reduce Western military arsenals (1991:xiv–xvi). Then, when the West least expects it, the Russians will revert to their previous communist ideology and attack the weakened Western world.

The Bayside apparitions epitomize these beliefs about Soviet deception and the persistence of the communist threat; the messages carry again the anti-communist ideas and the same basic themes expressed in the Cold War era. For example, in a message delivered to Veronica Lueken in 1991, the Virgin Mary cautions: "Do not be deceived. Their father is the father of all liars: satan. Their master plan is in motion. Pray for the light. Minds are clouded. I repeat: it is a ruse. Wake up America or you will suffer much" (*Directives from Heaven* 2, no. 10 [January 24, 1992]). Although some Roman Catholics interested in Marian apparitions believe that the transformations in the Soviet bloc have ushered in a Marian age of peace and prosperity, the Bayside messages continue to forewarn of imminent Soviet attack and emphasize that the democratic reforms in the Soviet Union are a ploy: "Russia is perpetuating one of the cruelest hoaxes in history . . . with its objectives remaining, as always, the same: communist enslavement of the world" (*Directives from Heaven* 4, no. 63 [February 4, 1994]: 2).

Predictably, the role of Gorbachev in this endtimes communist scheme received much attention in the Bayside messages during the thawing of the Cold War, and dispensationalists were preoccupied with his prophetic significance as well. The Bayside prophecies condemned Gorbachev as a satanic emissary, "the two-legged demon" who was planning to deceive the United States (*Directives from Heaven* 2, no. 10 [January 24, 1992]: 2). Pat Robertson, echoing a standard dispensationalist view, insisted that Gorbachev was not to be trusted and that he had an agenda for a new world order (1991:47). Grant Jeffrey, reminding readers that Gorbachev is an "unrepentant Marxist-communist," similarly asserted that he helped initiate the New World Order, in clandestine collaboration with the Vatican, and that he will continue to be instrumental in its development in the years ahead (1994:183).

Some post–Cold War prophecy writers even speculated as to whether Gorbachev might in fact be the Antichrist. According to popular interpretations of biblical scriptures, the Antichrist will have a charismatic and appealing personality and initially will bring a message of peace to the world before his reign of evil. The correlation between prophetic descriptions of the Antichrist and Gorbachev's personal qualities, political agenda, and rise to power was subsequently explored by Robert W. Faid in *Gorbachev! Has the Real Antichrist Come?* (1988). Faid not only analyzes Gorbachev's political career, but provides some numerical evidence that reinforces the Antichrist equation: the sum of "Mikhail S. Gorbachev" in Russian equals 1,332, or 666 x 2, two times the Mark of the Beast. In addition to those prophecy believers who viewed Gorbachev's peace efforts through perestroika, glasnost, and democratic reforms as Antichrist traits, some wondered whether the birthmark on his head might not be somehow related to the Mark of the Beast.

The persistence of such beliefs indicates that the end of the Cold War has not significantly altered long-standing ideas about Russia's sinister role in the endtimes because it is deemed a possibility that the Communist Party might regain political ascendancy. Like beliefs about the inevitable role of nuclear weapons in the last days, beliefs about the Russian threat are also firmly established in American apocalyptic prophecy traditions, reflecting decades of depictions of the former Soviet Union as an evil, apocalyptic adversary. As previously noted, when such long-standing and deeply held beliefs are challenged or disconfirmed, prophecy believers do not necessarily abandon them but often find ways to explain failed prophecies and may even assert the beliefs with greater intensity (see Festinger et al. 1956). For prophecy believers, the *seeming* end of the Cold War and the collapse of the Soviet Union have not irrefutably disconfirmed earlier predictions but are regarded as the latest fulfillments of God's endtimes plan.

Emergent Beliefs about the Role of Russia and Islam in the Endtimes

Various apocalyptic traditions continue to reflect Cold War ideologies and advance the notion that nuclear annihilation is inevitable, but new concerns also have emerged and some previous prophecy themes have been reemphasized in the 1990s. Lindsey's *Planet Earth—2000 A.D.* (1994) and *The Final Battle* (1995) exemplify several innovations that have occurred. Although retaining the basic endtimes narrative structure described in his previous writings, Lindsey has updated the scenario with references to recent geopolitical changes that he contends are fulfillments of prophecy. Covering all bases, Lindsey first asserts that Russia remains a major player in God's plan and then argues that the collapse of the Soviet Union, featured for decades as Gog, does not refute the prophecies in Ezekiel 38–39 but actually fulfills them. Modifying his previous stance slightly, he argues that Gog refers to *ethnic* Russians, not the Soviet Union with its various nationalities, and concludes that the recently formed Republic of Russia is the *real* Gog foreordained in prophecy. His explanation: during the Cold War the Soviet Union was moving toward world domination but this was not destined to occur. "I believe God's providential hand was working behind the scenes because it was never in the cards for the Kremlin to rule the world. . . . Prophecy declares the ethnic Russians will indeed play a significant role in those endtime events, but establishing a *Pax Sovieticus* over the world was never in the script" (1995:4). With characteristic ingenuity, Lindsey has explained the collapse of the Soviet Union without disconfirming long-standing beliefs about Russia's role in the endtimes, creatively reformulating and updating the dispensationalist prophecy tradition.

In addition to this subtle shift in interpretation, Lindsey pinpoints new developments in the Middle East and discusses the endtimes role of Islamic nations, further adapting the dispensationalist tradition to assimilate recent concerns and perceived threats. As Paul Boyer notes, the importance of Islam in apocalyptic prophecy is not a completely new idea but had been emphasized from the late thirteenth century to World War I, with the Ottoman Turks often identified as Gog, the evil aggressor from the north (1992:153). After the collapse of the Ottoman Empire and the 1917 Russian Revolution, the Soviet Union quickly became identified as the real Gog. The decades-later dissolution of the Soviet Union has resulted in a revival of interest in the eschatological role of Arabic nations and Islam as enemies of Christianity and the nation of Israel. The first chapter of Lindsey's *The Final Battle* (1995) is representative.

> Today, Communism appears to be on its way to the ash heap of history. But a greater threat—a more evil empire—is quietly, without fanfare, filling the void left by the break-up of the Soviet Union. This movement seeks not only to destroy the state of Israel but also the overthrow of the Judeo-Christian cul-

ture—the very foundation of our Western civilization. While Communism was only on the scene for seventy-five years, this evil empire is more than 1,300 years old. . . . The name of this movement—the greatest threat to freedom and world peace today—is Islamic fundamentalism. (1995:4–5)

Referring to Islamic fundamentalism as "a force more explosive than simple totalitarianism, Marxism-Leninism or Nazism" (1995:6), Lindsey devotes several chapters of *The Final Battle* to the "Islamic threat," discussing Muslim anti-Semitism and Muslim hatred of Christianity. He details how wealthy Islamic nations are developing chemical, biological, and nuclear weapons, and relative to Muslim fanaticism and terrorism asks readers to "imagine what this kind of zealotry means in the nuclear age—in the age where nuclear weapons can fit into a suitcase" (1995:8).

Former Soviet republics now Islamic nations—Turkmenistan, Kyrgyzstan, Kazakhstan, Tajikistan, Uzbekistan—are depicted in recent dispensationalist prophecy as having an instrumental role in the last days, joining forces with other Islamic countries to attack Israel. For example, Lindsey and other prophecy enthusiasts state that Kazakhstan's 1,150 strategic nuclear weapons, make it the world's third-largest nuclear power; they also point out that former Soviet nuclear scientists are working in Arabic nations and that Iran is actively pursuing nuclear weaponry, purportedly already having purchased three nuclear weapons from Kazakhstan and currently developing the technology to produce its own by the year 2000 (see Jeffrey 1994:194–196; Lindsey 1995:51–57). According to Lindsey, Islamic countries worldwide will eventually unite in an alliance that will eventually engage in a holy war, a jihad against Israel and Western civilization (1995:70). As these statements and beliefs indicate, by the time the Cold War had defrosted completely, prophecy enthusiasts had filled the void left by the decline of communism with the threat of "fanatical Muslims" foreordained to assault Western civilization with nuclear weaponry.

A number of dispensationalists (Lindsey, televangelist Jack Van Impe, and prophecy writers Salem Kirban and Grant Jeffrey, for example) have merged Cold War beliefs about the Soviets' role in the endtimes with recent fears of Islamic militarism to arrive at the prediction that Russia, because of its alliances with Islamic fundamentalist nations, will invade Israel, which will result in a nuclear conflagration; they cite passages in Zechariah that predict that the last war will originate in a dispute over Jerusalem (see Lindsey 1994:256–258). Lindsey interprets a passage in Ezekiel 38, about God putting "hooks into the jaws" of Gog and pulling it into battle, as a prophetic reference to Islamic influences on Moscow (the "hooks") that will draw Russia into an endtimes scenario leading to nuclear war (1994:200–201). Jeffrey declares that radical Arab groups may attack Jerusalem in the near future. "Russian KGB security officers have offered to sell tactical nuclear weapons, small enough to fit into a duffel bag, to Arab countries for $20 million each," and he adds that these alleged sales may allow the PLO, Hamas, or some other terrorist group to become nuclear powers (1994:196). This sense of the inevitability of a nuclear cataclysm brought about by Islamic forces is exemplified by prophecy writer Ed Hindson: "it probably won't be long before almost any well-funded dictator in the oil-rich Middle East will have nuclear warheads at his disposal. As the clock ticks onward, it is only a matter of time until the inevitable disaster strikes" (1996:88).

The Gulf War in Post–Cold War Prophecy

The increased attention to the eschatological role of Islam is not only related to the end of the Cold War and Islamic fundamentalism but also to the Iraqi invasion of Kuwait in August 1990. As previously mentioned, many prophecy believers interpreted the war in the Persian Gulf as the beginning of the endtimes countdown, with an estimated 15 percent of the American populace believing that the war was a fulfillment of prophecy and that Armageddon was at hand (Bezilla 1996:26). The intensified interest in prophecy beliefs during the war revealed the connection between perceptions of societal crisis and apocalyptic speculation nationwide; prophecy interpreters were interviewed on the national news about the role of the Middle East in endtimes traditions and booksellers reported huge sales of prophecy books (Maxwell 1991:60; Boyer 1992:329). Prophecy telephone hotlines even provided daily updates about the endtimes significance of the unfolding events in the Gulf: "For $2 a minute, you can be ready by calling the 900-number Tribulation Hotline and listen to . . . what the Bible says about The End and how events in the world fit into prophecy" (*Los Angeles Times*, January 28, 1991, D2). As noted, a revised edition of John Walvoord's *Armageddon, Oil and the Middle East Crisis* (1990) quickly sold upward of 600,000 copies from December 1990 to February 1991 (more copies sold in ten weeks than had sold from 1974 to 1984, when the first edition went out of print) and another 300,000 copies were ordered and distributed by Billy Graham (*Los Angeles Times*, February 7, 1991, E2). Walvoord, president of the Dallas Theological Seminary from 1952 to 1986 and author of twenty-seven books, states that conflicts over oil in the

Middle East will play a central role in the last days and asks, "Do current events point to the final global war, Armageddon? . . . This is exactly what the Bible anticipates in its prophecies of the end time. The world stage is set for a showdown" (1990:back cover).

Some prophecy theorists went further and suggested that Saddam Hussein might be the Antichrist. The following advertisement appeared in the *Los Angeles Times* (as well as other major newspapers) immediately after the Gulf War had ended:

> Will Saddam Hussein Rise From the Dead? Maybe that question seems pre-mature, since Saddam is still counted among the living. While he might be defeated and down for the time being, he just might be killed and come back from the dead. . . . Preposterous, you say? There are predictions of just such a thing happening—to a person called "the man of sin." He is sometimes also referred to by a number—"666." The same source predicts the political, eco-nomic and spiritual future of the Middle East, and in fact of our planet. It tells of wars and outcomes of wars, from ancient Babylon to modern-day Israel. That source is a book. The Bible. (March 28, 1991:A24)

The ad characterizes dispensationalist predictions about the recovery of the Antichrist from a fatal head wound, his uniting all nations against Israel, and the similarities between such prophecies and current events in the Middle East. Readers interested in learning more about apocalyptic prophecy are encouraged to request information from the nationwide organization Jews for Jesus, based in San Francisco.

The prophetic significance of Babylon in the last days and Saddam Hus-sein's role in the endtimes were addressed by various prophecy writers, includ-ing Charles Dyer, whose *The Rise of Babylon: Sign of the End Times* (1991) with its colorfully embossed cover featuring Hussein's face juxtaposed with the pro-file of Nebuchadnezzar, promptly sold 300,000 copies (Boyer 1992:330). Dyer, a colleague of John Walvoord's at the Dallas Theological Seminary, declares that Hussein not only looks like Nebuchadnezzar but is also similar in his desire to rule the world (1991:back cover). Although American dispensation-alists in the past have customarily interpreted the Babylon in Revelation 18 to be the Vatican, the United States, or a one-world economic or religious sys-tem, Dyer argues that the reference is to the literal rebuilding in the last days of the ancient city (1991:192). From his offered evidence (with photographs) of Hussein's reconstruction of Babylon, Dyer extrapolates that Hussein con-siders himself the new Nebuchadnezzar and predicts that someday this new Babylon will become a great economic power by controlling the oil wealth of the Middle East (1991:208–210). Dyer sees a rebuilt Babylon as the third-most-important endtimes sign, with the other two most significant prophetic events being the establishment of Israel as a nation and the revival of the Roman Empire in Europe. The city will eventually be destroyed, he says, by a multinational force (the revived Roman Empire led by the Antichrist), which will gain the oil resources before the end of the world. Dyer concludes, "Regardless of what happens to Saddam Hussein, the Bible makes it clear that Babylon will be rebuilt. The Middle East is the world's time bomb, and Babylon the fuse that will ignite the events of the end times" (1991:back cover). By focusing on the prophetic importance of Babylon rather than predictions about the Gulf War's escalating into a global conflagration, Dyer's interpretation was not disconfirmed once military actions ceased, unlike the speculations of various other prophecy interpreters.

A Moment of Peace before Armageddon

After the Iraqi forces were defeated and it became apparent that predictions of a global conflict initiated in the Middle East would not be fulfilled, some believers shifted their attention to the prophetic implications of peace in the endtimes scenario. For example, in his weekly television broadcasts from Troy, Michigan, Jack Van Impe predicted that the defeat of the Iraqi forces by the United States and the Iraqi surrender were the beginning of a period of international peace and the creation of a new world order prior to Armageddon (*Jack Van Impe Presents*, October 1994).

Since the end of the Cold War, many premillennialists have argued that there will be a "false peace," a period of security and concord prior to the rise of the Antichrist, a stance compatible with beliefs about Russia's grand deception and secret communist machinations in the endtimes. Numerous premillennialists, including Pat Robertson, cite Isaiah 2:2–4 as prophetic proof that a temporary peace will prevail in the latter days (Robertson 1991:226), and others cite 1 Thessalonians 5:3, which reads: "For when they say, 'Peace and safety!' then sudden destruction comes upon them, as labor pains upon a pregnant woman. And they shall not escape."

This fatalistic view of peace efforts is espoused by prophecy interpreter Dave Hunt of Bend, Oregon, whose books have sold more than three million copies. Asserting that the end of the Cold War is an endtimes sign prior to the emergence of a one-world order and the arrival of the Antichrist, Hunt states, "At long last, the prospect of a peace such as the world has never known before seems to have metamorphosed from an impossible dream to a realistic hope. In fact, the nations of the world will indeed establish an unprecedented international peace, and probably fairly soon. . . . That time of peace is mentioned, however, not with joy but with sorrow, for the prophets declared that it would precede a holocaust that would threaten the survival of all life on this planet" (1990:13). Hunt declares that peace negotiations cannot influence the foreordained course of events, and that although world leaders are compelled to work for peace, their efforts are unavailing within the context of the divine plan: "If mankind could by its own efforts establish a just and lasting peace, it would prove that the Bible—which declares that true peace can only come through Jesus Christ reigning upon earth—is not true. Therefore all such humanistic attempts are doomed" (Hunt 1990:14).

Other premillennialists say that attempts to reduce tensions in the Middle East also portend the rise of the Antichrist and the imminent destruction of the world. In his best-selling *Beginning of the End: The Assassination of Yitzhak Rabin and the Coming Antichrist* (1996), John Hagee argues that the assassination of Rabin fulfills endtimes prophecies and reveals humanity's place on the prophetic timetable. According to Hagee, the pastor of the fifteen-thousand-member Cornerstone Church in San Antonio, Texas, whose views are broadcast nationally and internationally on television and radio, the assassination "launched Bible prophecy onto the fast track" because it will lead to renewed peace efforts between Israel and Arabic nations (1996:8). Prior to Rabin's death, Hagee says, there was resistance to the peace process in Israel but now, to honor his life and memory, Israelis will do a wholehearted turnabout. In pursuit of peace, the nation will embrace the Antichrist, who will appear to be a peacemaker. Defenses down and lulled into a false sense of security, Israel will be attacked by Arabic nations, initiating an apocalyptic scenario.

As noted earlier, Lindsey predicts a similar series of events, concluding that Muslim nations will eventually attack an unsuspecting Israel, which will not be able to defend itself with conventional weapons but have to resort to nuclear weapons: "This latest phony peace deal in the Middle East thus only ensures that eventually there will be a thermonuclear holocaust in the Middle East . . . this seems to parallel predictions in Revelation and elsewhere to a T. Mark my words. It will happen" (1994:244).

Like other dispensationalists, Lindsey and Hagee assert that peace efforts in the Middle East are useless but nonetheless a foreordained part of the unalterable chronology of endtimes events. Such ideas reveal once again the deeply pessimistic underpinnings of apocalyptic worldviews and further indicate that despite the end of Cold War, fatalistic beliefs about the inevitability of nuclear annihilation and about the inability of human beings to create universal peace through their own efforts are intrinsic to dispensationalist thought at the end of the second millennium.

Global Unification and a One-World Government

Post–Cold War apocalyptic prophecy also has become increasingly preoccupied with recent attempts at political and economic unification, which are interpreted as a fulfillment of predictions about the revival of the Roman Empire (Daniel 7), an empire that, with the Antichrist as its leader, will dominate the world prior to the return of Christ. Prophetic indications of the empire are believed to include the reunification of Germany in 1990 and efforts to increase the power of the European Community and European Parliament, such as the Treaty of Maastricht, signed on December 10, 1991. Other international treaties also have been viewed through the lens of apocalyptic prophecy; for example, some premillennialists interpreted the signing of the North American Free Trade Agreement (NAFTA) in December 1993 by the United States, Canada, and Mexico as part of a secret agenda that eventually will lead to economic domination under the rule of the Antichrist.

The activities of the European Union, the European Community, and the European Common Market have been closely monitored by premillennialists and regarded by some as evidence of the coming of the Antichrist's one-world economy and one-world government. One prophecy interpreter states, "There is a chance that the European Community is making the throne on which the Beast could sit, covering not only Europe, but the whole world" (Arthur Berg, cited in Jeffrey 1994:122).

According to Lindsey, the imminence of the evil one-world system was revealed when Western Europe became a single economic market on January 1, 1993, linking twelve nations and eliminating tariffs and custom barriers; and it drew even closer when the 345 million citizens of those twelve nations became citizens of the new European Union on November 1, 1993 (Lindsey 1994:219). The fulfillment of prophecies about an encroaching one-world order is explored at length in Grant Jeffrey's *Prince of Darkness: Antichrist and the New World Order* (1994). He states that the one central bank and currency, one European citizenship and passport, one high court, one foreign policy, and the European army that have been established are all indications that an emergent "confederated superstate is destined to rule the world under the dictatorial control of the coming Prince of Darkness" (Jeffrey 1994:123).

The introduction of the European Currency Unit (ECU) on January 1, 1993, has been interpreted as an endtimes sign as well, but it is the symbolism of the ECU currency—Europa riding Zeus in the form of a bull—that has received particular attention; the symbol of the bull is interpreted as "the beast," and Europa is the "woman sitting on a scarlet beast" mentioned in Revelation 17:3. According to one interpretation, the woman is a symbol of the False Prophet and the beast represents the revived Roman Empire; together they symbolize an unholy alliance between the false ecumenical church and the new Roman Empire. Jeffrey exclaims, "It is amazing to see this prophetic symbol of the 'Mother of Harlots' and the revived Roman Empire appear on the new currency of the European Community. This same symbol was also engraved on the new stamp commemorating the election of the European Parliament" (1994:111).

Although much post–Cold War apocalyptic speculation about an emerging global system focuses on activities in Europe, President George Bush was suspected of being involved in the one-world-order conspiracy after his statements during the Gulf War about the beginning of a "New World Order." According to Pat Robertson in *The New World Order* (1991), Bush's reference was not just rhetoric but part of a "precise, systematic, and rigorously planned mechanism to manage people and nations collectively by proxy and by global authority" (1991:xi). Robertson examines "the invisible hand shaping U.S. government policies" and the trends in world politics that are leading to a one-world dictatorship. The ultimate goal, says Robertson, as foreordained by Bible prophecy, is the establishment of a one-world government under a centralized authority that will replace the old world order of Christianity (1991:14, 246). The Gulf War was especially significant because the military action against Iraq, authorized by the United Nations, "was the first time since Babel that all of the nations of the earth acted in concert with one another. . . . It is as if some power reached out from Babel, where the first world rebellion against God was quashed, and once again called the nations of the world to unity" (1991:252). The move toward a new world order, for Robertson, is inexplicable in terms of the desire for wealth or political power but springs "from the depth of something that is evil," an evil conspiracy controlled by secret societies and occult organizations (1991:8–9).

Robertson implicates the usual endtimes conspirators—the United Nations, the World Bank and the International Monetary Fund, the Society for Worldwide Interbank Financial Transactions (SWIFT), the Bilderberg Group, and the Federal Reserve Board—and explains that worldwide indoctrination to the values that will support a one-world government is being brought about through the mass media and popular culture as well. The pervasive and insidious urge for a unified world is exemplified, he argues, by the popular song "Imagine," by John Lennon, the deceased former Beatle. With its reference to a future in which there would be no countries, no religion, no heaven or hell, no possessions, and everyone living for today with the world "as one," it typifies the seemingly innocent desire for utopia on earth, which may lead to a one-world government, says Robertson. "George Bush and John Lennon are not alone in championing a new world order," he continues, and cites statements about establishing a world order by Woodrow Wilson, Nelson Rockefeller, Adolf Hitler, and Jimmy Carter, and writings from the secret society of the Illuminati in the eighteenth century (1991:4–6). The conspiracy is complex, unified by a "single thread [that] runs from the White House to the State Department to the Council on Foreign Relations to the Trilateral Commission to secret societies to extreme New Agers" (1991:6).

Robertson's book, publicized as a *New York Times* best-seller with more than half a million copies in print, reveals the degree to which conspiracy theories about secretive groups controlling worldly events continue to be a feature of apocalyptic worldviews. Exhibiting extreme xenophobia and perhaps anti-Semitism (fear of "international bankers" in the tradition of previous anti-Semitic publications), the widespread credence in global conspiracy reflects feelings of powerlessness about seemingly inexplicable or threatening global economic and political transformations. Post–Cold War beliefs about a one-world system and a sinister grand design for history assert that although such changes are overwhelmingly evil, externally determined, and completely beyond one's control, they are meaningful within a foreordained endtimes plan that promises their eventual destruction and the ultimate triumph of the faithful.

The Rise of the Antichrist

Endtimes ideas about worldwide conspiracy and monstrous evil are epitomized by contemporary beliefs about the primary antagonist in the apocalyptic drama: the Antichrist. Historically, legends about the Antichrist have emphasized his cruelty and great powers of deception, which will be used ruthlessly to maltreat the righteous. The Antichrist's tremendous deceit frequently has been associated with religious hypocrisy, and as a result a long-standing tradition exists among Protestants and Catholic dissenters of equating the pope with the Antichrist. Tyrants and persecutors of Christianity have also been identified as the Evil One; some of those labeled the Antichrist in the past have included Nero, Justinian, Saladin, Luther, Peter the Great, Napoleon, Kaiser Wilhelm, Mussolini, Hitler, Stalin, Khrushchev, Sun Myung Moon, Anwar el-Sadat, Moammar Qaddafi, King Juan Carlos of Spain, Jimmy Carter, David Rockefeller, Mikhail Gorbachev, and Boris Yeltsin. John F. Kennedy's Catholicism and his receiving 666 votes at the 1956 Democratic Convention was cause for much Antichrist speculation; some believed he would rule the world after making an alliance with the Vatican, African Americans, and communists. Henry Kissinger was a favorite candidate for the Antichrist in the 1970s because of his diplomatic successes in the Middle East (Antichrist as "a bringer of peace") and a calculation that his name added up to 666 (Alnor 1989:22). In the 1980s, President Ronald Wilson Reagan came under the scrutiny of Antichrist hunters (each of his names had six letters, and in 1988 Reagan changed the street number of the mansion given to him by wealthy friends from 666 to 668) (Boyer 1992:276). One popular belief is that the Antichrist will miraculously recover from a seemingly fatal wound: Reagan's recovery from an assassination attempt led to speculation about his role in the endtimes, and Pope John Paul II's similar recovery also evoked Antichrist accusations. Some persons have offered specifics concerning the Antichrist's personal history. Astrologer Jeanne Dixon said the Antichrist would be exactly thirty years old on February 5, 1992; in 1980, Pat Robertson speculated that the Antichrist was twenty-seven years old at the time (Alnor 1989:25). Robertson himself was accused of being a potential candidate for the Antichrist by some premillennial dispensationalists when he broke with conventional premillennialist views in declaring that the coming New World Order, the rise of the Antichrist, and the apocalypse could be averted if Christian America rallied to prevent a one-world government. According to Constance Cumbey, author of several books on the satanic underpinnings of the New Age movement and the coming of a New Age Antichrist, Robertson might be the Antichrist because of his activist theological views, political aspirations, and hypnotic powers (Alnor 1989:23).

Although Antichrist legends have always figured prominently in Christian apocalyptic speculation, in the post–Cold War era the figure of the Antichrist has received extensive attention, with particular emphasis on the fact that he will either bring peace to the world or rise to power during a time of peace. Prophecy interpreters cite a biblical passage about the first horseman of the apocalypse riding a white horse (Revelation 6:2), a symbol of the Antichrist coming in false peace, and have focused on the conspiratorial machinations that will allow him to become the ruler of the revived Roman

Empire, and his final reign over the entire world for a seven-year period through a one-world government, a one-world economy, and a one-world religion.

Many prophecy believers assert that the Antichrist will emerge from one country within the European Union or a country or confederation that was once part of the Roman Empire, and as a result have given special notice to powerful and charismatic individuals within the European Community. According to John Hagee, "In his rise to power, the Antichrist will weave his hypnotic spell first over one nation in the ten-kingdom federation, then over all ten" (1996:118). Popular beliefs also assert that the Antichrist will guarantee peace in the Middle East through a seven-year treaty with Israel that among its provisions will permit the Jews to rebuild the Temple. During this time, the Antichrist will rule with complete authority, but after three and a half years he will break the treaty, desecrate the Temple, and begin a reign of terror with the help of a religious leader identified as the False Prophet (2 Thessalonians 2; Revelation 13:11–18). The Antichrist will eventually declare himself divine and convince many Jews that he is their Messiah (for this reason, some prophecy enthusiasts assume the Antichrist will be Jewish). He will also convince Christians who remain after the Rapture that he is the true Christ, and many will worship him as a god (see Hagee 1996:117–131; Jeffrey 1994:184; Lindsey 1995:163–167; Robertson 1991:255).

Prophecy interpreters have gone to great lengths to describe the cruelty and powers of deception of the Antichrist that will be ruthlessly used against all who resist him. Lindsey refers to the Antichrist as "The Future Fuehrer," a charismatic, attractive man who will dazzle the world with miracles and yet be so evil that he will "make Adolph Hitler and Josef Stalin look like choir boys" (1994:232–233). Emphasizing the peace efforts that will be a part of the early career of the Antichrist, Hagee speculates that he might be a winner of the Nobel Peace Prize or perhaps the man who resolves the conflict between Serbia, Bosnia, and Croatia (1996:118).

Many dispensationalists believe that the Antichrist will not emerge until after the Rapture and that he will come from the revived Roman Empire, but a few eager Antichrist spotters see in President Bill Clinton a potential Antichrist and in Vice President Al Gore a potential False Prophet of a New Age nature religion, while others think that Hillary Clinton might be the False Prophet. Any connection, real or imagined, to the New Age, environmentalist issues, peace efforts, or "secular humanism" defined in the broadest sense continues to inspire Antichrist speculation among premillennialists.

References to the Antichrist have always been a part of the Bayside messages and have been increasingly emphasized in the recent literature distributed by the shrine organization. The prophecies describe the rise of the Antichrist and his cruelty and give details about his age and whereabouts, such as the following message attributed to the Virgin Mary, which states flatly that the Antichrist "now walks your earth. Earth-year 1940 was his beginning. He entered your country in 1970" (*OLR Book* 1986:111). One frequently cited message asserts that the Antichrist entered into the priesthood in 1971; another, that Satan entered into the body of a male practitioner of the occult in 1975 and once he is finished his mission using the man's body, he will possess another body (*OLR Book* 1986:96).

Formal theological discussions about the Antichrist look upon the concept as standing for evil in the world or an internal spiritual state of religious self-deception or resistance to Christ's message; popular beliefs and legends depict the Antichrist as an external force—the embodiment of ultimate evil in human form (McGinn 1994:4–5). Such beliefs and legends have reflected the fears and perceptions of ultimate evil held by Christians historically, underscoring the ways that Christian apocalyptic traditions are ultimately concerned with the struggle between the forces of good and evil, with evil regarded as an overwhelming, uncontrollable power that is foreordained to dominate in the endtimes.

New Technology and the Mark of the Beast, 666

In post–Cold War apocalyptic speculation, the sense of overpowering evil has been increasingly identified with computers and technological advancements, which many believe the Antichrist will use to enslave humanity. The association of computers with the Antichrist is revealed by beliefs that the Antichrist may in fact *be* a massive computer, such as the computer housed in the administration building of the headquarters of the Common Market in Brussels, Belgium, which employees supposedly have nicknamed "The Beast." According to numerous prophecy interpreters, this computer, which occupies three floors of the building, has the capacity to store financial and personal information on two billion people; "The Beast" allegedly will be replaced by a larger and more ominous computer currently being built in Luxembourg (see Relfe 1981:44–48).

A rumor that began circulating on the Internet and in oral tradition in 1994–1995 also associates the Antichrist with computers:

Warning! Bill Gates (president of Microsoft) may be the next Antichrist. Revelation 13:18 says, "Let anyone who has intelligence work out the number of the beast, for the number represents a man's name, and the numerical value of its letters is six hundred and sixty-six. Bill Gates' full name is William Henry Gates III. Nowadays he is known as Bill Gates (III). By converting the letters of his current name to their ASCII values, you get the following:

BILLGATES3

66+73+76+76+71+65+84+69+83+3=666

Daniel 7:23 says, "The explanation he gave was this: 'The fourth beast signifies a fourth kingdom which will appear on earth. It will differ from the other kingdoms; it will devour the whole earth, treading it down and crushing it.'" Current history knows three Antichrists: Adolf Hitler, Joseph Stalin, and the Pope. Is the fourth beast the Microsoft Corporation, which represents the power of money? (*Foaftale News* 37 [June 1995]: 11; Forteana News List on May 16, 1995)

Beliefs about the Antichrist being a computer mogul or somehow incarnated in computers are innovations on standard premillennialist notions about the Antichrist's being a peacemaker and political leader, epitomizing current ideas about the evil and apocalyptic ramifications of technology.

Apocalyptic prophecy interpreters have asserted for decades that technology will be used by the Antichrist to achieve worldwide worship. Some prophecy writers say that the Antichrist will require worship before two-way television consoles that will monitor the frequency of one's devotion to the image of the Beast (see Relfe 1981:127). Vigilantly assessing the prophetic possibilities of the latest technology, recent prophecy writers explain that the reference to the worship of the image of the Beast in Revelation 13:14–15 might be a description of an Antichrist image conveyed through the technology of "artificial reality" or created by the sophisticated use of computer graphics and holograms. Such an image might then be transmitted through television sets which would place a three-dimensional, life-like apparition of the Antichrist in living rooms throughout the world (see Kinman 1995:247).

Numerous premillennialists assert that the control of individuals through computer technology will be an inescapable part of the Antichrist's one-world order and that such technologies are already being implemented. Books such as *The Mark of the Beast: Your Money, Computers, and the End of the World* (Lalonde and Lalonde 1994; chapter headings include "Kiss Your Cash Goodbye," "Boy, Have I Got Your Number," and "Your Body: The Only ID You'll Ever Need") examine the current trends and the rationale leading inevitably to a cashless society controlled by computers (simplified monetary transactions, the elimination of much crime, and increased profit for businesses, for example). Like numerous other recent prophecy books, *The Mark of the Beast* asserts that for the first time in history the system of complete control described in the Book of Revelation has been made possible by advanced computer technology, laser scanning devices, and electronic surveillance. In *Prince of Darkness: Antichrist and the New World Order*, Grant Jeffrey describes the totalitarian use of technology in the coming brave New World Order:

> This system was technically impossible until the introduction during the last decade of laser scans, computer chips beneath the skin and computerized financial systems. . . . [T]he Mark of the Beast system will eliminate money, forcing men to buy and sell through a computerized system requiring each person to possess an individual Mark. The true horror of the coming New World Order is that its global and all-encompassing secret police state will be equipped with the most advanced technology making escape virtually impossible. (1994:293)

Pat Robertson imagines a similar future in *The New World Order*: computers able to process trillions of bits of information will contain the complete vital statistics and life record of every person in the world; all wealth and monetary transactions could be monitored and controlled; and tracking mechanisms could be implemented to observe the physical movements of everyone (1991:216). Advances in technology have made such tyrannical monitoring possible, Robertson ventures, and if a "demonized madman like Hitler could seize control of a worldwide, homogenized government," the world could be transformed into a massive prison (1991:216).

Numerous other prophecy interpreters also have examined the new technologies that are setting the stage for the totalitarian rule of the Antichrist, and discuss at length the prophetic significance of recent forms of surveillance: massive corporate and government computer databases; the FBI's fingerprint records and computer files on more than fifty million Americans; recent proposals for DNA genetic identification of all citizens; the future issuance of biometric health and identification cards that will contain each person's electronic fingerprint or voiceprint; the ability of the National Security Agency and other organizations to monitor every phone call, fax, and e-mail transmission in the world; voiceprint-recognition technology; credit-reporting agencies; and laser and optical scanning that allows objects and persons to be monitored from a distance (see Jeffrey 1994:92–104; Kah 1992:8–22; Kinman 1995).

In addition to expressing apprehensions about the loss of individual freedoms and the invasion of privacy by technology, post–Cold War apocalyptic beliefs reflect distrust of technological change and fear of economic control. This last concern is exemplified by the belief that no one will be able to buy or sell in the future cashless society without the Mark of the Beast, often believed to be a tattoo or emblem somehow related to the number 666. The Mark, it is maintained, will be required of all living under the Antichrist's reign, and those who refuse to accept the emblem will be killed or eventually starve to death. A common belief, based on the following passage from the Book of Revelation, is that the Mark will be placed on the forehead or top of the right hand:

> He causes all, both great and small, rich and poor, free and slave, to receive a mark on their right hand or on their foreheads, and that no one may buy or sell except one who has the mark or the name of the beast, or the number of his name. Here is wisdom. Let him who has understanding calculate the number of the beast, for it is the number of a man: His number is 666. (Revelation 13:16–18)

Beliefs about the design of the Mark—the symbolic embodiment of ultimate evil—often reflect perceptions about current societal threats. For instance, in the 1960s and 1970s, the peace symbol associated with the counterculture was frequently identified with the Antichrist and considered by some to be the potential Mark of the Beast. One prophecy writer said at the time, "We know that by peace the antichrist will gain some power over the nations, and we can think of no better anti-type of the cross than the broken cross" (Webber 1976:23). In the late 1970s, Veronica Lueken's messages continued to warn of the dangers of the peace symbol: "The broken cross, the sign of the Man of Perdition, the sign of the Antichrist, is the so-called 'Peace Symbol.' All who wear this are doomed" (*OLR Book* 1986:96). The adaptability and updating of the Mark of the Beast tradition is illustrated by the recent assertion among some prophecy believers that the current popularity of tattooing and body piercing among youth has prophetic implications because it may lead to a willingness in the future to accept a tattoo or body mark when the Antichrist's 666 economic system is implemented.

In the 1990s, the Mark of the Beast and his 666 system have become increasingly associated with computers, electronic banking, bar coding, lasers, and microchip implantation, revealing growing apprehensions about the intrusion of technology into human activities. In the tradition of earlier prophecy books such as *When Your Money Fails: The "666 System" Is Here* (Relfe 1981), numerous post–Cold War prophecy works are devoted to accumulating evidence that indicates that the 666 system is at hand.[3] For example, Dwight

Kinman, a pastor and prophecy interpreter from Canby, Oregon, writes in *The World's Last Dictator* (1995) that the emblem of the European Community is 666; that the symbol of the World Bank, Trilateral Commission, and New Age movement is 666; and that every person in the industrial world has an international eighteen-digit identification number that begins with 666 in the Common Market computer in Belgium (1995:259). The authors of *The Mark of the Beast* (Lalonde and Lalonde 1994) suggest that prophecies about the 666 Mark and a one-world economic system are being fulfilled in the form of electronic banking alternatives to cash transactions, by "smart cards," and by national identity cards containing a microchip with personal data. In *En Route to Global Occupation* (1992), Gary Kah similarly argues that the 666 economic system will initially be promoted through conveniences such as debit cards and electronic banking, which ultimately will pave the way for the Antichrist's worldwide monitoring system: "Once the debit card has become widely accepted, everything would be in place for the next and final step, which would be to force each individual to be tagged with a personal identification code without which he would be unable to buy or sell. The technology for such a worldwide electronic system is already in place, and experiments with such a mark have been conducted in several countries" (1992:12).

Prophetic significance also has been attributed to the international bar code, or Universal Product Code (UPC), which some prophecy believers see as being transformed into the Mark of the Beast in a future cashless society: "The mark will probably be similar to the bar code system of the Universal Product Code, each person tagged with their own permanent identification number easily read by scanners. The mark, however, will most likely come in the form of an invisible laser tattoo" (Kah 1992:150). In such scenarios the human body is physically altered and marked like a product, scanned, processed, monitored, and ultimately condemned to hell by involvement in the 666 system. A variation of this endtimes assault on the body is offered by Dwight Kinman, who asserts that by the year 2000, transponder microchip implantations will allow for the tracking and controlling of individuals. Providing photographs and illustrations, Kinman claims that these 666 biochips, encased in tiny glass tubes the size of a grain of rice, will be inserted in the back of the hand and used as a universal identification card. Supermarket checkout scanners will scan these microchip implants, making shopping and other financial transactions easier but also ultimately making tracking and control convenient during the Antichrist's reign (1995:259–262).

As Paul Boyer notes, for years prophecy writers have assigned advancements in technology a pivotal role in the endtimes, and recent notions about the evil use of technology to control people reinforce and update previous ideas (1992:267–269). Commonplace objects and everyday conveniences are infused with sinister meanings, and seemingly harmless daily activities seen as parts of an insidious, overall conspiracy that will lead to mass conformity and final enslavement. Technological advancements foretell of decline and imminent destruction, with "progress" viewed pessimistically and ultimately equated with dehumanization and doom. As the authors of *Computers and the Beast of Revelation* state, "In spite of all the scientific wizardry and political developments of our age, the world masses for the most part seem hypnotized with the wonder of it all. If we could go back one hundred years in time and look upon mankind [in the present] . . . , it would appear that the average person today is like a man caught in a nightmare, hoping that he wakes before he plunges over a precipice into oblivion" (Webber and Hutchings 1986:25).

Pervaded by the fear of manipulation by overwhelming evil powers, beliefs about the inescapable 666 system and the Mark of the Beast are inherently fatalistic, expressing a profound sense of helplessness in the face of an all-encompassing and unavoidable web of technological surveillance and control. Like developments in nuclear technology, recent technological changes have been readily interpreted as foreordained occurrences and incorporated into apocalyptic worldviews, and now complement the bomb in the endtimes countdown: technology initially will be used to dehumanize and enslave, and then, inevitably, to obliterate humanity.

The Beginning of Sorrows: Prophecies of Environmental Destruction and Pestilence

The prophetic significance of natural disasters, diseases, famine, and environmental destruction is another prominent theme in current apocalyptic speculation. Searching the Bible for prophecies describing recent crises, believers cite passages such as Matthew 24:7–8, which says that in the last days "there will be famines, pestilences, and earthquakes in various places. All of these are the beginning of sorrows." Putting a prophetic twist on the latest news reports, prophecy interpreters have explained the apocalyptic importance of current threats within the divine timetable, focusing increasingly on endtimes viruses and ecological disasters.

In various instances, previous interpretations of prophecy have been revised to account for new potential catastrophes. For example, during the Cold War, a biblical passage about a plague that would dissolve people's flesh (Zechariah

14:12–15) was interpreted by some prophecy writers as a reference to nuclear war and the effects of nuclear radiation. However, in the mid-1990s, the passage has been given an up-to-date prophetic relevance in the context of the ebola virus, dengue fever, and various emerging viruses referred to as "Apocalypse Bugs." John Hagee, citing Michael Preston's best-seller *The Hot Zone*, argues that an airborne strain of the ebola virus could emerge and in about six weeks create a worldwide epidemic that would devastate the world's population. He also says that new, mutated viruses and antibiotic-resistant bacteria could do the same, and if used in chemical or biological warfare, could create a plague similar to that described by Zechariah, and concludes that "AIDS, ebola, and killer viruses are a trumpet blast from the throne of God to the spiritually deaf. . . . *You are the terminal generation!*" (Hagee 1996:88, 98). Lindsey similarly suggests that AIDS, increased incidence of tuberculosis, malaria, and cholera, and the appearance of the hanta virus (related to the bubonic plague) are fulfilling endtimes prophecies (1994:114–116); and Jack Van Impe holds that the reference to the fourth horseman of the apocalypse who rides a "pale horse" (Revelation 6) and brings death through "beasts of the earth" may refer to deadly viruses in the last days (*Jack Van Impe Presents*, July 8, 1996).

Prophecy interpreters also have reevaluated biblical prophecies in light of ozone depletion, global warming, pollution, and other environmental threats (see Boyer 1992:331–337). Apocalyptic predictions about ecological devastation are largely based on prophecies in the Book of Revelation about the breaking of the seven seals and the pouring out of the seven vials of wrath, after which the seas are poisoned like "the blood of a dead man" and every living creature in the oceans dies (Revelation 16:3); the world is filled with darkness and yet people are "seared by intense heat" (Revelation 16:9–10); and the sun grows black, the moon becomes the color of blood, and a tremendous earthquake strikes (Revelation 6:12).

In the 1970s, Lindsey and others often viewed these prophecies in terms of the effects of nuclear destruction, and discussed how a global nuclear war would pollute the oceans, kill sea creatures, create a cloud that would obscure the sun, and burn the grass and trees (see Lindsey 1984 [1973]:117–121). Twenty years later, Lindsey still speaks of the effects of a "nuclear winter" on the environment but also analyzes the prophetic implications of the destruction of the ozone layer, mismanagement of natural resources, depletion of oil reserves, deforestation, and the greenhouse effect, and says that the Bible predicts a total breakdown of the earth's ecosystem in the endtimes (1994:83–100, 117).

By the mid-1990s, Lindsey's newsletter, *International Intelligence Briefing*, regularly had reports on environmental destruction and the increasing frequency of natural disasters, often referred to as a "quickening" of cataclysms prior to the return of Christ. In *Planet Earth—2000 A.D.* Lindsey provides specific examples of the fulfillment of prophecies concerning tribulations of the earth and the decay of the environment, declaring, for instance, that the depletion of the ozone layer combined with the greenhouse effect may result in the "scorching heat" and "horrible sores" described in Revelation 16 (9–11): "the Scripture refers to future events that sound strikingly similar to a plague of skin cancer that erupts among the population of the world" (1994:116). After detailing an assortment of other environmental endtimes signs, Lindsey's assessment of the current situation is predictably fatalistic: "There's nothing we as a people can do about it. It's too late to reverse the adverse effects of industrialization" (1994:309).

Although some prophecy believers view environmental devastation simply as a foreordained part of God's plan, others suggest that the suffering occasioned by ecological crises is the result of divine judgment upon humanity's careless destruction of the earth and cite a passage in Revelation that God would "destroy them which destroy the earth" (11:18). As Dave Hunt states, "A number of God's judgments are ecological in nature, devastating the grass and the trees and polluting the oceans and rivers. The implication is that man has brought the dire consequences upon himself" (1990:163–164).

Some premillennialists assert that although nothing can be done to avert environmental devastation, the ecological crisis may become so extreme that people will welcome a one-world government or perhaps an environmentally aware Antichrist to deal with the problem. Lindsey wrote in 1977 that a new world order may be embraced by people as the only solution to the environmental crisis; Dave Hunt, in 1991, declared that ecological crisis and the environmentalist movement may unite humanity in a common international cause, creating the global unity necessary for the rise of the Antichrist (Lindsey 1977:69–70; Hunt 1990:164).

Just as the possibility of nuclear annihilation has been embraced by premillennialists as divinely ordained, so too has environmental destruction been viewed as an endtimes sign, a certainty rather than a disaster that human beings might prevent through responsible action. Consistent with the broader fatalism of the premillennialist worldviews, humanity is powerless to save the earth and will inevitably destroy it in accordance with the divinely foreordained plan. The regeneration of the environment can be achieved only by God after the cataclysmic destruction of the earth; as Lindsey puts it, "Only a supernatural event—the return of Jesus—is able to restore the planet to health again, to allow it to support human life again" (1994:117). Although environmental destruction is unavoidable, believers are assured of planetary escape through the Rapture and promised that they will dwell in a cleansed and renewed earth with the arrival of the millennium.

Whether centered on the prophetic meanings of ecodisasters or nuclear bombs, global unification or Islamic fundamentalism, new technologies or a new world order, post–Cold War apocalyptic beliefs continue to reflect the view that today's society is in extreme crisis, that the world is unrecuperable by human effort, and that worldly cataclysm is imminent. Environmental destruction and deadly viruses have received greater emphasis in recent prophecy beliefs, yet visions of nuclear annihilation have not declined significantly in apocalyptic traditions and now are complemented by predictions of other disasters, evil conspiracies, and rising Antichrists. If nuclear destruction appears less imminent, it is still regarded as an inevitable event to occur after a period of false peace. In the meantime beliefs about overwhelming evil forces intensify.

Characterized by perceptions of overpowering evil and uncontrollable economic, political, and technological change, current prophecy beliefs reflect a complete loss of faith in government and dominant social institutions and reveal the depth of despair and alienation that exists among many Americans. The emphasis in post–Cold War prophecy beliefs on global conspiracies exemplifies the deeply rooted feelings of helplessness and fatalism intrinsic to apocalyptic worldviews. The preoccupation with the Mark of Beast and the encroaching 666 system epitomizes the sense of pervasive evil in the world, as everyday phenomena such as bar codes, ATM machines, televisions, and computers take on a sinister aura as potential tools of surveillance and enslavement.

These recent emphases within prophecy beliefs also illustrate the process of innovation within apocalyptic traditions; prophecy interpreters and believers have inventively reformulated and updated their belief systems to incorporate new technology, current crises, and perceived threats. In this regard, apocalyptic traditions are both ancient and emergent, continually being revised and made relevant in response to changing circumstances.

Some observers have speculated that premillennialist prophecy belief systems may collapse by the year 2002 if no redeeming supernatural event has occurred by then (see Chandler 1993:284). This prediction appears to be doomed to fail, considering the endurance of apocalyptic thinking, the adaptability of apocalyptic traditions, and the important religious and psychological needs that such beliefs fulfill. In a world believed by many to be increasingly evil and out of control, with even greater threats appearing on the horizon, apocalyptic beliefs explain current crises and suffering as meaningful within God's endtimes plan. The fact that Christian apocalyptic traditions have flourished at a grassroots level for two millennia demonstrates their enduring relevance and explanatory power and portends the continued appeal of such beliefs well into the third millennium.

8

Emergent Apocalyptic Beliefs about UFOs and Extraterrestrial Beings

> In the threatening situation of the world today, when people are begin-
> ning to see that everything is at stake, the projection-creating fantasy
> soars beyond the realm of earthly organizations and powers into the
> heavens, into interstellar space, where the rulers of human fate, the
> gods, once had their abode in the planets.
> —Carl G. Jung, *Flying Saucers*

Of the various eschatological ideas that have arisen in the nuclear age, those concerning the role of UFOs and extraterrestrial beings in the end-times offer particular insights into the emergence and transformation of apocalyptic traditions. As the third millennium approaches, a fascination with UFOs and aliens has arisen, and beliefs about sightings and encounters with extraterrestrials (ETs) have increased in frequency. Such beliefs often reflect apocalyptic anxieties and millennial yearnings, asserting that extraterrestrial entities will play a role in the destruction, transformation, salvation, or destiny of the world.

Despite overt differences, Christian apocalyptic traditions and the UFO phenomenon have concerns in common and express similar themes: a preoccupation with the threat of nuclear annihilation, environmental destruction, and other disasters; a sense of imminent crisis and the loss of confidence in the government to resolve current problems; cultural pessimism and an increasing emphasis on evil conspiracies; feelings of powerlessness and manipulation by external forces beyond one's control; and a yearning for worldly transformation by otherworldly beings. Like other millenarian traditions, the complex lore of UFOs also provides interpretations of events as being part of a meaningful plan, explains the existence of evil and suffering in the world, and offers the promise of salvation. A multivalent phenomenon that could have arisen only in the latter half of the twentieth century, beliefs about the destructive and redemptive aspects of UFOs reflect the apocalyptic fears and hopes of our era and constitute an emergent mythology of new gods and superhuman technology consisting of a synthesis of religious and secular ideas. According to psychiatrist Carl G. Jung, the emergence of beliefs about UFOs offers "a golden opportunity of seeing how a legend is formed, and how in a difficult and dark time for humanity a miraculous tale grows up of an attempted intervention by extra-terrestrial, 'heavenly' powers" (1978:16–17).

As a syncretic religious phenomenon, the flying saucer faith that arose in the 1950s and that continues today in varying forms is composed of an assortment of earlier mythologies, religious traditions, occult teachings, scientific notions, and American popular culture adapted and modified to express current concerns. A recurring belief amid this diversity of influences is that worldly destruction and transformation is imminent. The initial flying saucer movement expressed explicit apocalyptic themes, related primarily to anxieties about atomic testing and the fear of nuclear war. Early flying saucer enthusiasts advanced the notion that the detonation of atomic bombs had attracted benevolent, extraterrestrial beings to earth to warn humanity about nuclear catastrophes, to prevent a nuclear cataclysm, or to save a chosen people prior to nuclear apocalypse. Since the 1950s, wide-ranging endtimes scenarios associated with UFOs have developed, with continuing themes being that extraterrestrial entities will either invade earth in the last days, rescue human beings from worldly cataclysm, or help humanity transform the world and usher in a new age of peace and enlightenment.

The modern UFO era began when Kenneth Arnold, a businessman and pilot, reported seeing nine large disk-shaped objects "skipping" through the sky at an incredible speed near Mt. Rainer, Washington, on June 24, 1947. Less than two months later, according to a Gallup poll, 90 percent of the adult population had heard of flying saucers, and by the end of the year, more than eight hundred other sightings had occurred (Curran 1985:13–14). Millions of individuals have since reported sighting UFOs, and an elaborate body of lore has developed, giving rise to hundreds of UFO groups and a wealth of publications and films.[1] To date no conclusive physical evidence of the existence of UFOs has been produced, but this lack of tangible proof has not deterred widely held beliefs in UFOs and extraterrestrial intelligence. According to a November 1973 Gallup poll, 95 percent of adult Americans had read or heard about UFOs, an awareness of a topic that was one of the highest in the history of Gallup polls. The poll revealed that 51 percent of adult Americans believed that UFOs are "real" and not products of the imagination; 11 percent (a projected fifteen million people) said they had seen a UFO (Jacobs 1975:296). Subsequent polls indicate that beliefs about UFOs have not changed much since the 1970s. Gallup polls in 1978, 1981, and 1987 revealed that approximately 50 percent of North Americans believe that UFOs exist and that they are controlled by intelligent beings from another planet (Curran 1985:10; Gallup 1988:52–54).[2]

Some people think of these intelligent beings as benevolent. A more sinister view of ETs and UFOs has been offered by numerous Christian prophecy interpreters, including Hal Lindsey, who regards UFOs as satanic, endtimes manifestations. The role of UFOs in the endtimes also has been noted by Louis Farrakhan, the leader of the Nation of Islam, who asserts that UFOs will be used to destroy the white man's world and the enemies of Allah in an apocalyptic battle. At a press conference on October 24, 1989, Farrakhan described his encounter with a UFO, during which he received messages from the founder of the Nation of Islam, Elijah Muhammad, who purportedly dwells in a mother ship, whence he orchestrates the downfall of the six-thousand-year reign of the white man (Kossy 1994:27).[3] These divergent beliefs about and encounters with UFOs demonstrate the polysemic possibilities of the UFO phenomenon and the degree to which it may serve as a reflection and projection of current hopes and concerns.

Although beliefs about UFOs often have been ridiculed by academics, the lore that has arisen concerning contact with extraterrestrials has many of the attributes of a popular religious phenomenon: its own mythology, legends, and systems of belief, constructed from previous traditions about the supernatural, and affirmed and elaborated upon through personal encounters, visions, trance states, marvelous journeys, and other numinous experiences. Scholar of religion J. Gordon Melton argues that the flying saucer movement is essentially a religious phenomenon and that it constitutes a significant portion of the broader New Age movement in the United States (1995:9–10). According to folklorist Robert Flaherty, the UFO phenomenon has become a folk religious movement of global proportions, which has been transmitted by believers through rumors, legends, memorates, and various informal networks, and imbibed through science fiction literature, films, pulp magazines, and other forms of popular culture (1990:5).[4] Unlike religious movements that have been promoted and spread by ecclesiastical institutions, early beliefs about UFOs were not codified or co-opted by an institutional body, but diffused at a grassroots level and then formulated into an assortment of belief systems and traditions. This divergent lore is vast and includes legends about crop circles and cattle mutilations, abductions by invasive gray aliens who conduct bizarre medical examinations, mysterious men in black suits who attempt to silence those who have seen UFOs, and conspiracy theories about thoroughgoing government coverups, such as that concerning the rumored recovery of a crashed spaceship near Roswell, New Mexico, on July 8, 1947. Ideas about imminent societal disaster and worldly renewal often form the subtext for these eclectic beliefs, and apocalyptic themes have assumed greater prominence as the year 2000 approaches.

This chapter initially focuses on some of the recurring eschatological ideas associated with various well-known flying saucer groups and on assorted narrative accounts by individuals regarding their personal contact with extraterrestrial beings. It then examines narratives and beliefs about alien abductions, evil ETs and global conspiracies, and Christian prophecy beliefs about UFOs and ETs in the last days. The chapter concludes with a discussion of UFO beliefs that assert that a golden age will be brought about not by an apocalypse but by humans working in accordance with an extraterrestrial or cosmic plan.

Flying Saucers and Nuclear Apocalypse: The Beginnings of the UFO Movement

Traditionally, the appearance of enigmatic objects in the sky has been associated with divine portents and apocalyptic warnings, and it was not long after Kenneth Arnold's sighting of flying saucers in 1947 that people began speculating about the apocalyptic meanings of these objects as well as the possibility of salvation by beings from outer space. According to some UFO enthusiasts, the wave of more than eight hundred sightings in 1947 was directly related to the recent detonation of five atomic bombs (Alamogordo, Hiroshima, Nagasaki, Crossroads A, and Crossroads B). The sightings were frequently reported to have occurred near nuclear power plants, and a common belief was that nuclear bomb tests had drawn attention to planet earth. Flying saucers, some said, had come to warn humanity of the dangers of atomic weapons, to save us from destroying ourselves, or to keep us from endangering life on other planets, similar to the plot of the film *The Day the Earth Stood Still* (1951), in which a saucer lands near the White House and the Christ-like alien Klaatu forewarns of the threat of atomic bombs. UFO researcher Jacques Vallée observes that various UFO belief traditions suggest "that other galactic communities have kept a long-term routine watch on earth and may have been alarmed by the sight of our A-bombs as evidence that we are warlike and on the threshold of space exploration" (1985:47). The detonation of atomic bombs, some UFO enthusiasts conjectured, would cause a chain reaction that would disrupt the cosmos; others, that extraterrestrials feared for their own lives because of the development of nuclear weapons (see Beckley 1980:8). These notions assert that the development of the atomic bomb not only threatened the future of humanity but transgressed the laws of the universe, endangering life on other worlds and violating the cosmic order.

The UFO contactee narratives from the 1950s that describe encounters with benevolent space beings exhibit consistent eschatological themes that have informed subsequent beliefs about UFOs. The accounts resemble other types of visionary experiences and have frequently led to the formation of religious groups and spiritual movements. Because the contactee experience is often positive and tends to involve repeated communications with familiar extraterrestrial entities, an extensive body of narratives and beliefs has emerged, giving rise to assorted folk cosmologies. In the stories, the aliens often make contact in an isolated location with an ordinary and unsuspecting person, bringing the contactee aboard their craft, and sometimes explaining its technology or taking the person for a ride. Unlike the pre–World War II conceptions of bug-eyed monsters from outer space depicted in pulp fiction, the aliens encountered at the dawn of the atomic age are human-like in appearance and portrayed as rational, benevolent, and beautiful beings possessed of superhuman abilities. Coming from superior, utopian civilizations, these beings, like angels, often give messages through telepathy that forewarn of imminent disasters because of the failures of human beings, and usually express concern with the condition of humanity and planet earth. The world is said to be in a state of crisis, which is attributed variously to nuclear proliferation, ecological destruction, societal breakdown, human ignorance, violence, cruelty, and selfishness. The contactee is then given a crucial mission: to warn others of impending worldly catastrophe (Beckley 1980:5; Ellwood and Partin 1988:113).[5]

The sense of imminent doom that pervades the early contactee narratives and that persists in subsequent flying saucer lore usually is directly related to the threat of nuclear destruction. In the 1950s, four of the first flying saucer contactees who received national attention—George Adamski, Truman Bethurum, Daniel Fry, and Orfeo Angelucci—all conveyed messages from space people warning of the dangers of atomic bombs. Adamski was the first to declare that he had had actual contact with space people (in the California desert on November 20, 1952), and their primary message dealt with the danger of radioactivity to the inhabitants of earth and other planets.[6] The encounter narratives of other contactees contained similar forewarnings about atomic bombs and radiation. The space beings warned Orfeo Angelucci of a horrible war that would destroy the planet and urged him to alert the world: "For the present time you are our emissary, Orfeo, and you must act! Even though the people of Earth laugh derisively and mock you as a lunatic, tell them about us!" (Jacobs 1975:118).

Whether condemned as kooks, hoaxers, or pseudoreligious fanatics, or hailed as messianic shamans of the atomic age, these initial contactees have had a profound influence on subsequent UFO lore. Nearly all of them were ordinary men who were self-educated and came from working-class, manual-labor backgrounds. Their visions and accounts expressed the widespread apocalyptic apprehensions of the time and offered an escape from Cold War fears of inevitable nuclear annihilation. This sense of planetary crisis and otherworldly salvation is exemplified by the statements of Gabriel Green, founder of the Amalgamated Flying Saucer Clubs of America, a major organization in the movement: "To the Earth people they contacted, the Space People told of their advanced sciences and of their relatively Utopian way of life. To our planet, in the throes of social and political upheaval and teetering on the brink of self-annihilation by nuclear warfare, they had come, they said, to show us the way out of our crisis and the solutions to our problems" (Ellwood and Partin 1988:125).

In numerous contactee accounts, the apocalyptic danger of nuclear weapons is juxtaposed with descriptions of the space people's utopian life on their home planets, where no war, poverty, suffering, or unhappiness existed.[7] The space people frequently were said to live for thousands of years; some were immortal and nearly all could be reincarnated in another life (Jacobs 1975:115). Often earthlings were told that they also had eternal souls that would survive physical death. This emphasis on eternal life and reincarnation seems especially significant in the context of the nuclear era, in which the bomb threatens perceptions of symbolic immortality.

Worldly Destruction and Planetary Evacuation in the Flying Saucer Faith

Many contactee narratives assert that the space beings are communicating with earthlings to prevent nuclear destruction and other disasters; in some instances, however, worldly cataclysm is regarded as inevitable. A recurring idea in flying saucer lore is that a chosen few will be lifted off before earth is destroyed, a belief that occasionally has given rise to small UFO groups that center on a theology of imminent apocalypse and planetary escape. Perhaps the best-known case study of such beliefs is *When Prophecy Fails*, which focuses on a group in the 1950s led by Mrs. Marian Keech, who declared she was receiving channeled messages from space beings, who warned of worldly flood disaster and promised to rescue believers beforehand (Festinger, Riecken, and Schachter 1956).

The UFO group that has received the most extensive media attention and warrants some discussion is Heaven's Gate, thirty-nine members of which killed themselves by swallowing phenobarbital-laced applesauce chased with vodka on March 23–25, 1997. The collective suicide of members of the sect in the gated community of Rancho Santa Fe, near San Diego, California, was a media event—"the worst mass suicide in U.S. history"—with the group portrayed as a New Age-UFO doomsday "computer cult" of brainwashed devotees, sci-fi techno-millenarians, some of whom were castrated and all of whom were fans of the *X-Files* and *Star Trek*. The sect designed World Wide Web pages and used the Internet to disseminate their beliefs and recruit members.

Although so-called cults are not typical within the UFO movement and Heaven's Gate was much more dogmatic and authoritarian than typical UFO groups, aspects of its belief system resemble ideas present in other apocalyptic UFO groups (and American apocalypticism in general), particularly the sense of fatalism for a world regarded as evil and doomed, and the desire for planetary escape. Like other UFO groups, the theology of Heaven's Gate consists of a synthesis of concepts borrowed from Christianity, Theosophy, science fiction, Eastern religions, and New Age mysticism, as well as notions associated with Gnosticism, Mormonism, and Scientology, melded together and reinterpreted. A central idea among this diversity of beliefs is that doomsday is at hand and that by living an ascetic lifestyle one may transcend earthly existence and ultimately be transported by a UFO to a higher realm.

The group, which was started by Marshall Herff Applewhite and Bonnie Lu Nettles, first received national media attention in September 1975, after the couple gave a lecture on UFOs in Waldport, Oregon, and more than thirty people suddenly disappeared. Believers had sold their possessions and left family, friends, and jobs to relocate with Applewhite and Nettles and wait for their evacuation by flying saucers to the next "evolutionary level" (Balch 1995:138–142). Referring to themselves variously as "Do and Ti," "the Two" (after the two witnesses prophesied in Revelation 11), and "Bo and Peep," Applewhite and Nettles believed that their earthly mission was to lead the lost sheep of humanity back to heaven.

The group came to be called the Human Individual Metamorphosis and later the Total Overcomers Anonymous (references to the goal of overcoming human attachments) and developed a highly regimented lifestyle that included the abandonment of worldly pursuits, the effacement of one's ego, various physical deprivations, and isolation from outside influences that would jeopardize one's salvation. Believers attempted to control and conquer human instincts and desires (ranging from sexual urges to ties with their families), regarding such attachments as well as their bodies (or "vehicles") as a hindrance to salvation.

The beliefs of the sect changed over the years, especially after Nettles died in 1985, but a basic tenet was that aliens dwelling in the Kingdom of Heaven had planted human beings on earth as a gardening experiment to grow souls. Representatives from this Kingdom periodically make "soul deposits" in the bodies of humans, preparing them to be transplanted to a higher evolutionary level. Applewhite considered himself a messianic representative from this higher level, like Jesus, who was incarnated into a human body, and whose mission was to help earthly beings graduate from the human kingdom by overcoming human attachments. By bonding with Applewhite, the celestial messenger, and purifying themselves through the denial of their humanness, the elect could escape from an irredeemably corrupt world and progress to the next level.

The secretive group disappeared from public view until May 27, 1993, when it placed an ad in *USA Today* entitled "UFO Cult Resurfaces with Final Offer," which declared that societal institutions and mainstream religions are controlled by a conspiracy involving Satan and the evil Luciferians, and that the earth would soon be "recycled" and "spaded under." The group also warned of imminent worldly destruction through their Heaven's Gate World Wide Web site and by sending unsolicited messages (or "spamming") on Usenet newsgroups. The group's beliefs were generally ignored or ridiculed on the Internet and this response was interpreted by believers as a sign that they should begin to prepare to return to their home in the heavens, because "the weeds of humanity" had taken over earth's garden (*Newsweek*, April 7, 1997, 35).

The passing of Comet Hale-Bopp in late March 1997, was embraced as a final prophetic sign, the "marker" that believers had been waiting for, offering a sudden opportunity for planetary escape. Followers believed that the comet was being trailed by a gigantic spacecraft that would transport them to the "Evolutionary Kingdom Level Above Human"; collective suicide was viewed as a means of evacuating an evil world, a way to shed one's physical "container" and transport oneself onto this Next Level spacecraft and the Kingdom of Heaven.

Although depicted as a bizarre, occult UFO group, the basic theology of Heaven's Gate largely consists of vernacular and personal interpretations of Christian doctrine. Belief in UFOs was a key element in the group's constellation of beliefs, yet its rigid dualism, emphasis on demonic influences and conspiracies, rejection of the world as evil, and yearning for planetary escape clearly resemble various Christian premillennialist worldviews.

Few UFO groups are characterized by this degree of apocalyptic fervor; however, ideas about the imminent rescue of a chosen elect by space beings persist in the wider UFO movement today. The following full-page advertisement that regularly appears in UFO periodicals contains the basic elements of a more common disaster and evacuation prediction:

UFOS AND THE SPACE BROTHERS

WANT YOU TO SURVIVE

DOOMSDAY

Psychics, spiritual leaders, scientists and UFO contactees all agree that we are living in what has been called the END TIMES.

- The foundation of our civilization is about to crumble.

- The physical world as we know it is going to be destroyed.

- Psychic spiritual and "other-worldly" forces are about to *take over!*

THE TRUTH CAN NOW BE TOLD

. . . We are being told the Earth is rapidly entering the twelfth—AND FINAL!—hour for humankind. All indications are that a "time bomb of destruction" is about to go off ridding the planet of civilization as we have come to accept it. . . .

YOU CAN BE SAVED!

While utter chaos will take place all around us, all of those who have received this highly advanced, truly prophetic warning have said that the "Chosen Ones" who "are ready" will be saved and *taken off* this planet just in the nick of time. . . . [A] mass evacuation by space ship will take place in which hundreds of flying saucers will come down from the sky and "lift off" the worthy. (*UFO Review* 27 [1988]: 3)

The ad is for the publication *Psychic & UFO Revelations in the Last Days* (Beckley 1980), which provides a synthesis of assorted apocalyptic narratives and beliefs associated with the UFO movement compiled by Timothy ("Mr.

UFO") Beckley, editor and publisher of *UFO Review*. According to Beckley, the doomsday predictions collected in his volume were conveyed to more than twenty prominent UFO contactees, all of whom agree that worldly catastrophe is imminent, whether in the form of a global nuclear war, devastating ecological imbalances, land changes, or a shift in the earth's axis that will tip it out of its orbit and send it hurtling toward the sun. In addition, these contactees predict increased lawlessness, immense earthquakes, storms, volcanoes, and other natural disasters resulting in devastating famine and plagues in the last days. Although the world will soon go through a "doomsday phase," the chosen ones will be physically removed from the planet.

Similar to other catastrophic millenarian scenarios, the apocalypse anticipated within the UFO movement is often conceptualized as a cleansing of the world, to be followed by a terrestrial paradise of peace, fulfillment, and harmony. One tract describes it:

> After our rescue, the EARTH WILL BE CLEANSED. Then, after a sufficient time, we will be returned, to the earth . . . after which will be the Golden Age, the Age they speak of as the Millennium. We will be taken up into the sky; millions of earth people. Only to be returned in due time to repopulate and to bring into being the Golden Age; the Age of Wisdom and Purity; the Age of Christness! (Michael X. 1969:29)

The millennial visions, endtimes predictions, and evacuation scenarios in the flying saucer movement clearly resemble Christian beliefs about the Rapture prior to a period of worldly tribulation—although the criteria differ regarding who will be saved before the apocalypse. In some cases the chosen will be members of a specific UFO group; in others, everyone who believes in space beings as well as those who are metaphysically attuned or have the ability to evolve spiritually will be evacuated. Some scenarios include the salvation of children and "good people" with special skills and no criminal record (see Beckley 1980:30). A common belief is that the chosen ones will be "star children" and "cosmic blends"—people whose ancestors mated with space beings eons ago. Anyone interested in UFOs or who senses that they themselves come from "somewhere else" may be the star children referred to, people who are believed to have both earthly and alien genes or attributes (Beckley 1980:33–35).

Ideas about the planetary evacuation of "cosmic blends" may or may not be directly based on Rapture beliefs, but in many instances flying saucer enthusiasts are explicit about their reinterpretation of biblical passages within the framework of beliefs about UFOs and ETs. Searching the Bible for suggestive references to sky gods and unusual celestial phenomena, UFO believers have readily incorporated an assortment of Christian beliefs into the flying saucer pantheon. For example, Ezekiel's vision of spinning or revolving wheels making a rushing noise (Ezekiel 1:4–28) is frequently interpreted as a spaceship, as are the Star of the East that glowed brightly over Bethlehem and the light that blinded Paul on the way to Damascus. Some UFO enthusiasts say that Adam and Eve were extraterrestrials and that angels and various saints were space beings (e.g., the angel Gabriel was a spaceman who hypnotized Mary and artificially inseminated her); that Christ was an enlightened space being and that his numerous miracles, transfiguration, and ascension were caused by alien activity. Popular books such as *Chariots of the Gods?* (von Däniken 1969), *The Bible and Flying Saucers* (Downing 1968), and *God Drives a Flying Saucer* (Dione 1973) have fueled such speculation, asserting, for instance, that God was an astronaut, that UFOs may have parted the Red Sea and led the Israelites out of Egypt, that the ark of the covenant was some sort of radio transmitter, and that the destruction of Sodom and Gomorrah actually describes a nuclear cataclysm, with Lot's wife the victim of radiation.

Unlike Christian fundamentalism or other traditions that tend to reject or demonize the deities of other religions, the UFO faith actively seeks and assimilates Christian ideas and those from other belief systems as well as from popular culture. The UFO faith is thus a composite and repository of previously existing traditions, which imbue the UFO pantheon with historical depth and the authority of the past, even as it is recast in a space-age framework (Flaherty 1990:48–50).

The Ashtar Command, Religious Syncretism, and Apocalyptic Admonitions

The reworking and assimilation of previous beliefs into the UFO faith is illustrated by the numerous UFO groups and publications that assert that Jesus will return in the Rapture or in the Second Coming as the commander of a fleet of space ships. One group of this persuasion is the Guardian Action International organization, which is centered on the channeled messages of Ashtar, who is said to be a space being and commander of thousands of space ships that together are referred to as the Ashtar Command, which will descend prior to worldly catastrophe. When Jesus returns, according to one Ashtar Command leader named Romilar, he will not be alone: "For Jesus, the Christ figure, will not float down out of heaven unescorted. He will be surrounded by our messengers, the angels in the ships of gold, pure gold that will shine. He will lead the Armageddon, the armada of spaceships that will take those from this planet, who have been chosen" (Beckley 1982:55).

The beliefs associated with the Ashtar Command exemplify both the apocalyptic and syncretic aspects of the UFO faith. For decades, the space being known as Ashtar is purported to have channeled messages to hundreds of individuals, beginning in 1951 with George Van Tassel, a desert visionary who lived at Giant Rock, California, near Joshua Tree.[8] The Ashtar Command pantheon consists of a wide range of gods, goddesses, and spiritual masters from diverse planets, including a Trinity not of the Father, Son, and Holy Spirit but comprising a coalition of Commander Ashtar, Jesus Christ (known as Lord Sananda), and Lady Athena, the former Greek goddess.[9] According to devotees, Ashtar continues to transmit messages to various trance mediums, including the primary representative of the Ashtar Command, Thelma B. Terrell (whose spiritual name is Tuella), who began receiving messages from Ashtar in 1979. Believers hold that Ashtar may be "the wisest space being assigned to our solar system . . . [with] the task of bringing Earth more safely through the troubled times that will most certainly cross our path in the next few years" (Beckley 1980:25).

Beaming his messages to contactees from a colossal starship, Commander Ashtar predicts enormous natural disasters, shifting plates of land, nuclear cataclysm, and numerous other crises in the near future, warning that "such an event cannot be postponed much longer. Your planet's vibrations are very, very negative" (Beckley 1980:27). The sense of approaching catastrophe conveyed in the Ashtar Command messages resembles that of the Bayside prophecies, warning of imminent doom but holding out the slender hope that human beings will change their ways. For instance, in one message, when Ashtar is asked through a channeler if apocalypse can be prevented, he replies:

> There is a chance this can all be averted, but with each passing day, the chance gets less and less. If mankind could change the way it lives, if mankind were to put down its arms, then it could be averted. However, there is no sign that this will happen. Someday someone will take matters into their own hands and will push the button, the button that will end civilization as you have come to recognize it. Look to the sky. Tell those that you know who believe, to look up, that we are coming in greater numbers. We will do what we can. Tell those who believe, tell those who are righteous, that we are here, that we are watching over them, that we are praying for their safety. (Beckley 1980:29)

This and other messages from the Ashtar Command call for the reform of humanity yet repeatedly imply that human beings are incapable of changing and that future destruction will be the unavoidable result of human transgression: "It is impossible to change the course of history. . . . This is a natural occurrence, something you have brought upon yourselves, and you will have to pay the karmic consequences" (Beckley 1980:28–29). Although catastrophe is imminent, believers are assured that benevolent beings are observing earth and if need be will rescue the chosen ones.

When disasters intensify and apocalypse becomes inevitable, the Ashtar Command will rescue between 140,000 and 170,000 chosen individuals and take them to a safe place, to either another planet or a large mother ship, where they will be able to watch the destruction from afar. Evacuees will then be returned to repopulate the planet at some point in the future, depending on the degree of devastation and nuclear fallout (Beckley 1980:27). The rescued chosen ones will be believers in UFOs and others whose presence is essential for the repopulation of the planet. According to recent messages delivered to Tuella by the Ashtar Command, this endtimes evacuation scenario, referred to as the "Great Exodus of Human Souls," will occur in three phases by the year 2000 (Tuella 1993).

Aetherians, Ascended Masters, and Conditional Apocalyptic Beliefs

Numerous other UFO groups also warn that worldly catastrophe is imminent but assert that complete annihilation may be averted if people follow the directives of space entities. This conditional apocalypticism, which resembles the apocalyptic warnings delivered at various Marian apparition sites, maintains that if people change their behavior as prescribed by superhuman beings—put an end to violence, become spiritually attuned, or work for the transformation of planetary consciousness—the world may be saved.[10] The Aetherius Society, one of the best-known and longest-lived UFO contactee groups, has said for decades that imminent disasters may be averted through prayer and other spiritual practices. Based in Los Angeles, the society was founded by George King, who states that he has been selected as the primary channel for extraterrestrial messages transmitted from a being named Aetherius. According to King, he was contacted telepathically in 1954 by numerous Cosmic Intelligences orbiting earth in spacecraft and given messages concerning the salvation of the world: imminent worldly destruction may be avoided if the dangers of atomic weapons are acknowledged, and worldly redemption is possible through prayer and the promotion of the metaphysical teachings of the Cosmic Masters (including Jesus, Mars Sector 6, and Jupiter 92). King and his devotees use "Spiritual Energy Batteries" that harness and amplify their prayers for world salvation; this "Prayer Power," a form of psychic healing energy, is then discharged periodically to avert planetary catastrophes. Like the Baysiders, the Aetherians believe in the power of prayer to forestall or avert cataclysm, and the Aetherians declare that their prayers, amplified by the spiritual technology provided by the Masters, are responsible for the end of the Cold War and for averting various disasters such as a predicted earthquake that would have submerged California (Curran 1985:63–69).

In addition to the threat of earthly cataclysms, King declares that a constant threat of invasion by evil space beings exists, and that the Aetherians and the Cosmic Masters have fended off these nefarious beings on various occasions. In the late 1950s, for example, evil entities—scientists from the dying planet "Garouche"—were defeated by Master Aetherius and a fleet of nine thousand spaceships that encircled earth with an impenetrable shield (Saliba 1995:36). In other messages, the Masters have promised that the Aetherians will be warned if the apocalypse should occur, so that they may gather at certain sacred, spiritually charged mountains to await rescue from above. The goal of the society, however, is to prevent worldly annihilation, save every soul on the planet, and transform planetary consciousness.

In addition to UFO groups that venerate extraterrestrial entities in flying saucers who visit earth and make contact with human beings, numerous groups focus on Ascended Masters who exist on other planets but do not visit earth in vehicles. One such group, which has been anticipating an apocalypse for decades, is the Church Universal and Triumphant (the Summit Lighthouse), which has roughly thirty thousand devotees. Its followers say that the Ascended Masters in the cosmos communicate through paranormal means, channeling redemptive messages through Elizabeth Claire Prophet, the leader of the group. Like UFO groups, the doctrines of the church are syncretic and include ideas from Christianity, Eastern religions, Theosophy, and aspects of the I AM movement, an American depression-era sect.

Ms. Prophet, the "Anointed Messenger" of the Great White Brotherhood, has received numerous apocalyptic warnings from the Ascended Masters, who include Jesus, the Virgin Mary, Archangel Raphael, the eighteenth-century French nobleman St. Germain, the heroes of the American Revolution, Harriet Beecher Stowe, Albert Einstein, a mysterious entity named Ray-O-Light, and K-17, the supernatural director of the Cosmic Secret Police. These Masters are believed to guide the world and help humanity fulfill the "cosmic destiny of the millions of souls evolving on the planet earth" (Prophet 1987:i). In the early 1980s the church, which had its headquarters in Malibu, California, since the 1960s, purchased twelve thousand acres of land in Montana, several miles north of Yellowstone National Park. The church received extensive media coverage when reporters learned that bomb shelters were under construction on the property. Ms. Prophet announced that they were being built in preparation for twenty-five thousand years of negative karma that would soon be made manifest on earth in the form of cataclysmic disasters, including a Soviet missile attack.

Although the Church Universal and Triumphant, the Aetherians, and other groups within the wider UFO and New Age movements may differ in terms of specific theologies and endtimes scenarios, a fundamental belief shared by all is that a complete transformation of society and the human race is necessary to thwart humanity's destructive tendencies. Human beings are usually viewed by these groups as an unenlightened, lower life form, and extraterrestrials are said to be helping humanity attain a higher form of consciousness that will lead to the next level of evolutionary development. This widely held belief is espoused by Brad Steiger, a leader in the UFO movement and author of more than one hundred books on UFOs. Steiger maintains that UFOs are multidimensional, higher entities that are guiding human beings into a new age of harmony and enlightenment, and that these godlike beings have always assisted humanity but that since the 1950s have accelerated the interactions in preparation for the imminent transformation of the planet. The transition, which has been predicted for centuries, will inevitably involve apocalyptic trauma: "For generations our prophets and revelators have been referring to it as The Great Cleansing, Judgment Day, Armageddon. But we have been promised that, after a season of cataclysmic changes on the earth plane, a New Age consciousness will suffuse the planet. It is to this end that the gods have been utilizing the UFO as a transformative symbol" (Steiger 1983:39–40).

The Raelians, Cosmic Cloning, and the Syncretism of Science and Religion

The synthesis of religion and science, nuclear apocalyptic fears and space age millenarian hopes that characterizes beliefs about UFOs, finds full expression in the cosmology of the Raelians, a well-known UFO group that asserts that humanity will be transformed and saved by the arrival and guidance of super-human beings. The Raelian movement, which has more than twenty-five thousand members worldwide, was founded in 1973 by Rael (born Claude Vorilhon) after an encounter with space beings. In this and subsequent encounters Rael was informed that his mission is to warn humanity that it has entered the "Age of Apocalypse" since the bombing of Hiroshima and Nagasaki in 1945 and that human beings now must choose whether they will annihilate themselves in a global nuclear war or make a leap to a new planetary consciousness. Raelians contend that human beings were scientifically created by extraterrestrials, called the "Elohim," who fashioned humankind in their own image through the synthesis of DNA in their laboratories, and then set human beings on earth. The 1945 detonations alerted the Elohim, our extraterrestrial forefathers, to the fact that humanity is now sophisticated enough to learn about its origins, if it does not destroy itself first. Rael, as the messenger of the Elohim and the last of forty earth prophets, states that UFOs manned by the Elohim and the thirty-nine previous prophets (Jesus, Buddha, Mohammed, Joseph Smith, et al.) will arrive on earth *if* an Elohim embassy is built for the space beings in Jerusalem by the year 2025. If not, the Elohim will not come and earth will be destroyed.

Unlike many other UFO groups, the Raelians do not emphasize planetary bodily escape but, rather, personal salvation and a type of immortality achieved through a process of cosmic cloning. By attaining spiritual perfection, the Raelians believe that they will alter and perfect their DNA; it is hoped that duplicates of themselves will be cloned by the Elohim for future space travel and settlement on virgin planets. Raelians participate in four annual festivals in which they believe that their DNA codes are registered by the Elohim as they hover overhead in spacecraft. The Raelians each also sign a contract that permits a mortician to cut a piece of bone from one's forehead (the "third eye"), which is then frozen and saved for the arrival of the Elohim, who may use it to immortalize the devotee through DNA replication. In addition to saving themselves by being regenerated through superhuman technologies such as cloning, the Raelians work to save the world by informing others of the teachings of Rael and the Elohim and by advocating construction of an embassy for the space beings in Jerusalem (Palmer 1995:106–107).

Like the apocalyptic predictions of previous prophets, the techno-millenarian beliefs communicated by Rael, George King, and other UFO visionaries express the notion that the fate of humanity is determined by the arrival or guidance of superhuman beings and that worldly salvation is possible only if human beings act in ways prescribed by these messiah-like entities. Human beings, by themselves, are depicted as relatively powerless and having contributed very little to the development of human history and culture. The sense of fate and the powerlessness of humanity to save or transform itself that characterize these UFO beliefs is epitomized by the Raelian cosmology, which asserts that human beings are the products of an experiment conducted by space scientists. According to the Raelians, not only did the Elohim create human beings in test tubes long ago, but they have impregnated female earthlings in order to produce all the great spiritual leaders of the world, orchestrating the religious development of humanity and determining significant historical events.

Messages from the Ashtar Command similarly assert that the world's great cultural and spiritual leaders were either space entities or were influenced by ETs, and that messages from the space people inspired numerous American leaders and thinkers, including George Washington, Abraham Lincoln, Benjamin Franklin, and Franklin Roosevelt (see Beckley 1982:38). Related beliefs about ancient astronauts who were responsible for many of the achievements of humanity through the ages also reflect this sense of powerlessness: aliens, not human beings, oversaw construction of the pyramids and development of ancient civilizations and agriculture. Alone, humans are helpless and doomed; worldly salvation and transformation is possible only if they follow the mandates of superhuman entities who determine the fate of humanity and the planet.

Apocalypse, Technological Angels, and Fatalism in the UFO Faith

As various researchers have noted, beliefs and narratives about space beings resemble previous stories about intervention by supernatural entities, specifically encounters with angels (see Jung 1978; Godwin 1990; Flaherty 1990). These similarities have caught the attention of Christian writers as well, including evangelist Billy Graham, who notes, "UFOs are astonishingly angel-like in some of their reported appearances" (Curran 1985:10). Like angels, the space people are often depicted as superior otherworldly beings of light; they are gentle, benevolent, peaceful, helpful—the perfection of harmonious and youthful beauty. Both use remarkable means of aerial transport and are superior to humans intellectually, morally, spiritually, or technologically (Godwin 1990:184–185). Most important, perhaps, both angels and space beings are messengers, communicating God's principles or cosmic laws. However, encounters with angels tend to involve communications of a personal nature, whereas missives from space beings are often said to have global importance and to concern planetary crisis and threats to the future of the human race. These messages frequently reflect the view that the planet can no longer sustain human life; that although planet earth is hostile, the universe is friendly; and that angelic beings with benevolent technology will rescue believers. Like the prophets of old, UFO contactees warn of impending chastisements and worldly destruction unless humanity changes its behavior, and offer the hope of survival and salvation.

In his study of the psychological meanings of UFOs, *Flying Saucers: A Modern Myth of Things Seen in the Skies* (1978), Carl G. Jung wrote that traditional beliefs about supernatural beings change with the times and assume the cultural forms of particular historical periods. Documenting the antecedents to UFOs in past religious beliefs about a divine mediator, he suggested that space people were the equivalent of modern angels in technological guise who had emerged in popular belief traditions. Jung believed that early UFO sightings were a direct result of Cold War anxieties: with the world divided into two hostile superpowers with nuclear weapons, people yearned for a divine resolution of the crisis. Although many people may have trouble believing, in an increasingly secular age, that the human race will be saved by God's miraculous intervention, they are willing to believe in superhuman beings with advanced technology. According to Jung, "Anything that looks technological goes down without difficulty with modern man. The possibility of space travel has made the unpopular idea of a metaphysical intervention much more acceptable" (1978:22–23). Focusing in particular on visions of UFOs as luminous disks, Jung declared that flying saucers resembled mandalas, archetypal symbols of psychic totality and salvation found in mythologies through the world. UFOs might be psychological projections or perhaps "materialized psychisms" emerging from the collective unconscious that expressed people's yearning for harmony, reassurance, and reconciliation in the nuclear era (1978:14–23).

Although Jung's study was first published in 1958, the beliefs and lore of UFO movements and encounters with benevolent space beings since that time seem to support his thesis. One does not have to dig deep to uncover the apocalyptic ideas of UFO groups and contact narratives, and it is readily apparent that many of them are preoccupied with the threat of nuclear destruction and other perceived crises. As a popular religious response to the anxieties of the nuclear age, the UFO faith directly addresses apocalyptic fears, promising salvation by all-knowing beings with superior consciousness and technology who oversee the fate of humanity. In contrast to the destructive technology of atomic weapons and the inescapable specter of nuclear annihilation, UFOs represent a benevolent technology that offers the prospect of planetary escape and the possibility of a golden age of peace and harmony. Just as the image of the mushroom cloud has become a master symbol of destruction in the modern era, the UFO has emerged as a folk symbol of hope and salvation, promising rescue by means of a technological Rapture brought about by savior beings descending from the heavens, the traditional dwelling place of the gods in Western religions.

Like postwar apocalyptic beliefs in Christian traditions, the UFO faith often expresses the belief that nuclear annihilation and other cataclysms are imminent and uncontrollable by human beings. Although earthlings are encouraged by the space people to stop using nuclear weapons and work to avert worldly cataclysms by promoting peace and harmony, a sense of fatefulness and impending doom is often pervasive. As a message from the Ashtar Command states, "If you watch the news you can see that the earth is like a festering wound, a wound that keeps getting larger and larger. There is more hatred among mankind than ever before. The bomb is about ready to explode" (Beckley 1980:32). Helpless before the destructive power of the bomb and other impending disasters, humanity sees its only salvation in the planetary escape and protection offered by otherworldly beings.

The UFO faith exemplifies the ways that traditions arise from current eschatological and soteriological concerns and have been reinvented from existing beliefs and practices in accordance with the cultural and mythic forms of the atomic age. The continuing development and reformulation of traditions concerning the endtimes role of UFOs illustrate the ways that apocalyptic belief systems are constructed in response to the dominating concerns of the times.

The Transformation of UFO Lore: The Eschatological Meanings of Alien Abduction Narratives

In recent years a variety of new UFO traditions have emerged that center on the abduction of human beings by extraterrestrials. Alien abduction narratives are first-person accounts about encounters and captures by alien beings who are often described as small, gray-skinned creatures with large triangular heads and bulging black eyes. Although such encounters have been known in UFO circles since the mid-1960s, the phenomenon was popularized after the publication in 1987 of Whitley Strieber's *Communion*, which reached the top of the *New York Times* best-seller list in May that year. Strieber's account of his abduction was followed by extensive coverage of the phenomenon on television and radio talk shows and in a profusion of publications, including *Abduction: Human Encounters with Aliens* (1994) by Harvard psychiatrist John E. Mack, *Close Encounters of the Fourth Kind* (1995) by journalist C. B. D. Bryan, *Secret Life: Firsthand Accounts of UFO Abductions* (1992) by historian David M. Jacobs, and *Intruders* (1987) by ufologist Budd Hopkins. Ufologists make bold claims about the pervasiveness of the abduction phenomenon, estimating that anywhere between 900,000 and 3.7 million individuals have undergone abduction (Bryan 1995:256; Whitmore 1995:67). Although abduction accounts have come from countries other than the United States, some researchers see alien abductions as primarily an American phenomenon, with no other nation expressing the same intensity of interest in the subject (Whitmore 1995:80).

Despite the wealth of literature on abduction encounters, the apocalyptic aspects of such experiences have been largely neglected by researchers, even though abductees themselves often assign an eschatological meaning to their experiences, which frequently deal with imminent worldly destruction, human destiny, transformation, and a controlling power that oversees all existence. Some abductees (or "experiencers") assert that the aliens are evil beings who have a sinister plan for world domination or that they are amoral beings who are exploiting humanity for their own purposes in order to insure the survival of their race. The other, more predominant view, is that aliens are benevolent beings or multidimensional entities who are warning us of imminent disaster or overseeing the evolution of humanity, either by interbreeding with human beings or by directing human consciousness to a more advanced level. The latter view has obvious redemptive themes. In some scenarios, the salvation of humanity will not be brought about through worldly cataclysm but gradually through the genetic and spiritual perfection of human beings as directed by superhuman entities—a view that differs significantly from previous apocalyptic worldviews.

Recurring Eschatological Themes in Abduction Accounts

Folklorists such as Robert Flaherty (1990), Thomas Bullard (1989), and David Hufford (1977) have noted that although the abduction phenomenon has precipitated a variety of narratives, beliefs, and interpretations, the accounts share features with previous legends of supernatural encounters, abductions, and otherworldly journeys, particularly nightmare experiences, out-of-body experiences, shamanic journeys, and traditional encounters with fairies, dwarves, demons, and other diminutive creatures of the lower mythologies. According to these researchers, an actual core experience of some type may underlie the abduction reports, and the transcultural experience is then interpreted within the context of specific belief traditions, such as the "Old Hag" tradition, the fairy faith, or UFO beliefs (Bullard 1989:168; Flaherty 1990:373–482; Hufford 1982:232–234).

In addition to their parallels with earlier accounts of encounters with otherworldly beings, UFO abduction narratives have a consistent structure and are characterized by similar themes. First, aliens are interested in human reproduction and the genetic makeup of human beings, and abductees describe in vivid detail their often frightening encounters in which aliens conduct medical experiments. Abductees describe examinations often of a sexual nature in which they are penetrated or their body parts and organs removed and later reassembled (Bullard 1989:156; Whitmore 1995:70). According to some, aliens submit abductees to this gruesome ordeal so as to procure genetic materials to create hybrid breeding pools in an attempt to save their own race or to develop a new breed of human beings that will survive after the current world is destroyed. Other abductees declare that the aliens come from a "dying planet" that has been devastated by catastrophes, and because their planet and its inhabitants are no longer fertile, they seek human genetic materials to rejuvenate their race (Bullard 1989:156–158).

As numerous researchers have commented, abduction narratives not only share the features of traditional narratives about incubi and succubi, dwarves, and fairies (capture, paralysis, temporal distortions, "missing time," and sexual and reproductive themes) but also resemble accounts of shamanic initiations, in which individuals enter a deathlike trance and journey to other worlds where they endure torture and dismemberment and then are reassembled by supernatural beings and bestowed with sacred knowledge, often of an eschatological nature. Some abductees assert that some sort of spiritual transformation occurs after the encounter, a turning point in their lives (Bullard 1989:162–163; Whitmore 1995:70–72). Abductees regularly report that after the physical ordeal, they are subjected to a spiritual examination in which their souls are scrutinized for flaws—again, a parallel with the spiritual self-examination and transformation reported in traditional shamanic and visionary encounters.

After the physical and spiritual examination, the abductee is given messages by the beings, which usually take the form of prophecies and warnings about worldly destruction, the end of the human race, and the salvation of the planet (Bullard 1989:156–157; Bryan 1995:421). As Bullard states, the aliens warn "that humans are on a path to nuclear, ecological, or moral destruction and [deliver] prophecies of a coming time of tribulation or cataclysm. In other words, earth is well on its way to the fate already suffered by the aliens' planet" (1989:156–157). Often these messages resemble those delivered to early flying saucer contactees, similarly warning that if humanity does not change its ways, stop using nuclear weapons, and end world conflicts, some sort of catastrophe is inevitable. In some cases, abductees have been shown images of the world blowing up and of an otherworldly metropolis being built by aliens for those evacuated prior to worldly destruction. Although warnings of the dangers of nuclear weapons persist, current abduction lore is also preoccupied with apocalyptic scenarios involving environmental catastrophes, such as global warming, the destruction of the ozone layer, deforestation, and pollution of the oceans, with many in the UFO movement believing that the primary message of the aliens is the conservation of earth (Bryan 1995:421).

In some instances imminent catastrophe is regarded as a natural consequence of human error, with humans destroying themselves; in other instances it is spoken of as a chastisement, similar to the chastisements predicted in Marian apparitions, although inflicted for different reasons. Sometimes the aliens encourage the abductees to study metaphysics and to become more caring and thoughtful of others as a means of averting apocalypse, again similar to the religious message of many earlier flying saucer contactee experiences. Abductees are often informed that they have been chosen and that their experiences are part of a larger plan that is to be revealed at a later date. They are also told that humanity will survive the upcoming cataclysm in some way, if not through planetary escape, then through the process of hybridization in which a new human/alien being will be created (Bullard 1989:157).

In addition to the themes of worldly destruction and salvation, feelings of complete powerlessness also pervade UFO abduction accounts. Unlike the benevolent Space People and Cosmic Masters encountered by early UFO contactees, the beings in abduction accounts are often depicted as intergalactic vivisectionists, all-controlling extraterrestrial genetic engineers who conduct torturous experiments on human beings in order to save the human race, which cannot be saved through human effort. Many abductees not only feel helpless but sense that although aliens seem altruistic and courteous, in fact they are cold and indifferent, with little regard for human suffering or perhaps no understanding of it: "Some abductees complain that they were treated like guinea pigs and merely used by the beings. . . . Manipulativeness is another common complaint lodged against the abductors . . . some abductees realize they were compelled to obey some hypnotically repeated insistence" (Bullard 1989:157). Abductees often feel that the aliens have a hidden agenda and that they have completely controlled the abduction and are controlling worldly events as well. As one abductee put it, "They're doing things against our will. And the most frightening thing is, we have no control. . . . It doesn't matter what we do or think. They're going to do whatever they want anyway" (Bryan 1995:227–228). In these accounts, the gray aliens forcibly abduct victims and dissect them as if they were lab rats; the abductees often emerge from these experiences feeling traumatized, exploited, and abused. Some abductees even announce that beadlike objects have been implanted in their bodies for reasons of surveillance, control, or further exploitation. In any case, future abduction may be imminent—it could happen at any time, to anyone. Despite the feelings of transformation that some abductees report, these accounts are marked by an undeniable sense of helplessness and victimization by overwhelming forces beyond one's control.

Whatever one makes of such narratives, they are consistently apocalyptic, reflecting anxieties about the imminence of the end of the world and the end of the human species. The narratives may resemble traditional experiences of initiatory death and transformation involving otherworldly beings, but the broader and more explicit message concerns the destruction of the world and the salvation of humanity. Although not yet formulated into a cohesive apocalyptic worldview, abduction lore shares features with other apocalyptic belief systems: it is characterized by a sense of powerlessness, perceptions of societal crisis, and the belief in a superhuman plan or superhuman forces that are overseeing the salvation of humanity, in this case through extraterrestrial genetic engineering. Abduction narratives imply that the world is doomed unless the human race undergoes some sort of radical transformation that cannot be accomplished through human effort but only through the guidance of otherworldly or interdimensional entities.

Unlike earlier UFO evacuation scenarios, abduction lore expresses the idea that salvation will not necessarily come from above through sudden rescue by benevolent space beings but from within through the gradual transformation of humanity by means of unpleasant but necessary genetic manipulations. In *Abduction* (1994), John E. Mack writes that abductee experiences are characterized by an awareness of "the failure of the human experiment in its present form," as well as the necessity for alien/human hybridization and a radical change of human consciousness and behavior. According to Mack:

> Abduction experiencers come to feel deeply that the death of human beings and countless others will occur on a vast scale if we continue on our present course and that some sort of new life-form must evolve if the human biological and

spiritual essence is to be preserved. . . . [W]e may be witnessing . . . an awkward joining of two species, engineered by an intelligence we are unable to fathom, for a purpose that serves both our goals, with difficulties for each. (1994:415–416)

In an age in which notions of symbolic immortality and human continuity are threatened by visions of nuclear catastrophe, environmental destruction, deadly viruses, and other crises, beliefs about UFOs and ETs offer the hope that a superhuman plan exists for the salvation of humanity and the continuation of the human experiment.

The yearning for a sense of continuity and symbolic immortality is fulfilled through beliefs about millennial redemption and an immortal soul, and also through a sense of connection with one's ancestors as well as "living on" through one's children (Lifton 1987:10–27). In UFO lore aliens are depicted as not only our ancient ancestors but our children as well; ETs are a futuristic vision of what human beings will become as they continue to evolve. In some scenarios the aliens are believed to be our future descendants who have traveled back in time to visit earth and observe their primitive human ancestors. At a time in which humanity is confronted with images of ultimate extinction, extraterrestrials represent the symbolic recovery of the future and the continued existence and evolution of the human race (Flaherty 1990:710–712).

Like the alien/human hybrid spawned in these narratives, abduction lore is itself a hybrid of religious and secular ideas, an amalgam of motifs about worldly destruction and salvation expressed in terms of futuristic technology, evolution, and genetic manipulation. As superhuman genetic engineers with omnipotent technology, the aliens are a secularized counterpart of God in some scenarios; in others, they are depicted as some sort of transcendent consciousness or power in the universe, like "the Force" of *Star Wars*. In either case, extraterrestrials are otherworldly beings who fulfill many of the traditional functions of deities. Like the gods and goddesses of old who mated with mortals to create hybrid heroes with extraordinary powers, aliens interbreed with humans to create new beings who insure the survival and continued development of humanity. The extraterrestrials are said to be overseeing human evolution and, like gods, are believed by some to have created human beings, and they intervene in history and warn humankind of its moral transgressions (Whitmore 1995:74).

As noted previously, history is often presented as the unfolding of a superhuman plan controlled by extraterrestrials in UFO lore, similar to God's divine plan in Christian prophecy belief. Contactees and abductees have a critical role in this plan: to warn humanity of imminent destruction and to participate in crucial cosmic experiments involving the contribution of their blood, sperm, and ova to ensure the survival of human beings or to help create a new hybrid race. In these accounts the sacred and the profane go hand in hand, and salvation occurs through painful experiments and genetic recombination. Above all else, beliefs about aliens and UFOs assert that humans will survive worldly destruction as the result of superhuman guidance and ultimately transcend earthly existence, gaining the technology and wisdom of the aliens and perhaps becoming superhuman beings themselves.

Evil Aliens, Abductions, and Conspiracies

Although much alien abduction lore warns of imminent worldly catastrophe but offers the promise of survival, with the approach of the year 2000 increasingly sinister and unredemptive UFO lore about malevolent ETs who will usher in the apocalypse has emerged. These aliens are described as evil beings who are plotting to destroy the human race and sometimes are depicted as the demonic counterparts and enemies of the benevolent aliens. In this endtimes lore, good and evil aliens take on mythic dimensions and wage wars that will determine the fate of humanity and the world. Previous abduction experiences have been reinterpreted as part of this alien invasion plan. In some scenarios the human/alien hybrids from dying planets will invade and conquer earth in the future. In other scenarios the aliens are already walking among us and preparing to colonize earth.

This recent UFO lore offers little chance of averting imminent worldly destruction or humanity's enslavement by aliens. The hope of salvation promised by the early flying saucer faith has been replaced by beliefs and narratives about sinister abductions and cattle mutilations that are characterized by a sense of imminent crisis, overwhelming evil in the world, paranoia, and manipulation by uncontrollable forces. In a characteristically syncretic fashion, this UFO lore has adopted the conspiratorial themes that pervade Christian apocalyptic traditions, becoming more and more preoccupied with the rise of the New World Order, the Antichrist, and theories about the baleful machinations of organizations such as the Trilateral Commission, the United Nations, and the Bilderberg Group, to name a few.

Conspiracy theories about government cover-ups and secret organizations have been a theme in UFO lore from its beginnings. Stories have been told since 1947, for instance, about the menacing "Men-in-Black" (MIBs), dark-clothed strangers who stalk and threaten those who try to increase public awareness of UFOs (and who, as folklorist Peter Rojcewicz has discussed, resemble the devils of earlier folk traditions [Rojcewicz 1987]). The sense of helplessness and overwhelming evil that characterizes this lore is exemplified by recent beliefs about government cover-ups concerning a pact between the gray aliens and the MJ-12, a group of top-level scientists and military officers planning to establish a one-world dictatorship. In his chronology of the development of UFO phenomenon, aerospace historian Curtis Peebles states that recurring beliefs about UFOs from 1987 to 1993 assert that gray aliens who suffer from genetic disorders abduct human beings in order to survive, removing their sperm and ova, and combining them with their own genetic material to produce alien/human hybrids. In exchange for the aliens' knowledge of space technology (which has been used to build advanced weaponry), the MJ-12 granted the "Grays" permission to abduct earthlings for their experiments and for extracting the enzyme from the blood of humans and cattle (hence the cattle mutilations) necessary for their survival. It also built underground bases for them. According to some beliefs, the aliens then deceived the MJ-12 (referred to as the "Grand Deception") and now are increasing their assaults and preparing for invasion; this, according to some, was the underlying motivation for President Reagan's proposed "Star Wars" program for the construction of a protective shield (Bullard 1989:158; Peebles 1994:273).

Another common theme in this belief tradition is that the aliens and the MJ-12 are collaborating to establish a New World Order. According to this scenario, the MJ-12 and the Grays, in league with the Trilateral Commission, the Bilderberg Group, the Council on Foreign Relations, and international bankers, has formed a "Secret Government" that controls every aspect of politics, the military, industry, religion, commerce, banking, and the media, a view espoused by Milton William Cooper, perhaps the most infamous UFO conspiracy theorist. The beliefs assert that humanity ultimately will be enslaved or exterminated in concentration camps at the hands of the Grays, millions of whom now await in bases to invade the United States from within (Peebles 1994:281–282). Beliefs about the imminence of alien attack are reflected by the statements and publications of the influential ufologist John Lear (son of Learjet inventor Bill Lear), who has declared on various occasions that human beings have no hope of resisting this invasion, stating in one interview, "They're going to march us just exactly like the Holocaust" (Peebles 1994:274). Such beliefs not only reflect the view that humanity is doomed but imply that the cosmos itself is perhaps dying as sickly aliens from dead planets invade and destroy earth.

Unlike beliefs about aliens developing human/alien hybrids to ensure the survival of both races threatened with extinction, more recent lore has absolutely no redemptive themes; in this sense it resembles secular apocalyptic ideas about the imminence of nuclear cataclysm, expressing feelings of hopelessness and fatalism. The evil aliens have superior technology and intelligence, as well as the help of the U.S. government and the sinister Secret Government, a coalition that is all-powerful and that will enslave and exterminate humans, as the Grays conduct cruel experiments on the survivors. Fatalism, nihilism, and powerlessness—the trinity of secular apocalyptic thought—are characteristics of such beliefs and are distilled and amplified in this UFO tradition. Inexplicable and inescapable evil forces are everywhere; they are uncontrollable, and the creeping tentacles of the conspiracy entwine with every aspect of human existence.

The increasing secularization of UFO traditions is exemplified by yet another emergent tradition within broader UFO lore. This branch of lore does not involve aliens at all but holds instead that the increase in accounts of UFO visitations and abductions is the result of a global conspiracy by evil *earthly* powers: alien abductions have been faked, and UFOs have been developed by global organizations that are preparing to stage a UFO invasion in the future to frighten people into accepting a New World Order. The threat of alien attack would make the nations of the world forget their differences and unite to fend off the invasion. The global unification will then bring about a totalitarian society of surveillance and complete control. According to UFO researcher Nario Hayakawa, "Secret international banking groups and other global secret groups are going to forcefully eliminate international borders and create some kind of controlled society. . . . The most amazing weapon they will use to do this will be the extraterrestrial threat" (Kossy 1994:27). In this latest merging of traditions, UFO lore and Christian prophecy beliefs about a global dictatorship associated with the rise of Antichrist converge in a secularized endtimes conspiracy about overwhelming evil powers.

As the great diversity of religious and secular UFO lore indicates, the UFO phenomenon has become a Rorschach test of popular eschatological ideas. Debunkers and enthusiasts may debate the existence of UFOs, but unquestionably the UFO phenomenon has served as a barometer and projection of dominant psychosocial concerns in the postwar era. The range of UFO lore illustrates the protean qualities of apocalyptic beliefs and the ways new traditions reflect dominant concerns, fears, hopes, and preoccupations in American society. Despite the wide-ranging nature of this lore, common themes emerge— immense conspiracies, imminent destruction, and individual helplessness— that also characterize Christian apocalyptic traditions and that similarly express the extreme level of alienation and hopelessness felt by many in American society today. The fatalistic underpinnings of these varying systems of belief are revealed by the pervasiveness of conspiracy theories, which situate every event in a labyrinthine plan. The invention and use of nuclear weapons, the rise and fall of the Soviet Union, AIDS, the drug trade, recent trends in politics, commerce, and banking, and ultimately the destruction and salvation of humanity are explained as part of a grand design, whether foreordained by God, controlled by the Secret Government, or orchestrated by ETs. Conspiracy theories, like other fatalistic systems of belief, are appealing precisely because they provide reasons for perceived evils and directly address feelings of powerlessness and victimization, attributing these to sinister, impersonal forces beyond one's control. By naming actual enemies and revealing an underlying master plan, these differing eschatological traditions offer a sense of understanding, order, and symbolic control over otherwise inexplicable and uncontrollable events.

UFOs and Christian Apocalyptic Traditions

The multivalent meanings of UFOs and the adaptability of apocalyptic traditions are epitomized by the ways that UFOs have been emphasized in Christian prophecy belief and interpreted as part of God's endtimes plan. In Christian traditions throughout history, sightings of strange aerial phenomena have been associated with divine portents and apocalyptic warnings, inspired in part by the biblical passage in which Jesus says that "fearful sights and great signs shall there be from heaven" before the end of the world (Luke 21:11). Some have interpreted the more numerous UFO sightings as a portent that apocalypse draws near, but a goodly number of prophecy enthusiasts have interpreted UFOs as malevolent manifestations and ETs as demonic beings that will be involved in an apocalyptic scenario prior to Judgment Day.

According to Leon Bates of the Bible Believers' Evangelistic Association (Texas), the demonic features of ETs include their avoidance of strong light, foul odors reported at UFO landing sites, their purported telepathic powers, and their ghostlike attributes (1985:90). Christian author I. D. E. Thomas cites references in Genesis 6 about the Nephilim—sons of God who mated with the daughters of men—and concludes they may have been fallen angels who are returning in the last days to use UFOs as part of a plan to create a super race, conquer earthlings, and prepare the world for the Antichrist (1986:232).

Various other prophecy enthusiasts, including Hal Lindsey, paint UFOs as a satanic endtimes delusion devised to take the faithful away from God in the last days before Christ's return. In his *Planet Earth—2000 A.D.*, Lindsey devotes an entire chapter to the prophetic importance of UFOs, stating at the outset:

> Since the publication of the *Late Great Planet Earth*, I have become thoroughly convinced that UFOs are real. . . . And I believe they are operated by alien beings of great intelligence and power. Where I differ from most "ufologists" is in the question of origin. I believe these beings are not only extraterrestrial but supernatural in origin. To be blunt, I think they are demons. The Bible tells us that demons are spiritual beings at war with God. We are told that demons will be allowed to use their tremendous powers of deception in a grand way in the last days. (1994:68)

According to Lindsey, those who are unsaved will be deceived by the "great wonder" of UFOs; demons disguised as aliens from an advanced civilization will land their spacecraft and perhaps assert that they had planted human life on earth and that they have returned to help guide our evolution. This event will be so staggering in its implications that it will result in all the faiths of the world forgetting their differences and coming together. A New Age one world religion will then be created, which will pave the way for the acceptance of the Antichrist. Lindsey declares that the media have been preparing the world for such an event, conditioning humanity to accept the idea of superior alien beings (Lindsey 1994:69–71).

Numerous other Christian evangelicals have expressed the view that UFOs may intervene during a time of world crisis and present a "Divine One World Plan" that will eventually become the evil New World Order. "It's no accident that the incredible emphasis on alien beings, flying saucers, extraterrestrials, has burst upon humanity in recent times" says prophecy writer David Allen Lewis, "UFOs will be instrumental in preparing the minds of humanity for the reception of the Antichrist" (Chandler 1993:189). Other prophecy enthusiasts have noted the connections between the UFO phenomenon, the New Age movement, and occult-based spirituality, all of which are said to be part of Satan's conspiracy to lead people away from Christ. Former New Age author Randall Baer, now an evangelical Christian, states that UFOs are integral to the New Age movement and that they have demonic, "delusionary brainwashing effects on people . . . UFOs are *messengers of deception*, nothing else" (1989:109).

UFO enthusiasts have validated their faith through ambiguous biblical references to sky gods and heavenly phenomena; Christian prophecy believers, on the contrary, have found biblical evidence that UFOs and ETs are devils, fallen angels, and satanic manifestations that will lead to the rise of a global religion and the Antichrist. The demonization of UFOs and ETs by prophecy believers seems related in part to the threat that the actual existence of intelligent extraterrestrial beings would pose to conservative Christian theology. Some scholars have even speculated that fundamentalist Christianity might collapse as a result of the discovery of extraterrestrial intelligences. For example, in *God and the New Physics*, physicist and science author Paul Davies writes:

> The existence of extra-terrestrial intelligences would have a profound impact on religion, shattering completely the traditional perspective on God's relationship with man. The difficulties are particularly acute for Christianity, which postulates that Jesus Christ was God incarnate whose mission was to provide salvation for man on Earth. The prospect of a host of "alien Christs" systematically visiting every inhabited planet in the physical form of the local creatures has a rather absurd aspect. Yet how otherwise are the aliens to be saved? (1983:71)

According to Davies and others, the assumption that earth and humanity are at the center of the universe makes conservative Christianity especially vulnerable to an encounter with ETs. Furthermore, the popular view within the UFO movement that ETs have created human beings and have been responsible for human evolution obviously challenges literalist interpretations of the Bible. Although some devotees of the UFO faith assign a central role to Jesus Christ in their pantheon of deities, an underlying implication of the UFO phenomenon nonetheless is that the source of humanity's salvation is not only Jesus but a race of highly evolved beings with superior technology, which may include Jesus. The demonization of the UFO phenomenon by prophecy believers and other conservative Christians illustrates the extent to which its alternative mythology of creation and salvation poses a threat to Christian fundamentalist views and demonstrates once again the dynamic aspects of premillennialist prophecy traditions and the ability of prophecy interpreters to explain current phenomena in terms of God's divine plan.

Progressive Millennialism and UFO Beliefs

Endtimes ideas about malevolent aliens intensify and spawn new eschatological beliefs within both Christianity and the UFO movement, but the approach of the third millennium has also precipitated a renewal of ideas about benevolent beings and extraterrestrial intelligences that will help humanity attain a golden age on earth. Deemphasizing the idea of apocalypse and stressing notions of human evolution and progress, these ideas assert that if human beings follow a cosmic plan prescribed by an extraterrestrial force, they will establish a terrestrial paradise and achieve the salvation of humanity. Such ideas constitute a form of millennialism that differs significantly from apocalyptic traditions, which maintain that the world must be destroyed before it can be renewed. Relatively optimistic and noncatastrophic in emphasis, these ideas are an expression of what scholar of religion Catherine Wessinger calls "progressive millennialism," characterized by the notion that a golden age may be brought about gradually by human beings acting according to a divine plan or cooperating with the guidance of superhuman agents (Wessinger 1994:56; Wessinger 1995:2). A progressive millennialist view was held by Christian postmillennialists who preached the Social Gospel in the nineteenth century and declared that Christian principles would eventually prevail and defeat all evil, transforming the world into a place worthy of Christ's Second Coming. As noted in chapter 2, these postmillennialists had a reformist vision of the salvation of the world and worked to establish the millennial kingdom on earth through good works—they contributed to the abolition of slavery and of child labor, the temperance movement, and prison reform.

In the UFO movement, progressive millennialism takes a variety of forms, and is identified by the notion that instead of the apocalypse, a sweeping change will occur involving a transformation of planetary consciousness, behavioral patterns, energy fields, or the genetic code of all human beings. As manifestations of cosmic intelligences, UFOs and ETs are believed to be guiding human beings through this monumental transformation into a golden age of peace and prosperity.

In some scenarios collective transformation and terrestrial salvation is contingent upon the arrival and guidance of superhuman beings who will help to bring about the millennium. This view is promoted by the Unarius Academy of Science in El Cajon, near San Diego. Led until recently by Uriel, "Archangel and Cosmic Visionary" (otherwise known as Ruth Norman, 1900–1993), the Unariuns anticipate a spacefleet landing in 2001 involving thirty-two spacecraft from each planet of the Interplanetary Confederation. Each space ship will carry one thousand scientists who will work with human beings to save our dying world, spiritually transforming earth so that it will finally be advanced enough to join the other thirty-two enlightened planets. In anticipation of the arrival of these interplanetary beings, the Unariuns work to spread the teachings of the Interplanetary Confederation in order to transform the spiritual consciousness of humanity gradually. Rather than stressing the imminence of apocalypse, the Unariun worldview emphasizes the efforts of human beings working in harmony with space beings to create a golden age.

Other progressive millennialist UFO traditions assert that the salvation of humanity and the attainment of a terrestrial paradise will be brought about by human beings acting according to a divine plan as communicated by super-human beings. This view characterizes the "11:11 Doorway" movement led by Solara Antara Amaa-ra, who states that she channels messages from various extraterrestrial beings and asserts that human beings are angels originally descended from various stars in the cosmos. According to Solara and her thousands of followers, a cosmic "doorway of opportunity" for the salvation of humanity opened on January 11, 1992, and will close on December 31, 2011. During the twenty-year interval, humanity will be given the chance to elimi-nate evil, spiritually cleanse and transform itself, and then ascend to a new realm of consciousness. Like numerous other UFO and New Age millennial-ist movements, Solara holds that 144,000 believers (a number prophesied in the Book of Revelation) must unite worldwide in "conscious Oneness" to attain some sort of spiritual critical mass that in turn will launch all of human-ity into a higher level of consciousness that will usher in a golden age (Solara 1990). Although evil is acknowledged in progressive millennialist worldviews such as Solara's, the world is not considered to be irredeemably evil, and the spiritual actions of humans beings are believed to be essential for the salvation of the entire planet and the redemption of humanity.

Solara's "11:11 Doorway" movement is similar in its beliefs to the Harmonic Convergence, the most famous example of New Age/UFO progressive mil-lennialism. Coordinated by author José Argüelles, the Harmonic Conver-gence was celebrated by tens of thousands of people throughout the world on August 16–17, 1987. The event was centered on a variety of Mayan, Native American, and Christian prophecies, the end of specific cycles of the Aztec and Mayan calendars, and purported cosmic occurrences and planetary con-figurations. According to Argüelles, the ancient Mayans were cosmic vision-aries who left a "galactic calling card" in the form of coded messages in the Mayan calendar that reveal how human beings may transform themselves and join the Galactic Federation after the Mayan calendar ends in 2012. In *The Mayan Factor* (1987), Argüelles states that August 16–17, 1987, was a critical juncture in the history of the planet, a dangerous transition from one era to another during which the future of humanity would be determined. The world was to have plunged into a "negative cycle" toward apocalypse unless 144,000 people or more participated in this rite of planetary passage, which was to restore earth's solar and cosmic resonance. The event would create an atmosphere of increased spiritual understanding and trust of extraterrestrial and cosmic powers, triggering the Harmonic Convergence in which humanity would progress toward "galactic synchronization" and eventually join the federation of other enlightened planets after the aliens make contact in the year 2012.

Over the weekend of August 16–17, individuals gathered at renowned sacred sites such as Stonehenge, the Great Pyramid, Machu Picchu, and Mount Shasta, where they chanted, meditated, and engaged in various ceremonies in an attempt to transform the planet spiritually and connect humanity, earth, and universal energies. In this scenario, human effort would not only prevent Armageddon but also activate the return of the spirit of the Aztec god Quetzalcoatl and all the gods and goddesses and heroes and heroines that have ever existed in the human imagination (Argüelles 1987:170). The archetypal divine energy of these beings was to be reborn in the hearts of all people on August 16–17, 1987, instilling a new global consciousness that would result in a world in which humans beings would live in harmony with one another and the environment. Organizers and participants of the Harmonic Convergence emphasized that their spiritual efforts during the two-day event saved earth from destruction and allowed humanity to pursue its evolutionary cosmic destiny in establishing a new age. The progressive millennialist tendencies of the Harmonic Convergence event are exemplified by the belief that evil and worldly catastrophe may be overcome by humans who act in consonance with a cosmic plan for salvation.

Like other New Age and UFO progressive millennialist traditions, the Harmonic Convergence was characterized by the notion that all of humanity may achieve a terrestrial paradise, not just a select few. In contrast to apocalyptic traditions, which express a pessimistic and tragic view of the world as irredeemably evil, progressive millennialism regards evil as conquerable by humans with help from superhuman beings. A golden age is believed to be attainable through the incremental improvement of the world, an idea that has its secular equivalent in the notion of a utopia achieved through progress and human effort. According to Charles Strozier, New Age millennialists attempt "to get ahead of the apocalyptic and direct it," gradually bringing about the Age of Aquarius through personal spiritual transformations that affect the larger transformation of society (1994:231). Unlike apocalyptic belief systems that emphasize salvation for the righteous and destruction for the evil "others," progressive millennialism, at least within the UFO and New Age movements, tends to be less dualistic and to accept all humanity in its inclusive millennial embrace. UFO and New Age millennialists have taken ideas about worldly salvation from an assortment of previous traditions and cultural sources, and may anticipate not only the return of Jesus to redeem the world but also the arrival of Ashtar and Lady Athena, Quetzalcoatl and the Virgin Mary, Lady Gaia, Master Aetherius, the Elohim, the Kachina, Buddha, Mohammed, our extraterrestrial ancestors as well as our progeny in the form of human/alien hybrids, and potentially every god and goddess and culture hero that has ever existed.

Although UFO and New Age progressive millennialism places more emphasis on human action in bringing about the millennium and therefore appears less deterministic than apocalyptic worldviews, both forms of millenarianism reflect the view that history unfolds as part of a superhuman plan and that the fate of humanity is guided by external forces. Just as God's divine will determines and oversees events in Christian prophecy belief, so too in the UFO movement do the extraterrestrials oversee human history: they have created earth, directed the development of the human race, and have a plan for humanity's salvation. Within this cosmic drama human beings are said to have a foreordained role to play, and through spiritual effort, genetic transformation, and the guidance of the extraterrestrials, they will realize their destiny and perhaps become godlings themselves with the cosmic ability to create a golden age on earth. Like previous millenarian worldviews, these emergent UFO and New Age traditions provide systems of meaning for understanding human existence and promise that the universe is ordered, that evil and suffering will be eliminated, and that an age of harmony and justice will be established through the fulfillment of a cosmic plan.

Conclusion

With the approach of the year 2000, and in the aftermath of the events associated with the Branch Davidian, Solar Temple, Aum Shinri Kyo, and Heaven's Gate groups, understanding the varieties of apocalyptic belief has become increasingly important. Although various optimistic and noncataclysmic visions of humanity's inevitable progress to a golden age have emerged in recent years, they are in the minority, overshadowed and outnumbered by apocalyptic worldviews that predict imminent worldly destruction. As the twentieth century comes to an end, apocalyptic visions flourish, reflecting perceptions of overwhelming societal crisis and a pessimistic outlook for a world so corrupt that it can be redeemed only by superhuman forces through a worldly catastrophe.

Despite the diversity of visions, rhetoric, and beliefs about impending worldly cataclysm, four categories can be derived from the data examined in this study: (1) unconditional apocalypticism, (2) conditional apocalypticism, (3) unredemptive apocalypticism, and (4) cataclysmic forewarning. These categories do not constitute an absolute typology but are useful for conceptualizing the fatalistic aspects of endtimes discourse, and may serve as a framework for understanding the various expressions of apocalyptic belief that have existed in the past and that have emerged in recent years.

Unconditional apocalypticism is characterized by the belief that history is predetermined and that apocalypse is imminent and unalterable: the world is believed to be irredeemable by human effort; its cataclysmic destruction is regarded as inevitable; and a superhuman plan exists for collective salvation. Premillennial dispensationalism, exemplified by Hal Lindsey's writings, epitomizes unconditional apocalyptic thinking. Dispensationalists assert that a divine pattern controls all of history, that contemporary events are fulfilling God's plan for humanity, and that humans are completely powerless to alter these fated events in any way. Collective efforts cannot affect historical inevitability, and when certain preordained conditions are fulfilled (e.g., the rebuilding of the Temple in Jerusalem, the appearance of the Antichrist), the end of the world will occur. Although the destruction of the world is related to human sinfulness, sin is considered ineradicable and universal repentance not achievable. In the dispensationalist view, the world is irredeemably evil and unrecuperable through human action; even though God tests humanity in different stages, humanity will inevitably fail each stage and collective salvation may occur only through cataclysmic destruction. Unconditional apocalypticism has characterized the worldviews of many catastrophic millennialist movements other than dispensationalism, including the Millerites and the Branch Davidians. As noted, unconditional apocalypticism is also inherent in the beliefs of various UFO groups and endtimes traditions that predict inevitable worldly destruction and the salvation of the chosen ones either through planetary evacuation or genetic engineering and human/alien hybridization.

Conditional apocalypticism is characterized by the belief that apocalypse is imminent but may be postponed if human beings behave in ways prescribed by a superhuman power, such as God or extraterrestrials. Conditional apocalyptic worldviews assert that human beings cannot prevent worldly destruction through their own efforts but that within the broad constraints of history's inevitable progression, human beings may forestall worldly catastrophes if they act in accordance with divine will or a superhuman plan. This view is illustrated by the predictions of Veronica Lueken and the beliefs of the Baysiders, which assert that the end of the world is near but that human beings may postpone the day of doom if they follow God's will and if God permits that the world not be destroyed. In this scenario, human will is effectual in averting worldly destruction when it corresponds to God's decrees. This sense of an all-powerful divine will that characterizes the Bayside prophecies resembles Yahweh's will and Allah's kismet, which humans must carry out using their allotted ethical freedom (Brøndsted 1967:173). An assortment of UFO endtimes scenarios are structurally similar to the conditional apocalyptic ideas of the Baysiders in that humanity is warned of imminent apocalypse, but catastrophe may be averted if instead humans follow the decrees of extraterrestrials or a galactic plan. The messages from the Ashtar Command forewarn of impending worldly destruction and state that the course of history cannot be deflected, yet also maintain that if humanity improves its ways and increases its spiritual efforts, some worldly cataclysms may be averted. Both the Bayside and the Ashtar Command messages are characterized by an appeal for humanity to act in conformance with prescribed behaviors and the implication that change is impossible: "[T]he Warning is coming upon mankind . . . [but] man shall continue on their road to perdition, so hard are the hearts now, My child" says one Bayside prophecy, and a message from the Ashtar Command concludes, "[I]f mankind were to put down its arms, then it could be averted. However, there is no sign that this will happen. Someday someone . . . will push the button" (Beckley 1980:29). In these scenarios, apocalypse will occur as a consequence of humanity's destructive or evil behavior that is a violation of divine or cosmic laws.

Unredemptive apocalypticism, in contrast to these redemptive apocalyptic views, is characterized by the belief that apocalypse is imminent and unalterable and that no superhuman plan exists for worldly redemption or collective salvation. As discussed in chapter 5, unredemptive apocalyptic ideas are a relatively recent and rarely studied phenomenon; they are pervaded by a sense of hopelessness, futility, and nihilism. Specific worldly catastrophes—nuclear war, ecological destruction, a polar shift, widespread famine, disease—are regarded as inevitable and not subject to human agency. Instead of a superhuman plan or divine will as determinants of history, unredemptive apocalypticism expresses the view that the end of history will be determined by humans, technology, or impersonal forces under no one's direction that are progressing inexorably toward a cataclysmic culmination. Until recently, beliefs about the inevitability of nuclear annihilation were the most predominant expression of unredemptive apocalypticism, but in the post–Cold War era fears about an assortment of other apocalyptic scenarios (environmental destruction, deadly viruses, earth's collision with a large asteroid or comet, a catastrophic alien invasion) have become increasingly common.

Cataclysmic forewarning, another general category of endtimes thinking, includes various types of doomsday speculation in which apocalypse is said to be imminent but avoidable through human effort. Although cataclysmic forewarning resembles conditional apocalypticism, it is not inherently fatalistic because history and the future are not believed to be determined, nor do the warnings of imminent catastrophes reveal an operative superhuman plan or unalterable will underlying history. The predictions of potential disastrous scenarios described in books such as *The Fate of the Earth* (Schell 1982), *The Closing Circle* (Commoner 1971), and *The Limits to Growth* (Meadows et al. 1972) are presented with the hope of motivating people to act to avert possible catastrophes and save humanity from approaching, but not inevitable, doom.

The Future of Apocalyptic Belief: The Year 2000 and Beyond

Given the significance attributed to transitional numbers and dates, it is no surprise that the year 2000 has been invested with portentous meanings and inspired widespread feelings that something monumental will occur with the flip of the calendar page. Although the year is a subjective demarcation of the passage of time, it *seems* like a watershed in history, with its sense of an ending and a new beginning. The prospect of triple zeros may even suggest complete nullification. The endings of centuries have been viewed by many as critical junctures, weird liminal times that are betwixt and between, periods of danger and transition. Like previous epochs, this fin de siècle evokes feelings of crisis, exhaustion, and catastrophe, as well as hope of tremendous transformation and rejuvenation in the birth of a new era.

Although the end of the millennium is not assigned any particular significance in the Bible or other prophetic texts, it is the focal point for the projection of a wide range of popular eschatological concerns and hopes generated over the years that now permeate American culture and consciousness. The grassroots nature of end-of-the-millennium beliefs about imminent worldly destruction and salvation is revealed by the fact that even though most contemporary Christian prophecy interpreters are reluctant to predict a specific date for Christ's return, surveys indicate that many Christians believe that Jesus will arrive sometime around the year 2000. For example, in a Time/CNN poll conducted by Yankelovich Partners on April 28–29, 1993, 20 percent of the respondents answered yes to the question "Do you think that the second coming of Jesus Christ will occur sometime around the year 2000?"; 31 percent were not sure; and 49 percent answered no. Twenty percent is a significant number, but the 31 percent who believe that Christ *might* possibly return around the year 2000 perhaps reveals even more about the pervasiveness of millennial speculation.

Although most contemporary Christian prophecy interpreters have avoided endtimes date setting (a notable exception was Edgar Whisenant's *On Borrowed Time/88 Reasons Why the Rapture Will Be in 1988*), a number of them have implied that Christ will return by the year 2000. Pat Robertson and other prominent prophecy writers and lecturers such as Mary Stewart Relfe, Lester Sumrall (founder of LeSEA Broadcasting), and James McKeever (founder of Omega Ministries) have suggested that the turn of the millennium has endtimes importance; and televangelist Jack Van Impe has gone out on a limb and predicted the Rapture and Jesus' return for October 1999 (Alnor 1989:35–39; Boyer 1992:337–338; Chandler 1993:278). According to some Catholic folk beliefs, the apparitions of the Virgin Mary at Fatima and Garabandal included predictions that the world would end in 1999–2000, and the end of the century has prophetic significance for some Jehovah's Witnesses, whose founder, Charles Taze Russell, purportedly said that 1999 would be a time of doom when God's divine plan will be revealed (Mann 1992:xiii).

In addition to turn-of-the-millennium predictions associated with specific Christian prophecy traditions, the prophetic meanings of the cryptic quatrains of the French physician and astrologer Nostradamus (1503–1566) have stimulated an industry of prophecy interpretation. Various interpreters of the quatrains predict worldly cataclysms prior to the year 2000 (including a nuclear attack on New York City in 1997), and some declare that the following loosely translated quatrain predicts the final destruction of the world in July 1999:

> In the year 1999 and seven months
> The great King of Terror will come from the sky.
> He will resurrect Ghengis Khan.
> Before and after war rules happily.
> (*Century* X, quatrain 72; cited in Hogue 1987:204)

According to other prophecy enthusiasts, Nostradamus's visions of pestilence, famine, and natural catastrophes by the year 1999 were also foreseen by Edgar Cayce, the "sleeping prophet" of Virginia Beach, who predicted earthquakes, climate changes, the flooding of coastlines, and a cataclysmic shifting of the earth's axis sometime between 1998 and 2001. Astrologer Jeanne Dixon also predicts extensive floods, geographic changes, Armageddon, and Christ's return by the year 2000. Some maintain that these catastrophic earth changes and a shift of the polar axis will be caused by an unusual planetary alignment on August 18, 1999, or on May 5, 2000 (Mann 1992:xiii–xiv, 104–105, 112–113; Chandler 1993:278–280).

As end-of-the-millennium apocalyptic expectation intensifies and new doomsday dates are forecast, it is worth remembering that the end of the world has been predicted many times. Even though humanity has survived every one of these predicted doomsdays, current apocalyptic speculation has a ring of plausibility, given the potential disasters and the enormousness of the problems that confront humanity at the turn of the millennium. In an era plagued by the threat of nuclear weapons, environmental destruction, AIDS, famine, and other possible forms of extinction, apocalyptic traditions have an obvious appeal, directly addressing fears of collective death by offering the promise of salvation and the assurance that a divine plan underlies history. Steeped in images of catastrophe that reflect an awareness of our own endings and the widespread feeling that the world itself may be dying, apocalyptic beliefs allay fears of human extinction, provide the hope of continuity and renewal, and give expression to the desire for a meaningful narrative underlying individual existence and human history. In apocalyptic traditions, the desire for symbolic immortality converges with the yearning for a terrestrial paradise of happiness and human fulfillment, in which death and suffering will not exist and human beings will live in harmony and understand their purpose in the universe.

Although apocalyptic worldviews address issues of ultimate concern—the reasons for suffering and injustice, the awareness of death and the yearning for immortality, the nature of good and evil, human destiny and the fate of the earth—the belief that the world can be saved only by otherworldly beings may reinforce feelings of helplessness and serve as a substitute for confronting the actual problems that face humanity. Apocalyptic traditions tend to deny the efficacy of human effort to improve the world and may encourage a passive acceptance of human-made crises and potential disasters.

If the years 2000 and 2001 pass uneventfully, perhaps the emphasis in American millennialist beliefs will shift from visions of the world as irredeemably evil and inevitably doomed to more optimistic views in which human beings are compelled to bring about millennial transformations through their actions, confronting crises and working to overcome suffering in the tradition of the postmillennial social reformists of the nineteenth century. Whether or not reformist millennialist movements arise in the twenty-first century, apocalyptic traditions predicting inevitable worldly cataclysm most certainly will flourish as long as perceptions of overwhelming societal crises and uncontrollable evil exist.

Beliefs about worldly destruction and transformation have been an ongoing and significant part of the cultural and religious heritage of the United States and are an enduring way of interpreting the world. Developed thousands of years ago and up through the nuclear age, apocalyptic traditions provide comprehensive systems of belief that fulfill important religious and psychological needs. Despite predictions to the contrary, apocalyptic belief systems will not become outdated or "collapse from exhaustion" in the near future. Whether analyzing the prophetic implications of computers and recent global economic configurations, or recasting ancient apocalyptic ideas in terms of UFOs and extraterrestrial genetic engineering, endtimes enthusiasts have consistently updated eschatological beliefs and made them relevant and will continue to transform such ideas creatively in the years ahead.

At the turn of the millennium, ancient apocalyptic traditions converge with current concerns and popular-culture influences; individuals may choose from among a smorgasbord of endtimes ideas, reformulating these within the constraints of their respective traditions, expanding their belief systems, or constructing personalized apocalyptic scenarios that suit their own tastes.

With the development of communication on the Internet through e-mail and newsgroups, endtimes enthusiasts from diverse belief traditions now exchange ideas and debate everything from the symbolism of the Book of Revelation and Nostradamus's quatrains to the prophetic significance of the New Age movement and *Star Trek* episodes. Given the dynamic nature of apocalyptic traditions and the diversity of eschatological ideas that have emerged at the end of the twentieth century, one need not be a prophet to predict that at this moment a multitude of rough beasts, saviors, and doomsday scenarios are slouching toward Bethlehem to be born.

Notes

I. APPROACHING DOOMSDAY: THE CONTOURS OF AMERICAN
APOCALYPTIC BELIEF

1. Cited in the *Register Guard* (Eugene, Oregon), March 26, 1995, 4A; *Register Guard*, April 7, 1995, 20A.

2. The nature and range of such works are suggested by the bibliographical essays and surveys of American millenarianism by Ira V. Brown (1952), David E. Smith (1965), Leonard Sweet (1979), Dietrich G. Buss (1988), and Lois P. Zamora (1982a).

3. Some notable exceptions include Charles B. Strozier's important psychohistorical study, *Apocalypse: On the Psychology of Fundamentalism in America* (1994), which compares Christian fundamentalist beliefs with New Age ideas and Hopi prophecy beliefs; Barry Brummett's *Contemporary Apocalyptic Rhetoric* (1991), a rhetorical analysis of various religious and secular apocalyptic discourses; and Hillel Schwartz's *Century's End: A Cultural History of the Fin de Siècle from the 990s through the 1990s* (1990), a sweeping survey of a thousand years of fin de siècle thought.

4. There exists an extensive body of commentary on the literary genre of apocalypse, much of which has been written since the early 1960s. These works examine the genre from literary, theological, historical, and sociological perspectives. An overview of approaches is contained in *Apocalypse: The Morphology of a Genre* (published as a special issue of the journal *Semeia*), which surveys Jewish, Christian, Greco-Roman, Gnostic, and Persian apocalyptic literature (J. Collins 1979). A later issue of *Semeia* is devoted to the characteristics and definitions of early Christian apocalypticism (A. Collins 1986). Another anthology, *Apocalypticism in the Mediterranean World and the Near East* (Hellholm 1983), contains thirty-five essays on the literary genre of apocalypse, as well as discussions of the historical and sociological background of the literature, as expressed in a variety of societal and religious contexts, such as Egyptian, Iranian, Gnostic, Christian, Jewish, Akkadian, and Palestinian.

The 1979 special issue of *Semeia* mentioned above and John J. Collins's book on the subject define the term *apocalypse* as "a genre of revelatory literature with a narrative framework, in which a revelation is mediated by an otherworldly being to a human recipient, disclosing a transcendent reality which is both temporal, insofar as it envisages eschatological salvation, and spatial insofar as it invokes another, supernatural world" (J. Collins 1989:4). As a noun, *apocalyptic* is considered by some scholars to refer to a specific worldview or historical movement, to be distinguished from the term *apocalypse* as a literary genre (J. Collins 1989:1–15).

The term *apocalypticism* has multiple connotations as well. Some historians use it to characterize a particular worldview limited to a specific period: "Apocalypticism in the full sense of the word, a balance of myth, method, and way of life existed only for about 200 years, and formed a unique mentality" (Funkenstein 1985:57). One frequently cited terminological distinction defines *apocalypse* as a specific literary genre; *apocalyptic eschatology* as a specific religious perspective involving ideas and motifs that may exist in a variety of literary works and social contexts; and *apocalypticism* as a system of thought associated with visionary movements and related to specific social factors (Hanson 1976:27–34).

5. Millennialism is more commonly used to characterize Christian beliefs; millenarianism is frequently employed to designate any belief system or movement that includes expectations of a future age of perfection and salvation. Another synonymous term is *millenarism*, which has the advantage of being shorter than *millennialism* and *millenarianism*; however the word is infrequently used. The term *adventism* is sometimes applied to beliefs and movements that anticipate the coming of the millennium, specifically those that place particular emphasis on speculations about the return or "Second Advent" of Christ rather than his thousand-year reign. The Second Advent of Christ is also referred to as the *Parousia*, a Greek word that literally means "presence" and is used in the Bible to refer to the arrival of Christ. The term *chiliasm* (from the Greek word *chil*, "one thousand") is infrequently applied, although sometimes it is used to refer to expectations of a hedonistic, carnal, or bacchanalian millennium (Schwartz 1987:522). The word *Armageddon* (as in "Battle of Armageddon") comes from the Book of Revelation and is used in some Christian discourse to refer specifically to the anticipated final battle between Christ and the forces of good against the forces of evil, which will occur before or at the end of the world. Its root is somewhat unclear, although many premillennialists assert it refers to the name of a valley in northeast Israel called Megiddo, where, they believe, a final supernatural conflagration will occur involving the major armies of the world, as well as the Antichrist, who will be destroyed by Christ and the saints. Prophesied as the largest and bloodiest battle in history, Armageddon will usher in the millennium.

6. Apocalyptic movements frequently have centered on individuals believed to be endowed with supernatural abilities—charismatic leaders, culture saviors, visionaries, or prophets—who mediate between humanity and the supernatural, and convey a divine plan for worldly redemption (Wallis 1943; Lanternari 1963). Such individuals are not granted authority by official religious institutions but take it unto it themselves based on what Max Weber identified as "charisma": "a certain quality of an individual personality by virtue of which he is set apart from ordinary men and treated as endowed with . . . exceptional powers or qualities" (1947:358–359). Unlike priests, who have the role of administering the teachings of official religion and whose source of authority is an established religious organization, the authority of charismatic

prophets stems from direct religious experiences and special abilities, such as trance, prophecy, healing, divination, performance of miracles, or inspired preaching (Weber 1963:46–59). This extraecclesiastical authority results from a prophet's ability to convey messages found to be meaningful by believers and the willingness of believers to act on these pronouncements.

7. In a discussion of the folk religious nature of apocalyptic beliefs, historian Ernest Sandeen adopts and expands Robert Redfield's (1989 [1956]) notion of the "Little Tradition" to include not only agrarian and preindustrial societies but millenarian movements in industrial societies. Sandeen argues that contemporary millenarian beliefs are still part of the "Little Tradition," but differ from preindustrial millenarianism in the manner in which such beliefs are communicated: "[M]odernizing millenarian movements seek the expansion of their membership through centrally directed campaigns; concentrate upon the mass media to spread their message, historically through the printed page and, increasingly, in the second half of the twentieth century through television; authenticate their claims by reference to a printed source, the Bible; organize their beliefs into an ideology which is rationally defended; are male dominated; and discourage direct revelations, especially from women" (1980:175). Although Sandeen's observations accurately describe contemporary apocalyptic traditions such as premillennial dispensationalism, a number of current millenarian movements emphasize the direct revelations of female visionaries. Various Roman Catholic groups that center on apocalyptic Marian apparitions are founded on the visions of female seers, and several New Age millenarian movements celebrate the apocalyptic ideas communicated by female prophets, channelers, and visionaries (e.g., Elizabeth Claire Prophet, of the Church Universal and Triumphant). Assorted groups within the UFO movement also are founded on the revelations of female visionaries, contactees, or channelers (e.g., Uriel, of the Unarius Academy of Science; and Tuella, who channels messages from the Ashtar Command).

8. Although folklorists have tended to focus their studies on verbal lore, many have recognized the interdependence of oral and other types of communication, as well as the dynamic relationship between mass media communication, popular culture, and folklore (see Bausinger 1990; Dégh 1994; Dundes and Pagter 1992; Howard 1995; Mechling 1996; Santino 1996). Folklore is not only transmitted through printed sources and electronic media but now through the Internet and e-mail, as members of global subcultures who never interact face-to-face exchange and create folklore in cyberspace. Despite predictions to the contrary, technology and industrialization have not necessarily destroyed traditions but have altered the ways that traditions are expressed and communicated, and have helped to generate and perpetuate new types of folklore.

9. As Helmer Ringgren observes, "The question of man's attitude toward destiny has never, as far as I know, been treated systematically" (1967:16).

10. In his discussion of the nature of "inevitability doctrines," psychologist Leonard Doob notes that although the term *destiny* often suggests good fortune, *fate*

usually has negative implications. Accordingly, he defines *fate* based on its negative associations: "I assign fatalism to negative affect because often—though not always—fate is associated with doom, which usually has the same negative connotation" (1988:6).

11. As J. T. Hickey notes, "Fatalism maintains that the human will cannot affect the outcome of affairs, however, whereas determinism may or may not deny the efficacy of the will as cause" (1967:1324).

12. For example, Antti Aarne and Stith Thompson's *The Types of the Folktale* (1961) includes numerous stories in which fate plays a predominant role, such as the *Predestined Wife* (930A), *Prophecy of Future Greatness for Youth* (930, mt. 312), *The Youth to Die on his Wedding Day* (934B), *Oedipus* (931), and *The Predestined Death* (934A). For a study of the diffusion of the *Predestined Wife* tale, see Archer Taylor (1958). Thompson's *Motif-Index of Folk-Literature* (1955–1958) also contains the chapter "Chance and Fate," which has subheadings such as "Luck and Fate Personified" and "Determination of Luck and Fate."

13. Stories about the three Fates have ancient roots and were personified by the Greek poet Hesiod (eighth century B.C.E.) in his poem *Theogony* as three goddesses—Klotho, Lachesis, and Atropos, the daughters of Night—who control the destiny of mortals and punish the transgressions of humans and gods (*Theogony* 211–222). Later in *Theogony*, Hesiod says that the Fates are the daughters of Zeus and Themis, and that Zeus gave them the highest position: "they distribute to mortal people what people have, for good and for evil" (*Theogony* 905–906) (Lattimore 1977:178). Klotho spins the thread of life and thus one's destiny; Lachesis measures its length and weaves the threads of luck or chance into the fabric of one's life; and Atropos, the inescapable one, snips the thread and determines the moment of one's death. The sister of the three Fates is Nemesis, who was sent to chastise those who offended the gods and reward those who were good. Mortals might offend the gods by transgressing moral law, an act that made the gods angry, or by achieving too much success in life, which made them jealous; in either case, Nemesis was dispatched to punish offenders with death or disaster. A survival of the idea of offending the gods or the fates persists today in folk beliefs that caution against "tempting fate" ("Don't say 'I never have problems' or 'I never get sick' for fear of tempting fate"; or the idea that "pride comes before a fall").

14. The word *fairy* comes from the Latin *fata* (the Fates) and *fatum* (fate).

15. The role of fate in stories told by Greeks has been addressed by folklorist Robert A. Georges (1978), who notes that in some narratives, characters may be powerless, a pawn of fate's plan; in others, they may be able to supplicate, implore, or trick fate on certain auspicious occasions by themselves or with the help of magical or religious specialists. Folklorist Donald Ward (1972) has considered the way that humor in folk narratives functions to intensify the irony of tragic fate, providing people with a means of laughing at the inevitability of death and suffering and thus making tolerable that which might otherwise be insufferable.

16. Norse ideas about the three Norns, for instance, exemplify the belief in the omnipotence of fate and its relation to time and history. The Norns were believed not only to spin the thread of human life and death but to rule the fate of the gods and the universe as well, introducing time into the cosmos and therefore controlling the sequence of all events that must inevitably occur. Their control over all things is further represented by the belief that they watered and nourished the world tree Yggdrasil that connected heaven and hell (Leach 1972:797, 1190). From the beginning of time, it was believed, these Norse goddesses of fate decreed the annihilation of the world by destructive forces (Ragnarök) and the tragic doom of the gods.

2. THE AMERICAN APOCALYPTIC LEGACY

1. For a feminist analysis of the colonialist, racist, and sexist implications of Columbus's apocalyptic beliefs, see Catherine Keller's forthcoming work, *Apocalypse Now and Then: A Feminist Guide to the End of the World.*

2. Calvin's *Institutes of the Christian Religion* (1536) contains the primary tenets of his theological system. The idea of predestination also found full expression in the theologies of Martin Luther and Ulrich Zwingli, the other principal leaders of the Protestant Reformation.

3. The association of the forces of fate with God's divine will are also expressed in previous Christian doctrines of predestination that hold that God has predetermined each individual's salvation or damnation. According to Saint Augustine (354–430 C.E.), humans are so contaminated by sin that they cannot hope to enter the celestial realms through their own efforts but only if they have been chosen by God, who has destined some for salvation and others for damnation (Grambo 1988:13).

4. In *The Protestant Ethic and the Spirit of Capitalism* (1958 [1904–1905]), sociologist and political economist Max Weber discusses at length the concept of predestination, which he declares is Calvinism's most characteristic and influential doctrine. Weber argues that the doctrine of predestination and the attempt to determine one's fate ultimately motivated the Protestant ethic that contributed to the development of modern capitalism. The implications of the Calvinist view of a God that has predestined the salvation or damnation of every soul is described by Weber in the following manner:

> The Father in heaven of the New Testament, so human and understanding, who rejoices over the repentance of a sinner . . . [has been replaced in Calvinism] by a transcendental being, beyond the reach of human understanding, who with His quite incomprehensible decrees has decided the fate of every individual and regulated the tiniest details of the cosmos from eternity. . . . In its extreme inhumanity, this doctrine must above all have had one consequence for the life of a generation which surrendered to its magnificent consistency. That was a feeling of unprecedented inner loneliness of the single individual. (1958 [1904–1905]:104)

According to Weber, the doctrine of predestination not only evoked a profound spiritual loneliness but resulted in widespread religious anxiety at the popular level among believers who agonized over the fate of their souls: were they among God's predetermined elect or destined for eternal damnation? This intolerable psychological torment motivated believers to seek "signs" that indicated they had been chosen for eternal salvation. Despite Calvin's claim that one could not determine the final fate of one's soul, Calvinist folk theology asserted that living a godly life and fulfilling God's will through good works and success in a worldly calling were proof of one's faith and that one was among the elect and predestined for salvation (Weber 1958 [1904–1905]:110–115).

Yet because good works and proving one's faith through worldly activity were not a means of gaining salvation but interpreted as "signs" of one's predetermined salvation, even the slightest moral transgression might indicate that one was not among the elect but was condemned to damnation for eternity (Weber 1958 [1904–1905]:115–116). Therefore, the rigorous control of one's behavior was necessary to assure oneself that one was among the chosen, and as a result a moral code developed that emphasized hard work, a frugal lifestyle, and the rational organization of labor to accumulate wealth—what Weber calls the Protestant ethic. According to Weber, this asceticism unintentionally instilled the work ethic and drive necessary for successful capitalism; the original "capitalist spirit" was not motivated by the desire for worldly pleasure or power but by the religious anxiety associated with the doctrine of predestination and the ensuing attempt to prove one's salvation through success in a worldly calling assigned by God.

5. The affluent lifestyles of numerous premillennialist writers and TV ministers have contributed to suspicions about their motives. Hal Lindsey's literary success and lifestyle, for instance, have led some to question the sincerity of his writings. As one observer notes, "It's ironic, to say the least, that the writer of book after book proclaiming the soon-coming end of the world should sink a substantial portion of those book royalties into long-term real estate investments" (S. Graham 1989:253). Lindsey declares that his investments ensure the continuation of his ministry.

3. SIGNS OF THE ENDTIMES

1. At the time of the publication of *The Late Great Planet Earth* in 1970, Lindsey stated that a generation was approximately forty years, which would place the apocalypse sometime in the late 1980s, but he has since revised the length of a generation, saying that in biblical time generations may have spanned one hundred years.

2. Beliefs about doomsday reversals, such as animals chasing humans and riding in carriages on doomsday, are suggested by English local burial legends from the eighteenth and nineteenth centuries. These legends, about men being arranged to be buried upside down, supposedly resulted from the popular belief that the world would turn upside down on doomsday (Simpson 1978:559–564).

3. Eskeröd (1947) suggests that noncausal omens (e.g., "A red sunrise means bad weather" or "When ants leave their holes—good weather ahead") imply a belief in an a-causal relationship between the sign (whether animals, plants, human behavior, or forces of nature) and the result; causal superstitions (e.g., "If you break a mirror you will have seven years of bad luck") are characterized as involving "intentional or unintentional" cause-effect relationships.

4. APOCALYPTIC APPARITIONS OF THE VIRGIN MARY IN NEW YORK CITY

1. According to the most recent statement, issued on November 4, 1986, by Bishop Francis Mugavero of the Diocese of Brooklyn, an investigation revealed that the Bayside visions "completely lacked authenticity." "No credibility can be given to the so-called 'apparitions' reported by Veronica Lueken and her followers. . . . Because of my concern for their spiritual welfare, members of Christ's faithful are hereby directed to refrain from participating in the 'vigils' and from disseminating any propaganda related to the 'Bayside apparitions.' They are also discouraged from reading any such literature" (Mugavero 1989:210–211). The condemnation does not appear to have discouraged belief in the prophecies among Baysiders, however, and in fact may have motivated many of them to increase their efforts to disseminate the Bayside messages and gain ecclesiastical acceptance for Mrs. Lueken's visions. The Bayside literature declares that the Brooklyn Diocese did not conduct a thorough and proper investigation and notes that the apparitions at Lourdes and Fatima were initially condemned as well and that the church took years before it officially sanctioned these apparition sites. Baysiders believe that until a more extensive investigation is conducted, their involvement in the Bayside movement is ecclesiastically permissible (*OLR Book* 1986:40).

2. Although no studies have been published on the Bayside apparitions, research by the Turners (1978), Christian (1984), Matter (1986), Kselman and Avella (1986), and especially Zimdars-Swartz (1991) note the apocalyptic themes of previous Marian apparitions. In addition to these important works, other studies of the Virgin Mary and Marian devotion include attempts to trace the origins of the veneration of Mary to pre-Christian goddess and fertility cults (Gimbutas 1982; James 1959; Neumann 1963); to works that discuss the psychological needs fulfilled by Marian imagery and devotion (Cunningham 1982; Greeley 1977; Jung 1970); to psychoanalytical explanations (Carroll 1986); to feminist interpretations (Kristeva 1986; Warner 1976); and to the political implications of Marian devotion (Bax 1987; Perry and Echeverría 1988). A sampling of other significant studies include the Nolans' survey of pilgrimage in modern western Europe (1989), Orsi's history of devotion to the Virgin Mary in Italian Harlem (1985), and the historical analyses of Marian devotion in nineteenth-century France by Kselman (1983) and Pope (1985) and of Marian apparitions in rural Spain from 1399 to 1523 by Christian (1981).

3. For a more extensive consideration of the meaning of miraculous photography for Baysiders and a discussion of this practice as an innovation in regard to previous Roman Catholic traditions concerning miraculous images, see Wojcik (1996b).

4. Miraculous photography and the other unique features of the Bayside phenomenon and Mrs. Lueken's apparitions are linked by Baysiders to broader traditions of Marian apparitions and regarded as part of a progression of Marian sightings. Despite their various idiosyncratic elements, the Bayside messages do resemble other messages communicated at previous Marian apparition sites, particularly those communicated by the Virgin Mary to another American visionary, Mrs. Mary Ann Van Hoof, in the town of Necedah in rural Wisconsin during the 1950s. Mrs. Van Hoof's visions received extensive media coverage at the time, especially after approximately 100,000 people journeyed to her farm to witness her enter a state of ecstasy and converse with the Virgin Mary on the feast of the Assumption, August 15, 1950 (*Welcome to Queen of the Holy Rosary, Mediatrix of Peace, Mediatrix Between God and Man Shrine* n.d.). Like Mrs. Lueken's apparitions, the Van Hoof messages are lengthy and discursive, and express Cold War fears, anticommunist sentiments, a preoccupation with conspiracies, and apocalyptic apprehensions. The possibility that Mrs. Lueken consciously or unconsciously imitated the Necedah messages is noted by Michael Carroll (1986:139–140), who points out similarities in the language used by Mrs. Lueken and Mrs. Van Hoof.

5. In August 1995, Veronica Lueken died at the age of seventy-two. The most recent newsletter mailed by the shrine after her death calls for a renewed effort to disseminate the Bayside prophecies and carry on the mission of the Bayside movement. It notes that the Virgin Mary also died at the age of seventy-two and that Mrs. Lueken's death date, August 3, is

> not designated as a feast day for any saint in the Church—it's an open slot. All indications are that Veronica Lueken will eventually be canonized a saint of the Roman Catholic Church. . . . Our Lady of the Roses Shrine now enters a new and glorious phase of existence, just as its founder, Veronica, has now entered into a new and glorious phase of her existence. For being loosed from her earthly bindings, she is now at liberty to assist from Heaven the mission she so loved while on earth. When we reflect on the life of St. Theresa, we see that it wasn't until after her death that her message and sanctity became universally acclaimed. Such was the case with many other saints. So we should understand that Heaven has cued us up to this point, and has entrusted us with a great mission. ("Veronica of the Cross" n.d.:3)

The newsletter also reiterates the belief that the Virgin Mary and Jesus are always present at the apparition site vigils, even if Mrs. Lueken is not, and includes as proof of this heavenly presence a miraculous photo taken at a vigil held at the site in remembrance of Mrs. Lueken on August 5, 1995. Beneath the photograph the caption reads:

After the announcement was made of Veronica's death, an audio segment of timely and uplifting words from Jesus, Mary, and Veronica was played for the crowd. Just as it ended at 7:50 p.m., Mrs. Anne Scrivener, a Maryland organizer, snapped a Polaroid photo. A beam of light descends upon the statue of Our Lady of the Roses, Mary Help of Mothers. Heaven was punctuating Their own words with a wondrous and permanent sign to remember: that this Shrine is of Divine origin and that its growth and development will continue to be directed by Jesus, Mary and, of course, Veronica, from her new abode of the blessed. ("Veronica of the Cross" n.d.:photo insert)

Now that the messages from Mary and Jesus are no longer directly conveyed by Mrs. Lueken through apparitions, the practice of miraculous photography may come to play an even more important role in the religious lives of Baysiders as a means of determining the divine will, receiving apocalyptic messages, and experiencing the sacred at the apparition site.

5. SECULAR APOCALYPTIC THEMES IN THE NUCLEAR ERA

1. The atomic bomb also served as the inspiration for naming skimpy two-piece swimsuits "bikinis." French fashion designer Louis Reard introduced his swimsuit at the same time the United States began postwar atomic testing on the Bikini Atoll in the Marshall Islands in 1946. Reard supposedly selected the name "bikini" because the word was used extensively in the media coverage of the bombing and because he believed his design was "explosive."

2. The following account of an atomic age innovation in children's play was recorded in the *New Yorker* on August 18, 1945, twelve days after the bombing of Hiroshima and Nagasaki:

For years the playground in Washington Square has resounded to the high-strung anh-anh-anh of machine guns and the long-drawn-out whine of high-velocity shells. Last Saturday morning a great advance was made. We watched a military man of seven or eight climb onto a seesaw, gather a number of his staff officers around him, and explain the changed situation. "Look," he said, "I'm an atomic bomb. I just go 'boom.' Once. Like this." He raised his arms, puffed out his cheeks, jumped down from the seesaw, and went "Boom!" Then he led his army away, leaving Manhattan in ruins behind him. (*New Yorker*, August 18, 1945, 17)

3. For example, *Popular Mechanics* magazine featured a fallout shelter in its 1960 house of the year and included an article that began: "A bomb is dropped on a key target. But who cares, you live miles away. Fallout can't reach you. But soon, you and your family become ill, dangerously ill. Now you wish you had heeded the importance of a fallout shelter" (Hine 1989:135).

4. General advice was that fallout shelters should be stocked with a two-week sup-

ply of food and water, with standard fare consisting of canned and dried foods, evaporated milk, potatoes, cereal, and crackers. Also recommended were flashlights, batteries, candles, a radio, and, as one narrator of a civil defense film advised, "By all means, provide some tranquilizers to ease the strain and monotony of life in a shelter. A bottle of one hundred should be adequate for a family of four. Tranquilizers are *not* a narcotic, and are not habit forming." (Rafferty et al. 1982:105).

5. As Lois Zamora notes in an essay on American literature with end-of-the-world themes, "Our best writers have constantly questioned the nature of that end, and they have often framed their questions in the terms of the myth of the apocalypse" (1982b:97). Another writer states that "images of the end of the world abound in American literature, and with good reason: the very idea of America in history *is* apocalyptic, arising as it did out of the historicizing of apocalyptic hopes in the Protestant Reformation" (Robinson 1985:xi). Literary theorists have examined apocalyptic and millenarian themes expressed in the writings of American authors such as Herman Melville, Mark Twain, Edgar Allen Poe, Ralph Waldo Emerson, William Faulkner, Nathanael West, Ralph Ellison, Robert Coover, Susan Sontag, John Updike, Joan Didion, Don DeLillo, and Thomas Pynchon, among others (cf. Dewey 1990; Ketterer 1974; Kroes 1985; Lewicki 1984; May 1972; Robinson 1985; Wagar 1982; Yoke 1987; and Zamora 1982b).

6. Some artists did, however, address the idea of the nuclear destruction of humanity. Henry Moore's sculpture *Nuclear Energy* (1966) depicts a mushroom cloud in the shape of a skull; Jean Tinguely created a motorized device that destroyed itself before an audience at the New York Museum of Modern Art; and Jasper Johns assembled fragmented painted casts of scattered body parts—ear, nose, mouth, fingers, penis, toes—set in wooden containers above a target (Weart 1988:403–404, 394).

7. Jonathan Schell, in *The Fate of the Earth* (1982), asserts that contemporary artists may sense that all of art—their own creations as well as previous timeless masterpieces—may ultimately be destroyed by nuclear holocaust, and that posterity and history no longer offer the hope of saving art from time and destruction. The nuclear peril "threatens not each individual work but the world to which all works are offered, and makes us feel that even if we did accomplish our individual aims it would be pointless, thus undercutting our will to accomplish anything at all" (1982:164). Schell writes that action painting, performance art, and "happenings" are self-fulfilling forms of art that are "isolated from the past and the future—in the moment, thus giving up on communion with the dead and with the unborn: doing away, in fact, with art's whole dependence on the common world, which assumes the existence of the human future" (1982:164–165).

8. One of the few artists in "The End of the World" show at the New Museum of Contemporary Art whose work expressed the idea of a redemptive apocalypse was the Reverend Howard Finster, one of the few nationally renowned "folk artists" in the United States. Finster has been featured in *Life* magazine, the *Wall Street Journal,* and *People* magazine; he also has been a guest on the Johnny Carson show and designed

album covers for musical groups such as the Talking Heads and R.E.M. Although best known for the variety of his art and his prodigious output, and the two-acre folk art environment in his backyard in Pennville, Georgia, Finster turns out creations that are often explicitly apocalyptic. A number of his paintings and sculptures detail the various evils of contemporary society, announce the coming end and ensuing millennium, and depict his visions of heaven, hell, other worlds, and imagery from the Book of Revelation. Finster's apocalyptic visions are less horrifying and judgmental than most, and he often presents his message in an endearing and witty manner. His painting of the Four Horsemen of the Apocalypse, for instance, is entitled *Find the Four Horsemen of the Revelation* and portrays a ranch scene of dozens of horses, with the apocalyptic Four Horsemen hidden somewhere in their midst, disguised as saddled ponies. Yet Finster's own statements indicate the serious apocalyptic underpinnings of his work, as well as his sense of the inevitability of doomsday: "I have the whole world on my shoulders, and I feel responsible for this world, because it's livin' out its Last Days, and I'm here as a red light to warn this world about all o' that. God sent me here to preach His Word in the Last Days, and to be a Man of Visions, and to tell the world 'bout my visions through my sacred art and my garden, to bring out things where they wouldn't be forgotten. And that's what I'm adoin'. I'm fulfillin' God's plan for me on Earth's Planet" (Finster 1989:178).

9. I have heard people express similar sentiments with statements like "If they drop the bomb, I hope it lands on my house. The quicker the better."

10. Xeroxlore often the takes the form of parodies of office documents and letters, exemplified by the following memo regarding a union dispute concerning the end of the world:

MEMO

TO   ALL PERSONNEL

FROM   HEADQUARTERS

Due to the fact that the two unions involved have been unable to agree upon who shall blow the trumpets, the end of the world has been postponed for another two weeks. (Dundes and Pagter 1987:92)

11. One researcher, for instance, observes that the countercultural apocalypticism and millenarianism of the 1960s and 1970s was a response to widespread feelings of anomie among youth, and gives as an example the Charles Manson "Family," which he notes was millenarian in its expectations of a racist apocalypse and the transformation of society: "Manson thought of himself as leader, as father, as savior. His years at the Spahn movie ranch and in the desert mountains near Los Angeles, preparing for doomsday, seem like a perverse biblical image. Still, there was a promise of salvation here, too, with the otherworldly savior being replaced by a charismatic leader" (Bodemann 1974:444).

12. The punk aesthetic has persisted, in various forms, to the present day. Some original punks have declared that the punk subculture "died" soon after its inception, but there are still many individuals who consider themselves punks, postpunks, or "alternatives" (as well as many who refuse such labels altogether) and who continue to be inspired by the legacy of early punk in some way. Later incarnations of punk include hard-core, new wave, no wave, thrash, gloom, gothic, gloom-glam, speed metal, straight edge anarchist punk, grunge, industrial, and riot grrrls, among others. The music and ethos associated with these movements are occasionally nihilistic and apocalyptic as well.

6. FATALISM AND APOCALYPTIC BELIEFS

1. Among the better known studies are works by Barkun 1974, Chamberlain 1975, Cohn 1970, Festinger et al. 1956, Friedländer et al. 1985, Friedrich 1986, Garrett 1975, Hanson 1979, Harrison 1979, Hobsbawm 1965, McGinn 1979, Schmithals 1975, Schwartz 1990, and the studies of American millenarianism cited in chapter 1.

2. Primo Levi, recalling the psychological state of the Muselmänner, described them as "non-men who march and labor in silence, the divine spark dead within them, already too empty to suffer. One hesitates to call them living: one hesitates to call their death death, in the face of which they have no fear, as they are too tired to understand" (1961:82).

7. THE TRANSFORMATION OF APOCALYPTIC TRADITIONS IN THE POST–COLD WAR ERA

1. Reflecting on the persistence and variability of Christian apocalyptic traditions, Paul Boyer observes, "One is struck not only by the durability of apocalyptic belief, but also by its enormous adaptability. From second-century Asia Minor to eighteenth-century America, in vastly different historical circumstances, interpreters found vastly different meanings in the prophecies" (1992:77).

2. The variable content but underlying structural consistency of apocalyptic narratives suggest folklorist Vladimir Propp's observations about the morphological similarities in folktales that otherwise appear unrelated because of their seemingly different content (1968). As Propp noted, although the specific actions or characteristics of the dramatis personae may differ in folktales, the function, or "act," of these characters remains the same, thus constituting the fundamental elements of the tale. Apocalyptic narratives similarly contain certain formal regularities that serve as the basis for the stability of the tradition, but the content is variable and serves as the source for innovation.

3. Mary Stewart Relfe explains in *When Your Money Fails: The "666 System" Is Here* (which reportedly sold more than 600,000 copies within five months after publication) that before "Mr. 666" comes to power, the use of the number 666 to buy and sell must be established worldwide. Relfe then presents numerous examples of the cur-

rent use of the number 666: the World Bank code number, new credit cards in the United States, IRS forms, as well as various products, including computers, shoes made in countries of the European Community, menswear, gloves, and fertilizer, in an attempt to illustrate the imminence of the Antichrist's arrival (1981:15–20, 235).

8. EMERGENT APOCALYPTIC BELIEFS ABOUT UFOS AND
EXTRATERRESTRIAL BEINGS

1. As mainstays in American popular culture since the late 1940s, UFOs and extraterrestrials have been depicted in thousands of science fiction books and popularized further by hundreds of films, such as *2001: A Space Odyssey, E.T., Close Encounters of the Third Kind,* the *Star Wars* trilogy, *Independence Day, Star Man, Cocoon,* the various *Alien* movies, as well as dozens of such B-movie classics as *Mars Needs Women, I Married a Monster from Outer Space,* and *Devil Girl from Mars.* UFOs and ETs have pervaded television programs as well, ranging from *My Favorite Martian* to *Star Trek* and *The X-Files.*

2. In an August 6, 1990, Gallup poll, 14 percent of Americans asserted they had seen a UFO, up 3 percent from the 1973 poll. These polls indicate that UFO beliefs and sightings do not seem to be related to particular population groups or educational level; roughly 50 percent of those who believe in UFOs or have reported sightings have attended college (Jacobs 1975:296; Gallup 1988:52–54).

3. Farrakhan described his UFO encounter at a press conference on October 24, 1989: "A beam of light came from the Wheel and I was carried up on this beam of light into the Wheel. . . . At the center of the ceiling was a speaker and through the speaker I heard the voice of the Honorable Elijah Muhammad speaking to me as clearly as you are hearing my voice this morning" (Kossy 1994:27). The vision from Muhammad warned of the U.S. war planned against Moammar Qaddafi and also of the war being waged "against the rise of Black youth and Black people in America" (Kossy 1994:27). The role of UFOs in the endtimes also has been discussed in Farrakhan's newspaper, *The Final Call;* the lead story of the September 8, 1992, issue was entitled "UFOs and the New World Order," and it discusses a government plot to create a one-world order by staging a false UFO invasion in the future.

4. Flaherty's (1990) work is the most extensive study of the flying saucer faith from the perspectives of folkloristics and comparative mythology.

5. The following excerpt from a tract on UFOs and the endtimes role of space beings illustrates a number of the themes that characterize messages delivered to UFO contactees:

They tell us that they are coming here to assist humankind through these troubled times. They bring with them a general warning which tells us we are doomed unless we alter our ways. They say that they themselves have gone through similar periods and survived because they learned how to live in harmony with the Universe as well as their fellow beings. They are offering their hand in help if we will listen and heed their words. However, they have informed all those who are willing to listen that they are powerless to prevent the worst from taking place if we refuse to acknowledge their existence—something which world leaders and the military have refused to do. (Beckley 1980:5–6)

6. Adamski related that the elder philosopher of the space craft told him not only that atomic weapons would endanger earth, but that the radiation would harm other planets as well (Jacobs 1975:111). According to Adamski, the space people "were concerned with radiations going out from earth . . . I asked if this concern was due to the explosions of our bombs with their resultant vast radioactive clouds? He understood this readily and nodded in the affirmative. My next question was whether this was dangerous, and I pictured in my mind a scene of destruction. To this, too, he nodded his head in the affirmative, but upon his face there was no sign of resentment or judgment. His expression was one of understanding, and great compassion; as one would have toward a much loved child who had erred through ignorance and lack of understanding" (Leslie and Adamski 1967:59–60).

7. In contactee narratives descriptions of an idyllic life on other planets are often contrasted with life on earth, as conveyed by the following account from VIVENUS, an alleged space woman:

We wear no shoes, for the touch of our ground is blessed when we are moved to touch it. . . . We don't have money; we don't have wars; we don't have cars; we don't have bombs; we don't have guns; we don't have pain; we don't get lonely; we don't have misunderstanding; we don't have ridicule; we don't have misfortune. We don't have a lot that the Earth has—and there is no lack anywhere. (Beckley 1982:69)

8. Van Tassel was one of the most influential of the early organizers of the flying saucer movement, holding flying saucer conventions at Giant Rock from 1954 to 1974 (the first convention, in 1954, attracted more than five thousand people).

9. Although Commander Ashtar is a male, his name resembles that of Ashtoreth, the ancient Syrian and Phoenician goddess of love and fertility. In addition to Ashtar, other space deities from the Ashtar Command who frequently channel messages are a "beautiful spacewoman" named Aura Raines from the planet Clarion and the somewhat militaristic Monka from Mars (see Beckley 1982).

10. The statements of Gabriel Green, long-standing president of the Amalgamated Flying Saucer Clubs of America, exemplify the combination of conditional apocalypticism and an evacuation scenario that is frequently expressed in the UFO subculture. Green states that apocalypse is not inevitable as long as human beings abandon their destructive ways and learn, through the guidance of aliens, to develop positive attitudes and behaviors that will move humanity into an Aquarian Age of peace and harmony. However, if an apocalypse does occur, Green asserts that the space beings will

swoop down and evacuate one-tenth of the world's population in the Rapture: "only one-tenth of the population will be spiritually qualified to live in an environment of harmony, and there are some limitations on their ability to provide for us, to house us and so forth" (Fulcher 1984:2). In the universalist manner characteristic of the flying saucer worldview, Green declares not only that this UFO advent will fulfill biblical prophecies of the Second Coming but that it will "fulfill the purposes of all religions simultaneously" (Fulcher 1984:2).

Bibliography

Aarne, Antti, and Stith Thompson. 1961. *The Types of the Folktale: A Classification and Bibliography.* Folklore Fellows Communications 184, Helsinki.

Aberle, David. 1970. A note on relative deprivation theory as applied to millenarian and other cult movements. In *Millennial Dreams in Action: Studies in Revolutionary Religious Movements,* ed. Sylvia L. Thrupp, 209–214. The Hague: Mouton. Originally published 1962.

Abrams, M. H. 1971. *Natural Supernaturalism: Tradition and Revolution in Romantic Literature.* New York: Norton.

Abramson, L. Y., Judy Garber, and Martin E. P. Seligman. 1980. Learned helplessness in humans: An attributional analysis. In *Human Helplessness: Theory and Applications,* ed. Judy Garber and Martin E. P. Seligman, 3–34. New York: Academic Press.

Adams, Marilyn McCord, and Norman Kretzmann. 1969. Introduction to *Predestination, God's Foreknowledge, and Future Contingents,* by William Ockham, 1–33. New York: Appleton-Century-Crofts.

Alnor, William M. 1989. *Soothsayers of the Second Advent.* Old Tappan, NJ: Fleming H. Revell.

Alonso, J. M. 1979. *The Secret of Fatima: Fact and Legend.* Trans. Dominican Nuns of the Perpetual Rosary. Cambridge, MA: Ravengate Press.

Anders, Gunther. 1962. Reflections on the H bomb. In *Man Alone,* ed. Eric Josephson and Mary Josephson, 288–298. New York: Dell.

Argüelles, José. 1987. *The Mayan Factor.* Santa Fe, NM: Bear.

Asimov, Isaac. 1979. *A Choice of Catastrophes.* New York: Simon & Schuster.

Aune, David E. 1983. *Prophecy in Early Christianity and the Ancient Mediterranean World.* Grand Rapids, MI: Eerdmans.

Baer, Randall N. 1989. *Inside the New Age Nightmare.* Lafayette, LA: Huntington House.

Balch, Robert W. 1995. Waiting for the ships: Disillusion and the revitalization of faith in Bo and Peep's cult. In *The Gods Have Landed: New Religions from Other Worlds,* ed. James R. Lewis, 138–166. Albany: SUNY Press.

Balmer, Randall. 1988. Apocalypticism in America: The argot of premillennialism in popular culture. *Prospects* 13:417–433.

Barasch, Marc Ian. 1983. *The Little Black Book of Atomic War.* New York: Dell.

Barkun, Michael. 1974. *Disaster and the Millennium.* New Haven: Yale University Press.

——. 1983. Divided apocalypse: Thinking about the end in contemporary America. *Soundings* 66 (fall): 257–280.

——. 1987a. The language of apocalypse: Premillennialists and nuclear war. In *The God Pumpers: Religion in the Electronic Age,* ed. Marshall Fishwick and Ray B. Browne, 159–173. Bowling Green, OH: Bowling Green University Popular Press.

——. 1987b. "The wind sweeping over the country": John Humphrey Noyes and the rise of Millerism. In *The Disappointed: Millerism and Millenarianism in the Nineteenth Century,* ed. Ronald Numbers and Jonathan M. Butler, 153–172. Bloomington: Indiana University Press.

——. 1990. Racist apocalypse: Millennialism on the far right. *American Studies* 31:121–140.

——. 1994. *Religion and the Racist Right: The Origins of the Christian Identity Movement.* Chapel Hill: University of North Carolina Press.

Bartter, Martha A. 1988. *Ground Zero: The Atomic Bomb in American Science Fiction.* New York: Greenwood Press.

Bascom, William. 1965. The forms of folklore: Prose narratives. *Journal of American Folklore* 78:3–20.

Bates, Leon. 1985. *Projection for Survival.* Sherman, TX: Bible Believers' Evangelistic Association.

Baudrillard, Jean. 1988. *Selected Writings.* Ed. and intro. Mark Poster. Stanford: Stanford University Press.

——. 1994. *The Illusion of the End.* Trans. Chris Turner. Stanford: Stanford University Press.

Bauman, Richard. 1992. Folklore. In *Folklore, Cultural Performances, and Popular Entertainments.* Ed. and intro. Richard Bauman, 29–40. New York: Oxford University Press.

Bausinger, Hermann. 1990. *Folk Culture in a World of Technology.* Trans. Elke Dettmer. Bloomington: Indiana University Press.

Bax, Mart. 1987. Religious regimes and state formation: Towards a research perspective. *Anthropological Quarterly* 60:1–12.

Becker, Ernest. 1973. *The Denial of Death.* New York: Free Press.

Beckley, Timothy Green. 1980. *Psychic and UFO Revelations in the Last Days.* New Brunswick, NJ: Inner Light.

——. 1982. *The New World Order: Channeled Prophecies from Space.* New York: Global Communications.

Benét, William Rose, ed. 1987. *Benét's Reader's Encyclopedia.* 3d ed. New York: Harper & Row.

Bercovitch, Sacvan. 1978. *The American Jeremiad.* Madison: University of Wisconsin Press.

Berger, Peter, and Thomas Luckmann. 1967. *The Social Construction of Reality: A Treatise in the Sociology of Knowledge.* Garden City: NY: Doubleday-Anchor Books.

Berger-Gould, Benina, Susan Moon, and Judith Van Hoorn, eds. 1986. *Growing Up Scared? The Psychological Effect of the Nuclear Threat on Children.* Berkeley: Open Books.

Bergoffen, Debra. 1982. The apocalyptic meaning of history. In *The Apocalyptic Vision in America: Interdisciplinary Essays on Myth and Culture,* ed. Lois Parkinson Zamora, 11–36. Bowling Green, OH: Bowling Green University Popular Press.

Berlitz, Charles. 1981. *Doomsday: 1999 A.D.* Garden City, NY: Doubleday.

Bezilla, Robert, ed. 1996. *Religion in America 1996.* Princeton: Princeton Religion Research Center.

Blackwell, P. L., and J. C. Gessner. 1983. Fear and trembling: An inquiry into adolescent perceptions of living in the nuclear age. *Youth and Society* 15:237–255.

Bleeker, C. J. 1963. Die Idee des Schicksals in der alt-ägyptischen Religion. In C. J. Bleeker, *The Sacred Bridge,* 112–129. Leiden, the Netherlands: E. J. Brill.

Bloch, Ruth. 1985. *Visionary Republic: Millennial Themes in American Thought, 1756–1800.* Cambridge: Cambridge University Press.

Bloom, Harold. 1996. *Omens of the Millennium: The Gnosis of Angels, Dreams, and Resurrection.* New York: Riverhead Books.

Bodemann, Y. Michael. 1974. Mystical, satanic, and chiliastic forces in countercultural movements: Changing the world—or reconciling it. *Youth and Society* 5:433–447.

Bolle, Kees W. 1987. Fate. In *The Encyclopedia of Religion,* ed. Mircea Eliade, 5:290–298. New York: Macmillan.

Bourguignon, Erika. 1976. *Possession.* San Francisco: Chandler.

Boyer, Paul. 1985. *By the Bomb's Early Light: American Thought and Culture at the Dawn of the Atomic Age.* New York: Pantheon Books.

———. 1992. *When Time Shall Be No More: Prophecy Belief in Modern American Culture.* Cambridge: Belknap Press of Harvard University Press.

Bradbury, Ray. 1950. *The Martian Chronicles.* Garden City, NY: Doubleday.

Brake, Michael. 1985. *Comparative Youth Culture: The Sociology of Youth Culture and Youth Subcultures in America, Britain, and Canada.* London: Routledge & Kegan Paul.

Brednich, Rolf Wilhelm. 1964. *Volkserzählungen und Volksglaube von den Schicksalsfrauen.* Folklore Fellows Communications 193, Helsinki.

Broad, William. 1992. Dismantling arms creates new risks. *Register Guard* (Eugene, OR), July 6, A1, A4.

Bromley, Geoffrey. 1982. *The International Standard Bible Dictionary.* Vol. 2. Grand Rapids, MI: Eerdmans.

Brøndsted, Mogens. 1967. The transformations of the concept of fate in literature. In *Fatalistic Beliefs in Religion, Folklore, and Literature,* ed. Helmer Ringgren, 172–178. Stockholm: Almqvist & Wiksell.

Brown, Ira V. 1952. Watchers for the Second Coming: The Millenarian tradition in America. *Mississippi Valley Historical Review* 39:441–458.

Brummett, Barry. 1991. *Contemporary Apocalyptic Rhetoric.* New York: Praeger.

Brunvand, Jan Harold, ed. 1996. *American Folklore: An Encyclopedia.* New York: Garland.

Bryan, C. B. D. 1995. *Close Encounters of the Fourth Kind.* New York: Penguin.

Bryant, M. Darrol, and Donald W. Dayton, eds. 1983. *The Coming Kingdom: Essays in American Millennialism and Eschatology.* New York: New Era Books.

Buber, Martin. 1957. *Pointing the Way: Collected Essays.* Ed. and trans. Maurice Friedman. Baltimore: Johns Hopkins University Press.

Bullard, Thomas E. 1989. UFO abduction reports: The supernatural kidnap narrative returns in technological guise. *Journal of American Folklore* 102:147–170.

Burdick, Eugene, and Harvey Wheeler. 1962. *Fail-Safe.* New York: McGraw-Hill.

Burridge, Kenelm. 1969. *New Heaven, New Earth: A Study of Millenarian Activities.* Oxford: Basil Blackwell.

Burroughs, William S., Jr. 1966. *Naked Lunch.* New York: Grove Weidenfeld. Originally published 1959.

———. 1981. *Cities of the Red Night.* New York: Holt, Rinehart & Winston.

Burroughs, William S., Jr., and Keith Haring. 1988. *Apocalypse.* Amsterdam, New York, Miami Beach: George Mulder Fine Arts.

Buss, Dietrich G. 1988. Meeting of Heaven and Earth: A survey and analysis of the literature on millennialism in America, 1965–85. *Fides et historia: Official Publication of the Conference on Faith and History* 20 (January): 5–28.

Cantril, Hadley. 1965. *The Patterns of Human Concerns.* New Brunswick: Rutgers University Press.

Carey, Michael J. 1982. Psychological fallout. *Bulletin of the Atomic Scientists* 38 (January): 20–24.

Carroll, Michael P. 1986. *The Cult of the Virgin Mary: Psychological Origins.* Princeton: Princeton University Press.

Cassara, Ernest. 1982. The development of America's sense of mission. In *The Apocalyptic Vision in America: Interdisciplinary Essays on Myth and Culture,* ed. Lois Parkinson Zamora, 64–96. Bowling Green, OH: Bowling Green University Popular Press.

Chamberlain, E. R. 1975. *Antichrist and the Millennium.* New York: Dutton.

Chandler, Russell. 1993. *Doomsday: The End of the World—A View through Time.* Ann Arbor, MI: Servant Publications.

Chernus, Ira. 1986. *Dr. Strangegod: On the Symbolic Meaning of Nuclear Weapons.* Columbia: University of South Carolina Press.

Cherry, Conrad, ed. 1971. *God's New Israel: Religious Interpretations of American Destiny.* Englewood Cliffs, NJ: Prentice-Hall.

Chidester, David. 1988. *Salvation and Suicide: An Interpretation of Jim Jones, the Peoples Temple, and Jonestown.* Bloomington: Indiana University Press.

Chilton, Paul. 1986. Nukespeak: Nuclear language, culture, and propaganda. In *The Nuclear Predicament: A Sourcebook*, ed. Donna Uthus Gregory, 127–142. New York: St. Martin's Press.

Christian, William A., Jr. 1981. *Apparitions in Late Medieval and Renaissance Spain.* Princeton: Princeton University Press.

———. 1984. Religious apparitions and the Cold War in southern Europe. In *Religion, Power and Protest in Local Communities: The Northern Shore of the Mediterranean*, ed. Eric R. Wolf, 239–266. Berlin: Mouton.

Clarke, Doug. 1982. *Shockwaves of Armageddon.* Eugene, OR: Harvest Books.

Clayton, Bruce D. 1980. *Life After Doomsday: A Survivalist Guide to Nuclear War and Other Major Disasters.* Boulder, CO: Paladin Press.

Coates, James. 1987. *Armed and Dangerous: The Rise of the Survivalist Right.* New York: Noonday Press.

Cochrane, Glynn. 1979. Big men and cargo cults. In *Reader in Comparative Religion: An Anthropological Approach*, ed. W. Lessa and E. Vogt, 433–440. 4th ed. New York: Harper & Row.

Cohen, Daniel. 1983. *Waiting for the Apocalypse.* Buffalo: Prometheus Books.

Cohn, Norman. 1970. *The Pursuit of the Millennium: Revolutionary Millenarians and Mystical Anarchists of the Middle Ages.* Rev. and exp. ed. New York: Oxford University Press. Originally published 1957.

Collins, Adela Y., ed. 1986. *Early Christian Apocalypticism: Genre and Social Setting. Semeia* 36.

Collins, John J., ed. 1979. *Apocalypse: The Morphology of a Genre. Semeia* 14.

———. 1989. *The Apocalyptic Imagination: An Introduction to the Jewish Matrix of Christianity.* New York: Crossroad.

Commoner, Barry. 1971. *The Closing Circle: Nature, Man, and Technology.* New York: Knopf.

Cotton, John. 1642. *The Pouring Out of the Seven Vials.* London: Printed by R. S. for Henry Overton.

Cunningham, Lawrence. 1982. *Mother of God.* San Francisco: Harper & Row.

Curran, Douglas. 1985. *In Advance of the Landing: Folk Concepts of Outer Space.* New York: Abbeville Press.

Daniels, Ted. 1992. *Millennialism: An International Bibliography.* New York: Garland.

Davidson, James W. 1977. *The Logic of Millennial Thought: Eighteenth-Century New England.* New Haven: Yale University Press.

Davies, Paul. 1983. *God and the New Physics.* New York: Simon & Schuster, Touchstone.

Dégh, Linda. 1994. *American Folklore and the Mass Media.* Bloomington: Indiana University Press.

Dewey, Joseph. 1990. *In a Dark Time: The Apocalyptic Temper in the American Novel of the Nuclear Age.* West Lafayette: Purdue University Press.

Dial-a-Bummer. 1990. *Harper's Magazine* 281, no. 1687 (December): 22.

Dinges, William D. 1991. Roman Catholic traditionalism. In *Fundamentalisms Observed*, ed. Martin E. Marty and R. Scott Appleby, 66–101. Chicago: University of Chicago Press.

Dione, R. L. 1973. *God Drives a Flying Saucer.* New York: Bantam.

Doob, Leonard W. 1988. *Inevitability: Determinism, Fatalism, and Destiny.* New York: Greenwood Press.

Dorner, August. 1928. Fate. In *Encyclopedia of Religion and Ethics*, ed. James Hastings, 771–778. New York: Scribner's.

Dorson, Richard M. 1970. Is there a folk in the city? *Journal of American Folklore* 83:185–222.

———. 1973. *America in Legend: Folklore from the Colonial Period to the Present.* New York: Pantheon Books.

———. 1977. *American Folklore.* Chicago: University of Chicago Press. Originally published 1959.

Downing, Barry H., 1989. *The Bible and Flying Saucers.* New York: Berkley. Originally published in 1968.

Dugger, Ronnie. 1984. Does Reagan expect a nuclear Armageddon? *Washington Post*, April 8, C1, C4.

Duncan, Barry L., Mary Ann Kraus, and M. Bernadine Parks. 1986. Children's fears of nuclear war: A systems strategy for change. *Youth and Society* 18 (September): 28–44.

Dundes, Alan. 1961. Brown County superstitions. *Midwest Folklore* 11:25–56.

———. 1979. The dead baby joke cycle. *Western Folklore* 38:145–157.

———. 1987. *Cracking Jokes: Studies of Sick Humor Cycles and Stereotypes.* Berkeley: Ten Speed Press.

———, ed. 1965. *The Study of Folklore.* Englewood Cliffs, NJ: Prentice-Hall.

———, ed. 1984. *Sacred Narratives: Readings in the Theory of Myth.* Berkeley and Los Angeles: University of California Press.

———, ed. 1988. *The Flood Myth.* Berkeley and Los Angeles: University of California Press.

Dundes, Alan, and Carl R. Pagter. 1987. *When You're Up to Your Ass in Alligators . . .: More Urban Folklore from the Paperwork Empire.* Detroit: Wayne State University Press.

———. 1992. *Work Hard and You Shall Be Rewarded: Urban Folklore from the Paperwork Empire.* Detroit: Wayne State University Press. Originally published 1975.

Dupont, Ives. 1973. *Catholic Prophecy: The Coming Chastisement.* Rockford, IL: TAN Books and Publishers.

Durkheim, Emile. 1965. *The Elementary Forms of the Religious Life.* Trans. Joseph Ward Swain. New York: Free Press. Originally published 1915.

Dyer, Charles H. 1991. *The Rise of Babylon: Sign of the End Times.* Wheaton, IL: Tyndale House.

Eliade, Mircea. 1959. *The Sacred and the Profane: The Nature of Religion.* Trans. Willard R. Trask. New York: Harcourt, Brace & World.

———. 1974. *The Myth of the Eternal Return: or, Cosmos and History.* Trans. Willard R. Trask. Princeton: Princeton University Press. Originally published 1949.

———. 1975. *Myths, Dreams, and Mysteries: The Encounter Between Contemporary Faiths and Archaic Realities.* Trans. Philip Mairet. New York: Harper & Row. Originally published 1957.

Ellis, Bill. 1989. Introduction to *Contemporary Legends in Emergence,* special issue, *Western Folklore* 49:1–10

———. 1991. Cattle mutilation: Contemporary legends and contemporary mythologies. *Contemporary Legend* 1:39–80.

Ellwood, Robert S., and Harry B. Partin. 1988. *Religious and Spiritual Groups in Modern America.* 2d ed. Englewood Cliffs, NJ: Prentice-Hall.

Enroth, Ronald M., Edward E. Ericson, Jr., and C. Breckenridge Peters. 1972. *The Jesus People: Old-Time Religion in the Age of Aquarius.* Grand Rapids, MI: Eerdmans.

Erwin, John S. 1990. *The Millennialism of Cotton Mather: An Historical and Theological Analysis.* Lewiston, ME: Edwin Mellen Press.

Eskeröd, Albert. 1947. *Årets Äring* (The year's crop). Stockholm: Almqvist & Wiksell.

———. 1964. Needs, interests, values, and the supernatural. *Studia Ethnographica Upsaliensia* 21:81–98.

Evans-Pritchard, E. E. 1937. *Witchcraft, Oracles, and Magic among the Azande.* Oxford: Clarendon Press.

Faid, Robert W. 1988. *Gorbachev! Has the Real Antichrist Come?* Tulsa: Victory House.

Faulkner, William. 1954. William Faulkner's speech of acceptance upon the award of the Nobel Prize for Literature, December 10, 1950. In *The Faulkner Reader: Selections from the Works of William Faulkner,* ed. Malcolm Cowley. New York: Random House.

Festinger, Leon, Henry W. Riecken, and Stanley Schachter. 1956. *When Prophecy Fails: A Social and Psychological Study of a Modern Group That Predicted the Destruction of the World.* New York: Harper & Row.

Finster, Howard. 1989. *Stranger from Another World: Man of Visions Now on This Earth.* New York: Abbeville.

Flaherty, Robert Pearson. 1990. Flying saucers and the new angelology: Mythic projection of the Cold War and the convergence of opposites. Ph.D. diss., University of California, Los Angeles.

Foerster, Norman, ed. 1970. *American Poetry and Prose.* Boston: Houghton Mifflin.

Foster, George M. 1972. Divination. In *Funk and Wagnall's Standard Dictionary of Folklore, Mythology, and Legend,* ed. Maria Leach, 316–317. San Francisco: Harper & Row. Originally published in two volumes, 1949–1950.

Foster, Lawrence. 1987. Had prophecy failed? Contrasting perspectives of the Millerites and Shakers. In *The Disappointed: Millerism and Millenarianism in the Nineteenth Century,* ed. Ronald Numbers and Jonathan M. Butler, 173–188. Bloomington: Indiana University Press.

Frazer, James G. 1918. *Folk-lore in the Old Testament*. Vol. 1. London: Macmillan.
————. 1976. *The Golden Bough*. London: Macmillan. Originally published 1922.
Friedländer, Saul, Gerald Holton, Leo Marx, and Eugene Skolnikoff, eds. 1985. *Visions of Apocalypse: End or Rebirth?* New York: Holmes & Meier.
Friedrich, Otto. 1986. *The End of the World: A History*. New York: Fromm International.
Fulcher, Robb. 1984. Story of spacemen broadcast by man. *Oregonian*, May 8, B2
Funkenstein, Amos. 1985. A schedule for the end of the world: The origins and persistence of the apocalyptic mentality. In *Visions of Apocalypse: End or Rebirth?* ed. Saul Friedländer, Gerald Holton, Leo Marx, and Eugene Skolnikoff, 44–60. New York: Holmes & Meier.
Gallup, George, Jr. 1988. *The Gallup Poll: Public Opinion 1987*. Wilmington, DE: Scholarly Research.
Gallup, George, Jr., and Jim Castelli. 1989. *The People's Religion: American Faith in the Nineties*. New York: Macmillan.
Gallup, George H. 1972. *The Gallup Poll: Public Opinion 1935–1972*. 3 vols. New York: Random House.
Garrett, Clarke. 1975. *Respectable Folly: Millenarianism and the French Revolution in France and England*. Baltimore: Johns Hopkins University Press.
Geisendorfer, James V., ed. 1977. *Directory of Religious Organizations*. Washington, DC: McGrath.
Georges, Robert A. 1978. Conceptions of fate in stories told by Greeks. In *Folklore in the Modern World*, ed. Richard Dorson, 301–319. The Hague: Mouton.
Georges, Robert A., and Michael Owen Jones. 1980. *People Studying People: The Human Element in Fieldwork*. Berkeley and Los Angeles: University of California Press.
————. 1995. *Folkloristics: An Introduction*. Bloomington: Indiana University Press.
Gimbutas, Marija. 1982. *The Goddesses and Gods of Old Europe: Myths and Cult Images*. Berkeley and Los Angeles: University of California Press.
Ginsberg, Alan. 1965. *Howl and Other Poems*. San Francisco: City Lights Books.
Godwin, Malcolm. 1990. *Angels: An Endangered Species*. New York: Simon & Schuster.
Gordon, Stuart. 1993. *The Encyclopedia of Myths and Legends*. London: Headline.
Graef, Hilda. 1963. *Mary, A History of Doctrine and Devotion*. Vol. 1. *From the Beginnings to the Eve of the Reformation*. New York: Sheed & Ward.
Graham, Billy. 1983. *Approaching Hoofbeats: The Four Horsemen of the Apocalypse*. Waco, TX: Word Books.
Graham, Stephen R. 1989. Hal Lindsey. In *Twentieth-Century Shapers of American Popular Religion*, ed. Charles H. Lippy, 247–255. New York: Greenwood Press.
Grambo, Ronald. 1988. Problems of fatalism: A blueprint for further research. *Folklore* 99:11–29.
Greeley, Andrew. 1977. *The Mary Myth: On the Femininity of God*. New York: Seabury Press.

Griffin, William. 1979. *Endtime: The Doomsday Catalog.* New York: Macmillan.

Groves, Leslie R. 1962. *Now It Can Be Told: The Story of the Manhattan Project.* New York: Harper.

Grunig, James. 1971. Communications and economic decision-making processes of Colombian peasants. *Economic Development and Cultural Change* 19:584–598.

Gumpert, Lynn. 1983. *The End of the World: Contemporary Visions of the Apocalypse.* New York: New Museum of Contemporary Art.

Hadden, Jeffrey K., and Charles E. Swann. 1981. *Prime Time Preachers: The Rising Power of Televangelism.* Reading, MA: Addison-Wesley.

Hagee, John. 1996. *Beginning of the End: The Assassination of Yitzhak Rabin and the Coming Antichrist.* Nashville: Thomas Nelson.

Halsell, Grace. 1986. *Prophecy and Politics: Militant Evangelists on the Road to Nuclear War.* Westport, CT: Lawrence Hill.

Hand, Wayland D., ed. 1961–1964. *Popular Beliefs and Superstitions from North Carolina.* Vols. 6–7 of *The Frank C. Brown Collection of North Carolina Folklore.* Durham, NC: Duke University Press.

Hand, Wayland D., Anna Casetta, and Sondra Thiederman, eds. 1981. *Popular Beliefs and Superstitions: A Compendium of American Folklore from the Ohio Collection of Newbell Niles Puckett.* 3 vols. Boston: G. K. Hall.

Hand, Wayland D., and Jeannine E. Talley, eds. 1984. *Popular Beliefs and Superstitions from Utah,* coll. Anthon S. Cannon and others. Salt Lake City: University of Utah Press.

Hand, Wayland D., and Donald J. Ward. Forthcoming. *Encyclopedia of American Popular Belief and Superstition.* Berkeley and Los Angeles: University of California Press.

Hanson, Paul D. 1976. Apocalypse, genre; apocalypticism. In *The Interpreter's Dictionary of the Bible: Supplementary Volume,* ed. Keith Crim et al., 27–34. Nashville: Abingdon Press.

———. 1979. *The Dawn of Apocalyptic.* Rev. ed. Philadelphia: Fortress Press. Originally published 1975.

———. 1984. The apocalyptic consciousness. *Quarterly Review* 4:23–39.

Harris Survey. 1972. *Alienation in America.* New York: Louis Harris.

Harrison, J. F. C. 1979. *The Second Coming: Popular Millenarianism, 1780–1850.* New Brunswick: Rutgers University Press.

Hebdige, Dick. 1979. *Subculture: The Meaning of Style.* London: Methuen.

Heilbroner, Robert. 1974. *An Inquiry into the Human Prospect.* Rev. ed. New York: Norton.

Hellholm, David, ed. 1983. *Apocalypticism in the Mediterranean World and the Near East.* Tübingen: J. C. B. Mohr.

Henningsen, Gustav. 1967. Fatalism in systematic aspect and fatalism in its functional context. In *Fatalistic Beliefs in Religion, Folklore, and Literature,* ed. Helmer Ringgren, 183–186. Stockholm: Almqvist & Wiksell.

Henry, Tricia. 1989. *Break All Rules! Punk Rock and the Making of a Style*. Ann Arbor, MI: UMI Research Press.

Herbert, Albert J. 1986. *Prophecies, the Chastisement, and Purification*. Paulina, LA: Privately published.

Hickey, J. T. 1967. Fatalism. In *New Catholic Encyclopedia*, ed. Catholic University of America, 1323–1324. New York: McGraw-Hill.

Hindson, Ed. 1996. *Final Signs: Amazing Prophecies of the Endtimes*. Eugene, OR: Harvest House.

Hine, Thomas. 1989. *Populuxe*. New York: Knopf.

Hobsbawm, Eric J. 1965. *Primitive Rebels: Studies in Archaic Forms of Social Movement in the Nineteenth and Twentieth Centuries*. New York: Norton. Originally published 1959.

———. 1979. Millenarianism. In *Reader in Comparative Religion: An Anthropological Approach*, ed. William A. Lessa and Evon Z. Vogt, 440–444. 4th ed. New York: Harper Collins.

Hofstadter, Richard. 1967. *The Paranoid Style in American Politics and Other Essays*. New York: Vintage Books. Originally published 1952.

Hogue, John. 1987. *Nostradamus and the Millennium: Predictions of the Future*. New York: Doubleday/Dolphin.

Hopkins, Budd. 1987. *Intruders: The Incredible Visitation at Copley Woods*. New York: Random House.

Houglum, Robert Michael. 1986. A rhetorical perspective of the survivalist movement of the Pacific Northwest. Ph. D. diss., University of Oregon.

Howard, Robert Glenn. 1995. E-mailing the apocalypse: End-times communication on the Internet. Paper presented at the Annual Meeting of the American Folklore Society, Lafayette, Louisiana.

Hufford, David J. 1977. Humanoids and anomalous lights: Taxonomic and epistemological problems. *Fabula* 18:234–241.

———. 1982. *The Terror That Comes in the Night: An Experience-Centered Study of Supernatural Assault Traditions*. Philadelphia: University of Pennsylvania Press

Hunt, Dave. 1983. *Peace, Prosperity, and the Coming Holocaust: The New Age Movement in Prophecy*. Eugene, OR: Harvest House.

———. 1990. *Global Peace and the Rise of Antichrist*. Eugene, OR: Harvest House.

Incredible Bayside Prophecies on the United States and Canada. 1991. Lowell, MI: These Last Days Ministries.

Jacobs, David Michael. 1975. *The UFO Controversy in America*. Bloomington: Indiana University Press.

———. 1992. *Secret Life: Firsthand Accounts of UFO Abductions*. New York: Simon & Schuster.

James, E. O. 1959. *The Cult of the Mother Goddess*. New York: Barnes & Noble.

Jameson, Frederic. 1984. Postmodernism, or the cultural logic of late capitalism. *New Left Review* 146 (July–August): 53–92.

Jarvie, I. C. 1977. Explaining cargo cults. In *Rationality*, ed. Bryan R. Wilson, 50–61. Oxford: Basil Blackwell.

Jeffrey, Grant R. 1990. *Armageddon: Appointment with Destiny*. New York: Bantam Books. Originally published 1988.

———. 1994. *Prince of Darkness: Antichrist and the New World Order*. New York: Bantam Books.

Jewett, Robert. 1979. *Jesus against the Rapture: Seven Unexpected Prophecies*. Philadelphia: Westminster Press.

———. 1984. Coming to terms with the doom boom. *Quarterly Review* 4:9–22.

Jonas, Susan, and Marilyn Nissenson. 1994. *Going Going Gone: Vanishing America*. San Francisco: Chronicle Books.

Jones, Lawrence. 1985. Reagan's religion. *Journal of American Culture* 8:59–70.

Jones, Michael Owen. 1967. Folk beliefs: Knowledge and action. *Southern Folklore Quarterly* 31:304–309.

———. 1989. *Craftsman of the Cumberlands: Tradition and Creativity*. Lexington: University Press of Kentucky.

Jorstad, Erling. 1970. *The Politics of Doomsday: Fundamentalists of the Far Right*. Nashville: Abingdon Press.

Jung, Carl G. 1970. *Four Archetypes: Mother, Rebirth, Spirit, Trickster*. Princeton: Princeton University Press. Originally published 1959.

———. 1978. *Flying Saucers: A Modern Myth of Things Seen in the Skies*. Trans. R. F. C. Hull. Princeton: Princeton University Press. Originally published 1958.

Kah, Gary H. 1992. *En Route to Global Occupation*. Lafayette, LA: Huntington House.

Kamper, Dietmar, and Christoph Wulf, eds. 1989. *Looking Back on the End of the World*. New York: Semiotext(e).

Käsemann, Ernst. 1969. The beginnings of Christian theology. *Journal for Theology and the Church* 6:17–46

Kawada, Louise, ed. 1985. *The Apocalypse Anthology*. Boston: Rowan Tree Press.

Kazin, Alfred. 1988. Awaiting the crack of doom. *New York Times Book Review*, May 1, 1.

Keller, Catherine. Forthcoming. *Apocalypse Now and Then: A Feminist Guide to the End of the World*. Boston: Beacon Press.

Kermode, Frank. 1966. *The Sense of an Ending: Studies in the Theory of Fiction*. New York: Oxford University Press.

———. 1985. Apocalypse and the modern. In *Visions of Apocalypse: End or Rebirth?* ed. Saul Friedländer, Gerald Holton, Leo Marx, and Eugene Skolnikoff, 84–106. New York: Holmes & Meier.

Kester, Marian, Peter Belsito, and Bob Davis. 1981. *Streetart: The Punk Poster in San Francisco, 1977–1981*. Berkeley: Last Gasp.

Ketterer, David. 1974. *New Worlds for Old: The Apocalyptic Imagination, Science Fiction, and American Literature*. Garden City, NY: Anchor Press/Doubleday.

Kinman, Dwight L. 1995. *The World's Last Dictator*. 2d ed. Woodburn, OR: Solid Rock Books.

Kirban, Salem. 1973. *Guide to Survival.* Huntington Valley, PA: Salem Kirban.
———. 1981. *666 (Pictorial Format).* Huntington Valley, PA: Salem Kirban.
Kirsch, Jonathan. 1977. PW interviews: Hal Lindsey. *Publisher's Weekly,* March 14, 30–32.
Koch, Klaus. 1972. *The Rediscovery of Apocalyptic.* London: SCM Press.
Kossy, Donna. 1994. *Kooks.* Portland: Feral House.
Kristeva, Julia. 1986. Stabat Mater. In *The Kristeva Reader,* ed. Tori Moi, 160–186. New York: Columbia University Press.
Kroes, Rob, ed. 1985. *Nineteen Eighty-Four and the Apocalyptic Imagination in America.* Amsterdam: Free University Press.
Kroker, Arthur, and David Cook. 1986. *The Postmodern Scene: Excremental Culture and Hyper-Aesthetics.* New York: St. Martin's Press.
Kselman, Thomas A. 1983. *Miracles and Prophecies in Nineteenth-Century France.* New Brunswick: Rutgers University Press.
Kselman, Thomas A., and Steven Avella. 1986. Marian piety and the Cold War in the United States. *Catholic Historical Review* 72 (July): 403–424.
Kurti, Laszlo. 1988. The politics of joking: Popular response to Chernobyl. *Journal of American Folklore* 101:324–334.
LaBarre, Weston. 1971. Materials for a history of studies of crisis cults: A bibliographic essay. *Current Anthropology* 12:3–45.
———. 1972. *The Ghost Dance: The Origins of Religion.* New York: Dell.
La Farge, Phyllis. 1987. *The Strangelove Legacy: Children, Parents, and Teachers in the Nuclear Age.* New York: Harper & Row.
LaHaye, Tim. 1972. *The Beginning of the End.* Wheaton, IL: Tyndale House.
———. 1975. *Revelation: Illustrated and Made Plain.* Grand Rapids, MI: Zondervan.
Laing, Dave. 1978. Interpreting punk rock. *Marxism Today* (April): 123–128.
Lalonde, Peter, and Paul Lalonde. 1994. *The Mark of the Beast: Your Money, Computers, and the End of the World.* Eugene, OR: Harvest House.
Langer, Ellen J. 1983. *The Psychology of Control.* Beverly Hills: Sage.
Lanternari, Vittorio. 1963. *The Religions of the Oppressed: A Study of Modern Messianic Cults.* Trans. Lisa Sergio. New York: Knopf.
Lattimore, Richmond, trans. 1977. *Hesiod.* Ann Arbor: University of Michigan Press.
Leach, Maria. 1972. *Funk and Wagnall's Standard Dictionary of Folklore, Mythology, and Legend.* San Francisco: Harper & Row. Originally published in two volumes, 1949–1950.
Lefcourt, Herbert M. 1976. *Locus of Control: Current Trends in Theory and Research.* Hillsdale, NJ: Erlbaum.
Leslie, Desmond, and George Adamski. 1967. Visitor from Venus. In *The Flying Saucer Reader,* ed. Jay David, 51–72. New York: New American Library.
Levi, Primo. 1961. *Survival in Auschwitz.* New York: Collier.
Levin, Kim. 1988. *Beyond Modernism: Essays on Art from the '70s and '80s.* New York: Harper & Row.

Lewicki, Zbigniew. 1984. *The Bang and the Whimper: Apocalypse and Entropy in American Literature.* Westport, CT: Greenwood Press.

Lewis, David Allen. 1990. *Prophecy 2000.* Green Forest, AR: New Leaf Press.

Lewis, James R., ed. 1995. *The Gods Have Landed: New Religions from Other Worlds.* Albany: SUNY Press.

Lifton, Robert Jay. 1967. *Death in Life: Survivors of Hiroshima.* New York: Random House.

———. 1979. *The Broken Connection: On Death and the Continuity of Life.* New York: Simon & Schuster.

———. 1987. *The Future of Immortality and Other Essays for a Nuclear Age.* New York: Basic Books.

Lifton, Robert Jay, and Richard Falk. 1982. *Indefensible Weapons: The Political and Psychological Case against Nuclearism.* New York: Basic Books.

Lifton, Robert Jay, and Eric Olsen. 1984. The nuclear age. In *Death: Current Perspectives,* ed. Edwin S. Shneidman, 451–459. 3d ed. Palo Alto: Mayfield.

Linder, Stephen N. 1982. Survivalists: The ethnography of an urban millennial cult. Ph.D. diss., University of California, Los Angeles.

Lindsey, Hal. 1974. *The Liberation of Planet Earth.* Grand Rapids, MI: Zondervan.

———. 1976. *The World's Final Hour: Evacuation or Extinction?* Grand Rapids, MI: Zondervan.

———. 1977. *The Terminal Generation.* New York: Bantam Books.

———. 1981. *The 1980s: Countdown to Armageddon.* New York: Bantam Books.

———. 1983. *The Rapture: Truth or Consequences.* New York: Bantam Books.

———. 1984. *There's a New World Coming.* Updated version. Eugene, OR: Harvest House. Originally published 1973.

———. 1986. *Combat Faith.* New York: Bantam Books.

———. 1994. *Planet Earth—2000 A.D.: Will Mankind Survive?* Palos Verdes, CA: Western Front.

———. 1995. *The Final Battle.* Palos Verdes, CA: Western Front.

Lindsey, Hal, with C. C. Carlson. 1972. *Satan Is Alive and Well on Planet Earth.* Grand Rapids, MI: Zondervan.

———. 1973. *The Late Great Planet Earth.* New York: Bantam Books. Originally published 1970.

Linton, Ralph. 1943. Nativistic movements. *American Anthropologist* 45:230–240.

Lippy, Charles H. 1982. Waiting for the End: The social context of American apocalyptic religion. In *The Apocalyptic Vision in America: Interdisciplinary Essays on Myth and Culture,* ed. Lois Parkinson Zamora, 37–63. Bowling Green, OH: Bowling Green University Popular Press.

———. 1988. Millennialism and adventism. In *Encyclopedia of the American Religious Experience: Studies of Traditions and Movements,* ed. Charles H. Lippy and Peter W. Williams, 831–844. New York: Scribner's.

———, ed. 1989. *Twentieth-Century Shapers of American Popular Religion.* New York: Greenwood Press.

Lofland, John. 1966. *Doomsday Cult.* Englewood Cliffs, NJ: Prentice-Hall.

Luck, Georg. 1985. *Arcana Mundi: Magic and Occult in the Greek and Roman Worlds.* Baltimore: Johns Hopkins University Press.

Luckmann, Thomas. 1967. *The Invisible Religion: The Problem of Religion in Modern Society.* New York: Macmillan.

Lukacs, Anthony. 1986. The Rapture and the Bomb. *New York Times Book Review,* June 8, 7.

Mack, John E. 1982. Psychological trauma. In *The Final Epidemic: Physicians and Scientists on Nuclear War,* ed. Ruth Adams and Susan Cullen, 21–34. Chicago: Educational Foundation for Nuclear Science.

———. 1994. *Abduction: Human Encounters with Aliens.* New York: Scribner's.

Malinowski, Bronislaw. 1954. *Magic, Science, and Religion and Other Essays.* Garden City, NY: Doubleday. Originally published 1925.

Malsheimer, Lonna. 1986. Three Mile Island: Fact, frame, fiction. *American Quarterly* 38:35–52.

Mann, A. T. 1992. *Millennium Prophecies: Predictions for the Year 2000.* Shaftesbury, Dorset: Element.

Marcus, Greil. 1989. *Lipstick Traces: A Secret History of the Twentieth Century.* Cambridge: Harvard University Press.

Marsden, George. 1980. *Fundamentalism and American Culture: The Shaping of Twentieth Century Evangelicalism, 1870–1925.* New York: Oxford University Press.

Martin, William. 1982. Waiting for the End: The growing interest in apocalyptic prophecy. *Atlantic Monthly* 249 (June): 31–37.

Mather, Increase. 1669. *The Mystery of Israel's Salvation Explained and Applyed.* London: Printed for John Allen.

Matter, E. Ann. 1986. The Virgin Mary: A goddess? In *The Book of the Goddess, Past and Present: An Introduction to Her Religion,* ed. Carl Olson, 80–96. New York: Crossroad.

Maxwell, Joe. 1991. Prophecy books become big sellers. *Christianity Today,* March 11, 60.

May, John. 1972. *Toward a New Earth: Apocalypse in the American Novel.* Notre Dame: University of Notre Dame Press.

McGinn, Bernard. 1979. *Visions of the End: Apocalyptic Traditions in the Middle Ages.* New York: Columbia University Press.

———. 1994. *Antichrist: Two Thousand Years of Human Fascination with Evil.* New York: Harper Collins.

McKeever, James. 1987. *The Rapture Book: Victory in the End Times.* Medford, OR: Omega.

Meadows, Donella H., Dennis L. Meadows, Jorgen Randers, and William W. Behrens III. 1972. *The Limits to Growth: A Report for the Club of Rome's Project on the Predicament of Mankind.* New York: Universe Books.

Mechling, Jay. 1996. Mass media and folklore. In *American Folklore: An Encyclopedia*, ed. Jan Harold Brunvand, 462–463. New York: Garland.

Melton, J. Gordon. 1995. The contactees: A survey. In *The Gods Have Landed: New Religions from Other Worlds*, ed. James R. Lewis, 1–13. Albany: SUNY Press.

Melton, J. Gordon, and George M. Eberhart. 1995. The flying saucer contactee movement, 1950–1994. In *The Gods Have Landed: New Religions from Other Worlds*, ed. James R. Lewis, 251–332. Albany: SUNY Press.

Miller, Walter. 1982. *A Canticle for Leibowitz*. New York: Bantam Books. Originally published 1959.

Milspaw, Yvonne. 1981. Folklore and the nuclear age: The Harrisburg disaster at Three Mile Island. *International Folklore Review* 1:57–65.

Mojtabai, A. G. 1986. *Blessed Assurance: At Home with the Bomb in Amarillo, Texas*. Albuquerque: University of New Mexico Press.

Moore, Ward. 1947. *Greener Than You Think*. New York: Sloane.

Moorhead, James. 1978. *American Apocalypse: Yankee Protestants and the Civil War, 1860–1869*. New Haven: Yale University Press.

———. 1987. Searching for the millennium in America. *Princeton Seminary Bulletin* 8:17–33.

Morgan, Ted. 1988. *Literary Outlaw: The Life and Times of William S. Burroughs*. New York: Avon Books.

Mugavero, Bishop Francis. 1989. Declaration concerning the "Bayside Movement." In *Cults, Sects, and the New Age*, ed. the Rev. James J. LeBar, 209–211. Huntington, IN: Our Sunday Visitor Publishing Division.

Mullen, Patrick B. 1969. The function of magic folk belief among Texas coastal fishermen. *Journal of American Folklore* 82:214–225.

Myers, Edward. 1982. *The Chosen Few: Surviving the Nuclear Holocaust*. South Bend, IN: And Books.

Nelson, John Wiley. 1982. The apocalyptic vision in American popular culture. In *The Apocalyptic Vision in America: Interdisciplinary Essays on Myth and Culture*, ed. Lois Parkinson Zamora, 154–182. Bowling Green, OH: Bowling Green University Popular Press.

Neumann, Erich. 1963. *The Great Mother: An Analysis of the Archetype*. Princeton: Princeton University Press. Originally published 1955.

Nielsen, Richard P. 1975. Fatalism and type of information sensitivity. In *Psychological Anthropology*, ed. Thomas R. Williams, 389–398. The Hague: Mouton.

Nolan, Mary Lee, and Sidney Nolan. 1989. *Christian Pilgrimage in Modern Western Europe*. Chapel Hill: University of North Carolina Press.

Numbers, Ronald L., and Jonathan M. Butler, eds. 1987. *The Disappointed: Millerism and Millenarianism in the Nineteenth Century*. Bloomington: Indiana University Press.

O'Leary, Stephen D. 1994. *Arguing the Apocalypse: A Theory of Millennial Rhetoric*. New York: Oxford University Press.

Oring, Elliott, ed. 1986. *Folk Groups and Folklore Genres: An Introduction.* Logan: Utah State University Press.

Orsi, Robert Anthony. 1985. *The Madonna of 115th Street: Faith and Community in Italian Harlem, 1880–1950.* New Haven: Yale University Press.

Otto, Rudolph. 1958. *The Idea of the Holy: An Inquiry into the Non-Rational Factor in the Idea of the Divine and Its Relation to the Rational.* Trans. John W. Harvey. 2d ed. London: Oxford University Press. Originally published 1923.

Our Lady of the Roses, Mary Help of Mothers: A Book about the Heavenly Apparitions to Veronica Lueken at Bayside, New York. 1986. Lansing, MI: Apostles of Our Lady. Originally published 1981.

Our Lady of the Roses, Mary Help of Mothers: An Introductory Booklet on the Apparitions of Bayside. No date. Bayside, NY: Our Lady of the Roses, Mary Help of Mothers Shrine.

Overholt, Thomas W. 1989. *Channels of Prophecy: The Social Dynamics of Prophetic Activity.* Minneapolis: Fortress Press.

Palmer, Susan Jean. 1995. Women in the Raelian movement: New religious experiments in gender and authority. In *The Gods Have Landed: New Religions from Other Worlds*, ed. James R. Lewis, 105–135. Albany: SUNY Press.

Panter, Gary. 1988. *Jimbo, Adventures in Paradise.* New York: Pantheon Books.

Parfrey, Adam, ed. 1990. *Apocalypse Culture.* Rev and exp. ed. Los Angeles: Feral House. Originally published in 1987.

Peebles, Curtis. 1994. *Watch the Skies: A Chronicle of the Flying Saucer Myth.* Washington, DC: Smithsonian Institution Press.

Penton, M. J. 1983. The eschatology of the Jehovah's Witnesses. In *The Coming Kingdom: Essays in American Millennialism and Eschatology*, ed. Darrol M. Bryant and Donald W. Dayton, 169–207. New York: New Era Books.

Perry, Nicholas, and Loreto Echeverría. 1988. *Under the Heel of Mary.* London: Routledge.

Peters, Ted. 1995. Exo-theology: Speculations on extraterrestrial life. In *The Gods Have Landed: New Religions from Other Worlds*, ed. James R. Lewis, 187–206. Albany: SUNY Press.

Pope, Barbara Corrado. 1985. Immaculate and powerful: The Marian revival in the nineteenth century. In *Immaculate and Powerful: The Female in Sacred Image and Social Reality*, ed. Clarissa W. Atkinson, Constance H. Buchanan, and Margaret R. Miles, 173–200. Boston: Beacon Press.

Power, Eileen. 1928. Introduction to *Miracles of the Blessed Virgin Mary*, by J. Herolt. London: Routledge.

Preston, Richard. 1994. *The Hot Zone.* New York: Random House.

Primiano, Leonard Norman. 1995. Vernacular religion and the search for a method in religious folklife. *Western Folklore* 54:37–56.

Prophet, Elizabeth Claire. 1987. *The Great White Brotherhood in the Culture, History, and Religion of America.* Livingston, MT: Summit University Press. Originally published 1976.

Propp, Vladimir. 1968. *Morphology of the Folktale.* Trans. Laurence Scott. Rev. ed. Austin: University of Texas Press for the American Folklore Society and Indiana Research Center for Language Sciences. Originally published 1928.

Puckett, Newbell Niles. 1926. *Folk Beliefs of the Southern Negro.* Chapel Hill: University of North Carolina Press.

Quinby, Lee. 1994. *Anti-Apocalypse: Exercises in Genealogical Criticism.* Minneapolis: University of Minnesota Press.

Rabkin, Eric S., Martin H. Greenberg, and Joseph D. Olander, eds. 1983. *The End of the World.* Carbondale: Southern Illinois University Press.

Rafferty, Kevin, Jane Loader, and Pierce Rafferty. 1982. *The Atomic Cafe: The Book of the Film.* Toronto: Peacock Press/Bantam Books.

Rahner, Karl. 1963. *Visions and Prophecies.* Freiburg: Herder & Herder.

Redfield, Robert. 1989. *The Little Community and Peasant Society and Culture.* Midway Reprint ed. Chicago: University of Chicago Press. *Peasant Society and Culture* originally published 1956.

Reid, James. 1968. *God, the Atom, and the Universe.* Grand Rapids, MI: Zondervan.

Relfe, Mary Stewart. 1981. *When Your Money Fails: The "666 System" Is Here.* Montgomery, AL: Ministries.

Ringgren, Helmer. 1966. *Israelite Religion.* Philadelphia: Fortress Press.

———. 1967. The problem of fatalism. In *Fatalistic Beliefs in Religion, Folklore, and Literature,* ed. Helmer Ringgren, 7–18. Stockholm: Almqvist & Wiksell.

Robertson, Pat. 1991. *The New World Order.* Dallas: Word.

Robinson, Douglas. 1985. *American Apocalypses: The Image of the End of the World in American Literature.* Baltimore: Johns Hopkins University Press.

Rogers, Everett M., and Lynne Svenning. 1969. *Modernization among Peasants: The Impact of Communication.* New York: Holt, Rinehart & Winston.

Rojcewicz, Peter. 1987. The 'Men in Black' experience and tradition: Analogies with the traditional devil hypothesis. *Journal of American Folklore* 100:148–160.

Roses from Heaven: Jesus and Mary Speak to the World—1970–1976. N.d. Vol. 1. Orange, TX: Children of Mary.

Roses from Heaven: Jesus and Mary Speak to the World—1977–1986. N.d. Vol. 2. Orange, TX: Children of Mary.

Roshwald, Mordecai. 1989. *Level 7.* Chicago: Lawrence Hill Books. Originally published 1959.

Rotter, Julian B. 1966. Generalized expectancies for internal versus external control of reinforcement. *Psychological Monographs* 80:1–36.

Rovit, Earl. 1968. On the contemporary apocalyptic imagination. *American Scholar* 37 (summer): 458–463.

Rowland, Christopher. 1982. *The Open Heaven: A Study of Apocalyptic in Judaism and Early Christianity.* New York: Crossroad.

Russell, D. S. 1968. *Apocalyptic: Ancient and Modern.* Philadelphia: Fortress Press.

Sagan, Carl. 1986. Nuclear winter. In *The Nuclear Predicament: A Sourcebook*, ed. Donna Uthus Gregory, 13–18. New York: St. Martin's Press.

Saliba, John A. 1995. Religious dimensions of UFO phenomena. In *The Gods Have Landed: New Religions from Other Worlds*, ed. James R. Lewis, 15–64. Albany: SUNY Press.

Sandeen, Ernest R. 1970. *The Roots of Fundamentalism: British and American Millenarianism, 1800–1930*. Chicago: University of Chicago Press.

———. 1980. The "Little Tradition" and the form of modern millenarianism. *Annual Review of the Social Sciences of Religion* 4:165–181.

Santino, Jack. 1996. Popular culture and folklore. In *American Folklore: An Encyclopedia*, ed. Jan Harold Brunvand, 576–578. New York: Garland.

Savage, Jon. 1991. *England's Dreaming: Anarchy, Sex Pistols, Punk Rock, and Beyond*. New York: St. Martin's Press.

Schell, Jonathan. 1982. *The Fate of the Earth*. New York: Avon Books.

Schmithals, Walter. 1975. *The Apocalyptic Movement*. Trans. John G. Steeley. Nashville: Abingdon Press.

Schwartz, Hillel. 1976. The end of the beginning: Millenarian studies, 1969–1975. *Religious Studies Review* 2 (3):1–15.

———. 1987. Millenarianism: An overview. In *The Encyclopedia of Religion*, ed. Mircea Eliade, 9:521–532. New York: Macmillan.

———. 1990. *Century's End: A Cultural History of the Fin de Siècle from the 990s through the 1990s*. New York: Doubleday.

Schwebel, M. 1982. Effects of nuclear war threat on children and teenagers: Implications for professionals. *American Journal of Orthopsychiatry* 52:608–617.

Seligman, Martin E. F. 1975. *Helplessness*. San Francisco: Freedman.

Selzer, Michael. 1979. *Terrorist Chic: An Exploration of Violence in the Seventies*. New York: Hawthorn.

Shaffer, Leigh S. 1984. Fatalism as an animistic attribution process. *Journal of Mind and Behavior* 5:351–362.

Shelley, Mary. 1965. *The Last Man*. Lincoln: University of Nebraska Press. Originally published 1826.

Shinners, John. 1989. Mary and the people: The cult of Mary and popular belief. In *Mary, Woman of Nazareth: Biblical and Theological Perspectives*, ed. Doris Donnelly, 161–186. New York/Mahwah: Paulist Press.

Shute, Nevil [Nevil Shute Norway]. 1957. *On the Beach*. New York: William Morrow.

Simons, Elizabeth Radin. 1986. The NASA joke cycle: The astronauts and the teacher. *Western Folklore* 45:261–277.

Simpson, Jacqueline. 1978. The world upside down shall be: A note on the folklore of doomsday. *Journal of American Folklore* 91:559–567.

Skovmand, David Clyde. 1993. *The End Days: Breakdown of the Apocalypse*. Oakland: Our Lady's Worker of Northern California.

Smith, David E. 1965. Millenarian scholarship in America. *American Quarterly* 17:535–549.

Smyth, Willie. 1986. Challenger jokes and the humor of disaster. *Western Folklore* 45:243–260.

Solara Antara Amaa-ra, 1990. *11:11—The Opening of the Doorway.* Charlottesville, VA: Starne-Borne Unlimited.

Spilka, Bernard, Ralph W. Hood, Jr., and Richard L Gorsuch. 1985. *The Psychology of Religion: An Empirical Approach.* Englewood Cliffs, NJ: Prentice-Hall.

Stark, Rodney, and William Sims Bainbridge. 1985. *The Future of Religion: Secularization, Revival, and Cult Formation.* Berkeley and Los Angeles: University of California Press.

Stavrianos, L. S. 1976. *The Promise of the Coming Dark Age.* San Francisco: Freeman.

Steiger, Brad. 1983. *Gods of Aquarius.* New York: Berkley.

———. 1989. *The Fellowship.* New York: Ballantine.

Strieber, Whitley. 1987. *Communion: A True Story.* New York: Morrow.

Ström, Åke V. 1967. Scandinavian belief in fate: A comparison between pre-Christian and post-Christian times. In *Fatalistic Beliefs in Religion, Folklore, and Literature,* ed. Helmer Ringgren, 63–88. Stockholm: Almqvist & Wiksell.

Strout, Cushing. 1974. *New Heavens and New Earth: Political Religion in America.* New York: Harper & Row.

Strozier, Charles B. 1994. *Apocalypse: On the Psychology of Fundamentalism in America.* Boston: Beacon Press.

Strozier, Charles B., and Michael Flynn, eds. Forthcoming. *The Year 2000: Essays on the End.* New York: New York University Press.

Sweet, Leonard. 1979. Millennialism in America: Recent studies. *Theological Studies* 40:510–531.

Talmon, Yonina. 1968. Millenarism. In *International Encyclopedia of the Social Sciences,* ed. David L. Sills, 10:349–362. New York: Macmillan and Free Press.

Tappan, Mel. 1981. *Tappan on Survival.* Rogue River, OR: Janus.

Taylor, Archer. 1958. The predestined wife (Mt. 930*). *Fabula* 2:45–82.

Taylor, Richard. 1967. Determinism. In *Encyclopedia of Philosophy,* 2:359–373. New York: Macmillan.

Thomas, I. D. E. 1986. *The Omega Conspiracy.* Hendon, VA: Growth.

Thompson, E. P. 1982. *Beyond the Cold War: A New Approach to the Arms Race and Nuclear Annihilation.* New York: Pantheon Books.

Thompson, Stith. 1955–1958. *Motif-Index of Folk-Literature.* Rev. ed. Bloomington: Indiana University Press.

Thrupp, Sylvia L., ed. 1970. *Millennial Dreams in Action: Studies in Revolutionary Religious Movements.* New York: Schocken. Originally published 1962.

Timms, Moira. 1994. *Beyond Prophecies and Predictions: Everyone's Guide to the Coming Changes.* New York: Ballantine Books.

Tuella. 1993. *Project World Evacuation.* New Brunswick, NJ: Inner Light. Originally published in 1982.

Tufts, Marlene. 1986. Snatched away before the bomb: Rapture believers in the 1980s. Ph.D. diss., University of Hawaii.

Turner, Victor W. 1968. *The Drums of Affliction.* Oxford: Oxford University Press.

———. 1969. *The Ritual Process: Structure and Anti-Structure.* Chicago: Aldine.

Turner, Victor W., and Edith Turner. 1978. *Image and Pilgrimage in Christian Culture: Anthropological Perspectives.* New York: Columbia University Press.

Tuveson, Ernest L. 1949. *Millennium and Utopia: A Study in the Background of the Idea of Progress.* Berkeley and Los Angeles: University of California Press.

———. 1968. *Redeemer Nation: America's Millennial Role.* Chicago: University of Chicago Press.

UFO Review. 1988. UFOs and space brothers want you to survive doomsday. No. 27:3.

Vacca, Roberto. 1973. *The Coming Dark Age.* Trans. J. S. Whale. Garden City, NY: Doubleday.

Vallée, Jacques. 1985. *Anatomy of a Phenomenon: UFOs in Space.* Chicago: Regnery. Originally published 1965.

van Gennep, Arnold. 1960. *The Rites of Passage.* Trans. Monika B. Vizedo and Gabrielle L. Caffee. New ed. Chicago: University of Chicago Press. Originally published 1908.

Van Impe, Jack. 1987. *11:59 . . . and Counting.* Troy, MI: Jack Van Impe Ministries.

———. 1994–1996. *Jack Van Impe Presents.* Weekly broadcast. Troy, MI: Jack Van Impe Ministries.

Ventura, Michael. 1985. *Shadow Dancing in the U.S.A.* Los Angeles: Jeremy P. Tarcher.

Vogt, Evon Z. 1952. Water witching: An interpretation of a ritual pattern in a rural American community. *Scientific Monthly* 75 (September): 175–186.

von Däniken, Erich. 1969. *Chariots of the Gods? Unsolved Mysteries of the Past.* New York: Berkley.

Vonnegut, Kurt, Jr. 1981. *Cat's Cradle.* New York: Dell. Originally published 1963.

———. 1984. *Slaughterhouse Five or the Children's Crusade: A Duty-Dance with Death.* New York: Dell. Originally published 1969.

Wagar, W. Warren. 1982. *Terminal Visions: The Literature of Last Things.* Bloomington: Indiana University Press.

Wallace, Anthony F. C. 1956. Revitalization movements. *American Anthropologist* 58:264–281. Reprinted in *Reader in Comparative Religion: An Anthropological Approach,* ed. William A. Lessa and Evon Z. Vogt, 421–430. 4th ed. New York: Harper Collins, 1979.

Wallis, Wilson D. 1943. *Messiahs—Their Role in Civilization.* New York: F. S. Crofts.

Walvoord, John F. 1990. *Armageddon, Oil, and the Middle East Crisis: What the Bible Says about the Future of the Middle East and the End of Western Civilization.* Rev. ed. Grand Rapids, MI: Zondervan. Originally published 1974.

Ward, Donald. 1972. The fiddler and the beast: Modern evidence of an ancient theme. *Fabula* 13:108–121.

————. 1976. American and European narratives as socio-psychological indicators. In *Folk Narrative Research*, ed. J. Pentikainen, 348–356. *Studia Fennica* 20, Helsinki.

Warner, Marina. 1976. *Alone of All Her Sex: The Myth and Cult of the Virgin Mary.* New York: Wallaby Books.

Warshofsky, Fred. 1977. *Doomsday: The Science of Catastrophe.* New York: Reader's Digest.

Watchtower Bible and Tract Society of Pennsylvania. 1988. *Revelation: Its Grand Climax at Hand!* Brooklyn: Watchtower Bible and Tract Society of New York.

Watts, Pauline Moffit. 1985. Prophecy and discovery: On the spiritual origins of Christopher Columbus's "Enterprise of the Indies." *American Historical Review* 90:73–102.

Weart, Spencer R. 1988. *Nuclear Fear: A History of Images.* Cambridge: Harvard University Press.

Webber, David. 1976. *Countdown for Antichrist.* Oklahoma City: Southwest Radio Church.

Webber, David, and Noah Hutchings. 1979. *Is This the Last Century?* Nashville: Thomas Nelson.

————. 1986. *Computers and the Beast of Revelation.* Lafayette, LA: Huntington House.

Weber, Max. 1947. *The Theory of Social and Economic Organization.* Trans. A. M. Henderson and Talcott Parsons. New York: Free Press.

————. 1958. *The Protestant Ethic and the Spirit of Capitalism.* Trans. Talcott Parsons. New York: Scribner's. Originally published 1904–1905.

————. 1963. *The Sociology of Religion.* Trans. Ephraim Fischoff. Boston: Beacon Press. Originally published 1922.

Weber, Timothy P. 1987. *Living in the Shadow of the Second Coming: American Premillennialism, 1875–1982.* Rev. ed. Chicago: University of Chicago Press. Originally published 1979.

Welcome to Queen of the Holy Rosary, Mediatrix of Peace, Mediatrix Between God and Man Shrine. N.d. Necedah, WI: For My God and My Country.

Weldon, Michael. 1983. *The Psychotronic Encyclopedia of Film.* New York: Ballantine Books.

Werblowsky, R. J. Zwi. 1987. Eschatology. In *The Encyclopedia of Religion*, ed. Mircea Eliade, 5:148–151. New York: Macmillan.

Wessinger, Catherine. 1994. Varieties of millennialism and the issue of authority. In *From the Ashes: Making Sense of Waco*, ed. James R. Lewis, 55–62. Lanham, MD: Rowman & Littlefield.

————. 1995. Categories of millennialism and religious authority: Can we distinguish potentially volatile groups before violence occurs? Paper presented at the Annual Meeting of the American Folklore Society, Lafayette, LA.

————. Forthcoming. Millennialism with and without mayhem: Catastrophic and progressive expectations. In *Millennialism, Messiahs, and Mayhem*, ed. Thomas Robbins and Susan Palmer. New York: Routledge.

Whisenant, Edgar C. 1988. *On Borrowed Time/88 Reasons Why the Rapture Will Be in 1988*. Nashville: World Bible Society.

Whitmore, John. 1995. Religious dimensions of the UFO abductee experience. In *The Gods Have Landed: New Religions from Other Worlds*, ed. James R. Lewis, 66–84. Albany: SUNY Press.

Wigglesworth, Michael. 1867. *The Day of Doom; or a Poetical Description of the Great and Last Judgment*. New York: American News Company.

Wilburn, Gary. 1978. The doomsday chic. *Christianity Today*, January 27, 22–23.

Williams, Peter, W. 1989. *Popular Religion in America: Symbolic Change and the Modernization Process in Historical Perspective*. Urbana: University of Illinois Press.

————. 1990. *America's Religions: Traditions and Cultures*. New York: Macmillan.

Wilson, Bryan R. 1963. Millennialism in comparative perspective. *Comparative Studies in Society and History* 6:93–114.

————. 1973. *Magic and the Millennium: A Sociological Study of Religious Movements of Protest among Tribal and Third-World Peoples*. New York: Harper & Row.

Wilson, Dwight. 1977. *Armageddon Now! The Premillenarian Response to Russia and Israel Since 1917*. Grand Rapids, MI: Baker Book House.

Wojcik, Daniel. 1995. *Punk and Neo-Tribal Body Art*. Jackson: University Press of Mississippi.

————. 1996a. Nuclear lore. In *American Folklore: An Encyclopedia*, ed. Jan Harold Brunvand, 517–518. New York: Garland.

————. 1996b. Polaroids from heaven: Photography, folk religion, and the miraculous image tradition at a Marian apparition site. *Journal of American Folklore* 109 (432):129–148.

————. Forthcoming. Embracing doomsday: Faith, fatalism, and apocalyptic beliefs in the nuclear age. *Western Folklore* 55.

Woodward, Kenneth L., Dewey Gram, and Laurie Lisle. 1977. The boom in doom. *Newsweek*, January 10, 41, 51.

Worsley, Peter M. 1957. *The Trumpet Shall Sound: A Study of "Cargo" Cults in Melanesia*. London: Macgibbon & Kee.

————. 1959. Cargo cults. *Scientific American* 200 (May): 117–28.

X., Michael [Michael X. Barton]. 1969. *D-Day Seers Speak*. Clarksberg, WV: Saucerian Books. Originally published 1959.

Yoder, Don. 1974. Toward a definition of folk religion. *Western Folklore* 33:2–15.

Yoke, Carl B., ed. 1987. *Phoenix from the Ashes: The Literature of the Remade World*. New York: Greenwood Press.

Zamora, Lois Parkinson, ed. 1982a. *The Apocalyptic Vision in America: Interdisciplinary Essays on Myth and Culture*. Bowling Green, OH: Bowling Green University Popular Press.

————. 1982b. The myth of Apocalypse and the American literary imagination. In

The Apocalyptic Vision in America: Interdisciplinary Essays on Myth and Culture, ed. Lois Parkinson Zamora, 97–138. Bowling Green, OH: Bowling Green University Popular Press.

Zeitlin, Steven J. 1980. "An Alchemy of Mind": The family courtship story. *Western Folklore* 39:17–33.

Zimdars-Swartz, Sandra L. 1991. *Encountering Mary: From La Salette to Medjugorje.* Princeton: Princeton University Press.

Index